The Unravelling of the Postmodern Mind

Cristopher Nash

EDINBURGH UNIVERSITY PRESS

Edinburgh University Press Ltd
22 George Square, Edinburgh

Typeset in Monotype Apollo
by Norman Tilley Graphics, Northampton,
and printed and bound in Great Britain
by Creative Print and Design, Ebbw Vale, Wales

A CIP record for this book is available
from the British Library

ISBN 0 7486 1215 7 (paperback)

Contents

This is not a technical text for specialists – it's for a wide array of people in many fields who are curious about a culture around them and of which many, but not all, feel they're a part. It's about one of the most dedicatedly complex movements in history, and one that often speaks in purposefully, if not always consciously, abstract and deliberately ambiguous and 'eccentric' language, for reasons I hope to make clear. Thus a few of the ideas that I need to talk about will be unfamiliar to some, particularly at the start. In a sense, if post-moderns didn't in fact say things that people aren't used to thinking or even imagining, for my money there would be no need for such an essay. Specialists in fields it touches, meanwhile, will have a lot to say – and questions to raise – about things I've needed to tell more simply than I would have with more time and space.

The notes to be found at the end, then, aren't just adventitious afterthoughts – they are part of the argument, but at a different level, for those wishing, with the aid of references offered there, to explore further issues introduced in the main text.

Foreword

What I suggest is that we think again, in a different way this time.

For all the speculation about it, we have turned in the direction of a 'postmodern' culture because it suits us. Why that would be – for whom, what style of mind – is what this essay is about.

It is not an analysis – of the sort I'm glad to have given a good deal of my own energy to in the past – of the postmodern debate, of postmodern literature or of critical theory. It seeks to take another step. It's about the culture that produces a vast spectrum of artifacts and new patterns of speech and behaviour (*including* of course the theoretical and fictional literatures) that give vibrant substance to the postmodern experience.

This means that I look for assistance to specialists in many fields. My sense is that one of our most pressing needs is to try to shape a language allowing us to bring the diverse minds of today, with their divergent perspectives, to a shared awareness and interrogation of the impulses informing postmodernity, and to a realization that they're not alone as they in their various ways perceive its thrust, and prepare to engage fully with it.

Another thing that isn't this essay's intention is to attempt – as others have done and will do – to offer a survey or a chronicle of the contemporary world. To the contrary, my interest is in a specific culture, the postmodern, as quite distinct from other cultures around and 'about' us.[1] Postmodern thinking is only one of many kinds of radical thought and action at work today. A number of political activists – for sexual liberation, for ethnic freedom and identity, for women's and postcolonials' rights, for environmental action, for new modes of self-actualization, and more – designate their movements as 'postmodern'. Here are some of the most imaginative, vital, critically potent and productive social forces in our time. Postmodern theorists, on the other hand, can't be faulted for expressing bemusement on finding their ideas hooked to such programmes, and I need to warn that advocates of those projects will scarcely recognize themselves here, for reasons I'll describe.

In speaking of 'a postmodern culture', I would find it hard to take up this adventure if I didn't feel (and find it generally agreed) that it's important to think about culture. Now as perhaps never before it is common to believe that the study of cultural – including informational and communicational – forms and processes is increasingly central to any consideration of the distribution and control of material power. This is complemented by the broadly held belief, on the other side, that "the process of cultural globalization is increasingly delinking cultural production and consumption from a concrete polity and thus a realizable politics" (Garnham 1997: 71). The matter is compounded by the fact that, judged in economic terms, it is precisely where postmodernity has most direct influence – that is, in the 'Northern' or 'developed' nations – that cultural objects and practices (as compared with the commodities we need in order to survive) are the focus of people's prevailing material preoccupations.

The multiplicity of meanings of the word 'culture' is another issue. Do we consider it to be defined by the concepts people hold? the values they abide by? how they structure their relationships? what lifestyles distinguish them? For the purposes of this essay I speak of a specific 'culture' as a reasonably widespread cluster, within a broad society, of relatively distinct and closely interrelated beliefs, discursive and physical practices, and associated goods and services, shared by a significant body of people.

I take as my point of departure that not everyone sees things in the same way. For instance, postmodernity has not always been a favoured attitude shaping people's ideas and behaviour, and in a period when it is one favoured attitude, not everyone favours it. I go on to suggest that it takes some notion of different varieties of thinking to account for these differences in attitude. And I offer as an example a model of one particular variety of thinking (and feeling) – a model of a postmodern style of mind.

The argument for taking this line in the face of traditional objections – and in particular, traditional postmodern objections – to characterizing a culture in terms of the way its participants may think and feel will, I hope, unfold. Along with that, it will become apparent that in a sense much of what goes on here is rather inclined to turn inside out most popular and conventional perspectives. Instead of peering at the world through the filter of theoretical speculation, I invite an observation of the spectrum of postmodern cultural 'stuff' (its events and objects, *including* its theories), through the lens of human psychological and social experience, to see what patterns may be taking shape.

In the chapters to come I often behave in a manner radically different from the style I use when I think and speak as a postmodernist. My aim is to treat patterns or styles of human behaviour with the seriousness and dignity that the energy people commit to them deserves, to understand them in a way that tries to keep in touch with how they're experienced by those who live them. I regard such styles as more fully grasped in all their complexity in terms of the functions they might be felt to serve for their 'creators' or 'users'.

If anywhere I seem to distance myself from postmodernity, it happens here. Strive as I have throughout my intellectual life, I've ultimately not succeeded in becoming impressed with claims that there is nothing to be gained by thinking and asking questions about human thought processes as characterizable events, differing in kind from one style of mind to another, and about how they work as such. And about how a culture – the behaviour of a specific society of minds – may be usefully imagined, in analogous ways, as serving certain explicit and tacit human felt needs. Again, this is not a theory of a *Zeitgeist*, portraying ours as an 'era' with a ruling unified spirit; the evidence does everything to indicate otherwise.[2]

In the course of this inquiry, I turn to the toolkit of psychological thought for assistance. In doing so, I hold no brief with psychology as some final solution to the problems that postmodernism either seeks to resolve or creates for itself. It is no part of this book's intention to psychologize individual 'postmoderns', or to claim that here is what must be regarded as an 'abnormality' for which it offers a 'cure'. In fact to do so would be against the grain of the work, which solicits ways of *living with* a cultural movement that is in fact profound and multiplex. Far from seeking to 'fix' or transcend postmodernity, what's offered is not an example of disinterested winged overflight, but of one modest way that we can actively *engage* with the postmodern, by means of an *exchange* not merely of conjectural theories but of something more like 'living models'.[3]

I am certain that, with the same fundamental concerns, I might have chosen another model. A historical one is long overdue – a full-scale perspectived and far-ranging examination of postmodernity as the phenomenon of a local (and, it may be argued) necessarily transitory instance of a longer Western tradition. That story remains to be told. Philosophers will certainly wish to question the grounds for the very enterprise of the 'characterization' of recent theoretical discourses. I hope that out of a positive exchange among such divergent perspectives – the 'conversation' that in my view is largely what constitutes a working society – a richer sense of what is going on in our times may develop.

It is crucial that I give at the start two working principles. The first is a constraint: It's not the purpose of this book to elaborate dedicated critiques of other texts (which is an ongoing purpose and activity of a multititude of other works, to which I warmly recall readers' attention), except where that can help to sharpen the outlines of its own point of view. And the second is about one of the study's fundamental conceptions: *being postmodern isn't something we are but something we do*. It is a matter of ways of thinking, feeling, behaving. In my view, there are only postmodern *patterns* or *processes*, and these show up sometimes in the thinking and behaviour of all of us. In this sense, no one – in our times in 'the North' – is always or never postmodern. When I speak of 'a postmodern', I always mean someone who in a given situation is thinking, feeling, acting in a postmodern way; one who is in a sense 'postmodernizing'.

This is, as I have been calling it, an *essay*; an 'assay', a meditative experiment, 'trying out' a conception. It's meant to uncover not so much what we didn't know but what we possibly didn't realize. And here the watchword I have always in mind is not 'exhaustive' but '*suggestive*'. To 'cover' (take in) a whole culture, let alone a society, is inconceivable; to pretend to cover one can only 'cover' (conceal) most of it. What I wish is to locate *representative sites* – 'nodes in the network of signs' – where postmodernity seems to *articulate* itself most characteristically. This sampling is like the modest sample we take in when we scan the horizon and make note of the markers that help most to define the landscape as *this* landscape and not another, as a way of finding out where we are and where we can go from here. As an alternative way of seeing, like any 'template' laid over the landscape of a society at a given moment to expose for clearer observation axial features of the culture concerned, it covers some landmarks in order to highlight other ones, and to reveal the highroads that bring these into dynamic relation with one another. I allow this partly because anything else one might say would have this same effect, and I hope readers may feel that – as we 'find our feet' in this new culture – while it involves some imaginational risk, it may be one worth taking.

There will be some who feel that postmodernity and its claims seem so 'far from the truth' as not to be worth thinking about. Here it pays to remember what detectives (and lawyers) often say, that 'people come to me to solve a problem, not to find the truth'. This essay takes as one of its premises that until we've gained a full sense of how important humans feel *solving a problem* is, we'll miss what's going on when people seem to be offering a truth. What we'll be looking at has a great deal to do with the force of problem-solving, as much as truth-seeking, in people's thinking today.

For some readers, however well intentioned it may be, bestowing extended attention on what appears to go on in our minds – in the face of the immediate material hardships endured by the majority of the earth's population – can seem a classic case of how we get our priorities wrong today. I feel deeply in sympathy with this view. I hope that by the end it will have become evident why then I'll have persisted in proceeding in this way.

* * *

I wish to convey my profound gratitude to my colleagues and friends in the vast realm of psychology, theoretical and experimental and clinical, for their forbearance – dare I say downright tolerance? – in taking on board the ideas proposed here, in whatever ways they shall have ultimately chosen. And to warn that for what appears here, those dedicated women and men are entirely blameless; in its *ensemble* all its faults are mine. In particular, without the gift of the acute and fully, wittily and deeply lived insights of Mallory Nash this work might never have found its inspiration and its path.

I occasionally introduce neologisms, and some that skate blithely on the melt-edge of taste. This is simply for the uses of the discussion, to signal and allow easy reference to processes for which there haven't been suitable conventional names. We need to be game to *play* if we're to gain a feel for postmodernity's often deliberately transgressive language-games and why the culture must play them. But I feel as I have in writing elsewhere; few forms of busyness are less helpful than a great expense of energy on the gush of jargon, and I've no wish to add my *ad hoc* coinage to the permanent treasury of literary prattle. I hope readers will take what helps to articulate what is said in these pages with their own experience, and discard the rest.

About sources: times have changed. As always before, I've made every effort here to refer to texts readily accessible to readers in English. But this is no longer the task it was when I was writing fifteen years ago the book to which this is the sequel (1987). One of the most significant signs of the global force of postmodern culture is reflected in a local trait of this volume's Bibliography. Whereas, before, it was necessary to translate passages from some of the most influential texts in French, Italian and Spanish, not only have nearly all of those referred to there now appeared in English, but it is now not uncommon for texts 'transacting with' postmodern attitudes to be released conjointly in English as well as in their original languages. I signal instances where the translation is mine, and where I feel that a translation I quote presents problems, I give the original in brackets. Where words used normally require non-Roman character sets, with some unease I have transliterated them into Roman according to popular contemporary lexical practice, since they are normally introduced for the purposes of etymological discussion which may thus be more meaningful for more readers.

Page references are to the editions (translations for example) from which the relevant passages have finally been reproduced. Except where quotations are extensive, passages (many of which consist of only phrases) from *fictional* texts fully discussed and documented in Nash 1987/1993 are not referenced in detail here. Owing to their sometimes complex publishing history, sources used are organized in the Bibliography – and cited in the main text – according to the date of their most readily available recent English-language edition; further publication details are provided in the Bibliography. In the case of quotations, for accuracy and simplicity, where an ellipsis serves without confusion to link material from two sentences, '....' is employed without brackets.

I The Postmodern Tradition

Who would have predicted that with so much freedom could come so much anxiety? Having for millennia spent our lives wriggling through small economic, social, and moral spaces, we humans broke out into the open only to conclude that nothing, in fact, is ordained. When we can safely call on a system of beliefs, a body of theory that – proclaiming this profound uncertainty – says we exist and may thrive 'staring into the sun', into the very dissolution-of-categories-and-meanings, there can seem a guiding thread to our actions: we summon deep-gonging voices – Foucault, Lyotard, Lacan, Derrida, Baudrillard and Deleuze and Guattari.... Yet 'postmodern-*ism*', the gnarled body of theories that offered that poignant liberation a generation ago, is in mid-life crisis. While its prime creators are either deceased or in their closing years, we intone the theories, but the bell sounds quaint and increasingly cracked – and the world keeps changing. And *postmodernity* – a clamouring *culture* now – rolls on, half mindless of theory, gathering pace as it goes. What propels it so? Does it know? And can it tell?

Here, at the start of the twenty-first century, a commonplace among writers about postmodernism is that postmodernism is dead. On the other hand, all around us communities speak of themselves – for example, on the Internet – as postmodern engineers, geographers, management consultants, gardeners, religious devotees, travel agents, card players and much more. What is most vividly evident is that we live a life shaped by patterns of belief and behaviour that no one avows to be postmodernist, yet which fail to respond to any account of how we came to believe and behave that way that doesn't call on some model of 'postmodern thinking'. This broad, enigmatic gap between *'postmodernism'* (how we say we should behave, expressed in a body of theories) and the far-flung *culture of postmodernity* (how we seem to behave) asks for our attention, and that's what this and the next chapter are about. Since a great deal of what is believed the postmodern is for and about rests on ideas of language and what happens when we speak, we'll need to return often to what postmodernists have said – in literature and in theory – and listen to how they speak.

Here is a story.

It is the 1960s. The world has undergone a series of ordeals on a scale never before known to humankind. The nations' peoples struggle to make sense of two world wars' devastation, mass genocide and the palpable prospect of the nuclear annihilation of life itself. People on all sides are haunted by the apprehension that no one 'people' can be blamed; there had been Auschwitz, but there had also been the Gulag, and there had been Hiroshima and Nagasaki. Nor can war alone be accused. In the armed global truce that prevails, increasing numbers link 'peacetime police action' with words like 'Cambodia', 'My Lai' and 'napalm'; placenames such as 'Mississippi', 'Paris', 'Chicago', 'Belfast', mingle with 'riot tanks', 'tear-gas', 'mass detention', to signify a tide of power used with equally arbitrary indifference throughout ostensibly democratic nations' civic life. Rumours spread of the exhaustion of the earth's resources, of impending ecological catastrophe incurred by civilization's own concerted will to power. No one ideology, but the fact of *certitude itself* – of all history's systematic, totalistic thinking, exemplified in the totalitarianisms of racist and nationalist fervour and the monopolies of faith endorsed by the state and the organized opportunism of private purpose – is glimpsed as the mailed fist beneath the silken shimmer of societies. Many begin to propose that the rationalist, positivist enterprise of scientific and industrial progress is itself the instrument, the very sword and signature of terrors to come.

Thus now the world reaches a crossroads, and there must be a turning. Voices murmur of a new, peaceable revolution: a post-industrial worldview whose impulse, sustained by exponentially expanding technology, need no longer promote but may instead dissipate the power of monolithic systems of credo and control – in the 'flows' of a transnational information-based ethos. A fresh global culture can arise; a praxis may be cultivated for the disintegration of the illusions of so-called 'natural' verities and the false lifestyles they had enforced, and a release of the individual human 'subject' from the specious constraints of fixed normative notions of identity. Such 'things' as 'history' and 'truth' will be understood as mere constructions, nodes in a network of artificial signs, representations devoid of the 'foundational' status on which such terms – and their consequent modes of oppression – once depended for their very meaning. Many foresee a style of life for all that is open, plural, fluid, in which reality is what we make it.

* * *

This 'story' is so familiar that readers are likely both to assign much of it credence and to skip rather lightly through its recitation. Generations among us living today rehearse it, when called upon, with the kind of laconic, almost formulaic facility that, in an earlier, more traditional world, led both sceptics and the devout to lay the charge of 'mechanical lipservice, not felt-belief' at the door of those recounting the Christian story.

Obviously this narrative has problems. There are gaps – for instance, between the 'crisis' (the first part, paragraph one) and the 'resolution'. There is a puzzle, for example, as to why notions of 'truth' need be shed, since presumably the 'crisis' itself, to be a crisis, must be a 'truth' to which only a counter truth can be a suitable answer. And above all, since humans are given as the agents of the crisis: humans as agents alone, you might think, can resolve it; who then would imagine that the dissolution of personal being could help? But it isn't my aim to cast doubt on this tale, though we shall have to look into those problems. Rather, it is to 'take it as read', with all the ambiguity that that phrase entails. In other words, to accept it for what it's worth, but to consider it also, as we go along, as 'just one reading'. To ask why we favour this story, and to suggest a few thoughts about just how much it's worth – about where, more precisely, its force lies – and why it might appeal to us, why we might need it as an account of 'where we're coming from'.

Let me introduce some of these thoughts now. The first is that the story *is* in fact a grand narrative, one around which many of us today in the 'developed' world construct much of our lives. For some, it replaces the Mosaic, Christian, Marxian and Freudian narratives, for example. Or to put it more correctly, it half replaces them, so similar are many of the features of its beginning, its dynamics, its narrative premises, and even its invocation and repetition of certain stereotyped and incantatory phrases. It is actually these resemblances that beg most to be considered for a start. The story is, like those earlier ones, a tale on a global scale of the ordeal and the path taken by the forsaken child, an orphaned, abused or abandoned generation, left to make its own way in the face of heritage, tradition, truths, values and promises betrayed.

A second observation is that the virtually apocalyptic quality we frequently find associated with such a version of the origins and drama of postmodern life draws in part from something we're *not* talking about when we speak of it as merely a train of historically contingent events. It strikes a numinous note that we can identify and properly apprehend only when we see its affinity with the luminous chord struck by more ancient narratives (such as those of Moses and Christ) whose ceaseless rehearsal significantly sometimes exceeds the practical demands of immediate, concrete contemporary conditions.

Why such stories should bear that character and be felt worth such recitation is a question we'll need to unwrap when we come to Chapter 3.

The third matter is that there are in fact other accounts of the roots of postmodernity, including at least one that postmodernists themselves are more inclined to endorse. It makes sense, before anything else, to turn our eyes in that direction.

STYLES OF UNCERTAINTY

Not long ago, in the course of her analysis of contemporary lifestyles, a clinical psychologist and professor of the sociology of science, Sherry Turkle – assembling and developing the thoughts of writers in fields as diverse as social psychology, information technology, and Internet culture, and including others from a wide variety of 'walks of life' in America – recorded that (in the words of one field-worker and scholar) increasingly we:

> exist in a state of continuous construction and reconstruction; it is a world where anything goes that can be negotiated. Each reality of self gives way to reflexive questioning, irony, and ultimately the playful probing of yet another reality. The center fails to hold....[1]

"Individual notions of self vanish", Turkle said. "'We live in each other's brains, as voices, images, words on screens'."[2] "The life practice ... is that of a decentered self that exists in many worlds and plays many roles at the same time" (Turkle 1995: 14). In the cyberspace world, then, of multi-user virtual reality activities to which her study is principally (and positively) devoted and in which millions around the world now engage – there were 'only' hundreds of thousands when she wrote – "as players participate, they become authors not only of text but of themselves" (12). As one college junior put it, in communicating on the Net he was able to "turn pieces of my mind on and off".[3] "It isn't surprising", Turkle said, "that for some this play has become as real as what we conventionally think of as their lives, although" she adds "for them this is no longer a valid distinction" (14).

In these first chapters I'd like to begin to explore some of the more urgent reasons – many necessarily beyond the remit of Turkle's valuable study – why such fast-spreading accounts of experiences such as this, while they may astonish many, shouldn't be surprising.

But as we look at the history of ideas over the past century, we encounter in intellectual circles a now equally familiar, yet what at first seems a slightly different, story – or rather, a story congruent with the first, yet one with not only a rather different time-span but a different emphasis. The thrust appears similar; what we can know, what we can trust as 'the truth', and what we can believe in as the foundations of meaning itself, are 'put into question'. But here, the roots of doubt – and of freedom – are declared to arise not out of social and political circumstance but in the very nature, the 'ontological' character, of the universe and of mind.

Much of this second 'story' too, will be familiar to readers even faintly accustomed to the discussion of postmodern themes. But because it is the *processes of thinking* involved that will turn out to be essential later, I need to speak of it in some detail.

> After having proclaimed the omnipotence of scientific observation and deduction ... and after asserting that for its lenses and scalpels there did not exist a single mystery ... [m]an is still walking about in the midst of the same enigmas, in the same formidable unknown.... A great many scientists and scholars today have come to a halt discouraged. They realize that this experimental science, of which they were so proud, is a thousand times less certain than the most bizarre theogony, the maddest metaphysical reverie, the least acceptable poet's dream, and they have a presentiment that this haughty science which they proudly call 'positive' may perhaps be only a science of what is relative, of appearances, of 'shadows'....

This passage – in spite of its apparently explicit allusion to terms in more recently popular currency such as 'uncertainty' and 'relativity' – was published in April 1892 in support not of a philosophical position, but of the *symboliste* movement in painting (Aurier 1968: 93–4). With the mid-nineteenth-century decay of the Christian mythos and the subsequent spreading disillusionment with science as an alternative 'virtual religion', a ground swell of relativistic thinking in the late nineteenth century gained full cultural force after 1916 by way of Einstein's General Theory of Relativity and, in

1927, in the physicist Werner Heisenberg's now famous paper on 'the uncertainty principle'. By reason of this principle of 'uncertainty' or 'indeterminacy' no observer's apparatus can give an account of any observed system without the likelihood of so interfering with it that the system's 'reality' must be obscured or in fact altered. While there are natural forces at work in the universe, these are ones, as Heisenberg put it, "to which every approach from the world of natural experience ... is lacking". And further, at the level of subatomic physics (the 'foundations' of what we call 'the real world'), what we see 'happening' may also be seen from a second perspective incompatible with the first (1958: 101). Four years later, the mathematician Kurt Gödel published a paper on 'formally undecidable propositions' (1931) – later known as the 'incompleteness theorem' or simply 'Gödel's proof' – that had as vital an impact on the world of 'exact mathematical laws' as Heisenberg's had in the realm of physics. "It is impossible within the framework of an even relatively simple mathematical system", Gödel's theorem asserted, "to demonstrate the internal consistency (non-contradictoriness) of the system without using principles of inference whose own consistency is as much open to question as that of the principles of the system being tested" (Newman 1956: 1616). The consistency of mathematics or of logic cannot be established by any overarching reasoning which can be represented within mathematics' or logic's system. "Formal deduction has as its crowning achievement proved its own incapacity to make certain formal deductions" (Newman 1956: 1616).

Thus, put crudely, in such perspectives both our powers of empirical perception and our powers of pure logical conception are incapable by any rational means at any one time of ever making 'total' sense of – of 'totalizing' – or even of observing, all the facts that would make up 'the truth'; and what we do perceive or conceive may always be subject to some equally valid percept or concept that contradicts it.

While these propositions have since appealed powerfully to postmoderns, significantly (while philosophers were well aware of them from the start) they didn't produce anything resembling postmodern thinking. What was to make the difference, a full half-century later, and to which we attach the name *postmodernism*, was the extension of radical scepticism beyond the areas of mathematics and physics into the realm of language.

The failure of the hope of recovering the 'original meaning' or the 'foundational truth' behind a sign – of a word or for that matter a belief – will have vital significance for postmodern thought.

Whereas in Realistic traditions of thought an event 'read as a text' is in some important sense understood and defined by what's thought to come before it (for example a law of nature, an idea, the intentions of the author of an idea), here events are to be considered largely in terms of what comes after them (for example, in the act of 'reading' them, making sense of them). When you throw a ball or a brickbat at me, whereas traditionally we would understand the situation in terms of who you and I are and what a ball or a brickbat is, here we'd understand it in terms of who you and I are and what a ball or a brickbat is *in your and my systems of meanings at the time*. The difference between these 'systems' can seem small, but the effect of the difference may be large. (What if your meanings and mine are different? Actually, we deal every day with situations by asking such questions; when you threw that brickbat did you mean to kill me? did you mean to play catch?)

One way of grasping the kinds of difference it may make is to think in terms of two different perspectives associated with linguistic indeterminacy – that is, an indeterminism of *proliferation* and an indeterminism of *obliteration*. Let's trace their thematic outlines here in brief; we'll turn to their practical applications and implications shortly, and indeed at 'turning points' throughout this book.

Both begin with the proposition that, first, there is no natural reationship between signs and their referents (there's no reason in nature why in English we say 'dog' and in French we say 'chien'); signs are cultural artifacts. And that, second, we 'make out' what utterances signify in terms of (by contrasting them with) what they do not signify. This is the 'rule of difference' – the word 'black' invokes in our minds whatever it specifically invokes by being not, for example, 'white'.

In the perspective of a *proliferative indeterminacy* (as we may for this occasion call it) all utterances, all signs, are texts whose meanings – produced by the 'reader' – are merely 'nodes' in the total text, the network of the language of signs in operation in human experience. Thrown balls, thrown-up ideas, thrown-clay pots, thrown glances all belong to this arch-text, this 'semiotic universe'. (Thus in this essay, for its plain simplicity I'll often use the word 'language' where the meaning 'semiotic universe' seems to me clear.) As such, they continually modify each other, 'intertextually'. In making out a meaning for an utterance (by finding its relationships with other utterances) what we do is not to find a stable meaning, but merely to unfold the seamless fabric of possible utterances which the utterance in question draws into the open.

What makes for indeterminacy – in this in-some-respects 'positive, constructive' notion of indeterminacy – is a function of the multiplicity of relations between signs; a hyper- or over-determination. Each sign, instead of being finally 'underwritten' by an ultimately discovered meaning – since every system giving any sign its meaning is dependent on some system beyond it – is always being 'overwritten' with a potentially infinite number of meanings. A text – any event invoked in language, even if only in the language of our thoughts – appears to 'give us' too many 'things', which melt into further signs, which signify other 'things', which in their turn … ad infinitum; signs participate in a constant condition of flux, of becoming, their definitive individual identity forever displaced, 'deferred'. For this reason alone, if for no other, "the absence of an ultimate meaning opens an unbounded space for the play of signification".[4]

If the emblem of *proliferative indeterminacy* is 'infinity', the emblem of *obliterative indeterminacy* is 'impasse', or, as it's more often called in postmodern discussion, 'aporia' – an irresoluble hesitation between competing meanings. In this view, it becomes pressing to perceive that to say of events – including the events we call 'ideas' and the systems of value and meaning we may have built upon them – that they exist before they take form in language is to assign them a *metaphysical* foundation – a reality that is by its very definition ineffable, unspeakable and thus specious. Indeterminist thinking along these lines will thus frequently constitute (among deconstructionists for example) one vital flank of a radical attack upon Western culture's dualist habit of thought – God/Man, reason/unreason, nature/culture, right/wrong, truth/fiction, reality/imitation, mind/body, seriousness/play, inside (the text) and outside (the text). It works, for example, to reveal in the language of a culture the power it has (often covertly) grounded on some dogmatic, 'foundationalist' presumption or other as to what the 'primary' or 'original', 'true' meanings of certain signs and their associated values are. Among the assumptions now most famously thrown into question are, of course, the 'grand narratives' (the Christian story, the Marxist story, the Capitalist – e.g. Horatio Alger – story, the story of irresistible rational and scientific progress) by which our sense of ourselves and the role we're to play, and how, has been constructed.

Strange as it may at first seem, this mode of attack makes unrelenting use of precisely that same oppositional, binary way of thinking. It does so in recognition that one of the grounds on which Western rational (but now, in this view, 'metaphysical') thought has rested is the 'rule of identity' or of 'non-contradiction' – that is, the rule that a proposition must always mean (be identical to) itself and nothing other than itself; no meaningful utterance can in logic propose both one thing ('P') and its contradiction ('not P'). Following from the rule of difference, but subtly (yet significantly) modifying it, theorists committed to the observation of obliterative indeterminacy work to expose the contradictions spawned in the very processes of our producing meaning.

To appreciate the ambition of postmodern culture it will be important to see how far this mode of thinking may aim to reach into the roots of our experience. The conception of obliterative indeterminacy says that if indeed we discern what words signify in terms of (by contrasting them with) the latent 'traces' of what they do not signify, they thus actually call forth not the presence of things referred to but invoke their 'absence'. No text, no reading of any text, can logically be imagined to set before us – make 'present' to us – any immanent truth. This is so not merely because of the proliferation of possible meanings but because as soon as we regard anything as having meaning – even if what we say is that it means only itself – we have opened a chasm between the thing and us, by the act of paraphrase. Regarding a stone we name it a stone meaningfully by integrating it into a system of conceptual meanings; the 'thing' (the 'stone', say) is always beyond the text, is always absent. A paradox that obliterative indeterminism insists on is that even as we locate and identify the 'stone', it can be identified and located nowhere else but in its textuality, since even our ideas of 'location' and 'identity' themselves are constituted in, given meaning by, a text, by some field of signs and our reading of them. By this now famous literally interminable process of the deferring (*différance*) of any fixed and definitive differences among meanings, utterances generate only 'space' and (for many writers) move ever towards 'silence'.

The full potency of this in-some-sense 'negative' model of indeterminacy (often associated with deconstruction) needs watching: When 'stone' is uttered, not only is its absence 'traced' (the 'real' stone leaves only a trace of itself, in 'stead' of itself) but, in addition, what is *not* uttered is made significant by this invocation of its antithesis or 'other' or 'different'. The naming of the stone invokes the not-stone. The text 'speaks against' (contra-dicts) itself. Thus in every utterance we find, instead of mere amplification, a reciprocal cancellation, an endless production and erasure of meaning. In unqualified linguistic indeterminacy no text may exist but it destroys (deconstructs) itself. By this "subversive" activity, meaning "affects [sic] its own obliteration" (Ehrmann 1971: 251). Alongside the perpetual multiplication of meaning, this literal 'overturning' of such foundations of rational thinking as the law of non-contradiction will have extraordinary attractions for postmodern thought.

There is no efficient way of communicating how this model of thinking works except by giving at least a rough example, best illustrated in the practice of deconstruction. Here, seeking to tease out and explore the conditions of (the making of) meaning, and unable to rest on material or rational foundations for argument since final appeals to 'matter' or 'reason' are without foundation, deconstruction proceeds rather by a process of 'rigorous' reading of each utterance, exposing (deconstructing) the utterance's and its own contradictions. This quality of 'rigour', however indefinable (there being no descriptive words available for the process that might not risk resting on defined 'external' tests), is so essential to the success of the process that in deconstructionist discourse about *deconstruction* – that is, where deconstruction is commended – one will find the word 'rigour', one of the trademarks of the idiom, characteristically repeated many times per page. Perhaps the closest we can come to its meaning is that in rigour no readings may be considered better 'founded' than others and all readings must be unremittingly searched out and treated as equally tolerable. If – as an example – one wished to deconstruct a deconstructionist argument for itself (as one should, to be rigorous) one would read the word 'rigour' with rigour. One asks, for example, what is meant by 'deconstructive reading has rigour'? Where in the infinite network of signification does it get this evidently freestanding property from? who made it, defined it, and assigned it its powers, and according to what authority, rule or principle? Who said it was better than non-rigour (whatever that might mean)? If deconstructive reading simply 'is rigorous', what rule allows the deconstructive text the specific qualities of 'active testing' conventionally connected with 'rigour' (which it must allow) but seals it off from the qualities also associated with it, for instance, of – say (as a rigorous deconstructionist reading has to say) – pathological rigidity, numbness, inertia, and moribundity? if the deconstructive text is rigorous, how can we not see it as a corpse? If it is without closure (as it must in its own terms be), how is a deconstructive text's 'openness' not the grinning rictus of a cadaver? If, for example, I speak of deconstructive texts as dead, that doesn't mean I don't like them; in the context in which I imply this there must also be equally acceptable intimations of necrophilia. Thus, in my desire for the text's 'full-fillment', I desire both its and my termination and indetermination. What I've said above is circular, and *that is what* deconstruction shows, and (if it is rigorous) it shows it always, everywhere, in everything uttered. There is nothing 'wrong' or 'right' about this, it's simply how things work; each utterance is a perfect circle where all possible meanings are equidistant from 'reality', 'truth' and any 'ultimate meaning' itself.

I haven't written that 'interminable' paragraph for reasons of argument but – quite differently – to *re-enact* a very *particular quality of contemporary postmodernist thinking* that will become extremely important later; its interminable aspect.

But here there appears a further dramatic, even awesome dimension. As we 'read' the text of the world around us, who are we? We, as 'subjects', centres of consciousness, that is, striving to understand and engage with the universe that is the 'object' of our attention. A compact response to the question is this: the reader too, "this 'I' which approaches the text is already itself a plurality of other texts, of codes which are infinite or, more precisely, lost" (Barthes 1974: 10). 'I' as subject *am* always already engaged in the universe, I am but a 'node' in the arch-text of language, continually being shaped and reshaped by the potential infinity of meanings that are exposed there by the interminable play of the uses of language. The most that can be said of me with any precision is that I as subject am 'what I am constituted as' in the field in which I read and am read. My knowledge of my very being is composed of the multitude of associations that 'make up my mind', rolling back through all the history of the formation of the all words and deep into the world of all the meanings of which I am unconscious. There can be no terminus to the flood of my beings; at the moment that I'm 'found' I'm also 'lost'.

This conception of 'the decentring of the subject' – the vision of the 'person' as a lost-and-found-and-lost-again mere trope or twist in the network of language, where each of us as a conscious entity is diffused throughout the tumultuous web of signs – will permeate postmodern thought. In its most explicitly rigorous forms it underpins the view that Western culture must dispose of its essentially 'anthropocentric' humanism, its irrational privileging of the personal and human over the conditions of language in which our ideas of 'humanity' itself are continually constructed and reconstructed. The attractive force of the twentieth-century spectral vision of the disintegrating, 'dissolving human subject' has been so pervasive that it has brought about an otherwise unimaginable confluence of intellectual bedpartners – from Russian Formalists (Bakhtin) and Marxists (Althusser) to radical social historians (Foucault), psychoanalysts (Lacan) and deconstructionists (Derrida) – whose stated reasons for promoting it are so diverse and frequently incompatible (as theorists who have striven to marry them often observe) that what remains in view at last is rarely so much the coherence of their arguments for it as the expanse and urgency of the desire, as we'll observe, that it be received and attended to.

A way of understanding the prevailing difference between the 'proliferative' and the 'obliterative' voices of indeterminism is that the former says 'And thus we see that what is said can have infinite meanings', while the latter adds the rather surprisingly assertive conclusion, 'and they obliterate each other'. In the practices of postmodern theory, the two will always infiltrate one another, dissolving what boundaries might divide them. It is in the realm of postmodern life, and the sensations of people living it, that we'll find, later, the full force of the difference between them.

We're long past imagining that the central insight of indeterminist thinking – that it is both physically and logically impossible at any conceivable time to know or state the complete truth about anything – was a postmodern invention. The fact that, following intellectual developments along these lines in fields such as physics and mathematics, it had been in the 'public domain' for more than a generation before the invention of the word 'postmodernism', yet was never taken up with any significant interest in Western culture at large, is evidence in itself that something else was needed before a widespread movement could found central articles of faith on it (a paradox here if there ever was one). A reason for the coruscating power of the shift of attention to an indeterminacy in *language* – quite apart from other contemporaneous cultural changes – is easy to express: a more 'primary', semantic uncertainty, undecidability, was now at stake. The inherent fabric of our thoughts and utterances was more obviously in question.

We can see immediately that this kind of prioritizing of one variety of indeterminacy over another has extraordinary intuitive power (though, in keeping with the indeterminist rejection of prioritization, it can't be logically sustained). Once the meaning of the symbols in which our very thoughts are framed is indeterminate, it can make no great difference if mathematics and science question or don't question the determinacy of truth-statements, since there could be no fixed meanings for the symbols in which they couched their reasoning, or indeed for the very statements they made.

Postmodernism was now on its way.

* * *

I've put this discussion in the form of a 'story' (of 'the rise of twentieth-century indeterminism') not because its various proponents always tell it as a narrative ('we've come to indeterminacy by stages'), though some do. Many have argued that it is a timeless ontological truth of human existence intrinsic to the very act of thinking. It is, more simply and modestly, useful to see indeterminism's appearance as part of a (hi)story lest we forget, to our subsequent confusion, that people have not always thought in this way, but rather have been particularly disposed to do so since the late twentieth century.

But now we need to think further. For a third way of viewing both stories 'one' and 'two' – a 'third story', in effect – is that, in a larger perspective, something like this has happened before. The fact is that, historically, indeterminism has always been an available option. It has actually often been argued to have consistently surfaced in periods of major cultural change when dogma seems to have provided pressingly insufficient support or consolation for current experience.[5] A passage from an internationally famous reference work published decades before the first appearance of the word 'postmodern' discloses in a few lines the extent of the *recognition* of similar models in other eras. "Scepticism", says the fourteenth edition of the *Encyclopaedia Britannica*, means in Greek philosophical usage:

> to hesitate, to reflect, to examine, to consider pros and cons, to be unable to arrive at a decision or to rest content with surmise. Strictly defined, it is the denial of the possibility of knowing reality; that is to say, the human mind, by its very constitution, can never comprehend the ultimate nature of things.
>
> Scepticism, as a distinct school, begins with Pyrrho of Elis, who maintained that knowledge of things is impossible and that we must assume an attitude of reserve.... The Pyrrhonists were consistent enough to extend their doubt even to their own principle of doubt. They thus attempted to make their scepticism universal, and to escape the reproach of basing it upon a fresh dogmatism.
>
> Sextus Empiricus ... tries to show why a criterion of truth is impossible.... Men can know nothing save their own inward experiences.... The moods of precipients [sic] differ, and make it impossible to discern which affords true information about objects.... Objects differ according to their distance and position. ... hence objects cannot be known directly.... The modes of objects, never the objects themselves, appear to us.... Everything in the external world is relative, not merely to the percipient but to everything else.... no universal standard exists.... "nothing is self-evident.... nor can anything be made certain by proof; because we must either arrive in the process at something self-

> evident or involve ourselves in an endless regress." Accordingly, it is out of the question to argue from "signs" to things signified, and cause as an effective component of phenomena disappears.

The article goes on to cite, as subsequent examples of the sceptic position, Bayle's *Dictionnaire historique et critique* (1697) – "a quarry for contradictions calculated to set natural reason and supernatural revelation by the ears" – and Pascal (1623–62), as one who denies "the possibility of reaching by the unassisted reason a satisfactory theory of things.... [R]eason is unable to solve its own contradictions without aid from a higher source".[6]

We can easily recognize in these lines the now familiar insistence on – among other things – local contexts and the contingency of meanings as against universal truth (which, along with external objects, is seen as unknowable); the eminent distrust of language; the aim to search out inconstancy, inconsistency and contradiction; and the purpose of displacing rational philosophy in favour of the experience of the moment ('men's inward experiences').[7]

I tell this third 'story' – of what may appear to be recurrent cultural 'waves' throughout history – not to trivialize postmodern thought but, quite to the contrary, to prepare the ground for the apprehension that what we've recently called 'postmodern' themes may be invoked and sustained by still more persistent and possibly dramatic human dispositions. And that we may need to take into account a different, further story if we're to deal with this.

DWELLING IN FICTIONS

If language is the site where a postmodern consciousness locates the uncertainties that most beset and engross it, here is where postmodern culture's preoccupation with narrative comes in. It's in our thinking in story form – giving accounts of ourselves as actors in events 'spelled out' in time, in a compact drama of causes and effects – that we've routinely constructed and organized our lives and our import. And so, alongside the sophisticated theoretical apparatus that postmodernism has evolved for the critical analysis of our 'manners of speaking', postmodern fiction – with the radical freedom that its very fictionality allows – spreads out before us the extravagant array of options as we begin to 'think ourselves' in a postmodern way. To experience the 'reach' of the postmodern imagination – and to gain a sense of the shape and texture of human personal experience as it's articulated there – we need to spend some time in that house of mirrors.[8]

Postmodern fiction stirs the waters fundamentally in two different ways. It disturbs our conventional expectations in what is told (the story's 'substance') and in how it's told (the telling's form and language).

Stories

Establishing the order of things in terms of time seems irresistible. But as causality comes into question, one might instead conceive of actuality as an indifferent serial happening, as an aimless form-changing equilibrium, as an inevitable movement towards entropy, or as a condition of eternal stasis. In postmodern narrative, time-driven existence may give way – once again, as it has in the paintings and sculpture of theocentric eras where a transcendent providence is portrayed as placing us in a timeless 'design' – to a vision where events are flattened out into a 'still life', a tableau, a surface without depth or perspective. (Realism with its sense of perspective thus becomes a 'hiccup' in the history of human understanding.) In a novel, characters and events may be not 'lived out' in time so much as catalogued, as entries in an encyclopedia, a dictionary, a gazetteer of cities, as cards in a tarot deck, as pieces and moves in a game of chess. Space, too, may lose its substantiality. Sight – 'the realistic sense' ('seeing is believing'), that privileged faculty in Realist fiction – can become compulsive, and stretched to the limit.

Novels' entire action may be presented as seen through a window. Or – significantly, as we'll find – in a *mirror* – that perennial metaphor for the novel. Far from 'holding up a mirror to nature', postmodern texts repeatedly adopt as a capital object of their attention the mirror itself – the eternal symbol for the reflection of personal truth and self-knowledge and self-regard. Never neutral and 'transparent' as it seems but perforce opaque and distorting as they reflect, showing never our self but its double and in reverse, a negative we can never put right without a further mirror, ever distancing us from ourselves, mirrors – as emblems of both replication and contradiction, at once a multiplication and a displacement and estrangement from ourselves – appear everywhere. In mirrors characters see their doubles, their 'others'; characters lose time, shatter, go mad, pass out of reality, dissolve. And the novel 'speculates' upon itself as a speculum; the mirror-maze betokens the delusions of its own representations. In the chapters that follow this, the mirror will return 'with a vengeance'.

Now characters experience anomalies in what they see and understand. They encounter the ambiguity of their own acts. They watch events occurring where and when they shouldn't happen. Time moves backward, sideways, or stops; space is reduced, enlarged, displaced or evacuated; dimensionality is distorted or comes to seem illusory. Postmodern writings' obsessional figure of the circle comes into its own. The story finishes where it began, the protagonist ends where s/he started. As one of postmodern fiction's most vivid forerunners said of one of his novels, "In shape it is circular and by nature it is interminable, repetitive and very nearly unbearable".[9] If literature – writing and reading – must be linear, and traces above all that most elemental of human stories, the 'quest', the circle above all things is the sign of 'getting nowhere'. Action, activity itself, can seem emptied of effect, and subject to the play of chance. Stories now 'revolve' around the roulette wheel, the roll of the dice, the gamble at cards, the lottery, the book as a gaming-machine, gaming with words as a way of creating worlds, and the world as a game without end.

With this come some of postmodern writing's other most characteristic images – the labyrinth, and the toils of infinite regress. The labyrinth may appear as a garden, fortress, library, city, an entire culture, or an enigmatic idea; it may be the totality of 'creation'. Once caught in this ultimate emblem of both issueless frivolity and ineluctable confinement, both character and reader feel trapped in a medium where the urgency of choosing (which 'turning' or 'meaning' to take?) and the utter absence of grounds for decision are the very condition of its meaning. As the topos of 'infinite regression' emerges – in postmodern fiction, houses form within houses, labyrinths within labyrinths, people within persons – the postmodernist's celebrated dicta resonate that no closure is to be found and that there is no outside (no *hors-texte*) beyond the text. In this fiction of 'a-mazement', the text itself may be offered as an empty labyrinthine structure, an inert, inchoate, aimless, senseless shadow-world awaiting the entrance of the reader to lend it its ephemeral import.

In such a world, character itself is bound to undergo radical alteration. The 'self' multiplies; metamorphosis and transpeciation take effect. 'Persons' impersonate other 'persons', become invisible, become beasts; giantism, dwarfism and 'monstrosity' may emerge. Human values and feelings dissolve. A hospitalized character is endlessly nourished by tube with his own urine, a character's limbs and organs disintegrate, or s/he subjects another's by turns to ecstatic mystical adoration and nonchalant mutilation; butchery, rape and murder take place but as if 'without significance'. Where as-of-habit in our past reading we 'managed' such events – and so sheltered our anxieties – by casting them under the heading of 'satire' or of 'black humour', these were forms that were each founded on some decorum of sentiment. (By mutual assent we assumed that the young, the innocent, the vulnerable, the disadvantaged – in effect, the human, in the face of an indifferent nature, an indifferent regime – must in the end be given shelter.) But such models of moral decorum are now in question. 'Humour' itself is a matter of mere opinion, and 'satire' – grounded on some at least covert conceit as to what is 'right' – is but one of many outmoded games. Not only insentience and nescience, then – feeling nothing, knowing nothing – but the very degeneration, the 'decomposition' of personal being with its whims and wishes will become a postmodern topos with commanding resonances for us as we make our way forward.

It has long been a commonplace that if Realist fiction focuses our thinking on what we 'can' – what we can do and can know – postmodern fiction, contrarily, likes to leave us in the grip of the 'uncanny'; in a condition of irresoluble hesitation or aporia. The initial signs seem good. Postmodern novels may celebrate the power of fiction itself. Borrowing a conception from neo-Classical drama, the *lieu théatral*, fiction becomes a "space that truly contains all spaces ... a time which truly embodies all time" (Fuentes 1976: 705–6). But repeatedly, characters find themselves in a book, in an immortal library, in a point in space where (for example, in a Calvino story) there is

> no longer a container and a thing contained, but only a general thickness of signs ... occupying the whole volume of space.... There was no longer any way to establish a point of reference ... because it was clear that, independent of signs, space didn't exist and perhaps never had existed. (1965: 47–8)

The dream arises of a new kind of writing, expressed by a voice in Vonnegut's *Slaughterhouse-5*, of a novel where "there isn't any particular relationship between all the messages.... There is no beginning, no middle, no end, no suspense, no moral, no causes, no effects" (1991: 64).

The Telling of Stories

A key to postmodern thinking about writing is that it should be understood not as mimetic but as *diegetic*; the events that count are not events in an 'always-already-there' world which the text merely mimics, but in the world where they get 'spoken', narrated into being.[10] The strategies postmodern fiction uses to turn our minds in that direction – for example by parataxis, ellipsis, multilinearity, nesting, regression, recursion, assertion/negation, metalepsis, a vast array of randomization techniques, non-locutionary transcriptional ploys and 'metaplastic' grammatical, syntactic, aural/oral, arithmetic and machinic 'regulatory mechanisms' – come in profusion.[11] Most commonly of all, postmodern texts critique their own processes; narrators pause to doubt their own words, scorn their lapses into Realism, condemn their own forms, or come to a halt in mid-sentence, unable to go on.

But there's more to it still. The question of *persons* and of *personal identity* lies at the heart of the matter. Now in a novel (for example by Robert Pinget) an occurrence may happen to one person in different times or places, at one time to different people or in different places, in one place but to different people or at different times; a single occurrence may seem variably to form part of two or three or more different sequences of events. People's and places' names change apparently ad lib, and all things they're said to have done in the past may be uniformly described as having 'happened ten years ago'. 'People' refuse to stay where they belong. But what does 'belonging' mean? Does personal identity – 'I am the same person I was' (where 'identity' stems from the Latin 'idem', 'the same') – exist? By a 'leap' between the story and its telling, events may erupt into the realm of causality of the hypothetical writer and reader themselves. (Famously, the reader of a novel in a story by Julio Cortázar is killed by one of his characters.) For 'writer' and 'reader', in such stories, are of course only hypothetical – they too are only parts of the fiction. In the novels of Kurt Vonnegut there's an invented character, a rather second-rate science-fiction writer called Kilgore Trout; but I can presently go into a bookshop and buy science-fiction books whose title pages announce that they are by Kilgore Trout. And no, Vonnegut did not write them.[12]

The message is plain: while we'd assumed that 'people' were the agents of their actions within the worlds they inhabited, and that fiction was created and contained within reality and must be kept there, fiction may escape reality, create reality and destroy it, and ideas of 'person' disintegrate. When, in novels by writers like Philippe Sollers, "she" (*elle*) may equally allude to a woman or to the page (*LA page*) in the book about 'her' – where we're uncertain whether "I" stands for a character, for the narrator, for the text itself – who says we were right to have devoted ourselves so diligently to this person-orientated way of sorting things out? It is pure 'Narration', as a famous critic proclaims, 'that speaks'.[13] Thus even the narrator, the 'author' as person, disappears.

This, then – we've seen it coming – is the crucial postmodern shift. One advocate of a revolutionary brand of literature wrote in 1976 that the "humanistic concept of the self" was now eclipsed. The function of characterization – in fiction and in our lives – "has become obsolete".[14] Not only must story as such be obliterated; as the novelists Nathalie Sarraute and Alain Robbe-Grillet had already expressed it by 1957: the reader "has watched the watertight partitions that used to separate characters give way"; "the novel that contains characters belongs well and truly to the past".[15] There may or may not be such a thing as the human mind, but the old Realist concept of person simply doesn't produce a useful model for its representation.

A narrative, now, is in no way tied to laws of identity or continuity outside itself; it is governed simply by the rules of language. (Who am I? Who are you? define yourself – and try doing it outside language while you're at it.) What we call 'a person' is no more than a string of linguistic signs.[16] We must watch this central vision's shifting shape and import as we move through the chapters to come.

But for all the apparent nullifications in the air – of person, time, cause, order, reason, truth, meaning – there is no place for tragedy. In this 'no-man's land' of pure language, that would entail our regarding loss from a fixed vantage point that postmodern thinking cannot recognize. What is left in the 'infinite play of signification' is exactly that: *play*; a field in which 'the ultimate' and the 'serious' must be perpetually crosscut, bracketed by the absurd, the lunatic, by release, by not only dissolution but also innovation; alternately grave and ludic – swinging high, swinging low, turning all upside down – it is a state of eternal oscillation. Ever losing *because* it's also ever finding, the postmodern is not nihilism; it makes its way through a condition of ceaseless creation. The 'motivation' of writing moves from the wearily (and always-at-best hybridly) mimetic to the frankly, wholly and often rapturously diegetic. With a single blow, writing, now – as sheer surface, without 'immanent meaning' – is unshackled in principle from all the strictures that have bound literature both to cultural, ideological conventions and to so-called 'natural' material reality. It breeds an infinity of new tellings, new tales to be drawn ever back into and reclaimed by the vortex of language.

The generic, ruling theme running throughout such fiction (and unceasingly reiterated by its analysts) is that, far from (re)presenting the world, it is unremittingly *'self-referential'*, *'self-reflexive'*, *'self-conscious'*. We have awakened from the manifold delusion that our words and our thinking 'transparently' discover the real world to our direct, unmediated, unconstructed gaze – and that we *ourselves* could ever be 'natural' beings with simple, unfabricated identities. 'Depth' (and with it 'gravity') is dissolved; 'surface' is all; through collage and pastiche we may now freely 'mix' and 'paste' together side by side icons, images, 'realities' from all places and times. If writing like this brings shock, it's in its very logic that this experience may invoke all-at-once, literally 'indifferently', the gamut of sensations – pathos, horror, arousal, outrage, 'outlandish' laughter. It may leave us with the suspicion (which it can't deny and may often solicit) that its objective is the cultivation of the sheer *sensation of itself*. It's an intimation that will return, in unexpected ways.

We would be mistaken to miss the exhilarating allurements in the act of writing, for writers now. Postmodern thinking has brought forth an idea about writing so simple that it's difficult to apprehend at once just how powerful it is. If narratives are made only of language, what 'happens' in *any* narrative may take place not in 'the world ' but solely in *the words* of its telling. 'The story', or indeed what we call *history*, may be conceived to spring from the slightest shifts at the level of the most basic units of language, of speech itself. The sensation of liberation and creation may be vast. We have only to ask: liberation, but from what? and to create what? Can freedom from social or philosophical convention be the whole answer? This is what we might – borrowing the title-word of a novel of Samuel Beckett's – call the problem of 'the unnamable'. In the postmodern's having established the 'thickness of signs occupying the whole volume of space, where there is no longer any way to establish a point of reference' – where it cannot finally fix a name for the thing from which it ultimately seeks release, why might it seem so relentlessly driven, so possessed?

FICTIONALIZING DWELLINGS

In the early part of the twentieth century, on the Portmeirion peninsula in Wales, a wealthy gentleman, Sir Clough Williams-Ellis, created a fantasy village, constructed of a cluster of replicas – in miniature but still to a human scale – of Mediterranean buildings he had long adored. Here, as the years went by, he erected – in a multitude of styles that now include Romanesque, Palladian and Georgian as well as Renaissance Gothic, Jacobean Gothic and Victorian Gothic, but whose presiding essence is of the Italianate Baroque – what has now long been a collection of prospects favoured by tourists of the British Isles, and the locale for numerous television and film productions.

In 1996, Jools Holland, a musician and one of the most widely celebrated presenters of rock in Britain of the decade, introduced on BBC television the 'office' he had built for himself in London. He laid the groundwork for this by communicating first his sense of the beauty and invention of Portmeirion.[17] The building constituting Holland's 'office' was, in fact, a compound reconstruction of what he found the most entrancing features and spirit of the elegant petite edifices of Portmeirion – only now further reduced in scale to a size suiting his own wallet and his practical needs. Here, in this minute copy of miniature replicas, this further diminuated yet still 'liveable' and workable array – a 'regression of realities', Portmeirion looking toward Portofino, Holland peering at Portmeirion and inviting us to watch him gazing at both – was an eclectic collage of arches, dens, corridors, windows and balustrades encompassing the history of public and vernacular architecture of southern Europe of the past four centuries, all in a workplace on a street in London. Not only were the facades of his structure imitations of Portmeirion (or similar) facades – each revealed within to be built not of, say, marble but of breezeblock and synthetic 'stone' – but (an element central to his pleasure) interior walls too were 'facades'; this 'bookcase', for example, was actually a door; not an object but an opening toward objects yet to be seen....

In his film of his new 'habitat', as he leads us through his rooms, Holland's rapture is unconcealed. He leaves no question but that his has been the longing of those who have sought to recapture for their own experience (their notions of) certain bygone times – ones where (for Holland, as he portrays it) life's living 'goods' were symmetrical, ordered, and tinctured in kindly pastels. Yet more, in his recapitulation of the Baroque, the period he dreams most to recapture and the very heyday of *trompe l'œil*, in rescuing for himself fragments of the Baroque's extravagant pseudo-reality he celebrates, all-at-the-same-time, the art of surface and dissimulation. The hope – the fantasy – of authenticity is abandoned as an issue. Holland knows well that his model, Portmeirion, has from its inception been a paragon of hoaxes and the setting for the dramatization of lives ruled by fantasy and deception. Their very titles tell the tale: the television series *Dr Who, Danger Man, The Prisoner, Secret Agent, Brideshead Revisited*, the films *The Inn of the Sixth Happiness* and *Under Suspicion*. Peculiarly, in their miniaturization to accommodate their shifting styles, Holland's building's rooms are queerly cramped, as if in his office's portmanteau version of a half-millennium of time there may be no occupant but Jools Holland. The fundamental focus of the 'show' in which he displayed his self-proclaimed triumph was never in fact on living or working there (which he never spoke of), but on the structure as observing and reflecting other structures, past and present. Devoted not to his needs as the structure's 'user', the attention was dedicated to appearances, to the continuously unfolding, mercurial aspect of the building as an object to be seen. (Here differences between postmodern and Modernist gestures become conspicuous.)[18] Among – and culminating – these needs was his enthusiastic, patently overflowing desire to be seen to present it to the public's uncertain and perhaps perplexed but fascinated gaze.

* * *

In 1996, Bill Gates, founder-chairman and CEO of Microsoft Corporation (which in 1998 replaced GEC on the stock exchange as the most powerful company in the world), published a description of the house he was building for himself – which, as he put it, "might suggest things about the future of homes in general". "I am certainly not comparing my house to [Hearst's famous] San Simeon, one of the West Coast's monuments to excess", he wrote. "While it has its pool, its sports court, and a reception hall to entertain one hundred for dinner comfortably ... privacy is important. I want a house that will still feel private even when guests are enjoying other parts of it".

> First thing, as you come in, you'll be presented with an electronic pin to clip to your clothes. The pin will connect you up to the electronic services of the house.... Recessed into the east wall will be twenty-four video monitors stacked four high and six across, each with a 40-inch picture tube.... [T]he monitors disappear behind wood panels when we're not using them.... The electronic pin you wear will tell the house who and where you are, and the house will use this information to try to meet and even anticipate your needs.... When it's dark outside, the pin will cause a zone of light to move with you through the house.... [T]he lights ahead of you gradually coming up to full brightness and the lights behind you fading. Music will move with you too. It will seem to be everywhere, although in fact people in other parts of the house will be hearing entirely different music or nothing at all. A movie or the news will be able to follow you around the house too. You'll use [a] remote to tell the monitors in a room to become visible and what to display.

The building is modelled on a guest 'cottage' previously built on the property, where "because some people like the temperature warmer than others do, the cottage's software sets the temperature in reaction to who's inside and the time of day" and the cottage "matches its inside brightness to the brightness of the outdoors". A central feature of the future house:

> is a database of more than a million still images, including photographs and reproductions of paintings. If you're a guest, you'll be able to call up on screens throughout the house almost any image you like – presidential portraits, reproductions of High Renaissance paintings, pictures of sunsets, airplanes, skiers in the Andes, a rare French stamp, the Beatles in 1965.... You'll be able to ask the house system to play ... songs that were performed at Woodstock, or music composed in eighteenth-century Vienna, or songs with the word "Yellow" in their titles.... [T]he images will actually materialize on the walls of rooms just before you walk in and vanish after you leave. If you and I are watching different things and one of us walks into a room where the other is sitting, the house will follow mediating guidelines. The house might continue the audio and visual imagery for the person who was in the room first, or it might change programming to something it knows we both like.... The house will be instrumented so that it records statistics on the operations of all systems, and we'll be able to analyze that information to tune the systems. This presages an instrumented world. (1996: 247–57)

Times *have* changed. While it can't escape us that, significantly, both Hearst and he made their fortunes as developers of the technology and distribution of information, Gates' house – to put it in a way that he would certainly enjoy – is a monument not to excess but to 'access', one of his success' most public and crucial bywords. San Simeon, like the Rockefellers' Cloisters, in New York – each composed of objects, rooms, spaces captured (some would say pillaged) from the stony remains of earlier cultures – is a memorial to an age of material empire. Gates' house, quite differently, is itself a world of reproductions in *electronically stored code, as information,* in 'pure language', virtually as evanescent – by choice – as imagination or hearing/seeing itself.

This word 'information' will prove essential. As we use it now, with more precision than before, it is not knowledge but consists merely of raw 'bits' of transmissible data (in information technology "on/off", "1/0") which may or may not be organized into 'meaningful' images or ideas (by someone, applying some rule), at which point it may come to resemble 'knowledge' but still never carries the warranty of 'fact'. As such, it is subject to radical 'modulation'. Thus as Gates says, aided by information technology "You might watch *Gone With the Wind* with your own face and voice replacing Vivien Leigh's (or Clark Gable's). Or see yourself walking down a runway wearing the latest Paris fashions adjusted to fit your own body or the one you wish you had" (1996: 101).

There's much that's familiar here. We easily recognize now the emphasis on surface, and on simulation and the artificial production of self-contained 'worlds'; the cultivation of pastiche; the unconstrained recombination and collage of sensations, and the active scattering and dispersal of categories, of material and cultural constraints conventionally placed on sensation itself. We feel prepared for the impulse toward the tuning of experience to the desires and values of the immediate moment, including matters of taste and even of essential sensory values – temperature, light, sound. We can understand the promotion of fluidity, of the even literal 'reduction', the melting down of 'matter' to a fluently transmitted repertoire of encoded and readily decoded but now unstable, shifting signs, where by means of the imaginational and material affluence of a Holland or a Gates all spaces and times and personal beings – including our own and those of our favoured icons – merge as we enter and submerge as we depart.

Moreover, perspectives that appear new in these examples of postmodern material culture are illuminating. They reveal on the horizon dimensions we might never have predicted, yet that have actually been long associated now with postmodernity. For instance, arising with a sense of the 'loss of time' and of the past is the culture's recurrent and well-known invocation of nostalgia, and the urge to reproduce and collect 'dead and gone' history as a kaleidoscopic mosaic of ephemeral aesthetic artifacts in an iridiscent fleeting present. And as to our workplaces and dwellings, we can grasp now the intimation that a habitat may become not so much a place to which one regularly returns (as to a 'home'), but more a space from which one regularly goes to an infinity of other places; not so much a 'lodging', where you are, as a reaching after where and what you're not.

There are, however, real riddles before us in the after-all quite characteristic contemporary examples placed on show by Gates and Holland; something cryptic, equivocal, even baffling. Some of them may come as a relief. For a start, things don't seem so melancholy as one might have thought, looking back over the earlier stages of this chapter. Rather, there are disturbing ups and downs, in rapid succession or as if in the same breath. In fact, in the two samples we've just glimpsed, intentions are benign – perhaps even to the extent of insouciance as to moral concerns; a modest, discreet 'indifference'. And, almost in the manner of early twentieth-century Continental futurism and utopianism but purged of the latter two's political resonances, they seem quite positive, frenetically positivistic in fact. Gates' and Hollands' creating for themselves simulative environments – ones whose consciously extravagant heterogeneity explicitly outruns the neat categories of time – coincides unproblematically with the liberality of the postmodern. Yet questions raised by the juxtaposition of this with, for example, the image that a Gates cuts of monolithic corporate power seems problematic. We may begin to wonder how we are to account for the following: the unmistakable signs we detect of an insistent, restless dedication to the meticulous and frankly *masterly* management of the environment, and of people's experiences within it. The unsettling fluctuation we perceive between the impulses toward utter *liberation* and toward total *control*. The inescapable themes of *watching, surveillance, concealment* and almost feverish *display*. And, most striking of all – as we follow each of our hosts, broadcasting to the world his 'private accommodations', lingering eagerly in the camera's eye, travelling through rooms in an ever-following spotlight: the strange, unforetold, subtly vibrant accent on some species of unnamed and discreet but omnivorous desire. The *desire of the individual, personal being*. Can we be seeing, rising slowly to the postmodern surface, quite exactly the thing that in theory we thought had been most crucially lost: the centred self? Just how does that work, exactly? ... Such a reading can't be right; but something is wrong, something more needs to be understood.

There's no need to stress these developments here; it would be premature; if there's anything to them, they'll come again. Clearly there are – as postmodern writing says – gaps, ruptures, 'chasms' that we must explore.

2 A Fantasy

I would like to bring into the open something only hinted at before. A certain dividing of the ways between the paths of postmodernism and postmodernity.

As a culture feeling ourselves caught in a position where both the 'straightforward' passage to new certainties and any possibility of retreat to some earlier, safer ground seem indefinitely obstructed, in postmodernism, so far, we appear drawn to two radical ('root') options. To seek, in *pluralism*, a way to allow all alternatives to stand at once, each choice regarded as a perfectly good one for the occasion, a choice worth making. Or to find, in *indeterminacy*, an attitude and practice allowing the issue of choosing to become a matter of – literally – indifference. As we'll see, however strikingly divergent these options can turn out to be when it comes to living a postmodern life, in current culture they are never entirely distinct from one another. The urge toward the former, the 'pluralization' of values and of lifestyles, is a universally perceived feature of postmodern culture and we'll need later to explore in detail some of the events it produces. But in practice as well as in logic, we frequently speak as though the sheer attractive force of the second of those options, the indeterminacy of our very meanings, makes it the ultimate foundation on which plurality itself must rest. (That is, that *if* choosing makes no difference, then all choice may be left to the individual and to the occasion.) And so it's right that we explore this notion early and with some care.

Here is where we feel the full weight of the classic description of experience in our times that was cited (from Kenneth Gergen, representing the view of many) in the first pages of this essay. We "exist in a state of continuous construction and reconstruction; it is a world where anything goes ...". The formula 'anything goes' has been so energetically attributed to postmodernist theories that it has – as a token of the moral and philosophical bankruptcy of our times – been a whipping-post-of-choice among opponents of postmodern thought. A problem we'll have to deal with is that anti-postmoderns are far from being the only people crying up and decrying this catchphrase. Today as I write, one single scan of the Internet, using one search engine only, yields 4,225,510 matches for 'anything goes', published by groups with interests ranging from postmodern literature and postmodern law to erotic multimedia and turkey management; a poll-rating no doubt exceeding Cole Porter's wildest dreams. Unlike anti-postmoderns 'out to get' anyone believing that anything goes, we need to take on board the current and vigorous reality of such notions' appeal, and to recognize the possibility that while the impulse they express might in fact have very little to do with postmodernism it may have a great deal to do with postmodernity. Whatever power the idea exerts in the contemporary imagination – that any value, any meaning, is as good as any other – it draws what *argumentational* force it might have from its association with a conception with which we're now familiar: unqualified linguistic indeterminacy. How strong, and of what sort, is the bond between postmodern theory and popular postmodern attitudes?

Linguistic indeterminism asks (as the Gergen quotation above reminds us) that we see that utterances depend for their meaning on the 'construction we put on them', and we need further to see that there are many different ways that we can read indeterminism – indeterminist thinking – itself. Does it mean to say that specific utterances are subject to a variety of specifiable meanings? Or that specific utterances are prone to a variety of specifiable meanings each of which is itself subject to a variety of meanings? Or that specific utterances are subject to an infinite number of meanings? Or that all utterances mean equally anything-and-everything? Or that all utterances mean nothing? Current in our times there are in fact all kinds of theories of linguistic indeterminacy. Among the arguments in support of deconstructionist thought, for example, we can discern one that conceives of an abyssal undecidability at the core of all 'literary' language (de Man); another putting forward the possibility, and indeed the urgency, of an anti-rationalist writing in the context of philosophy and philosophical discourse (Derrida); and others finding there the potential for a constructive critical practice in the context of social and political life (Norris, Spivak); and so forth. The subject of this chapter, however, is the most sweeping form of all such thinking: that is, unqualified linguistic indeterminism. For here alone is the theory that makes possible the widespread and enthusiastically welcomed – because so liberating – conception that postmodernism (and thus postmodern life) means 'anything goes'. We shall have to pay so many visits to unqualified linguistic or semantic indeterminism that, with due apologies for what may to some seem an indecent familiarity, I'll simply call it 'Unqle Sim', and those speaking for it 'Unqle Sims'.

It is crucial to perceive, now, that unqualified linguistic indeterminism as popularly understood – the idea that because of the nature of language 'anything can mean anything' – is a hypothesis for which no one has actually argued a fully developed, systematic case. (Indeed, the concept of anything so stable as a 'systematic case' would be anathema to it.) It is ultimately the power of the notion in the contemporary imagination, rather than any argument for it, that constitutes its greatest force. The aim of the following observations is not to assess the value of Unqle Sim or the work of its proponents but to offer some clarification of its actual range, as a contrastive background to the claims commonly made for it, to bring into somewhat higher relief the preoccupations and impulses of the culture that is drawn to those claims. Actually, it is technically difficult to 'hold' to a theoretical unqualified linguistic indeterminism, and a few reasons are these.[1]

1. Unqle Sim's propositions themselves rest on avowedly insecure foundations. For example, it cannot argue successfully for itself. (In fact, writers moving near to an Unqle-Sim position pledge with some consistency that they don't intend to do so. For example, Unqle Sim as a form of scepticism can't deal with, or account for, scepticism about scepticism.)
2. The Unqle Sim reading of utterances, once in train, cannot prevent itself from infecting Unqle Sim propositions. For example, Unqle Sim cannot name a boundary, a limit or turning point at which it will 'make a difference' what is said, and it can't defend its assertions against opponent assertions.
3. Unqle Sims can't provide reasons for differentiations advanced by them. For example, they can allow no rules or tests for the appropriateness or merit of any specific reading, including any Unqle Sim reading. Unqle Sims propose, for instance, 'rigour' in place of 'rational' analysis, but can't 'determine' rigour's meaning. While for Unqle Sim all readings of an utterance are necessarily equally 'good' (or equally problematical), Unqle Sim readings, as well as Unqle Sim utterances themselves, depend for their cogency on the faith that this is not so.
4. Contrary to the frequent claim that they find difference everywhere deferred, readings of utterances offered as Unqle Sim readings rely on differences between contexts for which they can't account. For example: (1) Unqle Sims characteristically

argue from history – that is, that it makes a difference that their view exists, where it didn't (or was ignored) 'before' – but can't fit this into an account (such as a 'historical narrative') that could be both comprehensible and acceptable to Unqle Sim. And (2) in their assertion of the inevitability of any reading's sensitivity to its context, Unqle Sim propositions must themselves fail to respond equally – that is, with indeterminate 'parity' – to, for example, cultural differences in reading (a Western academic's reading of an Unqle Sim proposition, say, as compared with one proffered by one's local National Front). They imply faith in a developmental feature of mind (where different readers at different stages will read differently and some are more competent than others) that they can't justify. Unqle Sim thinking thus rests on an asymmetry of readership, disclosing an emphasis on expertise or mastery whose seeming arrogance sits ill with its ostensible problematization of authority and authoritative reading. It cannot secure sufficient distance from (stand 'outside' of) or 'put into question' its own authority as it claims 'rigorously' and evenhandedly to do with all manifestations of authority.

5. Insofar as Unqle Sim propositions are logical they must be so logically strong as to be pragmatically impotent. In a given comparative reading of any two texts (say *Finnegan's Wake* and the Book of Ruth), in the light of Unqle Sim nothing changes. That is, while both texts will reveal themselves to be equally indeterminate, until something else is said (about, say, their different dictions) they remain in the same 'different' positions relative to each other. (*Finnegan's Wake* remains different from the Book of Ruth, if for no other reason than that, to work, the language of a practice finding each indeterminate needs to be different. Unqle Sim has given its account, but everything about the differences between the two texts remains to be explained.) In the same way, Unqle Sim propositions, to make sense as Unqle Sim propositions, need the 'differences' from them associated with propositions advanced by say Descartes, Kant, Hegel. This in itself would make little difference except that – given that all texts under Unqle Sim must 'come to' the same thing – it is unclear why Unqle Sims write. (One can easily imagine someone asking 'Why write more than is written, since except perhaps in some aesthetic, non-semantic way, any writing says not more but the same, that is, "everything"'. We'll come back to the matter of aesthetics later.) In other words Unqle Sim must try to dissolve differences it *needs*. If one says, for example, 'Deconstructionism

= Realism', while we might expect Unqle Sim to seek to endure such elisions, it's not clear that it could.

6. Unqle Sim cannot extricate itself from the charge that, in its particular procedure for the (ostensible) problematizing of metaphysics, it is a metaphysical position. In its proposition that indeterminacy is a product of the ontological nature of language, it smuggles an idea of 'nature' (in language) which it can provide no framework to defend. That is, it replaces Realism's 'always-already-there' material universe with a metaphysical always-already-there dynamism or force. If for example one were to ask: 'Who operates language?' the Unqle Sim answer must be (as it frequently is thought to be) that it operates itself, which is to propose a priority of language which Unqle Sim's own theory must repel.

   (A way of seeing this in Unqle Sim's terms shows up in its handling of the 'rule of difference'. For the word 'language' to mean anything, we must be able to conceive of a 'not-language'; Unqle Sim finds this both reasonable and intolerable, but tries to put it away by saying that reason is – as always – inadequate. Yet it must also acknowledge that to be so explicitly unreasonable – to speak with specific disregard for frames of reference such as those advanced in the name of rational deduction and empirical induction and yet to rely on another frame of reference invoking a difference between language and not-language – must be in some sense metaphysical if not downright mystical if 'language', which is where such words show up, is to be worth talking about at all. To deal with what seems unpleasant in this conclusion, it says 'It's only a contradiction. That's what I've been telling you, it's in the nature of language that we must defer, we cannot decide one way or the other.' But it gets to that point by presuming that we agree that there can be nothing outside language – or if there is, *something* must be inadequate, something in our way of speaking must not be working properly, because whatever's 'outside' can't inscribe itself in language. But the idea that *language* could be inadequate – if something must be – is just another of those intolerable things. Unqle Sim is actually a theory of the omnipotence of language. More about 'omnipotence' later.)

Claiming to renounce essential, unitary (foundational and totally unified) systems, people speaking for Unqle Sim invoke an 'essential' medium (language) that takes in and absorbs (and in fact in some sense creates) all that is spoken of as 'reality' – and whose analysis is regarded as more powerful, all-embracing, and literally significant than our thoughts about reality – in a way that can't, in its own terms, be satisfactorily distinguished from the discourse either of conventional rationalism and positivism or the metaphysics which positivism and rationalism seek to supplant.

7. Actually, as language-users, people seeking to support Unqle Sim constantly shift frames between different 'languages'. They lead a double life, and Unqle Sim can't offer an adequate account of this, of how such things work. As one advocate of postmodernity famously said, 'Even Derrida brushes his teeth' – that is, someone this spectator took to be powerfully on the side of Unqle Sim lives nevertheless as though he believes in a frame (material reality?) in which certain behaviour can be named in a relatively stable, 'determinate' way, whatever language is used for it. Here, as with many of the questions raised so far, Unqle Sim would say that it is not a matter of either/or, that the point is that there is an interminable oscillation between any two such positions. This appeal to the perception of oscillation will turn out later to be crucial. But meanwhile, as an argument it is, if not disingenuous, inadequate, for it conceals the fact that to observe this oscillation it must keep to a pseudo-meta-frame of reference that obscures the frame in which one believes reasonably wholeheartedly in brushing one's teeth. In the idiom of Unqle Sim, propositions must concertedly suppress the urgency of their staying within one language frame suitable to them.

Put in crude day-to-day terms, it seems 'sensible' that I may be consistently convinced, for example, that it's meaningful to think such things as that I am hungry, that I will die, and that if I get on a plane in Chicago whose advertised destination is Detroit, even if I don't get to Detroit I am more likely to end up in Detroit than in Hong Kong, and of knowing that I won't slip out of that frame without being able to assess why – that is, what were the conditions of the frame-shifting that has taken place. Now, it does not requiring shifting to a 'merely realistic' or 'commonsense' frame to determine this; the whole thing *can* be said to 'happen within language' if we wish. But to say so fails to vitiate the effect that certain very large clusters of things said – such as those referring to 'what we call' material events – have, consistently and in many contexts, a stability about them that neither qualitatively nor quantitatively fits snugly into the accounts of language characteristically given by Unqle Sims. Above all, for all its continual alterations, language itself is notoriously one of the most conservative of human artifacts, and could not function as language without being so. Unqle Sim can't account for that 'odd stability'. This problem (the 'suppression of the urgency of staying within a determinate frame of reference') extends further. Unqle Sim needs both to think that 'frames' do not exist and to depend on one frame (one special kind of discourse – the National Front's or the Detroit-plane's pilot's discourse will not do) in order to 'think' that they don't. And Unqle Sim can't find its way to a position where it can describe its rules for allowing both frames, or admit that they operate as (discrete) frames when at the same time it requires that they do.

8. As widely understood, in many of its cases Unqle Sim – by way of another kind of frame-shifting – confounds the violations, which are essential to it, of the rule of non-contradiction (two mutually exclusive things cannot be said of the same event) with a rule of homology (in two different places the same rules must apply), and thus claims to have found indeterminacy when it's not there.
9. Unqle Sim can allow no rules for these kinds of frame-shifting (since support for such 'meta-rules' would appear to be the endorsement of some overarching and 'enclosing' system). Unqle Sim can't account for either the existence like this of two or more frames, or how it comes to encourage our shifting between them in a way that seems, itself, to have remarkable ('odd') regularity about it.
10. Far from being indeterminate, in its diction, syntax, tropes, locutions, thematic topoi and governing propositions (as we've seen and will see further), the specific traits of Unqle Sim discourse can be classified and predicted.
11. Far from being indeterminate, Unqle Sim readings of specified texts can, to a striking ('odd') degree (as we've seen and will see further) be predicted.
12. Since for Unqle Sim it is supposed to be of the nature of language for unqualified linguistic indeterminacy to happen 'indifferently' everywhere in language, it should be impossible for Unqle Sim 'activity' to appear more in some writers or texts than in others; but a determinate Unqle Sim canon of texts can be identified, and in fact a list of such texts and of canonical authors is often declared by linguistic indeterminists. (These are characteristically referred to as falling into two categories, texts that can be shown to deconstruct themselves – for instance ones by Rousseau – and ones that show themselves deconstructing themselves – for instance ones by Sollers. This pattern of

categorical thinking – problematic in itself – is troubled by the added difficulty that one must ask, 'What rule (of "presence", unmistakably) allows for this differential showing/not showing to be found in different texts?')

* * *

In these suggestions I've spoken in extremely 'coarse-textured' terms, but I think they can serve our present purposes. The topic here is not the 'truth' of what 'serious' theorists might have said of linguistic indeterminism, but the contours of what *postmoderns* have *taken* to be its truth, and the power and implications of that. Certainly in Unqle Sim itself there appear to be 'logical contradictions' at each 'turn', but this fact finally has scarcely any of the interest that it held for its early respondents; Unqle Sim *wants* to enact contradiction. A sequel to this that is a good deal more remarkable than its apparent logical consequences is that while unqualified linguistic indeterminacy can't be *'effective'* in ways that realists would judge effect, postmoderns widely show the need to speak as though it can be. (The 'anything goes' phenomenon returns here.) By definition – and by its own design, since it is inconceivable that it could name a positive effect as its aim – it can't bring about a 'significant change' or 'difference'; it articulates a frame of mind. I want to begin to suggest the tenor of that in postmodern life.

Because it will be vital, this needs looking into with some care. However 'pure' or 'empty' utterances may seem, however they appear not to tell us 'about' anything (renouncing 'subject', in the sense both of the what and the who 'behind' them), every utterance visibly represses another, the one it leaves out, an alternative construction of signs. One of the by-products of many of our recent theories' proper exhortation that we stop settling easily on what utterances seem to 'say' (constatively) is the acute realization that we must start looking more closely at what utterances (performatively) 'do'. Each thing said is someone's model of how to behave: of the kinds of things to say to ourselves and to each other, of what comes first, what comes last, what doesn't matter and what shouldn't be said or thought at all, at least not in public.

This places us in an unexpected position with relation to the ideas discussed so far. Once we've set our mind on some determination of meaning (once we've found any intimation in a thing said that we believe we might return to, find still there, find portable enough to use in the same way in another context) – which we must do at the very least if we're to sustain an argument for indeterminacy itself – there is no way of distinguishing a categorical difference (though there are sometimes rich differences in texture) between postmodern indeterminist speaking and writing and the articulations of ambiguity that have for millennia been the meat of interpretation in the spheres of traditional philosophical, theological and aesthetic debate. All declared indeterminisms are necessarily provisional indeterminisms, never 'Unqle Sims'. Implied at the start of any statement of unqualified linguistic indeterminacy is the phrase: '(*I say but I can never mean* –)'. We are always adopting also, along with our indeterminism, some mode of positive assertion – whether rationalistic, materialist, metaphysical, or other. Only in a dedicated faith in Unqle Sim, in its being unqualified, is a revolutionary postmodern indeterminism launched. Since to date no theorist has gone consistently that far, postmodern gestures toward unqualified indeterminacy inscribe not a discrete philosophy – and indeed postmodern theorists have regularly though in various ways declined to present theirs as such – but an aesthetic or a psychological predilection; not a coherent proposition but something that we're obliged to call a wish. Our perceiving this alerts us to the pregnant fact that indeterminist-speaking in itself asserts a specific model of thinking, and the question is, who wishes to assert it? Who needs it?

This is not about discrediting indeterminism. Quite apart from the deep imaginative attachment many of us feel for the treasures of perception and conception it can stir, there can ultimately be little benefit in devoting energy to seeking the overthrow of radical indeterminist thinking, broadly speaking, if only because any local detailed engagement with it must imbue its opponents' discourse with the liabilities they seek to discount, and we become tangled in the round of contradictions that must end in the question pointed up in the past few pages, 'Why do we claim to say we're "totally free" when we know we're not?' What is of real interest now, rather, is not the way the *arguments* for an 'unqualified' indeterminism appear to paint themselves into a corner. It is rather the way postmodern culture will frequently seem inclined to act on a belief in what it conceives to be indeterminist thought's overwhelming *conclusions*, without regard for its arguments and their peculiar implications, as though, so to speak, nothing had happened.

To sense the weight of this – if not yet its full burden – it can help to look at what has commonly occurred in recent times among those who do try to keep the arguments alive: in the preceding pages we'll have easily noticed that a quick and efficient way of appearing to address Unqle Sim is to point out that it can't function without establishing a ground of its own that would seem to contradict its own thesis. This is actually a response readily produced by beginning undergraduates, who are quite familiar with the 'feel' of the indeterminist themes around them, and indeed it is now applied with satisfaction as standard fare among anti-postmodern theorists – to the point where it begins actually to show lacklustre signs of weariness rather than creative engagement.[2] What stands out here is not whether indeterminist thinking is good or bad. It is that the over-exertion, the fatigue and evident etiolation of both the Unqle Sim thesis and its rebuttal, *combined with the continued recitation of both*, form a compulsive circle of commotion (it might seem unkind to say fuss) which is the truly piquant, historically vital phenomenon that quite literally 'cries for our attention', our examination and understanding.

Recognizing that *no* substantially elaborated 'postmodernist' theory has *actually supported* unqualified indeterminism[3] – that radical linguistic indeterminism is not able to behave as postmoderns with telling regularity have imagined it could – we're able to grasp that it is only at the level of desire that Unqle Sim and postmodernist meet 'in reality'.

As differences between postmodernism and postmodernity become clear, we must recognize that they seldom entirely part company.[4] It could gratify some to say that as a theoretical tenet unqualified linguistic indeterminism itself has silted into a philosophical pond, narrowly isolated from the mainstream of contemporary life. But little could be further from the case. While philosophies may by their very logics need to leave it aside, as a current of popular opinion it flows vigorously on. When it comes to radical belief, postmodern attitudes are of a different order of magnitude in their wider social, economic and political effect than any consistent postmodern (say, poststructuralist) theory; but there should be no surprise in this. Postmodernism as a body of theories is not and never was 'the foundation' of postmodern life (the very phrase would bring a chill to the mind of a postmodernist). Instead, it constitutes a cluster of local and transitory artifacts, one subtly vibrant fraction of the vast myriad culture of postmodernity.

Because it is often the most articulate and literally vociferous ('voicing') part, we'll need to come back to it regularly. But by its at least superficial difference from the larger culture it trenchantly reveals a formidable feature *of* the culture. At the start of Chapter 1, I said that scepticism has always, historically, been an 'available opton'. I meant to highlight in that way that reasons given to sustain it are not a force of nature or some 'finally recognized' ontological truth but a matter of cognitive choice, there to be adopted and equally ready for discard. Given every chance throughout the millennia, philosophical scepticism doesn't always produce either postmodernism or postmodernity. Sceptical philosophy never seems to turn out to be a sufficient cause for the social adoption of scepticism; it achieves the role of something resembling a cultural force only with the intervention of some further stimulus on some other front.[5]

It's for this reason that the differences need to be kept in mind between the actual character of unqualified indeterminism and the character of what it's thought to be. It has a significant place in postmodernity – as a *cultural fantasy*.[6] The ultimate ground of the idea of the unqualified linguistic indeterminacy of all things said and thought is actually 'modal'. That is, a matter of affective tonality – a substrate of volition, of *psychological disposition*. It is what someone wants, rather than an absolute truth underlying all. We can observe that, as an 'optative' attitude – one may elect it (we may 'read' through its filter, even while questioning the viability of so filtering or 'framing' one's reading in this way) or not – it has a *special character of its own*. It expresses certain quite distinct preoccupations and predilections about which we really need to do some positive thinking.

* * *

If it is difficult to hold to an unqualified indeterminism, in our everyday lives we live and deal with relative or provisional uncertainties of meaning. In practice, each time someone points out to us some indeterminacy, a question we ask (most often without being aware of it) and that it can be crucial to ask in future is: do we see this (the impossibility of ending) as the end of the discussion? Quite apart from the illogicality of doing so, we certainly know from experience that one alternative can be: 'We agree to differ as to interpretations; now let's – by the most workable means we can find – get on with the business at hand.' In contrast to this, as we'll see, for many postmoderns indeterminacy is the (perhaps tragic) end to the discussion, which the indeterminist (perhaps in a spirit of pathos) nevertheless cannot bring to a close.

This is the obsessional aspect of much of postmodern thought's indeterminism. Literally, we are 'beseiged', 'sat down before' (*obsedere*) something from which we feel it impossible to 'move on'; beset, blockaded, held hostage as we may be in a fortress of our own making – in this case in the closed dwelling of our language. It might seem enough to say that that's the point; that no utterance is ever finished, in the sense that every utterance will inevitably, in every new moment, be reread but differently. But that fails to explain why then more utterances need be *produced*. We don't 'move', yet we're feverishly active, seeking always a new utterance and a new meaning for each utterance. The activity has about it what can be called an inclination to 'delirium'.[7] For reasons I hope to show, instead of 'closing' we may relentlessly swerve in our thinking, our interpreting and uttering, as if we can't stop 'running on' in a way that may significantly resemble – as in delirium and dream – running in place.

But an obsession is a discrete pattern of behaviour and, as we know, never exists by itself. Characteristically, obsessional activity comes – when it comes – as part of an effort to solve or extinguish or manage some worse disquiet, some greater bedevilment. In fact, we can't in indeterminism's own terms take an indeterminist utterance itself as a definitive statement, but must consider it as constituted by its function in its context. What *can* be the function of this inability to finish; what can we imagine to be its context?

When it comes to literature, texts published in the 1950s that many regard as the groundbreakers of postmodern fiction bear titles like these: *The Voyeur*, *Jealousy*, *The Age of Suspicion*.[8] The theme, as it was phrased in the next generation by theorists, was in no way confined to fiction. "Language can be described, and has been usefully described by de Man and Derrida, as making promises it cannot keep."[9] "Language promises", wrote J. Hillis Miller, "but what it promises is itself. This promise it can never keep. It is this fact of language, a necessity beyond the control of any user of language, which makes things happen as they do happen in the material world of history" (1987: 35).

The outline of a figure in the postmodern carpet, dimly glimpsed in the previous chapter, emerges now with more intensity and persistence. The past and promise belied; the suspicion of utterance; the anxiety of control; the fastidium of doubt; the compulsion of watching; the fixation upon 'undersides' and sedulous exposures; the urgency of disbelief; the obsessional multiplication of meanings beyond the limits of mundane reason. Far in excess of our most ready-to-hand explanations of its roots – such as the one offered in the compact materialist story of postmodern origins tidily told at this book's outset, and which had already revealed unsettling gaps – there rises before us a tumbled range of new questions.

We've come to the point where the matter of desire, for all the difficulties that it raises, can't be intelligently put off. As one of the principals in the postmodern debate has typically suggested, speaking of the indeterminist enterprise as a matter of ethos,

> if following Lyotard's luminous formula, we accustom ourselves to thinking of [contemporary ideological] strategies not so much

> as philosophical stances as rather in terms of desires – the desire called antifoundationalism, the desire called antiessentialism – we will be better able to bracket the content of such positions provisionally and to turn to the more historically interesting question of why intellectual or social strata in contemporary society have found the new ethical doxa congenial and useful. This is the only question that can lead us to any increase in collective self-knowledge. (Jameson 1994: 35)

If we have entertained a belief that the theoretical texts a postmodern might allude to as his or her authorities (in an appeal, for example, to a new openness of meaning) register merely the discourse of the dispassionate intellectual observation and documentation of an interesting and important aspect of language, it appears that we're obliged to let that thought go. While postmodern theoretical statements frequently propose to found a 'new science' (as Derrida called deconstruction), their tonality is rarely if ever that of the conventional modest inquirer, serenely content to have noted a new and significant 'fact'. A brittleness is here, something abrasive, corrosive, that we would find hard to read elsewhere without associating it with some note of '(out)rage'. This is actually rarely denied; the aim to overthrow logocentric, metaphysical and positivist thinking is often declared at the outset and – as writers believing in the Oedipal model have noted in analysing indeterminists' utterances – in much the manner of one intent on 'the slaying of the Father'. Whether or not we accept that psychoanalytic mythos, light laughter is scarce, here, and in its place wit, of which there is an abundance, shows little of the equilibrium, the *equanimity* of humour. As has often been remarked, for instance, of poststructuralist writing, a kind of ponderous intensity, gravity, self-seriousness prevails, with a curiously homogeneous urgency matching that of the diction of protest that is difficult to explain or to account for in the terms of what in principle is historically, after all, the most dedicated and powerful case against homogeneity and against seriousness. That this trait of writing under Continental influence is counterbalanced in the American postmodern writing tradition by a tone (from its beginnings with Hassan) of often strenuously bristling polemic euphoria simply sharpens the point. There is a 'cause' here – if we may allow play with the word 'cause' – suggesting an unexpected end-directed (if 'passive') aggression that can be bewildering when we seek a place for it alongside the report that language is but the infinite play of signification.

There is no high-power alternative theoretical programme concealed in these observations. It's more simply to signal that in postmodern thinking there is an unprecedented attention to *rhetoric* as an arena of unrelieved delusions, and that the laying bare of utterances' gaps and voids – together with the vigorous and self-consciously displayed overturning of the linguistic furniture of received understandings – has become a consuming postmodern intent. Whatever we may come to feel about its motive force, it may situate itself in the impulse to *locate sites,* and *reenact scenes,* of *betrayal.*

We may sense that with this, as the other side of the same coin (as if its 'stamp', its 'proof'), there may be a pressing *strategy for dealing* with betrayal. As though, caught within the system, in the network of the betrayer, one may hope to deploy its own language against itself, to disintegrate the very fabric of both truth and deceit. The term 'suicide-bomber' may spring to mind. But, catchy as that sounds, it leaves a lot to be desired. For one thing, as we will have perceived and as we'll need to consider seriously, the further each theoretical argument proceeds toward indeterminacy, the further away it moves from any discrete social or political engagement of the sort normally associated with protest. It becomes difficult not to ask, 'What protest is this, that would lay seige to the world's beliefs in personal being and meaning?'

Linguistic suicide-bombing can be one postmodern dream. But as we've noted, it can't exceed the bounds of a dream, and it leaves too much unaccounted for. Alongside it are the ecstatic vision of liberation and the rival and harrowing imminence of infinite uncertainty. And, winding through it all, the unspent apparent white nightmare of betrayal. Moved by the postmodern hope of a transcendent medium – such as language – in which all deceptions can be at once exposed and dissolved, we may go on to wonder what order of experience might inspire so effulgent and multiplex a reverie. Who, with so many disparate voices as we'll hear, would dream such dreams – ones, as we've seen, invoking principles beyond the power of the most radical philosophical and theoretical practices to sustain?

3 Ambivalence

Is it possible that in the past we've been asking the wrong questions? or seeking answers in the wrong place? When it confronts us with its enigmas, can postmodernity really be expected to 'explain itself'? And how would the postmodern regard our trying models by which we might give coherent accounts of it?

TALKING ABOUT MINDS

One of the first things postmodernism helped us to see was that no system is freestanding, or can provide a complete rationale for itself. No work 'containing its own critique' doesn't also institute a programme of attitudes that remain unproblematized. When it seeks to express what it means, for example, the postmodern has always been obliged to draw on some system of meanings – some language, say, for speaking intelligibly about language – that it would in principle much rather throw into question. In other words, it must always be craning its neck, reaching for some view of itself from some vantage point, by way of some idiom, 'outside' itself; one worth trying, for the occasion. This catch is never more evident, in fact, than when a 'meta-view', some ontological theory is advanced – as is so often the case – of how things can or ought to work in a postmodern way. For it is thus unable to explain people's different relations to the theory. How can it be that so many having essentially the same apparent background (social, political, economic), and espousing the same outlook, act out so many different – and apparently conflicting, mutually exclusive – kinds of 'postmodernness'? It's as though elemental things about itself must be effaced from postmodern thinking as it speaks of itself in its own terms.

Once again we're obliged to try our hand at finding a language that postmodernism on its own may logically have to fail to offer, to put into more precise words not merely how diverse, oscillating, shimmering a thing postmodernity is (which the postmodern certainly welcomes in principle), but how it can come to *be* so, and still call itself by one name.

The real trouble shows up when it comes to the matter of the marked instability in postmoderns' own ideas and ways of behaving. We see it, for instance, as soon as people speak (as many of us do) of the sensations of both extreme solitude and of solidarity with others – of both the tranquility and the excitement – that arise in cyberspace or in dancing at an Ecstasy-inspired rave; of our 'return to nature, to the elements' in exotic sites, and yet of the frankly artificial construction of such venues for our tourist gaze. We see it in our favouring shopping malls lined with mirrors and our fascination with new modes of body modification, together with our repudiation of concern for glamour and our own outward appearance; in our obsession with 'information', together with our lack of interest in the provenance of it that might make it genuinely informative; in our belief in the dissolution of values and of 'the subject', together with our assertion of the rights of the individual and his or her values; in our calls for the deconstruction of institutional social systems, together with our desire for still more closely knit communal life; in our appeals for peace and the gentle life, together with our paying for ever more aggressive and sensational violence in our favoured media images; in our declared wish to live for the moment and for the ephemeral, and our opinion that history is dead and the past is without present meaning, together with our ceaseless retro nostalgia. In saying that 'many of us' live in these apparently complicated contradictory ways, I've meant to leave it clear that not all people in our times do so to the same degree. Other millions appear to organize their lives (often with expressions of fulfilment) around some more unified understanding, whether its 'centre' be vocation or family or some social, political, scientific or religious belief or a moderately harmonious amalgam of these. The complexity I've described – some will say 'a complex' – is the very essence, specifically, of 'postmodern being'.

We need some kind of understanding that can help us to imagine how one may come to be postmodern, and hear a specifically 'postmodern lifestyle' advertised and solicited everywhere – to think along such unique and even predictable lines as those we can identify as postmodern – yet to be so apparently *contradictory* in our acts and attitudes toward ourselves.

Let us begin with an example from human personal life. In our encounters with one another: an elemental thing we know and act on as if by instinct is that in any given moment, if we're to respond in a way that's in keeping with 'what's really going on', when someone speaks to us there are at least three things in play. There is, first, 'the *text*' (what s/he says). And second, the *subtext* or *agenda*, which seems to be its *content* – the 'reason' the person gives or might be understood to give for saying it, the general pattern of beliefs the person holds. And third, the *need* beneath, for which even the hard-to-find 'content' is often a disguise, not uncommonly concealed even from the person whose need it is. (One: 'Don't drive that way!' Two: 'It's against the law.' Three: 'I'm scared.') This three-tiered way of 'reading things' is not just a postmodern discovery (though it's essential to much postmodern thought about 'texts'); it's at the core of our daily understanding and getting along. (If we engage only with 'One' and 'Two', we know that we may end up in discord that leaves silence and scars, when if we'd engaged with 'Three' we might have moved closer rather than further apart, and have made adjustments in, say, the driver's speed, and/or the passenger's attitude to it, that satisfied both – for the moment anyway.) Dealing with human events – often reflexively and out of our awareness, sometimes through hard conscious struggle – we manage situations and relationships successfully and honestly by asking, *what function* does this action or thing-said serve? *What need might it be felt or hoped to satisfy?*

In trying to understand a culture and how it shapes our lives, there is no reason why we should – and there may be powerful reasons why we shouldn't – bring the enterprise to a halt by saying of its ideas simply that 'The statement of idea X functions to communicate idea X'. I suggest that as we proceed we ask not merely 'What is the underlying belief behind X idea?' but '*What problem might it solve to believe this?*' This is not, in other words, another analysis of beliefs. It's a study of the *needs* for certain beliefs as opposed to others. It's inescapably about the dynamics of human beings in their interactions with others and with themselves.[1] This way of reading, of thinking about what people say and do, is close to that of Nietzsche (as Deleuze stressed) when in essence he asks, as a starting point for an inquiry into the predisposition of the ostensibly objective philosopher/scientist: 'Who is seeking truth? In other words: what does the one who seeks truth want?' (Deleuze 1983: 94). Glancing ahead, postmodern concepts need particularly to be reviewed in such a light, for reasons having to do with an investment postmodernity has already begun to show in *concealment*. We need to have some compassionate understanding of that.

Theories of language, of reading and writing, theories of nature and society as constructs, theories of degrees of certainty and decidability, and indeed theories of meaning, are all theories – and in fact specific representations – of the mind.[2] They are psychological modes of speaking and understanding, and it's that line of inquiry that I wish simply to pursue further. This means including our thinking about not merely the conceptual, philosophical but also the affective experience of the postmodern as postmoderns describe it.

Strange as it may seem, I'm not going to put a case here for the logical foundations of psychology. In my view it is a perspective, a language game, like any other; one idiom among many by which we seek to put into words and acts the qualities of our experience. As we've seen, a centrepiece of postmodern thinking is the insight that whatever we say appears to travel in a circle; that every inquiry is a bootstrap operation. When the question of the validity of psychology is the topic, the circle of thinking looks something like this: 'Anyone's meanings – including mine – are uncertain' (a philosophical position) —> 'The meaning of I – including my experience of myself – is uncertain' (a psychological position) —> 'My meanings – and so anyone's – are uncertain'. Yet whenever we speak, we act as though it is reasonable to focus our attention on things from just one of the particular vantage points along some such circle. Thus we're content to hear it said that (philosophical) matters of meaning arise before (psychological) thinking organisms arise to think them.[3] A simple rider I mean to add in this essay is that not all but only some styles of mind think this way. And I would like to propose that for the time being we pause at a *different* point on this undeniable circle, and consider what happens when we try the viewpoint of a psychological position, to look more closely at some styles of mind, and focus on the one that says 'The meaning of I – including my experience of myself – is uncertain'.[4]

Unwilling as I was to clutter our initial meeting with too many characters, I must now introduce a new voice to the party. I've already borrowed his intonations from time to time to lend a cutting edge, for clarity, to ideas I might normally have wished to leave untouched by inflections intimating – as his often do – the self-complacent adoption of a moral highground combined with an irascible antagonism toward radical scepticism. He will play an important part in our encounter with postmodernity, if only because his is often the most dedicated voice against it, and I mean to let him be heard with – for the time being – as little critical comment as possible. Since he stands for Unqualified Truth, tailoring his terms to befit a foundationalist moral conservatism, I'll call him 'Unqle Trim'. Unqle Trim, for example – in contrast to postmoderns calling the 'subject' into question[5] – wishes to support the counter-idea that real discrete subjects exist and that each of them carries on relatively compactly in one place, namely in some body. He would say that we can't meaningfully think of anything as 'called into question' until we have asked: 'Who is asking?' ('I love these abstractions', Unqle Trim would say, 'but – let's be fair – what allows you to make an exception of yourself as agent of this "putting into question"?') For him this is not just a polemic strategy, to elicit the maieutically useful answer, 'I (a *subject*) am asking'. For him it would leave in our hands the end of a thread of information which it would be unreasonable and graceless not to draw out; that is, 'Someone is asking while others are not. How come?' It seems safe to go along with Unqle Trim this far.

If I do, then, speak of persons and their affects and effects – while I want to keep in sympathetic touch with the many who prefer to think of 'persons' as where sensations arise and where ideas come from (including, for instance, ones for which we might feel a strong wish to hold someone responsible) – I'd like to devote some thought to how and why, under what conditions, increasingly more of us should come to feel that this is more easily said than believed.

It's worth registering the fact that postmodern thinking itself not only can't avoid a psychological frame of reference, but persistently sponsors it in detail. Postmodern theorists and postmodern fictionalists frequently make vociferous and popular appeal, as we'll see, to what are conventionally regarded as 'abnormal' psychological states ('paranoia', for example, and 'schizophrenia') as icons for revolt, and often expressly commend these as alternative ideals for the reconstruction of human thought and action. The lead taken by Lacan and those among Lacan's successors in psychology itself in the elaboration of an account of the dissolution of the subject is only one of the more celebrated theoretical examples of the 'postmodern/psychological connection'. The influence of Foucault on postmodern thought is grounded on a psychology of power, and Lyotard's on a psychological theory of libidinal economy. Baudrillard's attacks on Freudian psychoanalysis as reductive are founded on psychological counter-theories of the Symbolic and, subsequently, of psychological seduction. For Deleuze and Guattari, there exists a materially located psyche with a capacity to invest itself in the repressive social formation that is the target of their attack – it must have the capacity to actualize, for example, Oedipus within itself – and they adopt what they consider to be a bona fide psychological model, that of 'schizoanalysis', as the optimal medium for social action. And Derrida, not without reason often regarded as the most resistant to the foundations on which psychology is based, makes perhaps the most consistent use of strategies whose origins he acknowledges to have gained their primary force (if not in fact their origin) in psychological analysis; he relies regularly on postulations of 'unconscious' processes, and writes as aggressively as he can against cultural 'resistances' to psychoanalysis.[6]

So long as this habit persists, we have unfinished business. We need to bring into the open a few recent assumptions and anomalies that have been sometimes left covert. A striking feature of contemporary culture is a constellation of developments in psychological thought – ones that are themselves reciprocally interwoven with events in postmodern thinking, yet that are ironically *not foreseen* in the classic psychological propositions popularly regarded as essential in postmodernity's own 'founding' theories. Among these recent developments are certain altered, more sceptical attitudes toward themes previously leant on by inspirational figures associated with postmodernism such as Lacan, Lyotard, Deleuze and Guattari, as well as (not infrequently), Foucault, Derrida and others.

1. The Oedipal mythos and the Family Romance are no longer nearly so widely held as the dominant psychological drama of human mental life and culture. Among those working nevertheless to hold fast to a Freudian model, the emphasis has shifted to what they themselves often call problems of a 'pre-Oedipal' self.
2. Previously dominant notions of libidinal *drives* (and their repression) governing human mental life from birth to death have lost their privileged place in reconstructions of psychological dynamics, in favour of relational psychology and an emphasis on the functions of patterns of thought, affect and behaviour in the formation and continual reformation of the self in local relational fields.[7]
3. Seeing the mind as the register of a drama of struggle between horizontal (layered) levels within the psychic being (such as consciousness/subconscious, id/ego/superego) has come to be regarded as unnecessarily reliant on a still rigidly structured notion of mind, and as placing fallacious emphasis on notions of 'self' as an entity identical with what is more correctly one aspect of the self, namely the ego. And that – apart from theoretical and empirical dilemmas it poses – this too easily obliterates what happens in relational fields between people (where 'vertical' divisions and dividedness are crucial), and leads to serious failures not only in general understanding but in clinical treatment.

I've invoked the growing tendency to lay aside Oedipal, drive or hydraulic and repression theories in favour of relational theory, for example, not as an event accredited by some notion of progress or by the happy discovery of some absolute meta-posture, but merely to make clear that contemporary culture 'has its mind on' something else, and that we can't do better than to watch where we're going. This 'cohabitation' of altered attitudes – of current postmodern perspectives and a more current psychological model of the human mind – is significant, and makes it pressing that we explore each in the light of the other. While we'll frequently need to think more about the changes I've mentioned under 1 and 2, I must say more, immediately, about issue 3, whose import is most immediately eventful for the project ahead, since it's concerned with the matter of 'the subject'. Let's call it, for the moment, the 'ego mistake'.

We recall how a *sine qua non* of radical indeterminism is the indeterminacy of the subject. Indeterminism cannot leave the Observer (that exotic primate the 'I/Eye') untouched by indeterminacy attributed to the Observed, for fear of either one of two uncongenial possible outcomes: either 'The universe is deranged but I'm all right Jack' or 'So far as I know everything's all right and I have significant mental problems'. How the first option could come about is difficult to conceive. And the latter would itself entail assigning authority to some psychological model of effective subjects. What, then, does postmodern thinking refer to when it considers this problematic thing, the subject?

Unquestionably a need described by humans (as 'organisms') is that experiences (sensations, emotions, thoughts) 'come together' or cohere, with a feeling of mutual 'belongingness' and discreteness sufficient to sustain a workable sense of the difference between self and other, and to support the motivation (indeed the belief that it is possible) to live from one moment to the next. Much of what we speak of as one's 'self' is made up of these very feelings of some experiences' seeming especially 'present', 'near', somehow coherent, discrete and continuous; and when – for any reason – these experiences weaken, the sense of self seems to weaken. On the other hand the project of identifying difficulties with the centred subject has at its core the realization that a *'subject' defined as 'ego'* – as the 'person' who thinks and speaks consciously of him/herself as 'I', as some Cartesian unified and fixed being – is not a good representation of how things work in the actually far more dynamic sphere of mental and linguistic processes. Logically, either 'subject' does mean 'ego', and must – as an inadequate representation of the site of such complex events as thinking, feeling and image- and idea-formation – be distinguished from something broader (such as 'self') that's going on in the organism, or (if it's offered as another word for what goes on there) it must be treated as simply inadequate.

Unfortunately, in some mid-twentieth-century thinking, this logic was set aside in favour of another, the 'ego mistake': With the spread of Freudian theory, the special term, 'ego', had come into ever wider circulation as a word for precisely that function (or 'structural' part) of the psychic self serving to *organize* and *promote* the self's definition or identity – its coherence, discreteness and continuity. A fundamental problem in the history of the century's thinking arose as certain schools of thought, including postmodern theory, came for a considerable time to identify the whole self – under the name of 'the subject' – with this idea of the ego.

Yet a conception fundamental to psychology, since the time Freud himself made it plain by differentiating the 'ich'/ego from other functions of the psyche, is that there is a vast difference between the complex and shifting field that constitutes the self and the spuriously compact balloon called 'the Subject' (ego) that postmodern thinking subsequently came to inflate in order to see it pop. The sensation of self-presence rarely comes in the form that ego organizes for us for special purposes on critical occasions. For most psychologists, *including* those most influenced by postmodern thought, problems associated with 'the subject' have never been quite the problems postmodern theorists saw in them. This is because psychologists have long made active use of the notion of '*self*', of which the (for postmodernists) troublesome, objectionable bit, 'ego' is regarded as only a quite limited part. To think that the self is nothing more than the portion, the formalized identity, which the ego makes it its business to designate and 'present' (make present) and promote in the world would to the psychologist be pointlessly asking for disaster. Indeed for psychologists (including now ego-therapists), as we'll see, problems of the self are only compounded by premature efforts to strengthen the rule of the ego.[8]

For vastly influential psychologists as early as Jung's break with Freud nearly a century ago, a proper understanding of the self has always *accommodated* virtually all of the fluidity, multiplexity, and instability of margins that mid-twentieth century (e.g. poststructural and postmodern) theorists said disproved the idea of the subject-as-ego. The ego *can* give a sense of 'centre' to the self, but no one in psychology has seriously suggested that that centre is the same as the totality of the self. Put simply, decentre the subject and you throw the ego into question, but have done nothing to dissolve or otherwise threaten psychological notions of the self – and of many problems of the self.[9] I'm suggesting, and hope to unfold later, that unlike contemporary ideas of the self, 'the subject' presented for decentring by traditional postmodern theories is something of a 'straw man'. That is, a conception that no one is disposed to regard as meaningful or practicable in actual life. This becomes all the more important when we observe in it a striking ambivalence toward 'the subject' (always rejecting, always covertly appealing to it) that certainly can subtend a conceptual (philosophical) position, but can't coherently be considered as conveying a universally agreed human truth more than as a symptom worth examining.

Who might it be that regards the fantasy of the total competence of language, for example, as so urgent – such that the pronoun 'I' can be not just a tag-name for the self but can eternally 'fix' and be co-extensive with it – that its failing to serve perfectly raises difficulties of an ontological order?

The number of humans feeling that the task of assembling a unified definition of themselves-as-wholes (such as the ego represents) is worth stopping to do when there is so much else they've wished to do before it was all over – and the number of those feeling that the task's impossibility should become the basis of their view of existence – appear in the past to have been so small as to be 'statistically insignificant'. What makes the issue *vital* is that the historical moment in which such attitudes *have* increasingly swept through people's thinking is the moment in which we now live. We may learn much about the postmodern if we can come to understand this extraordinary development.

* * *

I want to recall a way of seeing things that many contemporary psychologists (as well as sociologists) – influenced by attitudes from which postmodern thinking also springs – regard as fundamental to our understanding of how the self takes shape. This is the conception of the *field*.[10]

As Kurt Lewin put it a half century ago in bringing field theory from physics and mathematics into the social sciences (where it has been virtually seamlessly assimilated), each individual is 'of a field', a "life space" (1951: 57). We are not placed in an environment as entities separate from it, but *live* as part of and are *shaped in* the total array of physical and social events in contact *at a given time*: all those events, that is, however minute and however inchoately perceived, that *at some level* affect us and which we affect, including all those features and anticipations of the world that are constituted in our minds *at the time*, whether 'real' or imagined.

The field is close to what Fritz Perls called a '*Mitwelt*', a 'between' or shared world as a process. Seen from the standpoint of the therapist,

> the reality of the client ... changes constantly: there is not one configuration of the field on offer ... the field is constantly being reconfigured.... In the course of an hour's encounter the person may be a young, plaintive child, an oppressed manager re-enacting a work situation, a strong adolescent remembering leaving home, or someone negotiating with the therapist regarding vacation dates and fees. These different configurations of the field represent different states of being: involving perhaps shifts in the person's body positions, voice, thinking patterns, and mode of relating.

To be alive and contactful in the field, says the psychologist, "I need to recognise these shifts and ... that I'm witnessing varied 'selfings'". In this process one must in turn bring positively to bear an equal awareness of one's own alterations in relation to the other (Parlett 1991: 78).

There is no question here of some 'multiple personality disorder'. As a cloud passes, as you enter the room, as I recall a word, as you blink when I utter the word – during the course of every encounter at the fluid, ever-changing boundary between our selves and our environment – the field of our relations continually alters, so that for each of us the experience of our selves can finally be described only as a process – a continuous 'selfing'. One's self – not infinite in its nature, but a rich whole (whose full potential one can never 'finally realize', and that thus seems infinite) – is shaped differently from every other self by the particular conditions of one's biological and environmental history. Yet in each moment, some new sensation, feeling, valuing, desire, engenders a new prevailing 'figure' against the background of one's total being, and one's self thus manifests in a new way.[11] The figure in the field-of-the-moment is not the same as one's self, which is the fullness of all one's 'presents' even while – crucially – the array of this self is limited by the conditions, organic and relational, that have formed it.

Taken as wholes, we *can* be characterized in the sense that, over the span of our lives, patterns unique to each of us (for instance, in our different ways of dealing with seemingly similar situations) unquestionably reveal themselves. But – so long as we remain alive to what is actually and uniquely happening at what many therapists call the 'contact boundary' – these are continually modified and replaced. Thus we live at two paces – in the rhythm of our lives as wholes, and in the rhythm of our moment-to-moment 'self-presents'

– each interpenetrating and influencing the sense of the other. But when, for any reason, this flow from one state to another is arrested, locked into a form or pattern of thought and behaviour, then genuine relating and the possibility of growth – and of effective responsiveness to the reality of situations (which, however it seems, are always new) – are lost. In other words, it is in those *particular* conditions when the individual is rigidly 'fixed' as a 'person', in the way that postmoderns have imagined that the conventional 'subject' *universally* is, that his or her self's viability becomes genuinely 'problematic'. While it's getting ahead of the game to say so, in this perspective postmodern critiques of 'the subject' begin to reveal themselves to be in fact articulations of a profound unease *not* with the 'reality' of the subject – or self – but with profound problems that can develop *in connection with it*.

It's right to ask then by what means a sense of self – with its apparent coherence and discreteness – might arise and remain sustained, without our insistence on its having a fixed 'I'. The complexities of this perennial question make it impossible to develop a full-scale theory here, but a distinction put forward by Schafer and others may prove valuable and sufficient for the needs of this essay. They distinguish between the experiences of 'self-as-agent (I)' and 'self-as-object (me)', on one hand, and the experience of 'self-as-place', on the other hand, with no pronoun attaching to it – an experience perhaps (but not necessarily) prior to the emergence of such pronominal linguistic formulations for self as those we associate with 'I' or 'ego'.[12] In the organism in its field emerges – and continues – a sense of 'self-as-place' to which some sensations are felt to belong more intimately than others, and of a consequent sense of 'self as difference' from what is other, which we call – more for clarity in speaking than as the description of an absolute entity – a boundary between self and other. (A moment's settling quietly back into feeling what it's like simply 'to be' may confirm an almost intuitive rightness in this description of one's self, as compulsive labels such as 'I' and 'me' are allowed to dissolve away.) A vital feature of the mind-styles to which this essay is devoted will be an unusually acute and insistent attention to the inevitable plasticity of that boundary, of the nature of what is felt to be 'of the self' and 'of the other'.[13]

One of the pieces of evidence for a field notion of the self is that most people have experienced and made their way through profound conflicts among their diverse 'presents', occasionally with momentous effects on the course of their lives,[14] and with the sensation that their reality and identity were in cataclysmic danger, without imagining their very selves continuously to be on the edge of disintegration. That is, that often human beings appear to have lived with a sense of themselves as just such 'open-plan', open weave beings, somewhat more flexible and resilient, than writers have implied who in recent times have felt a more rigidly conceived subject to be a major crisis in their lives – as something that has failed or betrayed them. Again, who is it that has felt such a stark conception of the self to be an obligation, and for whom a more open and natural ('field') understanding of self seems so interdicted as to require fierce theoretical defence? And why?

* * *

I want to say something about the terms I use (and ones I don't use) in what follows. Ones that are in special need of mention are 'the unconscious', the idea of 'narratives' of psychological development, and the words 'symptom', 'fantasy' and 'psychology' itself.

An essential trait of the twentieth century – brought to the fore in science and made via technology to transform our everyday lives – was that we learned to live with 'truths' running counter to commonsense experience. Much of postmodern theory rests its persuasive power on our acceptance of that principle; we have to trust that what we think we see cannot be trusted. Psychology, too, concerns itself with what is not always 'commonly sensed' but may be, rather, powerful in us yet out of our day-to-day awareness. I can't think of a reason for making an exception of psychological thinking by declaring unilaterally that, unlike those other disciplines, it should stop doing this. Like everything else, its ideas must 'simply' be tested in the light of considered experience.

But, save when dealing with someone else's theory necessitating it, I don't refer to 'the unconscious'. While I have thought most of my life about the variety of ideas of a place called the unconscious (and have indeed been persuaded about important aspects of some of them), concerted theories about it frequently have as central to them some developed and relatively elaborate map of its *structure* that I feel is unnecessary for the purposes of this discussion. I believe deeply in the importance of things we do and say as a result of events in us (events certainly not to be 'mapped' elsewhere) that prove to be *out of our awareness*, and that these things we do and say can tell much about what is active in us out of our awareness, and that pivotal patterns of feelings, beliefs and expectations in us are revealed in this way. It is these patterns themselves, exposed in what we do and say, and the dynamics of their interaction with – or their failure to respond to – the changing fields of our experience, that concern me within this essay. I am interested in making no more claims than I need to make my point in a way that's consistent, and I don't plan to unpack any intricate chart of the unconscious in order to talk about those things here.

There will be frequent allusion in these pages to ideas of child development, and particularly of children's relations with parents (or their 'primary carers').[15] This kind of thing invariably makes some people feel queasy; most notably those who take mention of such matters as introducing undue speculation, tones of moral or political self-indulgence, or other sentimental thematic contaminants where they are trying to conduct 'properly serious' and 'pure' quasi-scientific or philosophical discourse about the nature of existence.[16] Yet to consider 'the nature of existence' – or indeed to consider any thought as 'pure' and free of formative context – is itself not something we do without developmental influence. How discourses might rule out the consideration of relational contexts within which human mentalities take their first form, while devoting unlimited speculation to further (social, theological, economic, political, linguistic) manifestations of formative relationships, is likely to be beyond readers who stop to think for a moment.[17]

The discussion to come is not an account of maladies, a nosography. When, for example, I use the word 'symptom' (as I've already done), it is not to enlist a theory of disease, but rather to point out some gesture or manner of speaking that recurrently 'falls in the company of' (*sympiptein*) some particular kind of thought and may be indicative of a previously unnoticed pattern of thinking.[18] Similarly, I've occasionally spoken of 'fantasies' we carry with us. (I said in Chapter 2, for example, that Unqle Sim was a fantasy.) The word 'phantasy', however, will also appear, and I intend both terms in the way that psychologists characteristically do. First, neither bears with it any pejorative connotation. And second, as distinguished from 'fantasy', 'phantasy' refers to a mental model of how things are, or would ideally be, that is *out of awareness*. We take it from the behaviour of an infant, for example, that it wants to survive yet we never imagine that it's thinking consciously: 'It would be good to survive'. While every case is of course subject to its own forms, it looks likely that we couldn't make sense of much of our behaviour without the assumption that it is in part informed by phantasy. *Both* fantasy and phantasy are held, among psychologists to whom I refer, to be powerfully active in influencing thought and action.

There is no generic word for the vast spectrum of disciplines dedicated to the understanding of mental processes. From the beginning, specialists in fields called theoretical, experimental and clinical psychology, psychiatry, and psychoanalysis and other forms of psychotherapy have followed teemingly diverse approaches and under many different appellations to which they have frequently assigned considerable significance. In this essay, cases will often arise where the very breadth of agreement among disciplines poses the greatest lexical problem, since there is no term including them all and it would be impracticable – and unkindly tedious if not downright fatuous – to itemize them individually each time. After much thought (and not infrequent desperation), in such cases I've elected to use the words most widely *believed* – though often erroneously – to embrace them in a generic way, that is, 'psychology' and 'psychologists'. But I must beg readers to bear in mind that this may well not be the epithet that all those to whom it refers would prefer to have applied to themselves, and that when I cite *specific* 'authorities', for every proposition advanced there will be some 'authority' offering an alternative. Indeed, it's in the spirit of this study, as an experiment in conjectural modelling, that I hope it will provoke positive testing – not least among 'psychologists' – in the light of alternative constructive models and evidence.

* * *

As we've begun to see, any effort to extinguish all rationales for reading postmodernity in the light of psychological observation is likely to end in logical and empirical tangles, not to say tears. It seems time to do something else. One 'something else' is to carry out the project we as postmoderns initiated of describing postmodernity in terms of the metaphors of psychology and, more importantly, to consider what can be the significance of a persistent and striking resemblance between the metaphors of postmodern culture and those of psychological culture. Or, as Christopher Norris in the closing sentence of a recent book recommended we do, to "reexamine" postmodernity's relation to one of "the dominant self-images of the age" (1993: 304). I feel that we'd be remiss to let slip the occasion to place the one kind of discourse into a dynamic frame with the other – the postmodern with the psychological; to search out with some honesty the interplay between their emblems and what this might tell about each. To put back into circulation in postmodern discourse, in other words, one of the modes of speaking about which it is most explicitly ambivalent – and to test and learn about the limits and forms of that ambivalence. If that seems to be a challenge, I believe both that postmodernism is strong enough to respond, and that it needs to.

I claim no priority nor any overarching ontological truth for psychological models. I pray no one will be deceived by my adopting themes from what are often regarded as therapeutic settings. While the observation of common practices will be important, this is not a normative psychology, in terms of good and bad, sick and well. It means instead to weave a slightly different fabric of understanding in which current ideas and activities may themselves be discovered in some of their otherwise unperceived relations to our broader experience. If the model seems to match postmodernity, then the two may have a 'family relationship'; understanding the one may offer some value in reading the other. Though I'll make frank use of strategies to show connections or how they may be found, I'd be pleased if the following chapters were thought not so much an 'explanation' as a work of poeisis, of constructive imag(in)ing around a pressing material topic.[19]

A MODEL

Something that critical thought has been particularly if not surprisingly disinclined to accommodate in its traditional dedication to the psychological interpretation of works – for example in the study of literature – is that, seen from the standpoint of psychology itself, some form of 'ambivalence' is not merely poignantly inevitable but an essential for life and health. There isn't in human experience the possibility of a fixed, unified feeling toward any object of our attention or indeed toward our selves. From the first moments of an individual existence no child can attain all that it wishes, no environment can satisfy all our native needs, and yet we keep going. (If in what follows, against my native impulse, I speak of a child as 'it', it's solely to avail myself of the luxury that English permits to avoid the gender trap that catches us all when we come to speak of adults.) The most elemental human dream, the phantasy of attachment to some never-ending life-source, has two unconditional countermarkers: separation at birth, and separation at death. Throughout our existence we're shaped by our responses to the disjunction between some sense of an 'ideal' and the reality of the limitations of our individual being. A simple unitary vision of existence either obstructs our response to the conflicting actualities of our condition or is so broad as to be without effect if not altogether meaningless. It's not difficult to conceive how the sight of such persistent conflicts and disillusionments might lead some to abandon existence. Only the 'mixed feelings' of ambivalence allow us genuine contactful relations with the mixed conditions of reality, and the possibility of carrying on.

Early in our lives we find primitive and crucial ways of dealing with life's 'mixed bag'. One that is repeatedly described in psychology is that until a *readiness for ambivalence* has grown, opposed values are dealt with by *splitting*, by keeping them separate in our awareness.[20] In our development as infants, for example, where a mother as carer is also one who *must* sometimes fail to appear to care 'in time': for its mental stability, for its survival, a child – unable, unready to accept that its mother is *both* these things – spontaneously divides in its mind the 'caring' from the 'uncaring' mother. Indeed, it's at the point that a child becomes able to think of, to live with thoughts of a mother (or primary carer) as that more complicated thing, a 'mixed being', that it begins – *needs* – to feel itself to be separate from her, from the perplex that she is.

So at important stages, for psychology, *division*, *separation* is a fundamental and in fact urgent feature of our unfolding. One is separated from one's first source, one separates qualities from one another, and one separates oneself from others. This kind of formative 'turning' happens also to be one on which, in some form or other, virtually all postmodern writers concentrate a great proportion of their attention.

Traditionally, and in fact commonly in postmodernists' view, this is the turning toward – among other things – 'reason', toward rational thought. Reasoning, conventionally seen, is the process of discrimination, of 'splitting' – of the division of both things we perceive and conceive into classes, together with the acceptance of certain accompanying principles or rules of thought of which the 'law of non-contradiction', as we've seen, is one of the most crucial; two mutually exclusive things can't be said of the same event. What contemporary indeterminism insists we observe is that the categories of reason 'do not hold (still)', and that – just as the child with a 'realistic' relationship to 'mother' must learn to live with the fact that it does not have two mothers (one nasty, one nice) but one complex one – we must leave simple, discrete divisions behind as in some sense delusory.

Psychologists tend to take a further step, to say that we need to learn to live in a state of ambi-valence – a condition of mind in which conflicting values are allowed to share the space and investment of our attention. It's a state many have called 'the depressive position'.[21]

As psychologists themselves often ruefully note, the term 'depressive position' is easily confused with 'depression', from which it's vitally different. 'Living in the depressive position' one may experience depression (about which we'll have much to say), but also many other things. For this and other reasons, and for its greater accuracy generally – partly since in fact it means precisely to have exceeded 'mere' depression – I speak of it instead as 'the ambivalence threshold'.

Something crucial for the future is that while it is a psychological position, the ambivalence threshold is never a 'solid state', a finally achieved 'resting place', but is a liminal condition of mind from which one may always fall back, that must continually be 'worked for' and 'worked through' in the face of life's vicissitudes – where, for example, *both* a fantasy of harmonious unity *and* a knowledge of the crushing impossibility of it are 'held' together in the mind. The special, leftover value of the more conventional term 'depressive position' is that it communicates something of the anguish and fear that may be forever anticipated in the potentially disintegrative experience of so directly and perpetually confronting, in full awareness, (1) what is desired with (2) its impossibility. For some, the fearsome aspect of the ambivalence threshold may seem so unapproachable that they will 'do anything' in their psychic lives to evade it, with (as we'll discover) important sequelae in their life stories.

A central theme in this book is that a great deal in what is commonly understood to be postmodern has its foundation in a particular pair of responses to the problem of ambivalence, to which postmoderns rightly sense that rationalist modes of 'splitting' are inadequate. That, in other words, in place of rational solutions arrived at by means of the systematic classification and hierarchical ordering of experiences, *and* – also – in lieu of moving to the ambivalence threshhold, postmodern thinking would promote instead, a third way, or pair of ways: the *radical 'splitting'* (a pluralist response), and the *radical 'merging'* (an indeterminist response), of our options, of the 'matter' of our experiences. I want soon to explore openly the possibility that these have their parallel in a particular process of mind. And – in subsequent chapters – what the implications of this might be.

For some four decades coinciding remarkably with the dates normally given for the establishment of postmodernism, numerous psychologists (along with many social historians and journalists) have been writing that 'narcissism' is the new and the predominant form of 'mental malaise' of our time. As one social critic, Christopher Lasch – with whom I shall take rather pugnacious issue in later chapters – famously (and influentially) expressed it, "Each society tries to solve the universal crises of childhood – the trauma of separation from the mother, the fear of abandonment, the pain of competing with others for the mother's love – in its own way", and for Lasch at the time that he wrote it a generation ago, as for many others since, "the character traits associated with pathological narcissism", "appear in ... profusion in the everyday life of our age".[22]

For the history of psychology itself the emergence of this perspective in the second half of the twentieth century marks a significant event, for it represents the replacement in many professionals' minds of what had been regarded as the conditions whose treatment had always been considered the very province of psychoanalysis – of neuroses thought to stem from conflicts among socially repressed desires within the individual psyche. I want to discuss the style of mind to which recent psychology has thus turned much of its attention. The words they use for it – narcissism, narcissist – carry common associations that do it no favours, and I mean to suggest an alternative term, but preserve the former's 'echo'. The term is 'narcissance'. I'll say more about it soon; but for the moment, just this:

In speaking of *narcissance* I mean to refer *not* to a *type of person*, but to a *type of process*.

I can best convey the qualities of this process if I begin with a brief account of what has been conventionally meant by 'narcissism'. Among psychologists themselves the fight was won a century ago both to hold onto the term 'narcissist' for its ancient and evocative metaphorical associations – the mythical hero Narcissus, first seeing his image reflected in a pool, pining after a beauty he cannot embrace or 'possess', kills himself – and to strip it of its unhelpful 'street' associations with 'self-centred' self-admiration and pleasure-seeking self-indulgence. The fact is that many of the latter connotations seem quite useful in the street but are virtually the opposite of what is meant in human psychology.[23] For here, 'narcissism' (as Karen Horney said sixty years ago) is not about self-centredness but to the contrary is about the loss of a sense of a centre and about self-alienation; it's in the end not about self-admiration and pleasure in oneself but is precisely about suffering.

The Narcissus we understand in a psychological way gazes into the mirror *longing* to see a face that might look back with love. 'Narcissism' relates to a mental disposition in which the *boundaries between the self and objects are not clearly defined*. The narcissant's quest is for objects – crucial above all being other humans-as-objects – that may somehow reflect back and thus confirm the image of his or her self.

As first elaborated by Freud, there are two phases in 'narcissism's' manifestation. 'Primary narcissism' occurs notionally in an infant prior to the concentration ('investment' or 'cathexis') of its psychic energy on external objects (principally the parents, parent surrogates and subsequent objects of desire), and is thought to be experienced as an undifferentiated or 'oceanic' union with a constant, certain and omnipotent being or force.[24] As we come to greater awareness of the external world, in this view, our investment shifts to some external object or objects. But when a child's primary 'object' has failed to fulfil or has abused the omnipotence s/he attributes to it – for example where a parent has gone or otherwise failed to provide the spontaneously (perhaps 'naturally') desired consistent love and care – 'narcissistic injury' may be the product, and 'secondary narcissism' can emerge. To defend the psyche against the disappointment, anxiety and pain that the child has come to associate with emotionally investing in an object (such as a parent or first carer), psychic attachment is stalled or arrested. The area of desire for relationships with others as separate from the self is disturbed. Desire is withdrawn, and diverted back to circulate within the self; a self now uncertain of its intrinsic worth outside of that undifferentiated union of which it still dreams and for which it continues to strive. Difficulties for the individual thus arise – in determining boundaries between the self and the objects of his or her attention, in determining what is 'real, out there' and what is part of the self. 'Secondary narcissism' – customarily spoken of simply as 'narcissism', as 'narcissistic disturbance' or as a 'disorder of the self' ("disturbances in the continuity, cohesion, vigour and value of the self") – is the result, and becomes a subject of psychotherapy's concern.[25]

Here is where, instead of speaking of 'malaise', 'neurosis', 'disturbance' or 'disorder' (unless I'm quoting someone else) with their heavy normative connotations, I begin to use the word 'process'. And where, instead of speaking of 'narcissist' (a personality type), I speak of the process – the procession of mental events – of 'narcissance'.

In psychological terms, living at the ambivalence threshold consists in 'owning', living with, the fact of separation; in containing and enduring value-dividedness (ambi-valence). It allows for an experience of self-as-place, of self-presence, within the shifting field. In a deep sense, one no longer takes either separation or dividedness – or a realistically measured dependence on others – 'personally'. It is felt not as a defect in oneself but as a feature of daily conscious being. No longer driven, dispersed and dissipated by the often necessarily buried yet endless struggle to elude the problem, one may be free to be oneself, to own one's personal, ever-modifying boundaries, and to move '*as* one' through the world.

But with any arrest or failure in this process – wherever it becomes impossible to achieve or maintain the depressive position, where the mind loses its footing at the ambivalence threshold – comes the dilemma. The point of focus for theories of 'narcissism' is the process that takes place as a consequence of separation, of breaches that have not been made tolerable at a pace, at a manageable scale, and in a context – an environment – capable of sustaining the child as it moves through such life-shaking changes.[26] Narcissant processes begin where true ambivalence can't be achieved, where cognitive splitting fails to fulfil its intended function, where attachment is withdrawn, and fragmentation erupts within the child's own sense of itself.

This turning point – the dramatic experience of psychic separation and loss – has been a centre of attention since modern psychology's inception, whether in the interests of the understanding of 'narcissism' or of any other dynamic in the development of mind. People often think of it – become aware of it first – in adolescence, with the loss of that never-to-be-replaced 'first true' love. Behaviourists are sometimes inclined tacitly to regard it as occurring incessantly throughout life in the repeated movement from satiety to hunger, or contentment to pain. Dynamic or 'depth' psychologists have variously seen it as arising as the child encounters the insufficiency of the parent as parent, or at the point of entrance into language or the realm of the Symbolic, or at the moment of realization of oneself as (also) other. Or earlier, with the awareness of the separateness of the breast. Or at birth, with the loss of 'oceanic oneness'. This last, while it seems to be getting down to basics, stripping away those alternatives that may be only reenactments of a 'birth trauma', may seem to many a fiction, resting on a myth of a blissful pre-natal 'symbiotic' condition (intra-uterine experience must itself, after all, be quite different in each individual case). But what is fundamental is that characteristically in narcissance one doesn't experience this 'trauma' as a one-off event. The sense of separation and loss is always there, ready to leap upon us (again), taking its most vivid form *by virtue of* its contrast with a vision, a phantasy, however fictitious and however out of awareness, of oneness or harmony. (The companion piece seeming to confirm such a vision is the awareness – and sometimes obsessional denial, which amounts to the same thing, psychologically – of the separation that awaits all, in death.) This figure of how-things-go *dominates the field* in what I will call a narcissant style of thinking, feeling and perceiving.

In this context, by a seemingly infinite variety of mechanisms, in narcissance one seeks some connection (fusion) with what is 'other' – a fusion that might obliterate the experience of separation and the depression and fear that come with it. Or one seeks to offset the loss of that hope by some turning inward, toward a 'self' that becomes all the more elusive since one's very difference from what is other is too painful to face. Narcissance emerges where in its development the mind isn't given to feel safe – to feel indeed that it will survive – as it confronts any crisis involving separation. Deprived of the chance to evolve a sense of self strong enough to carry out the job alone, or to build adequate self-boundaries to 'keep at bay' the barrage of conflicting options characteristic of life, it can form an unrelieved distrust of the peopled world outside. Thus stalled, it is incessantly riven through and through by feelings of dividedness and uncertainty that it might otherwise have perceived to be no fault of its own. The world, instead of being a mixed and frequently but tolerably messy place to live, becomes the constantly shifting mirror to what the mind itself both desires and fears most; a place both of warmth, welcome and safety, and of ceaseless danger and menace ready to drown the mind's being at every turn. (Here, in this incessant mirroring, the persistence and force of the mythic image becomes intensely real – the interminable ordeal of Narcissus, endlessly reflected in the pool yet ever rippling out of reach.[27])

Perpetually perplexed as to where responsibility and power lie, a narcissant mind can vacillate incessantly between the obsessional externalization of these (in feelings of inferiority and shame, or in paranoia) and identification with them (in manifestations of omnipotence, grandiosity). Striving to situate itself between such conflicting options, understandings, it becomes the site of the ceaseless production of interminable decodings, inferences and explications. Only, lingering within the depths of these turbulent cross-currents of projected and introjected identity and of infinitely proliferated meanings, concealed from its ever-raw self-consciousness and material scepticism ('realism'), is one luminous and unwavering but secret fantasy: the possibility – through an act of ideal intellection or imagination, through love, through spiritual devotion or through some form of solidarity with nature or with the human collective – of a transcendent oceanic union where it may merge ('again') with All in an eternally undivided One.

Clinically, then, traits commonly identified as typical of 'narcissism' (and more precisely, in this discussion, of narcissance) are a marked accentuation of:

1. a need and restless search for ideal infinite love, with admiration

or other forms of 'tribute' ('narcissistic supplies') solicited and temporarily accepted as substitute;
2. alternating feelings of omnipotence or 'grandiosity' and of helplessness, worthlessness or 'shame';
3. intense shyness, fears of abandonment/rejection, and a relentlessly sensitive self-reference in 'reading' others' behaviour;
4. a deep-running distrust of others, echoing an equivalent distrust for the self and a persistent sense of the world's and the self's own falseness, unreality;
5. a need to entertain, engage and charm – the compulsion to 'glamour' those whose qualities, aggressively idealized, can in turn be re-absorbed and exploited – alternating with a potentially cold ruthless contempt for, and the impulse to 'shame', others from whom no support is expected;
6. a shallowness of emotional life in relation to others and a shunning of intimacy – combined with a self-protective winning display of sympathy, and of confluence with others, secured by means of projection in place of genuine empathy for others' feelings;
7. extreme depression and feelings of emptiness alternating with manic hyperactivity and elation;
8. 'inexplicable' alterations between self-effacing compliance and explosive 'blind rage';
9. a sensation of standing at the brink of breakdown and irreversible desolation, a chronic need to damp-down deeper-running emotional affect, to resist uncontrolled excitement and the peril of explosive fragmentation and disintegration – coupled accordingly with feelings of depleting anxiety, exhaustion and hopelessness.

In the quality of these we can see that *narcissance* (literally, 'narcissing', 'narcissizing') is a process in which perceptions, understandings and behaviour are ruled by what appears to be a perilous struggle to achieve the equilibrium of a sense of self. Many of these features will in some form be familiar to every reader. We are narcissant – we all 'narcissize' – at times. 'What did he/she/you mean by that?' 'You were looking at me when you said that.' 'Nobody understands me.' 'I don't need anyone – I can do it myself.' 'What does that have to do with me?' 'I'm useless.' 'You're the most beautiful person in the world.' 'I'm suffocating, I want to be alone.' Sentiments like these are some of the tools of our existing. Many psychotherapists regard 'narcissism' as healthily positive at certain junctures in life, and it would be unexpected and perhaps worrisome if one's narcissance weren't engaged when one was, for example, thrust into conditions of severe social exclusion, personal danger or mental or physical abuse.[28])

In this essay I'll sometimes freely say 'as narcissants *we* – '. I'm not calling names. I'm speaking of what goes on when we 'narcissize', as we may when we feel our being's continuity inwardly troubled. (The phrase 'feel our being's continuity inwardly troubled' is important, since – by contrast – when we are free of narcissance we may often sense that our being is attacked from without, yet may be in little doubt inside as to where and who we are.) *To be 'a narcissant' is not to be a 'narcissant type of person'*. It is to be someone currently influenced by processes of narcissance. When these come to dominate our lives we may seem trapped forever in this style of being; narcissance *can* become self-perpetuating, and unless a means of transformation is found, the outcome may appear fateful and even catastrophic. But no one is fated to be 'a permanent narcissant'.

We can see now a quintessential, defining and pervasive predisposition of narcissance: *oscillation*.[29] Instead of holding to the complex attitude of authentic (and, incidentally, perhaps more 'realistic') ambivalence, in narcissance there is an inclination toward a kind of volatility characterized by 'swings' between opposed ('bi-polar') extremes of feeling and/or belief. I'll point out just three examples of the pattern, so recurrently evident in the traits I've indicated above.

One of these is the circle of *grandiosity* – or the feeling of omnipotence – and *shame*; of *idealization* and *contempt*. Common and crucial misunderstandings have to be made clear here. One is that, psychologically, 'shame' and 'guilt' are radically different things. In the simplest terms, guilt is felt as remorse for something one has done. Shame is felt as remorse for what one *is*. While an incident may elicit it – particularly for the narcissant – it is not about any specific incident but about the whole self, about one's worth and right to exist. (Frequently remarked among contemporary psychologists is the extent to which the misunderstanding of this difference – or the simple failure to *observe* shame – characterizes, and endangers the effectiveness of, conventional practices based on Freudian drive-repression theory with its attention to guilt.[30])

A second thing that has to be better understood is that grandiosity or a feeling of omnipotence is far from always "noisily proclaimed". As a resource called on, not infrequently in desperation, to overcome very private feelings of shame, it may more often in fact be "secretly and shamefully harbored".[31] Grandiosity is *not* always brought into play (visibly) to rival and outdo others. It *may* appear as exhibitionist self-display ('I am here!') to stimulate interest (without which in the first instance no child can survive), or as glamour in whose warm aura one envelops others, to elicit a return of warmth for the self. Conversely it may sometimes arise to fend off what are felt to be others' dangerous incursions. But as a way of defending against anxieties of terrible *dependence* it is fundamentally drawn on to 'save the self', to secure the sense that 'I *can* – and am *needed* to – survive'. With it, typical thoughts are: 'I am solely responsible for his/her unhappiness.' 'I can keep this friendship/partnership/business/marriage/family together singlehanded.' 'I alone can solve this.' 'No one can save him/her but me.' 'They will not survive without me.' 'I am the sole cause of my illness.' 'If I hadn't made that mistake we'd be in business / they'd be alive today.' 'I must watch every word I utter – the slightest inflection of my voice now may kill her.' Crucially, if such feelings *were* revealed, many of the problems they bring about (with others and within oneself) could be drawn into the open and dealt with. But contrary to popular impression, a feeling of *omnipotence may be the last aspect of oneself that one can face*. As the preceding examples make plain, it can be 'a rod for one's own back'. Not unsurprisingly, as the other side of shame – while it may often rescue us from certain immediate self-doubts and angsts – grandiosity can be the most punishing instrument of self-persecution.

With the phrase 'as the other side of shame', the force of oscillation becomes apparent. As many regularly observe, in a 'narcissist', there is seldom idealization of the other without an under-running shame for oneself, rarely a feeling of omnipotence without a current of contempt for the other. Omnipotence and shame are locked together in a state of permanent oscillation; where one appears, the other is not far behind, lurking. A classic trace of this oscillation is revealed in our common intuition that if (as we well understand) shame leads to our 'hiding', displays of grandiosity can be a form of hiding. In narcissance, each is continually 'overturning' the other to redress the internal balance for the survival of the psyche.

In this book examples of the grandiosity/shame nexus will recur with a frequency out of proportion to its significance in narcissance as a whole. This is because it is grandiosity that people most typically associate with 'narcissism', and by keeping an eye on its actual role and operation in narcissance we can bring our everyday thinking into touch with the dynamic qualities and real complexity of each of the many processes of narcissance, of which this is just one.

Thus narcissants are, as we've seen and as psychologists put it, intensely *field-dependent*. The world and the immediate environment are taken as reflections – and in fact as inextricable aspects – of one's self. Narcissance demands reassurance of belonging, as though belonging were virtually the institution and essence of self-as-place, of the feeling of being, and so a narcissant has a sometimes desperate (often out-of-awareness yet driving) need to 'attune'. Again oscillation emerges, now in the mixed desire for both intimacy and flight, existing side by side. In narcissance one is wrenched between the feeling that survival itself depends on there being no separation or difference from another and the terror of the 'suffocating' loss of self in an all-engulfing dependence on and merger with the other.[32] It's difficult to conceive of relationships' taking place without a dimension of confluence. From common (and romantic) exchange ('We think exactly alike, you and I!') to team spirit, to orgasm, some of our most intense feelings of 'health' come with the experience of solidarity or union with others. In narcissance, however, boundaries in the field may be obsessively obliterated and, alternately, re-erected as impenetrable fortress-walls between the self and others.[33]

A way to begin to apprehend in full the disconcerting power of narcissant oscillation is to see that when we find depression but also manic behaviour, or grandiosity but also shame, contempt but also idealization, confluence but also withdrawal into isolation, we are often in each case considering one event – that is, one axis of value and feeling in the urgent almost viscerally cycling search for equilibrium. The process – in a perpetual round of self/other contempt, for instance – may powerfully perplex one's perception of and relations with others. Polarization and oscillation together form a mechanism on which a narcissant mind seizes in its struggle to find a 'clear', 'hard-and-fast-enough' definition of its self to 'stand' – to stand firm against the bewildering tide of choices, conditions, qualifications, inflections of the other, the morasses of compromise, the sea of detail ('Who am I, to judge?'). Extremes, opposed feelings can be concurrent; spiralling together. Many will recognize this who have, in the midst of the manic exhilaration of a party or a dance – or in the presence of someone who's been the focus of all their desires – felt a wave of depression or loneliness.

Here, 'extremes' is vital. It may often seem that so many features are associated with the model before us that it surely must in the end be so expansive a model as to be ultimately meaningless. But narcissant oscillation is *not* merely instability or uncertainty. What at first glance seems to open the way to an infinity of attitudes and feelings actually turns out, as we look more closely, to be an example not of infinite options but of *contradictions*, a tension and flux between *polar contrarieties*. Oscillation, a product not of openness but of ambivalence, is Either/Or. What is precisely *not* available is an open array of positions and the possibility of living both responsively and at relative rest with the rich and continuous, unbroken *spectrum* of meanings and choices that characterize the experience of an openness to the vicissitudes of life.

This is crucial. *Neither* feelings of helplessness nor of potency, for example (each of which is sometimes experienced, after all, in all our lives) is proof of narcissance. Nor is the conflict between self and other, wish and fear, pleasure and pain, reality and desire, depression and manic excitement, between the impulses of confluence and withdrawal, between impulse and compulsion, between aim and necessity – each a conflict sometimes experienced, after all, in all our 'normal' lives. What *is*, is an unmistakeable volatility (or 'lability'), marked by the irresistible *oscillation between them.*[34]

But isn't this only a description of how we all are – of our aiming (in ways of which we're well aware) toward equilibrium, requiring continually condition-sensitive management and compromise? The difference appears in the very words we use. For in narcissance, far more often, the shifts are: (1) out of awareness; (2) out of contact ('tune') ultimately with the circumstances, following rather a course of dynamic internal events often governed, as we'll see, by a spectrum of relation-defeating mechanisms; (3) uncompromising, never establishing equilibrium; and (4) unmanageable, 'beyond control'. What characterizes narcissance in this way is not merely extreme fluctuations in time and extreme ambivalence at a given time, but a marked rigidity in the pattern of this behaviour in a field. If one feature appears (such as grandiose feelings), another radically opposed feature (such as feelings of shame) is close behind. It is not a fixed personality but *a stereotyped pattern of relations*, of processing experiences, that a narcissant is more disposed to *bring with* him or her to a field, when another person in the same field might be inclined more openly to 'take things as they come', to be prepared for surprise. This difference between 're-acting' (acting again, as before) and responding – living authentically in a way that's responsive to what *is unique* in the field, growing and changing with experience – will prove vital.

* * *

Something more needs to be said now about 'causes'. Among contemporary theories of human psychological development (with which postmodernism can't in the end part, as I've said) the most widely favoured story associates the crucial onset of consciousness and the entrance into the realm of signs, of language (the Symbolic) – and the separation from or division in the self – with some form of separation from the mother.[35] References to 'the matter (*matière*) of mother' will appear unseemly to many, when they seem to place biographical constructions on concerns of philosophical high-seriousness. While clinical reports abound with what would seem to be evidence for such causal accounts and I'll occasionally refer to these, I don't intend in the end to lean heavily on them.[36] This is not simply because the discussion's *ultimate* destination is a consideration of widescale (cultural) developments rather than 'merely' personal ones. It's because the pivotal, critical dimension in the account is not the loss of a personal mother but something else, as I'd like now to make clear.

What is *not* accounted for in that story of separation and its effects is that narcissance doesn't arise with everyone to the same degree. We have all been separated from our mothers. What differentiates narcissant responses from others is that the separation and the processes of self-formation have been *unsupported*. They have been unsustained by forms of caring, that is, that (1) reflect back to the developing individual a clear sense of his or her own worth, in and of his/her self as an individual, rather than as one there on sufferance, to fill another's needs; that (2) reinforce for him or her – by some form of 'holding' and by buffering and filtering the otherwise potentially crushing bombardment of ever-new external and internal events – a sense of the relative safety, the survivability of change and separation; that (3) convey a language – a gathering of conceptual and emotional tools and strategies – that s/he may use in refreshing for him- or herself this sense of survivability, a set of ways to 'speak to oneself' that can meliorate tension and provide comfort in moments of crisis; and (4) impart a sustaining sense of the richness and vitality of fresh experience, of the life-giving benefits of change, and of the worth of trying, of value in living and of life itself. Whatever the elemental matrix is imagined to be, the sense of a separation from it *unsupported* in this way is what perpetuates narcissance.[37] In matters of support and its absence, the biological/non-biological facts of parenting seem actually of limited relevance, and the scope of the issues at hand reach far further than the word 'mother' might traditionally have suggested. We'll consider in more depth later the sense of support and how a culture may affect it.

At this point I need to leave behind the sort of etiological exploration of narcissance that I might have been expected to unfold. That is, I'm not going to spin out some more elaborate determinist explanatory narrative of the origins, in individuals or indeed in a culture, of narcissance. The narrative examples offered in these and future pages are generally confined to illustrations and each is given fundamentally as a heuristic scenario rather than a historical account of narcissance's causes. Some readers will be interested in finding 'the precise biographical story' of, say, traumatic experiences – so often associated with the subject-matter and procedure of traditional 'psychoanalysis' – leading to narcissance, but I want to forestall any disappointment that might stem from my failure to trade in detailed and lengthy speculations of that sort here.[38] My subject is – to borrow a therapists' term, in a spirit that postmoderns will recognize – the 'phenomenology of the here and now'.

If narcissance revolves around difficulties in discerning difference between self and other, are we talking then about a species of people who are typically social failures? It needs to be pointed out here, as it often is by psychologists, that narcissants may often be among society's 'highest-achievers'.[39] Indeed it's in the particular felt interest of narcissants more than most to gain outward success, even at extreme actual cost to their inward lives.

Narcissance is only one complex constellation of mental processes.[40] As psychologists have frequently put it, it is in 'narcissism' that the concern regarding self "is in the foreground of awareness instead of being comfortably in the background" (Mollon 1993: 9). There are other kinds of mind-style. In the lives of many people, far greater attention and energy – and levels of distress, to which narcissants have no overriding claim – are focused on what is true and what's false, what's right and what's wrong, what's logical and what's not, what's pleasurable and what isn't, what's the best thing to do to achieve what they desire, or even what a deity might wish them to believe and be. For *them*, challenges to the self – for all the turmoil they may bring – are something they recognize and *feel they can live with*. The quality of their lives is thus markedly different from that of narcissant living.

In view of the familiarity of many of its traits it may seem strange that we aren't more aware of narcissance as such – as the sweeping force it can be in individuals' lives. For a number of profound reasons, narcissance makes it its business not to be detected, and society makes it its business not to detect it. As matters unfold, it can prove increasingly urgent that society take full intelligent stock of these forms of evasion.[41]

An unexpected resource in bringing 'narcissism' to public light, however – if one that presented problems of its own – was the introduction into the discussion of recent history it was afforded by late twentieth-century conservative social historians I've mentioned (such as Christopher Lasch), joined by journalists and publicists (such as Peter Marin), and even political figures of the interesting stature of Vice-President Spiro Agnew. A characteristic of this movement was its explicit discomfort with, if not an invariably hostile view of, the influence of 'narcissism' as a 'malaise' infecting current society.[42] In spite of their shrewd and often imaginative perception of connections between certain socio-economic forces and a selectively envisioned species of narcissism, this was essentially a '*Zeitgeist* approach', meant to describe a whole society as imminently self-indulgent, passively immobile, hypochondriacal, and finally indolent. And with few if any exceptions, they accorded this same generalized antipathy to postmodernity – when they felt prepared to name it.

A characteristic of many such writers has been that, while they've been vociferous in calling this culture 'postmodern', they have declined to discuss what postmodern thinking itself might actually consist of or how it worked – for reasons sometimes candidly revealing their hesitation to argue directly with postmodernism's propositions. (Lasch, for example, rarely referred to and showed no signal interest in examining the massive body of contemporary postmodern theory.)

This doesn't in itself invalidate their suggestions; often, in their historical moment, it wasn't within their conceived remit or their disciplines' purview – or necessary expertise – to do so. But at least two difficulties were produced by these fitful habits of accounting. One, their reports of the (ostensibly postmodern) 'culture of narcissism' were so tied to preconceived agendas (of a socially monitory variety) as to be, from an intellectual prospect, pointlessly divisive. Pointlessly, that is, exactly in the sense that they would not engage with postmodernity's 'point' or the 'points' it put in making it. And, two, that – bent as they were on *uncovering* 'malaise' as a collective *outcome* – they failed to inquire into what processes, precisely, might link what they saw as the looming shadow of 'narcissism' with the actual discourse and practice of the times. These have left a kind of vacuum in the discussion of contemporary culture, where those speaking of it as 'narcissist' were confined to a narrow group who were unprepared to consider in any depth the *experience of the culture where and as it has spoken for itself*. This seems to me unhelpful. At least, that is, if there is any sense in the thought that you can't 'use' psychology unless you're prepared to test it by a relatively close examination of the specificities (the terms, claims and behaviour) of the culture you've engaged to 'use' it on.

It can be helpful here, for clarity, to convey something of the idiom of the 'malaise' view. Lasch and his adherents have often expressed a sentiment that the 'new' generation speaks all too much about one's 'inner child', about 'realizing oneself for one's self', and about the responsibilities of the 'good enough mother', and that such a vocabulary intimates a 'narcissistic self-concern' that tends inevitably to 'baby' the individual by laying all the blame for our state of mind and behaviour on parents in an irreversible past. We can fully sympathize with the social-critical implications of this perspective, if it's correct. The difficulty is that it discloses a consummate disregard – as though out of a desperation whose own sources deserve attention – for the most fundamental aspects of how 'narcissism' actually works.

The protest against 'narcissistic self-babying' is a classic case, and is worth a pause: as is regularly and forcefully insisted by psychologists, if a 'narcissistic' patient is told he or she "could not help how he/she is, the shame may be increased. If the parenting was so bad that the patient had no choice, the patient is then seen as so damaged and crippled as to be beyond hope" (Yontef 1993: 337). For this reason, a vital part of contemporary therapeutic process is to make it possible for the patient to see how he or she is part of a field of reciprocal influence in which s/he has always been an active agent, and to open the way to a balanced sense of his or her own responsibility. The therapist knows well that to undermine this perception, instead (for the sake of, say, the therapist's own self-esteem in having given empathy or consolation or the easy assuagement of shame), risks only to perpetuate narcissance – to swell to overwhelming proportions the very sense of shame that is near the heart of narcissance.

It would be wrong to ignore such perspectives as the malaise view. Because the narcissant lives not in a vacuum but in a field of relations, an essential in describing the place of narcissance in contemporary culture must be to show how it is articulated with processes of mind most actively in opposition to it. This is a field of exchange fraught with tensions. In our times, a strong voice is heard that takes the 'narcissist' to task. There are signs – in the febrile passion of the response to the narcissance it seems to detect (however intuitively and without fully exercised intelligence or commitment) in postmodern trends – that this is not simply a rationally neutral counterposition but an acerbic 'rival' voice, that of the headmasterly 'pull your sox up' school. It appears to be one of the voices of Unqle Trim. The case of malaise critics' own patent unease may in fact be especially useful. Few kinds of discourse can be so illuminating as those produced by people whose responses to the 'uncomely' phenomonon of human narcissance are violent, and they need to be examined. In the end, culture in the developed world is and will be shaped in part by these counterpositions, locked in combat, and we must be prepared to review the implications of that.[43]

* * *

A few themes have insisted on being heard so far in these pages. One is that just as I've suggested that postmodernity is but one local response to 'the way things are', so is narcissance. And that as far as narcissance and its struggle with ambivalence are concerned, it will be apparent now that ambivalences at root are not about simply the frustration or confusion or conflict of 'desires' – they engage us with questions concerning the quality of reality itself.[44] That, moreover, these can allow in at *psychological* levels what seem to be metaphysical or ontological problems for humans, having to do with self and meaning, that have now a strangely familiar ring about them in a postmodern context. And that this coupled with the peculiar historical coincidence in contemporary life in the developed world of the widely reported spread of 'narcissistic' thinking alongside 'postmodern' thinking suggests that we'd do well to begin to have a closer look at them, side by side.

4 Ways of Speaking

In this chapter we look at things people say who have come to be identified with the tradition of postmodernity, and in the next at some of the things we do as we make our way into a postmodern style of life.

PROCESSES

Separation and Loss

Perhaps one of the most unusual features of postmodernist thinking is that in spite of its widely proclaimed resistance to grand narratives, it regularly offers a story of its own, an account of separation and loss, a momentous and irreversible *rupture*, in the formation of human consciousness. In Baudrillard's model of existence, for example, humanity is the victim of "a perfect crime". The "world as it is, before it even shows itself", is "misappropriated", stolen in a moment analogous to "the first few seconds of the Big Bang". "After that, our destiny is the accomplishment of this crime ... the continuation of the nothing" where Reality never returns, but is something only represented by us (1996: 1–2). For Deleuze and Guattari, the conflicts and repressions that characterize the social/Oedipal drama are ultimately ones where the process of desire-production they wish to endorse is interrupted, where desire is 'cut off'. "The child is separated from the mother's body by means of the socially imposed prohibitions which found their separate identities."[1]

This adoption of the vision of the separation from the mother as an essential metaphor for the inaugural crisis in human experience signalled by postmodernism is not confined, of course, to Deleuze and Guattari. Wherever experience is represented – as it frequently is in postmodern writing – as a dramatic ebb-and-flow of desire, a specific and determinate situation is foregrounded: that of '*lack*'. The initiating event for the emergence of the individual psyche for Lacan (whose schema's subtle and rich thematic profusion it is impossible to represent adequately in this space and which must itself be a matter for consideration later) is a 'biographical' one, the separation from the mother.[2] Relentlessly thereafter, for Lacan, this 'split' or 'cut' will resonate throughout the language in which the mind constitutes itself, and the 'subject' will be forever in search of an object, a site of infinite plenitude (an *'objet petit a'*) that can never be attained but in whose vain quest the subject interminably pursues human others who might take its place. For here is where we fantasize that we might 'recover' our identity, in our contact with – at some boundary marking out the difference between us and – the other. This fantasy is complemented and in fact driven, paradoxically, by a further or more fundamental, inchoate phantasy that identity itself might be *forsaken* in the interest of a more luminous and blissful dissolution in an originary oneness, in our merging once again with the other, imagined in terms of the 'mOther', from whom we have – by a fateful 'cut' (the first of many) – been forever severed. "This relation to nature is altered by a certain dehiscence at the heart of the organism, a primordial Discord".[3]

It is this *lack* and the mechanisms that arise in response to it, in Lacan's view, that haunt and impel the dynamics of mind. In the absence, for example, of the 'things' to which our utterances may seem to refer, and of the definitive meanings of the signifiers by which we would do the referring, it is inscribed in the very conditions of the language in which we think. Here the decentring of the subject is most dramatically enacted. By the very marks of lack – those 'nothings' we encounter where we had anticipated fulfilment at the point of contact with others – the subject's identity is 'defined'. Yet in this 'definition' – our being 'merely other' than what we can neither be nor possess – the nullity of our 'selves' is to be known. In this, and in what emerges in increasingly more refined form the more deeply we study Lacan – almost as though his very language enacts the search for the language with which to articulate this virtually unspeakable 'tragedy' (as he often calls it) – is an unmistakable recapitulation of the narcissant drama.

But there are a great number of writers intimately linked with the postmodern who, as we've seen, have every express reason to stand clear of psychological theories and the stories of 'tragedy' at the level of individual experience of which Lacan spoke. One of the supreme achievements of the linguistic indeterminism near the heart of postmodern thought has been its philosophically dedicated argument that there is no 'original text' and thus no 'original author' or creator. A prevailing effect, then, is that there emerges a condition, among such readings, where 'absence' becomes *figural*. This new, unique 'lack', this 'disappearance of origins', this 'void', this *absence itself*, has become one of the most pre-eminent and persistent themes in postmodern thought.

Jacques Derrida vividly dramatizes the case. Following decades' dazzling – and enormously influential – commitment to the exposure of that absence, in a series of interviews he demonstrates how the process works in his own experience. Speaking of a recurrent dramatic motif in his writing, he tells of "a kind of philosophy of cinders" (Derrida 1995: 210).

> The cinder is that thing ... that remains after a material has burned, the cinders or ashes of a cigarette, of a cigar, of a human body, of a burned town.... [T]he body of which cinders is the trace has totally disappeared, it has totally lost its contours, its form, its natural determination. Non-identifiable.[4]

In an interview that he chose to publish under the title "Passages – from Traumatism to Promise", Derrida speaks at length of a *singular wound* that takes place at the date of an utterance (for example, of a published text). At the text's individual inception, its very *difference* initiates its *différance*. That is, the singular date of the text being no longer present, the event of its creation is lost. This is its "*wound*", an "incision" that a poem, say, "carries in its body", at the point of its being cut off from its own birth, from the 'promises' it makes. "It loses what it wants to keep. It burns what it wants to save.... [T]his wound or this pain of the effacing in memory itself ... is a pain reawakened in itself." Philosophy, too, then, is "the question about its own source.... [P]hilosophical discourse goes from jolt to jolt, from traumatism to traumatism" (376–81). Derrida agrees to the interviewer's explication that "the effacement of the wound, of the date ... would be ... the source, not to say the origin, for example of philosophy" (382). Thus, says Derrida,

> this place, which for the moment I cannot identify ... is perhaps what I am looking for.... I see the journey of my brief existence as a journey in view of determining and naming the place from which I will have had the experience of exteriority.... [W]hat I suffer from inconsolably always has the form ... of loss ... as if an appeal for a witness had no witness ... not even the witness that I could be for what I have lived. This for me is the very experience of death, of catastrophe. (206–7)

At this point it is absolutely essential for me, personally, to insist that, here and in what is to follow, we do not for a moment confuse the exploration of the discourse of a culture with the exploitation of personal lives. Jacques Derrida, like Baudrillard, Deleuze, Guattari, and Lacan, can be taken as making use of the language customarily attributed to personal experience *for metaphorical purposes*. In a sense, a truly 'clean' scholarly report would resist the slightest thought of our being moved, in the way that one would be moved by an encounter with a 'real person' saying what Derrida says here – on the grounds that what was at hand was too much more widely significant, 'too important for that'. Try as I may, I can't go quite that far. But the net thematics of such discourse seen *as discourse* are beyond doubt, and stark: an inconsolable suffering; a catastrophic trauma carried forward and ever repeated, a wound, a loss, a burning away of origins and, with this, the effacement of the material self-image (the body) and the 'emergence' of a non-identifiable identity; and the perpetuation of a quest whose central desire is for the reflection, the recovery of a conviction of 'exteriority', of difference from what or who is other. In this account of an interminably unanswered appeal 'for a witness that I could be', we intimately and unmistakably recognize the unique model of experience of the bereft to which it belongs.

Betrayal

Something essential in our practical lives is our ability, after loss, to make restorative, trusting contact with others and with our momentarily 'shaken' selves; without this, human relations can't be expected to go on. In narcissance, however, exactly this kind of readiness to trust in others is under threat. And why not? With a child's entire being in the hands of its first carers, where for any reason it feels their will imposed without a matching valuation of its own independent being, the humiliation and the experience of worthlessness seem hard to avoid. Indeed where a child is *unsupported* in its encounter with the natural train of comings and goings, of disappearances, of absences of those who give it life itself, is it possible for its spreading apprehension of betrayal to be simply reasoned away? As children, when we're old enough to utter it, we may find ourselves saying to our parents, our carers, 'But you said –!' The very fact of *being* a parent, of being the one accountable for our very life – mightn't that itself be 'saying', 'promising' something? Perhaps, in our most elemental phantasy, an apparent promise so omnipotent and benevolent that it *must* sometime be 'betrayed'? May we all actually have sometime felt like crying out something like 'But you said –!'?

In narcissance one cannot let go – cannot relinquish the grief, the anxiety, the anger that has accrued from such occasions.[5] To make this worse, in narcissance one cannot allow oneself to *feel* these in so dependent-on-others a way that it might crush the sense of one's very own worth. Instead – and here will be one of the seeming paradoxes of narcissance, one having as much import as it is hard to grasp – certain distinguishing diagnostic features of narcissance appear: there is (1) an inability to return to a state of peace and of interest in the surrounding world *when the carer* (or the sense of the carer's care) *has returned*. There is (2) an inclination to regard others as using oneself to fill their own needs. And (3) instead of flexibility of reaction to changes in situation such as the removal and return of desired objects, there sets in a more all-consuming, rigid and portentous stereotyping of responses. In narcissance, one builds a counterstructure, a continuity of grief, anger, anxiety and distrust; that is, one consolidates a *system for the dissolution of systems* of belief and trust. In effect, a kind of constitutional affective (emotive) scepticism is moved into place. The sense of a world in which *exploitation and betrayal are the background* becomes an ever-present reality.[6]

It's easy to miss the subtlety of this chain of events. In fact we can easily ignore its extent – the number of those it may touch – in a society. Does it happen only in explicitly, graphically 'unhappy families'? Let's think back. The sense of betrayal is about the sense of promise and its abuse. Yet children behaving as ones who've been abusively deceived far from always feel themselves consciously to have been abused. People whose habits of mind turn out to be deeply narcissant often actually seem at first glance not only to be supremely confident, but to have come from 'adoring', 'ideal' homes. 'Ideal', the word so frequently applied, is well-chosen. Parents who idealize their children – that is, who are unable moderately to accept their own limitations and consequently act under the compulsion to see their children as ideal(ized) extensions of themselves – *do* frequently 'produce' children who seem buoyantly inflated. They are exactly that: pumped up, inflated to fill their parents' airy dreams, and otherwise – as they learn – often empty within.[7] Here in precisely this 'emptiness' – the compulsively, even meticulously staged 'perfection' of their material origins, this *lack of material explanation* for the sensation of loss, of this absence, this void – is one of several sources we'll encounter for the marked inclination of narcissants to *look to abstractions* for their bleakness' cause, and for its cure.

We can recognize now the roots of a life-practice among narcissants in their relations with others. When we're caught in a situation, back to the wall, where our dignity, our hard-won few values, our very survival perhaps, seems to depend on the articulation of a difference, a disagreement with another – how should we behave? Where a deepest wish and need is to merge, to harmonize with others – and above all when the *injunction* set for one's life has been the icon of unbroken harmony like that of 'the ideal family' – what to do? Dare confrontation and the hazards of separation, regardless? The 'solution' to this is a form of behaviour that few children don't sometimes use, but that some adults will call on throughout the course of their experience as narcissants. 'But you said –!' ceases to be merely a cry; it becomes a strategy. The charge 'You *betray yourself*' becomes the retort and the face-saving if not life-saving theme. Like the child, a narcissant unpicks and teases out in fine-gleaned and long-gathered detail the *other's self-contradiction*. (Is there a parent who doesn't know with pleasure, not to mention occasional desperation, what can be the fierce logic, the 'rigour' of a child?) Inch-by-inch, the betrayer is hoist to his/her own petard. Confrontation (full-frontal difference) seems averted, while 'justice is done'.[8]

Along with this frequently comes a further process – one that Kernberg and others have called a 'disappointment reaction'. "Behind the consciously remembered ... 'disappointments'" come "devaluations of the parental images ... in order to avoid the underlying conflict with them". Narcissants here "reveal dramatically" a "*total devaluation*" of the parents or others in whom power has been invested. By means of the 'disappointment reaction', the child's anguish is transmuted into a typically narcissant 'theory': that the *parent* is a disappointment, a being lamentably damaged beyond repair. As Kernberg has paraphrased the voice, "'Either you are as I want you, or you cease to exist'."[9]

By the grace of the deconstructive 'But you said' manoeuvre, exposing the counterplay of the other's very utterances, managed often with tact and characteristically with infinitely sensitive finesse, the foundations of authority are dismantled and dispersed. In this way, anger is 'retroflected', 'swallowed', and there seems to be a chance for the narcissant to obliterate dependency, erase conflict, displace grief, and dissolve the anxiety of separation. For a time.

We're under no compulsion to say that it is postmodern to be invariably concerned with 'betrayal'. But there are signs – in postmodernism's vigilant and diligent regard for local contexts and the contingency of meanings, its eminent 'lack of trust' in language as a medium for the representation of truth, its unsleeping attention to the fineprint of what is said, its rigorous aim to search out inconstancy, inconsistency and contradiction, and its express intent on the dismemberment of foundational authority – that we may be on the right track in conceiving of a connection. The theme becomes more explicit as we 'get down to cases'. Deconstruction, for example (as its leading proponent in Britain throughout its founding years often said), is "a technique for drawing out those ruses of 'unconscious' signification that haunt" our utterances (Norris 1986: 11–12). In *"unconscious"* and *"haunt"*, Norris effectively invokes a psychology at the core of deconstructive activity and, in *"ruses"*, a resonance most particularly of suspicion. As Derrida says, the 'displacement' of 'the centrality of the subject', so essential to deconstruction's enterprise, was from the beginning part of what was commonly called a "discourse of 'suspicion'" (1995: 257–8, 264). We have returned full-circle to that poignant refrain we've noted in Derrida and others – one of the most frequently reiterated abstractions or 'displacements' in postmodern discourse of the child's sentiment of betrayal: 'language promises a promise it can never keep'.[10]

This phenomenon is readily observed in Baudrillard's vision of a supreme ultimate deception whereby reality has been perfectly and invisibly 'murdered' and we find ourselves dissolved as selves by cultural – if not metaphysical – powers utterly beyond control. It can be glimpsed in the web of socio-economic, political and cultural treachery as portrayed by Deleuze and Guattari, whose first project is to attack the foundations of processes by which humans are severed from the conditions of the production of desire by the dominant structures of meaning and the colonization of the individual psyche. Narcissant echoes don't end here. Perhaps the most widely celebrated model for postmodern dissent and a watchword for postmodern solidarity is the reiterated defiant 'distrust' of and concerted attack on the articles of faith promoted by an Enlightenment patriarchy and its 'grand narratives'. Jean-François Lyotard's famous injunction to Western culture to cease and desist from *nous raconter des histoires* is cited more often than any other as the first point of postmodern revolt against a civilization that had universally misled us. An accompaniment to these has been the enormously popular topos in postmodern literature, perhaps most passionately theorized by Paul de Man, that – lest any reader ever be further deceived (as Realism had deceived us) – it was the first task of fiction itself to foreground its deceptions. We are so accustomed to this formula now that we forget how extraordinary it is (as is Lyotard's narrative appeal for the overthrow of narrative) in the traces of obsessionality it discloses.[11] The indelible value of such texts lies in their poetic power, and what is 'betrayed' in them more than most things is their anxiety of betrayal.

Alongside these, in the discussion not only of art, literature and philosophy but in the social sciences and the study of economic and political forces, recent discourse has everywhere carried traces of the representation of an elemental deception unfolded by Lacan in his account of 'the mirror stage'. At a point between the ages of six months and two years, this says, every child sees itself as a coordinated, unified whole reflected in a mirror, only to find this delusory ideal thwarted ever after – a promise to be endlessly and irresistibly betrayed – by the infinity of subsequent part-self reflections it must meet in the world and in its own shuffling efforts to construct a stable self. While the mirror stage is not itself a fiction (or wasn't when Lacan appropriated the conception of it from others' early and limited clinical observations), the speculative use he made of it is an important one. In Lacan's reaching out paradoxically for some concrete and palpable object in the 'external, material' world around which to construct a drama of catastrophic psychic delusion occurring in the realm of language, he exposed the urgency of an imaginational need to whose echoes many throughout the subsequent generation have responded.[12]

Jacques Derrida, meanwhile, unfolds a meditation on 'the tears of the victim' – on the default of all utterances as he sees it, the failed promise – that for many will be harrowing:

> The absolute victim is a victim who cannot even protest. One cannot even identify the victim *as* victim. He or she cannot even present himself or herself as such. He or she is totally excluded or covered over by language, annihilated by history, a victim one cannot identify.... [The victims] cannot even testify to it themselves. The meditation on writing is a meditation on this *absolute weakness*.... (1995: 389)

Here the absence infecting the very word and conception of 'present' converges with the crises of personal being, of self – one cannot *present* one's self. It is an apprehension of a condition of infinite distrust, where the decentring of the subject is identical to the narcissant's anguished sense of wounding, and the awe-filled dread of annihilation of his or her own person – by a force, a destiny beyond control.

The projects of Lacanian analysis and of deconstruction illustrate in the most intense colours how a characteristic mission of postmodern thinking is, as it is of narcissance, to *seek out sites of betrayal*.[13] In the consolidation of a mental process for the dissolution of systems of trust and belief we are face-to-face with a phenomonen that embraces both narcissant and postmodern thinking. But it's important from now on to perceive the potential intimacy – and in fact the entanglement and confusion, of which we may not always be aware – of the relationship between narcissant feelings of betrayal and feelings of betrayal on a larger, cultural and social/political scale. In Deleuze and Guattari, in Baudrillard, and in the language of Derrida the psychological and social strands of suspicion, of *méfiance*, are commonly interwoven. And disillusionment with a previous generation, together with the active project of devaluing its foundations, does play an indispensable part in civic responsibility. In narcissance, the project outdoes itself. Yet it would be immensely destructive to conceive of social revolt as a product of pure narcissance, and I mean never to suggest it. For the moment, it is enough to note that the abuse of power and its effects turn out to be far from always matters of 'purely political and economic' concern arising exclusively on a philosophical or a collective, public stage.

Oscillation

Much of what is most explicit in postmodernity is its celebration of heterogeneity and contradiction. But postmodern thinking is much of the time not about heterogeneity and contradiction, as it seems, but about calling a halt, about the seemingly categorical necessity to relinquish the effort to make headway, to 'move on' in the face of them. More often than we think, it's not a neutral observation but an acting-out – in the way of a mystery or passion play (or 'the human tragedy', as Lacan calls it), where a human dilemma is regularly ritually redramatized. It stages the experience of 'overload'. Contemporary parlance, both sociological and journalistic, repeatedly rehearses this, and we recognize the theme. But here I want to stress the role played by 'trust'. The primary source of our experience of incoherent 'overload' is not that we have trouble in *accumulating* categories and sense-making procedures – which postmodernity does richly, for example in collage and pastiche – but that we don't trust any one of them. That is, we have no faith in any of the protocols, procedures for resolution, for prioritizing, for sorting things out. This is a psychological dilemma for which postmodern thinking regularly (and now understandably) expresses an urgent need to give philosophical reasons, without always accepting the implications of the fact that favouring (philosophical) rationales for deciding/not deciding is itself a matter of trust – a trusting in not trusting – a manifestation of a certain 'turn of mind', and one that now strikes a familiar chord.

Postmodern thinking is not 'sheer chaos'. It is patterned. And a pattern quintessential to it is *oscillation*.

Something working its way to the surface now is that narcissants' anxiety to respond to context – that is, their extremely sensitive field-dependence, whether in the interests of confluence or of wishes to secure power over any threatening opposition – does not in any way guarantee an accurate engagement with what is actually 'going on', and may often suppress awareness of it. Commonly, its aim is not so much to find out the 'truth' as it is to establish a level of comfort with self and/or with self-uncertainty, whatever the 'external realities'. It may be directed by principles of oscillation such as '*suitable vacillation*', '*wasting*' and '*parity routines*' and the '*description/prescription routine*'. Their centrality to a consideration of postmodern thinking will in some cases be immediately apparent here; in future pages their full effect is likely to 'grow' on us.

In early stages in the formation of our information about the world, much of what we 'learn to say' is assimilated as part of – is often reflexively, invisibly merged with – what we 'learn to believe'. The development of our understanding of the world, and of things we should and should not believe about it, is perpetually constrained and shaped by the fact that the sources of our most essential information are also the very same as the sources of our personal nourishment, shelter, safety and love at our lives' most naked and vulnerable inception and will be moulded by the complex and often contradictory felt needs and desires of those in whose care we find ourselves. Bearing this in mind, how narcissance assesses things can be illuminated by a look at an example from childhood.

There are sometimes cases in law where the validity of the testimony of children is a critical concern. It's frequently observed that when asked a question and then asked it for a second time, children (of say two or three years of age) are more inclined than adults to *change* the answer, thinking that the first answer had been 'wrong' and that what was wanted was a different one. Asked for 'the truth', a child may think of this thing truth as 'what is suitable for the occasion'; the desideratum is felt by the child not to be *consistency* – an essential element in most conventional ideas of 'truth' – but *confluence*. A particularly revealing aspect of examples like this is that they arise – or are brought to attention – perhaps most frequently in cases where the possible neglect or abuse of the child is what is the issue. That is, where what is at stake is precisely what is felt to be at stake by a child who may well be *en route* to narcissance – where an anxiety of relationships powerfully colours what is said and, for the sake of survival, even what is believed. The salient difference between the less narcissant child's thinking and narcissant thinking is that the former develops an 'overview' in which what it may be socially desired to be said and what is true are separated out, distinguished from one another. For a potentially narcissant child, by contrast – impelled to change what it says and even believes, according to the field, to contextual need – the behaviour that seems best is not constancy but *suitable vacillation*.

The crisis that arises – what the narcissant child's 'overview' produces, in the end – is something additional: a *kind of behaviour* that itself constitutes a vital factor in the child's relationship to saying and believing. The act of saying and making oneself believe what in another part of one's being one also does not believe (after all, to the child those 'first answers' *had felt right*) can engender resentment, anger, confusion, and not merely vacillation at a given moment but *oscillation as a continuous, often relentless way of behaving, of being*. Oscillation becomes more than a strategy for confluent living and a mode of (unstable, 'shifty') believing. It becomes a pattern linked to what in psychology (in cases, for example, of emotional deprivation) would be called 'learned confusion', and – in a manner of response with which we can't help but sympathize – of simultaneous ironic and aggressive self-assertion. 'I am free of what others require of me and what I fear I must be for them, I am free of the world of commitment with its impossible demands, and I will actively demonstrate this – to myself above all; I adopt and enact uncertainty as my mode of being, *by consistent oscillation*, by persistently affirming my detachment from the world of personal accountability and the false regimes of so-called fact and fixed "truth".'

The second new principle shaping patterns of oscillation is that, in narcissance, oscillation can be intimately connected with anger, and produce habits of '*spoiling*'. It's a kind of experience that many others have occasionally had, particularly in periods of stress, where our self-esteem feels at a low-ebb. Here is an example: it's night; lying at last in bed and feeling the pleasurable warmth and comfort of it, one begins almost to rejoice for a moment in this simple enveloping pleasure – only, suddenly, there floods a searing flash-image across the mind of how close lying-here is to lying in bed in illness, perhaps mute and helpless before oncoming death. In narcissance, the mind may actually be haunted by this habit of counterflashing oscillation, where no pleasure, joy, or meaning can be retained, sustained, allowed its space, its 'natural survival-time', its reality. We can best understand this process when we consider the child who, having been 'abandoned' for a time, will not give the returning parent the pleasure of an embrace and a smile, and will thus, inevitably, not have these *for itself*. The message, complex in itself – 'I won't let you have (back) this moment's pleasure I feel because you don't give me enough of it' – imperceptibly becomes 'I won't let *myself* have this pleasure because it would betray the feeling of pain and anger I have – the need-full person I am.' In narcissance this pattern of oscillatory self-giving and self-deprivation can be a chronic configuration. A practice of sabotage, not uncommonly in psychology called 'spoiling', this *wasting routine* is literally 'devastating' (*gâter*); it swiftly converts pleasure into pain, emptying and laying waste whatever potential for explicit gratification it happens to uncover.[14] In narcissance it becomes a 'default protocol', as if a sub-program were installed alongside and triggered by the individual's most basic system for the 'computing' of value, acting to shunt the mind to-and-fro between elation and despair.

It should be understood, with this, that narcissant oscillation isn't something we always observe as such at the time. What *is* seen is often more a kind of layering or overwriting, much like the effect produced in photo-processing by '*solarization*' where say half the tones of a photographic image are left intact and half are reversed, and where in observing the image we are uncertain as to whether we're looking at a positive or a negative picture. We feel a wavering push-pull between figure and ground, like the one we experience on seeing the Gestalt theorist's duck/rabbit image. In a solarized portrait, 'life-like' fleshtones characteristically dissolve, and the 'subject' takes on an odd synthetic, metallic appearance – that of an idealized, chrome-shining 'inanimate object'. This glamourous and shimmering yet simultaneously flat and eerily inanimate, 'dead' quality of living persons is something narcissants often convey to observers and feel in themselves, and is an effect notably reiterated throughout postmodern film and art and in the popular media and commercial advertising.

The intimacy of the connection between postmodern problematizations of the stability of meaning, on one hand, and of narcissant problems of the stability of the self, on the other, will by now be vividly clear. A stumbling block for those trying in the past to think with clarity about the relations between postmodernity and personal psychology was not that postmodernists didn't think there was a connection but that for a long time they did, and called it 'schizophrenia'. (Following the publication in 1965 of the immensely influential psychiatrist R. D. Laing's *The Divided Self*, postmodernism in its early days liked to cover issues of personal oscillation with this word. In its subtitle Kurt Vonnegut's *Slaughterhouse-5*, a book rapidly adopted in various quarters as a model 'postmodern' text, is described as a novel 'in a schizophrenic manner'. Postmodern fictions and critical discourse have been widely embroidered with the epithet. Deleuze and Guattari proposed – and stimulated many with – a 'schizophrenic' paradigm for human life, to be supported by 'schizoanalytic' procedures for social criticism.) The intuition was right, but the label, the 'explanation' was unhelpful.[15] It's by the processes of narcissant oscillation that the instabilities of meaning mistakenly linked to 'schizophrenic' thinking actually take their most vital effect. This is where *parity routines* come into play.

The course of cultural change has been largely a history of people's 'reading' events and ideas about events differently over the course of time: a perception or conception is reinterpreted in such a way that it is modified or replaced. Contemporary indeterminist thinking is different; it *declines* either to moderate or to replace one perception or conception with another. The impulsion to seek mutually exclusive versions of an idea and maintain that any 'rigorous' reading retains both ideas, understood as a mode of oscillation, is a 'parity routine'. In 'real life', we never give equal value to all things thought. You wouldn't be able to read these words if you allowed all the things going on in and around you the same degree of attention, nor could you *decide* to read them if you assigned the same value to everything else you think of doing. This leaves philosophical indeterminism with an inscrutable problem: to understand why the rule of the parity of all propositions must prevail, we're obliged to look to some level of believing somehow 'outside' the plane of such propositions. Many have argued that such a plane must be a metaphysical one. But as we've also seen, *affective processes* can – without providing (rational philosophical or metaphysical) *'reasons'* – engender the same outcome. A psychological predisposition, oscillation, effectively interrupts prioritization, and blocks our 'coming down on one side' or another.

The *description/prescription routine* is, as we'll see, a form of oscillation that is a pervasive manner of postmodern speaking. What seems to be offered as a description of how things are, or how we behave, merges imperceptibly into an exhortation telling how things should be or how we should behave. Famous examples are postmodern writers' maintaining – often within the same sentence – that literature has exhausted its themes (and we should exhaust literature by showing how it is exhausted); the author is dead (and writing should kill – be seen to be killing – the author); literature is fiction (and literature should work to display the truth that it is fiction); texts deconstruct themselves (but we must deconstruct them); meaning is indeterminate (and we should work to show how its indeterminacy is determined); we despair of uncertainty (and we should celebrate our certain liberation from limits); and the subject is always-already decentred (and we should exert every effort to decentre it).

We might feel tempted to question the uses of description/prescription routines. They may suggest *schadenfreude*, a way of making the best of a bad deal, a kind of retaliatory or at least-and-best 'homeopathic' impulse – a form of 'pre-emptive remedy' (as in 'pre-emptive strike') – a variety of 'cognitive cross-dressing' unsuitable in serious debate. But psychologically, like other forms of oscillation, the process is actually not up for intellectual negotiation; in narcissance, it simply will take place. In postmodern discourse, the practice far from always produces clear and present confusion. Rather, ideas and actions that people subsequently try to base on it fall foul of the fact that what they thought was an exhortation was actually a protest or a lament, or that a statement of a 'truth' was actually a hope.

We begin to see how, as with narcissance, postmodern thinking is not merely an outcome of the theoretical observation of instability and uncertainty. The dedicated invocation of these is rooted in psychological processes – the *processing* – of contradiction. Styles of 'unravelling' that seem to occur in two quite different dimensions of our experience – the philosophical perception of the uncertainty of meaning and the psychological perception of the uncertainty of the self – strangely and significantly trace their courses along the same paths and are reached by the same means: the reflexive, even seemingly 'visceral' attack on the integrity of meaning and the disintegration of the integrity of the self, by processes of interminable oscillation between polar extremes. If postmodern thinking is sometimes decried as a form of 'stalling', it needs to be understood that it springs from a consuming and distinctive process of mind in which thinking itself is – urgently – stalled.

Dissolution

As we now understand, narcissance is a pathway toward a *felt* (and not merely philosophically rationalized) 'decentring of the subject'. The question of the self as *subject* – as the active agent of events – is essential. A narcissant feels "a deep loss of the sense of the continuity of his self in time and of its cohesiveness in space" (Kohut and Wolf 1986: 185); when "the child's own initiatives towards separation-individuation and autonomy are not encouraged ... a deficient sense of agency is expected" (Mollon 1993: 132). Sensing itself devalued as an autonomous being, it is left without a reliable perceptual apparatus (or dependable 'set of instincts') of its own, and can only cling to a system of illusions, as psychologists say, 'owned' by the carer.[16] The self is left literally the 'subject' of nothing.

For someone in narcissance, clinging to what many since Winnicott have called a "false self" – a self-image that is *performed* in order literally to 'secure' relationships – can actually produce the sensation of non-entity. The splitting of the false self from what may secretly be felt to be a 'true' but somehow less real, alien and even dangerous self is not merely emotionally disturbing: in narcissance one "may leap from one isolated or more or less coherent self image to the next without any intervening connections to maintain the continuity of self experience" (Meissner 1986: 426). Thus 'spinning', *circling*, a narcissant feels ungrounded and may fall into phobias, manic excitement and depression – as if forever excluded from the somehow more substantial experience of desiring and of periodically attaining at least moderate closure in the various realms of living. In this spin, a feeling of 'disappearing', of being 'invisible' – finely articulated in Lacan, Derrida, Baudrillard – is an archetypal narcissant experience.

The effects of this inescapably penetrate every part of the individual's daily life. They make it impossible to feel the difference between events having a specific local, momentary significance and events determining one's whole being. Consider these mundane occasions: someone straightens out a fold in your collar, or picks a thread from your sleeve or a particle from your chin, or steps in to help handle a heavy object for you. A salesperson snaps at you. A car horn blasts. A friend says 'Look at this room – your place is a mess!' or 'Your brother – saying that – he's a real idiot!' Your partner says 'You're late – I hate you!' When you're feeling 'within yourself' in situations like these you can say 'Thanks' or 'Sorry' or even 'Shut up!'; you can clean your rooms, accept that the other is physically stronger, have a word with your brother (knowing that he *was* an idiot that time but that he's really smart most of the time and you love him whatever anybody says), you can recall that the one saying 'I hate you' really did show wrath at the time but on balance seems to love you – and you can go on about your business.

In a state of narcissance, things are different. No matter how far you remove yourself from what's just happened, *you have been injured*; and you carry with you – for minutes, perhaps hours or days – the wounding gesture, the voice, the horn, and the ache that it's produced, an ache that may seem to spread throughout your body and extend even beyond, into the world around you. The mundane is ontological. *You* are weak, ugly, dirty, stupid – that is *you*, through and through. Because all these objects that have been 'attacked' (your possessions, your people) are *parts of you*, are inseparable from the boundless precarious field of links and attachments that define your existence – the slightest tic (or tick) penetrates, strikes without resistance through your entire being. Events like this will not go unanswered. You can fight back with 'everything that's in you' (as anyone knows who has picked a thread from your sleeve and met with a seemingly 'mad' bluster of blushes or an astonishing barrage of rage); you can clean your house night and day, you can keep an eye on yourself endlessly in mirrors – to make sure you are *perfect*. Knowing, with ever greater acuteness as the years go by, how hopeless that fight is.

As witnessed in psychology, 'narcissistic wounding' happens early, yet is experienced as reiterated wounding, a wound that *returns and threatens to return again*, for howsoever long as narcissance itself prevails. The struggle to avoid it becomes an interminable circle; in spreading waves, exhaustion becomes profound; you may feel yourself 'burn out'. It's not merely a matter of psychological interest that in narcissance one is a potential suicide. Someone for whom this liability, this burden of 'self' – which s/he must carry and somehow make presentable, 'make good' – feels co-terminous with nothing less than the full weight of the world. The worst part of being 'subject', an 'I', is not its 'fictionality' but that one can *not* be merely a fiction. To be an 'I' can, simultaneously, be an unfulfillable charge, a *reality* that the narcissant – all the while that s/he strives to define it – also profoundly wants in the name of silence, of peace, to be 'done with'. In narcissance pressed to the extreme, the 'death of the subject' – that ostensibly cool philosophically universal 'truth' and personally chilling ultimate reality – is both the only conceivable freedom and the only binding and consummate logic. A narcissant, in a sense, merely awaits the catastrophe that will bring this logic into final force; awaits it, and also strives with all the strength he or she possesses, to escape it.

In a very real sense, if we ever find postmoderns' preoccupation with the decentring of the subject 'overplayed', while this may disclose an obsession at work, the 'elevation' of the matter to the level of a philosophical perception is in fact a way of 'underplaying', of occluding an important dynamic of human exchange in material life. Narcissants often choose vocations entailing solitude (scholarship, art, writing are often cited), allowing one to 'be oneself' without 'having to perform', or professions where their meticulously accredited expertise and authority permit them to keep an 'understandable' distance from others. Yet this may alternate with an active social life – one revolving around a quest for another/others who may give total and unqualified care. But at either pole, life must be ideal; a narcissant can be self-persecutorily perfectionist in both vocation and in personal connections; s/he may be quick to abandon a 'relationship' failing to answer, and to go in further search of that essentially unattainable unreserved, uncritical, undemanding love. Appearing outwardly ready with great assurance at any time to 'assert' their 'identity' – whether by, say, ostentatious display or flight – narcissants may yet vacillate between what appear to be extraordinarily different kinds of being.

A capital result is that in relationships, in *society*, this oscillation multiplies. Narcissance in one individual inevitably stirs up whatever latent narcissance resides in others. (We recall that all of us have it in us.) In the refusal to be counted, to give, to 'be real', a narcissant excites the *impulse in others* to make extreme demands, to exert omnipotent power, to try repulsion or flight. The apparent 'decentring of subjects' thus becomes an ever-spreading social process. Seen as a function of narcissance, it is not merely an abstract concept but a palpable social eventuality.

The resemblance that has begun to rise into view between narcissant self-uncertainty and the dissolution of the subject that so absorbs postmodern thinking may seem to make sense – in a general way. Yet I've described narcissance as bound up with a spectrum of further, specific emotions and impulses that seem far removed from postmodernity's most obvious themes. Might we expect the similarity to vanish when in considering narcissance we must take into account the matter, say, of the feelings of shame and grandiosity? Let's look more closely at this pair, by way of example.

It takes little to realize that shame will be instrumental in producing self-effacement. With the haste toward concealment and the hunger for attachment to idealized others it subtends, shame presses the mind into extreme field-dependence. Boundaries are harder to justify and maintain, and the very conception of self as agent can be repulsed as abhorrent. Few mind-sets could seem more attuned to a postmodern prepossession with the notion of the self as the subject of nothing than a narcissant condition of shame. But what of its inextricable counterpart: grandiosity? Rarely, in fact, is the effacement of self more powerfully achieved than here. An all-too-obvious illustration appears where the narcissant seems to wish to stand out, to claim all our attention. What is essential in this is that the grandiose are, above all, non-contactful. Ostensibly the most proactive assertion of self-certainty, grandiosity is one of the most effective strategies that humans possess for deferring engagement, for keeping people at bay, and for delaying 'laying themselves on the line'. This is never more the case than where it appears as exhibitionist charm; in their very 'attractiveness' narcissants call attention not to themselves – their selves – but exactly to the decoy of their 'false selves', to their socially safe and endorsed self-*images*. By a glossy exterior, the world's perception is obstructed of an inner life whose felt 'contemptible' needs, fears and angers might be tested and condemned. The fullness of the self and its potential unfolding is withheld from the field. An enchanting person whose enchantments are bound to a narcissant desire to enchant is a person who is removed, gone. Often well out of his own awareness, Elvis has left the building.

What happens when, whether with some intimate or some rival, the issue is joined and the narcissant's grandiosity is challenged? We know the answer: it will not be without a 'grand fight'. Typically, the scene becomes a classic social enactment of the process of the mutual 'nullification of self'. The narcissant induces accusations of grandiosity, and savagely defends against them; the other's position hardens into barren righteousness or melts with the sense of increasing 'invisibility', as though s/he is 'talking to the air'. In the heat of the moment, while the other may sense that they are moving ever further from what is 'really going on', the more they collude in the fantasy that grandiosity is the issue truly at stake, the greater its success as a veil over the self-uncertainties that actually inspire it. In the final truce, while one may seem to win and one seem to surrender, their fuller selves go 'unrealized'. On the field of battle, the narcissant stands feeling drained, a 'hollow shell'; and the other feels that for all its restored silence, the room is somehow empty. Together by a process of psychological interaction they have manufactured precisely the conditions to which the postmodern attaches the philosophical label of the 'decentring of the subject', and this is found repeated in diverse ways throughout the realm of social interactions with narcissant processes whether these are to do with grandiosity/shame, confluence/withdrawal, or any other.

Popular postmodernism often genuinely needs to insist that the problem of 'the subject' begins a step before all this; that it is not about 'disturbances of the self' but about the very idea of 'the self'. But the two are enmeshed, and such prioritizations may be assessed only in the light of what happens in any actual field. In the field in which postmodernism theorizes the decentring of the subject, we encounter a greater abundance of conflicting explicit rationales and intentions than reason can cope with. It's the very incompatibility among these – where pivotal arguments cannot be made logically to agree or complement one another – that leaves the dissolution of the subject as evidence not of a consummate argument but of a consuming preoccupation.

We're in a position now to ask, What condition of mind, so plangently illustrated by writers like Derrida and Lacan, needs to 'make figural' – to put first, 'beyond all reason' – the vexed nature of questions of the self? When Jacques Lacan says (and Derrida echoes) that "when the subject appears somewhere as meaning, he is manifested elsewhere as 'fading', as disappearance" (1977b: 218), we recognize the process. Just as the narcissant's feeling 'They lied to me' is generalized by postmodern thinking into 'They lied to us', so the narcissant's 'I am meaningless' is 'sublimated' into the abstraction '"I" is meaningless'. Postmodern thinking's stress on the impossibility of the subject's self-definition finds its resounding echo in the narcissant's interminable oscillation among a multitude of modes of self-conception and behaviour. In its further accent on intersubjectivity and 'de-differentiation' – a term shared by postmodern theorists, sociologists and psychologists – postmodernity enacts an even more central narcissant trait: the failure to differentiate self from other. Out of the vortex of the obsessive field-dependence of narcissant thinking, the very essence of decentred-subject theory comes roiling to the surface.

A profound unreadiness, in confrontation with others, to represent the self as an independent subject, to declare a firm, personally assignable position, may have formidable effect. In the rush to silence the menace of others' harrowing incursions a narcissant may *feel compelled to theorize* his or her retreats, asserting new rules for the games people are to play. In defence against difference, one may proclaim the moral turpitude, say – or the *philosophical untenability* – of all (self) assertions.[17]

But there is another, immensely costly side to this. In a condition of narcissance one can feel that, in the mere swatting of an insect, by a giant hurtling tragic blow one is oneself in an instant struck down. Narcissants may remain childless because there is no felt room in their lives for *another* child, or because the world is already filled with children's cries – when the children they hear weeping may in fact be themselves. Feelings like these exemplify boundary confusion and self/other fusion. Not everyone undergoes them equally; but for those who do, they are real. The burning postmodern formula takes shape: that the difference between 'inside' and 'outside', between 'subject' and 'object', is so fugitive and equivocal as to be a matter beyond the reach of reason.

In the world of postmodern fiction from the time of its first heralds, writers have emblazoned their pages with the emblems of just such images of self-dissolution. (I'll mention a few at random; from the United States, Russia, Ireland, Argentina, Italy, Poland, France, they can give a glimpse of the issue's cultural expanse.) A character may merge with and lose himself or herself in other persons or things, or disappear into a dark solipsistic void. Nabokov's narrator in *Pale Fire* identifies himself with (and protests against his identification with) the man whose poem's analysis he claims to be writing, and thinks himself to be the various characters about whom he fantasizes the poet writes. In "Axolotl", Cortázar's narrator turns into the caged salamander he adores; in "Cockroaches" Bruno Schulz's narrator becomes the insect he abhors. In Calvino's *The Non-Existent Knight*, where the protagonist is nothing but outward appearances, defined by the suit of armour he wears, his servant becomes everything he 'steps into' – imagining he's a duck, leaves, earth, soup, in a world "in which all things dissolved and tinged all else with itself". For the narrator of Sollers' *The Park*

> in the cinema, I find myself at one among the characters before me on the screen.... I became that wall. A crack in that wall. I was that leaf-strewn path; that stretch of stagnant water by which an invading army passed. I was the queen's comb; the ship's flag.

In Le Clézio's *Le Procès-verbal* the protagonist is, variously, a vegetable, moss or lichen, the sea, an oyster; in his novel *War* the only 'clear character' becomes a mechanized doll, a kind of car, a tower, a manatee, a thought, the sun. While the narrator of Calvino's *If on a Winter's Night a Traveller* concludes "that everything that surrounds me is a part of me", the sole voice in Samuel Beckett's *The Unnamable* murmurs that "only I and this black void have ever been" and for the speaker in Sollers' *Lois*, "I have as a base only my own nullity". "I see I see myself as a halt narrative ... contentless form" says the narrator of John Barth's "Autobiography". "I must compose myself.... Look, I'm writing. No, listen, I'm nothing but talk."

Self-consciousness

The experience of helplessness is only half the story. In swift recompense, narcissance seeks out forms of mastery. That leading motif of the postmodern imagination – the mirror – returns, with the understanding that it's also the very emblem of Narcissus. "In the jarring between the collusive fitting in with the desire of the other and the actual separateness of the self", in narcissance above all, "self-consciousness" arises. There develops a "compulsive, and hypochondriacal preoccupation with the self: a compelling need to look in mirrors and to evoke mirror-responses from others.... The more total this identification with the observing other, the more intense the self-consciousness" (Mollon 1993: 54–6, 74). In this way, *without awareness* of how one feels but with acute *self-consciousness of how one appears*, narcissance evolves some of the most intricate and powerful mechanisms conceivable for 'managing the boundaries' shaping the relations between self and other. Among these the best known are: *projection* (disowning feelings or aspects of oneself and ascribing them to others)[18]; *identification* (feeling merged with – and assuming to be one's own – the qualities and feelings of another); *introjection* ('swallowing whole' and submitting to the rule of others' attitudes and beliefs, however incompatible with one's own inner life and needs); and *projective identification* (responding to others as though their feelings toward oneself – for example, fear, contempt – are one's own). In reaction to others, one may bring to bear *deflection* (tactically or passively averting interaction); *retroflection* (turning responses to others back toward or against oneself); and *reaction formation* (warding off threatening emotions – including others' – by repressing or failing to identify with one's own feelings). By such means, narcissance can skirt authentic confrontation and forestall the sensation of separation by dissolving the very apprehension of boundaries.[19]

Through self-consciousness (*rather than awareness*), by literally 'checking' oneself (as if in a mirror), by avoiding actions that might produce perilous conflict – one may deal with ambivalence by quarantining. Controlling how one's meanings and intentions are presented, severing them from their roots in deeper-running needs, one may detach oneself from the public shame of a seemingly infinitely spreading desire. An attitude is split off and manageably 'detached', 'boxed away' in its non-communicating compartment from other attitudes with which it might have compared notes. By dynamic framing manoeuvres like this, narcissance achieves *something like distance* (however lively the exchange may seem at the time), and defers engagement with the more hazardous feelings, beliefs, and needs of the fuller – some would say more authentic and profound – self.

It will be plain where this is leading. To exactly the degree that a narcissant *glimpses* these disparities, and yet remains unaware of the processes underlying them, what comes to the fore is the seemingly irreconcilable multiplicity of being, and the irreality, the apparent 'falsity' of any one state of being. In this sensation of the irreality of the self, self-consciousness thus promotes further self-consciousness, in an endless round.

Something on which both it and its adversaries universally agree is that *postmodernism* is unceasingly 'self-conscious'. Many of the first wave of its leading critical texts celebrated postmodern literature – even in their titles – as 'the literature of self-consciousness'. Not only in writing but in the gestures, the very body-language of conversational 'postmodern-speak', the signature by which we may recognize it first is the quotation mark. As we converse, that brief finger-sign that we make (like pairs of wiggled ears, and revealingly called 'scare-quotes') can signal the postmodern attitude: 'Someone else said this, not me – it's another's feeling, not mine.' 'The "real, original me" is buried, lost in the fun(house) of false voices.' Here is a piece of dialogue from a story within a story (within a story…) by John Barth:[20]

> "'(") ('(("What?"))') (")'
> "'"'"'*Why?*' I repeated," I repeated,' I repeated," I repeated,' I repeated," I repeat. "'"'"And the woman, with a bride-shy smile and hushed voice, replied: 'Why what?'

I've several times spoken of 'bracketing', a term brought into common use by poststructural and postmodern theorists for the procedure of enclosing a word or an idea within an impermeable semantic barrier in such a way that it may be observed but not allowed to interact with the context in which it's found – so that it is neutralized, 'depotentiated', drained of its customary force, and may be analysed and 'ironized'. On all sides, postmodern thinking is portrayed (and is proud to represent itself) as an impulse that is dedicatedly ironic.[21] Striving to represent all that it says as 'under erasure', it deploys a copious array of means by which to stand back from seriousness and from resolved, committed statements of meaning and value. Here is a passage from another of Barth's short stories (1969: 103–4), one with the definitively self-conscious title, "Title":

> How sophisticated we are today. I'll ignore her, he vowed, and went on. In this dehuman, exhausted, ultimate adjective hour, when every humane value has become untenable, and not only love, decency, and beauty but even compassion and intelligibility

are no more than one or two subjective complements to complete the sentence....

This is a story? It's a story, he replied equably, or will be if the author can finish it. Without interruption I suppose you mean? she broke in. I can't finish anything; that is my final word. Yet it's the interruptions that make it a story. Escalate the conflict further. Please let me start over.

This is that 'self-referential' literature whose techniques for cultivating 'critical distance' a generation of students have been warmly encouraged to adopt as their own as they learn to read with suitable *savoir*. In the flood of examples I mentioned as this book began, of the strategies by which postmodern fiction exhibits its self-reflexive vigilance – its deluge of diegetic techniques, its tireless self-critique – here at last was a genuinely sophisticated tradition that was truly, revolutionarily conscious of itself. Alert to the strategems of writing; on the watch for the illusions by which in all our discourse we were deceived by others and deluded ourselves; sleeplessly wary of the abysses of feeling in which they had been permitted to take form. In its crackling display of self-reference and critical self-regard it discloses its wit-bristling import. Splitting ominously affect-laden sentiments into a glitter of words and dispersing their whispering spent particles into the anxious silence, literature would at once call attention to and consume with cool laughter its troubled sense of itself.

The ultimate effect becomes clearer when we compare this with the effective processes of narcissance. Fastening its eye on the classifications of rhetoric in the name of self-conscious analysis, what postmodern thinking 'loosens', 'breaks apart' (analyses) is the relation not between the parts of speech but – as is the case in narcissance – between speech and the parts that hurt. By 'honeycomb manoeuvres' not unlike those of narcissant thought, it 'hives off' the different potentials of a situation into controllable 'cells' to 'keep things sweet' – sticks and stones can be resolved into textual events, into names, and names will never hurt us. The narcissant's 'the world is a mirror' is modestly stretched – the world is further 'distanced', placed at one more step's remove – by the postmodern's 'the world is a text is a mirror'. The move to a position of self-consciousness resembles a leap to a meta-posture that postmodern reading strongly promotes wherever it can,[22] even while it knows in theory that no ultimate transcendence can ever be achieved; we'll need to examine this in its own right later. But it is also, psychologically, a routine by which participants in a potentially confrontational situation may be induced into mild compliance; 'emotional involvement' is depotentiated, differences are 'purely academic', and no harm is done, for *'no harm' was meant*. Beyond superficial, harmless levels, 'users' make sure not to let exchange take place. But the procedure does take unfaltering self-consciousness; for without that, eruptions of parlous awareness may not be denied.

This isn't meant to sound provocative. A vital distinction must be made here. For many psychologists, *awareness*, unlike self-consciousness, includes 'owning' of oneself, where owning is literally knowing one's "response-ability, ability to respond, to be the primary agent in determining one's own behavior". "The act of acknowledgement of how 'I am' does not mean one transcends that which is being acknowledged" (Yontef 1993: 183–4). Varieties of self-consciousness characteristic of narcissance that seem produced in a desperate triumphalist spirit of mastery – where one writes, circum-scribes, makes a shrewdly observed character of oneself – are, as Yontef puts it, the equivalent of:

> saying both 'I am' and at the same time denying the 'I am' by saying it as if it were an observation of another person, declaring in effect: 'I was that way, but now that I confess, I who confess am not that way.' Such is not direct knowing *of* oneself, but a way of not really knowing. It is both a knowing *about* oneself and a denial of oneself. (183–4)

In this condition of self-consciousness, in "the failure in development of a spontaneous, stable, taken-for-granted self-experience" where "the individual tends not to feel himself at the center of his own life", one is "prevented from full involvement in living because he is developmentally stuck between 'the mirror and the mask'.... Living becomes a process of controlling the environment and other people from behind a mask". The outcome is a distinct "quality of unrelatedness" (Bromberg 1986: 439–40). Narcissant self-consciousness contributes to a *failure*, for example, to sense feelings in *others*, except insofar as these may key in with anxieties the narcissant may feel about him- or herself.

The confusion between self-consciousness and awareness is famously illustrated in postmodern fiction's perennial use of nesting images – rooms within rooms, frames within frames, characters within characters, like Chinese boxes or Russian dolls. In theory, philosophically, as postmodern criticism never ceases to reiterate, these serve as metaphors for infinite regression. A social analogue is narcissants' often cited tendency toward 'serial' or even simultaneous 'promiscuity' in the unending search for 'the ideal mate'. But *psychologically* what actually distinguishes both obsessive patterns – multiple lovers in life, infinite regressions in fiction – is the *lack* of interaction between 'compartments'; they almost invariably 'present' as mutually exclusive, mutually secret multiple lives, existences. The 'promiscuous' narcissant keeps his/her lovers apart. (The case of Lacan – who for many years lived two lives in two places with two different wives – is a classic example; we must consider the important matter of 'promiscuity' in the next chapter.) The problem in postmodern narratives of voices within voices (for example in the Barth story, "Menelaiad", from which the 'quotes-within-quotes' passage occurs, and whose closing line 'defines' the story's theme as "the absurd, unending possibility of love") is that characters and their stories do not interact, engage, don't negotiate with each other. Contrary to the logic of postmodern propositions regarding the dissolution of boundaries between multiple perspectives, the 'problems' articulated in the majority of postmodern *narratives* (by writers as diverse as Barth, Calvino, Beckett, Nabokov, Sollers) depend on the entirely 'impermeable' nature of 'contact boundaries', the unique and often elaborately contrived *absence* of engagement between characters across the boundaries described. Postmodern narratives typically turn on remorselessly compartmentalized situations where 'people don't talk to each other'. In this contrivance, as in narcissance, the endless struggle with the instability and fluidity of being is made manifest.

Here we must recall postmodern literature's constant reminder that 'there are no people in here', in fiction. The text is meant to be seen as pure surface, depthless, flat – a play of mere words. We know the enormous intellectual and imaginational benefits to be drawn from writing grounded on this proposal. But the psychological parallel is irresistible. In narcissance – in its processes of splitting and depotentiation of conceivably unsettling forces both in the self and others, and its inclination to delay processes of self-awareness and other-awareness – individuals experience "other people as lifeless shadows or marionettes". "The self becomes as if two-dimensional."[23]

This resemblance between what narcissants report and what postmodern writers say has strange and illuminating sequels for both. In narcissance, because 'anything happening' at the border between narcissant and other is thus often stalled, narcissants frequently feel '*boredom*', '*indifference*' and '*emptiness*'.[24] Still more strikingly, psychologists often note that, as "a very human response to the patient's state of non-relatedness", others' reaction – including therapists' – to "this warding off is a feeling of sleepiness and boredom".[25] The quality of sensations in the contact field yields clues to the function of the behaviour taking place there. Narcissant blocking processes can have a sedative, tranquilizing effect for both the narcissant and his/her witness. In an unsettling similar way, readers of self-conscious fiction often say that it is an 'intellectually intriguing exercise' that nevertheless 'leaves them cold'. Emotional engagements (for example with situations and characters) – which are essential *materials and tools of relatedness* in real life – are meticulously suspended.

The brief closing paragraph of Barth's "Title" begins "Oh God comma I abhor self-consciousness". There is a telling reason for this abhorrence. The sedation of feeling by 'objective', self-conscious mirroring has its eventual penalties. As a psychotherapist, Mollon observes, "The 'short circuit' effect of focusing on one's self can be extremely disorganising". There may be "an anxious ... sense of the bodily or mental self breaking up or altering shape" along with "the absence or breaking of a stabilising relationship with an empathic selfobject.... The person may become incoherent" (1993: 74, 75). The narrator of Calvino's novel *If on a Winter's Night a Traveller*, imprisoned in a room of mirrors with the woman with whom he'd make love, discovers that "I can distinguish no longer what belongs to one and what belongs to the other, I am lost, I seem to have lost myself, I cannot see my reflection but only theirs". In a short story called "Signs and Symbols", Vladimir Nabokov wrote of his protagonist, a child, that he "imagines that everything happening around him is a veiled reference to his personality and existence.... Everything is a cipher and of everything he is the theme. He must be always on his guard and devote every minute and module of life to the decoding of the undulation of things." Concluding an early story powerfully invoking the transition from the modernist to the postmodern, Nabokov's narrator says:

> The more insistently I told myself 'This is I' ... the less clear it became *why* this should be 'I', the harder I found it to make the face in the mirror merge with that 'I' whose identity I failed to grasp.... All the time I was aware of the feeling that I absolutely must maintain rigid control over myself.... My head seemed made of glass.... You see, we find comfort in telling ourselves that the world could not exist without us, that it exists only inasmuch as we ourselves exist, inasmuch as we can represent it to ourselves. ... My line of communication with the world snapped.... I understood the horror of a human face. Anatomy, sexual distinctions,

the notion of 'legs,' 'arms,' 'clothes' – all that was abolished, and there remained in front of me a mere something... .I was no longer a man, but a naked eye, an aimless glance moving in an absurd world. The very sight of a human face made me want to scream.... And I know that my brain is doomed, that the terror I experienced once, the helpless fear of existing, will sometime overtake me again, and that then there will be no salvation.[26]

The promotion of a 'self-conscious text' may or may not have 'philosophically therapeutic' critical merit. But it is perhaps always also enacting a style that may have a quite different psychological root and result.

Performance

But in narcissance – and in postmodern thinking – omnipotence, a sheer capacity to override all bounds, may come to the rescue. The belief that we can "reinvent ourselves" is not simply a characteristic fantasy of individual narcissance, it is a topos pervading contemporary popular culture. Postmodern fiction is filled with 'persons' who invent their own lives and the lives of other 'persons'. We may think that it's merely a local matter of abnormal psychology to say that "The narcissistic wish is: (1) not to have originated from two parents, but to have created oneself, to owe nothing to anyone; and (2) to go on for ever".[27] But in psychological theory, as we recall, a particular style of omnipotence recurrent throughout human culture but noted specifically as a feature of 'narcissism' is the belief in "the magical power of thought".[28] The form in which this most insistently appears in twentieth-century thinking is still more significant – in, as Freud put it, "a belief in the thaumaturgic force of words" (1957, vol. 14: 75). That is, we create and shape reality and ourselves through the power of human utterance, of language.

The implications are paramount for our reading of postmodern traditions grounded in linguistic indeterminacy (such as that of deconstructionism). As Mauro Mancia intimates in his notion of a 'libidinal hypercathexis of thoughts', 'an intellectual type of narcissism': in placing the onus of our apprehension of ourselves and the world entirely on the operations of language, on our processes of verbalization, we were already on course toward a special theory of the 'total competence of language'. In other words, we can't exclude the possibility that here is not so much a 'rigorously' neutral philosophical demonstration of an ontological rule of existence, but a psychological predisposition of a specifically narcissant kind.

There have been few epochs when the belief in the Logos – the mythos that 'In the beginning was the Word' – has been more fiercely held than it has in recent times. Postmodern thinking's extraordinary dedication to the notion of the all-encompassing potency of language – and postmodernism's virtually unexcelled success in reshaping certain cultural attitudes by the unalloyed linguistic manipulation of written texts and the demonstration of meaning's production and dissolution in the act of uttering – is a matter of historical record. We've noted how fictional postmodern writing has worked not only to produce extraordinary new strategems for the construction of 'events' by radical transformative procedures but to motivate the very generation of texts on the basis of diegesis – by the purported 'unfolding of language itself'. Fictions now revel in staging the power of the word in the 'user's hands', creating narrators creating their own worlds and characters before our eyes. Fictions by Borges, Calvino, Nabokov, Lem, Fuentes and others are famously littered with literally 'word-centred universes'. In Calvino, 'characters' (people) are made physically pliant to the 'characters' (letters) of the text, so that the narrator "could seize" Ursula H'x "by the hair and bend her against a d or t just as I write them now, in haste, bent, so you can recline against them". A figure in a novel of Fuentes' declares that "only what is written is real". Still to be addressed in our times is the extent to which in expository, theoretical writing this 'reshaping' of recent thinking about language has been pre-eminently achieved less by conceptual argument than by specific specialized techniques in the strategic textual management of language itself.[29] Some critics have shown an intuition of this but have yet to apprehend its full dimensions, when in thinking in particular of deconstruction they speak of "deconstructive technologism".[30]

An intense preoccupation of postmodernity is in fact the matter of *tekhne*, technology, the array of skills and arts by which we manipulate the world. We enter now the complex realm of *performance*. It is a region that for many is charged with ambivalence whose sources may run deeper than we think. The first intimations of this appear in the growing tension in recent decades between our feelings of omnipotence and impotence. This is graphically illustrated in our belief in the infinite power of technology, combined with a felt weakening of the boundaries of reality and our growing doubts about our capacity to 'manage things in time'. Postmodernism's potent 'technology of language', on one hand, and its uncovering in language of meaning's indeterminacy, on the other, is more than just emblematic of this predicament. The issue is 'grandiosity' and its effects. A common misunderstanding is that omnipotence always 'feels good'. An easy way of grasping how wrong that can be is to consider one of the axial experiences of someone in a state of grandiosity: '*I am responsible for everything*.' For some human beings, this sentiment is in the end grounds for suicide. Grandiosity is not fun; it's simply one of the basic mechanisms of a mind looking for a way of defining and managing itself. We all experience it; the jolt that the sensation of omnipotence gives us can rescue us from disaster. In the face of an unabating tide of anxieties, it may be urgent. But we pay a price for it. In *narcissance*, feeling omnipotent can be frightening.[31] This is where 'performance' comes in.

When you meet a narcissant you aren't meeting him or her, you're meeting his or her representative. The matter is adumbrated in postmodern fiction. In the first instance it seems merely playful. 'Impersonations' abound, together with 'mistaken' and 'double' identities; novels' events turn on counterfeiting, charlatanry, camouflage and hoax, with casts of clowns, masqueraders, actors and non-actors; dolls, manikins and dummies take the place of humans and humans uncannily replace dolls. The very creation of whole pseudo-realities will be the principal act of certain characters; we may be told (as we are in Nabokov's *Pale Fire*) of a central figure that "his whole being constituted a mask".

Invention and self-invention can be exciting. Perhaps we've nothing to worry about. In a very vital sense narcissance, like postmodern thinking, is a preoccupation with *tekhne*. For people fearing they have no intrinsic worth, no 'substance', what often keeps them going is the belief that they survive by the grace of their performance. An extremely common feeling in narcissance is that "'I will not be loved for myself but only in response to specific performances.'... 'If I don't perform I will be alone and unloved'" (Rothstein 1986: 315). This is abetted by the fact that "lack of emotional depth and commitment may permit a better social functioning, for example, in certain political and bureaucratic organizations in which lack of commitment means survival and access to the top" (Kernberg 1986: 286–7).

Frequently narcissants actually say that 'from the beginning' they were 'taught to lie'; that this is a necessity of life.[32] A child's intuition, when she's applauded for a dance or a song she provides on demand, or for a splendid school report – if she senses she has any reason to feel, as she may in the depths of her being, that these rewards are accorded *in place of* the simple love she would far prefer – only confirms her in the sense that it's not her self that's valued, but her performance.[33] A narcissant may often work for, and not uncommonly achieve, great material success – or social or amorous conquest. But s/he has to do it over and over, in new ways, with new objects of desire, obsessively; the brief-lived approbation and assurance it brings has the uniquely *hollow* feeling we experience when we take gratification from what we know or feel to be *a substitute*, leaving an ineradicable shadow of anger rather than of solace. The substitution of appearances for what is suspected might feel more 'real' is exactly what is in operation. As a culminating irony, from childhood a narcissant feels obliged to '*take it philosophically*', to smile and transmute these very sensations of constant manoeuvring into some sociable and conceptually fluent useful 'attitude'; s/he is selectively rewarded for developing precocious intellectual and verbal skills. Information and language may come to seem to secure the 'only true power'.

The effects of the sense of the urgency of actively performing are momentous. One must – in a vicious circle typical of narcissance – pile performance upon performance, as a shield against the anxiety of exposure. 'I am a liar, I play you false. Only my constant ploys make you value me. I am nothing but my utterances, my gift of gab. You will discover me, expose me. *I am all talk*.' No amount of protest saves the situation. Partners in the relationship may feel driven off their rails by this denial of their own openly expressed feelings – and relationships may collapse in the vortex of projective identification and denial.[34]

Anger is on its way. Narcissants' silent logic now can have a corrosive effect on the very underpinnings of their relations with the world. In their performed "compliance there is massive unconscious defiance. There is the implicit attitude that 'if you are fooled into accepting the feeling I display as the truth, you are contemptible'" (Modell 1986: 301). The sentiment can be intricate and fierce: 'Just as in accepting your idealized view of me that I've provided in idealizing myself for you (and that I've guaranteed by idealizing you yourself), in accepting your acceptance of my contemptible self I find both you and myself more contemptible.' The plowing-up of the boundaries between 'fields' of value drags a harrow with it across the borders between truth and fiction.

With this, a person's relations with *the world* change. In narcissance, one feels more and more depleted, emptied of 'reality'. (Analysts sometimes say that the "self is in danger of destruction by being siphoned off into its own performance".[35]) Postmodernism's well-praised problematization of the boundary between fact and fiction is, *par excellence*, the preoccupation – the special business – of narcissance. Narcissance can bear within itself a profound ambivalence toward reality itself. As by sheer attrition the mundane wears away the ideal that has been sleekly projected onto other people and situations, the narcissant – in the interests of confluence, alternately taking all the blame and repelling all blame – experiences a progressively more unbearable association of 'reality' with pain and uncertainty, shame, inadequacy, exhaustion – and, now, falsehood. It will have a potent effect in shaping postmodern lifestyles.[36]

The brilliant mathematician Alan Turing, often called the inventor of the computer, exquisitely presented his response to this minefield when, reputedly, he attended committee meetings with a paper bag over his head. In the end, he committed suicide. With the defensive withdrawal of investment in the world, and with the subtle erosion of any personally felt sense of value that can be set in motion by the urge toward compliance, the sensation emerges not only that one is merely an actor in another's body, but that the world itself is merely a play, a 'show'. The fabric of what pose as relationships, with relationships' measures of worth – their goods and ideals – can come to seem a tissue of lies. 'Don't trust me – trust nothing. The reality we live in – is created by my words.' Where, in narcissance, prediction and management as goals persistently and radically predominate over other aims and pleasures (such as the experiencing of the fullness of the moment and of the self in the moment), an insatiable hunger may arise, and a sense of the world as a mechanical, 'hollow', artificial place – a sham. Just as postmoderns describe 'reality' as artificial, depressive narcissance renders everything – people, buildings, landscapes – unreal, like cardboard cut-outs, two-dimensional, synthetic. The cognition of 'meanings' may be well developed, but the feeling of 'meaningfulness' – the sense of the possibility of *living* with meaning, the feeling of *vitality* and of things being literally 'vital' – may become etiolated, may decay and wither. Like postmodern indeterminist thinking, narcissance may seem driven by the apprehension of emptiness, of the void. The postmodern percept that at the bottom of every sign there's only another sign matches the narcissant sense that behind the panoply of others' gestures there is no one there. Under the burden, the pall, of our 'performance', echoing only the apparent performance of all the others: the foundations disintegrate on which any value and any a sense of reality might have been thought to rest. 'Reality? I can't enter. Because I'm not really here – nor is *it*.'

This is the scene where postmodern thinking plays out its wakeful – and often bitter, punishing – view of the world as increasingly false, a simulation of reality. The anger that comes with the felt obligation to perform ('you've murdered my reality') – converted into a ludic 'philosophy' ('they've murdered our reality') – can scarcely be better dramatized (acted out?) than it is in the vision of the world as a simulacrum that theorists such as Baudrillard proclaim. Critics and observers are often perplexed as to whether, in this, a Baudrillard is protesting against postmodern life or is himself postmodern. The perplexed vision of an incorrigible universality of dissimulation vividly re-enacts and illuminates the oscillation – and the pre-emptive remedy – of narcissant ambivalence.[37]

The conception of existence as hovering in a marginal realm between truth and illusion is not a specifically postmodern problem. *La vida es sueño* was written in the seventeenth, not the twentieth century. The belief that we (like no one before in history) are the special, singled-out victims of illusion is, we're obliged to admit, an instance of grandiose thinking. Whether it comes in a spirit of protest (disclosing a convulsive wish to 'preserve' a fixed unitary 'reality' that no culture seems to have found more readily than we) or in celebration (suggesting that at last we've overcome the constraints of material reality), the lavish lyric apocalyptic rush that the language of a Baudrillard brings to the theme doesn't actually make it seem less grandiose. What makes the postmodern difference is the self-persecutory omnipotent belief that *we* are the cause. That is, that we bring reality into being – and are made accountable for all – by our peculiarly powerful symbol-making mental constitution, our very utterance. Once again it appears that in the habits of postmodern thinking we may be 'narcissizing' the human condition. Never were we more likely to need to invent another theory (this time one about language) – to find another 'cause' – for the 'unreliability' of experience than at the terrible moment when we began to need to feel that we were omnipotent.

As it's unfolded in postmodern fiction, the illimitable power and burden of self-invention can become a nightmare. Characters, as if reliving the narcissant dream, become entangled and lost in their own fictions.[38] In Calvino's most famous novel, the teller turns a wrestling match into an ontological agon.

> In the tangle of male limbs opposing and identical, I try ... to strike myself, perhaps the other self that is about to take my place in the house or else the self most mine that I want to snatch away from that other, but which I feel pressing against me and which is only the alienness of the other, as if that other had already taken my place and any other place, and I were erased from the world.

Desperation and Aspiration

If in narcissance there seems to be a ceaseless oscillation between 'desperation' and 'aspiration', it may be apparent by now that there may be signs of a similar pattern in contemporary experience on a wider scale. In a fundamental sense, both narcissant and postmodern thinking shift continually between two competing radical urges: toward an infinite pluralism, and – perhaps to our initial surprise, thinking of postmodernism – toward something approaching a universal monism. Let's look at these alternative positions one at a time.

"The blood drains from my head", thinks Samuel Beckett's character Molloy; "the noise of things bursting, merging, avoiding one another, assails me on all sides, my eyes search in vain for two things alike, each pinpoint of skin screams a different message, I drown in the spray of phenomena".

We've run into this motif before, in the notion of 'overload'; and we hear of it every day, in the encroaching dread of 'data smog', systems overloads, and 'the information explosion'. The sensation of bombardment, of drowning in the spray of phenomena, is one that colours people's ideas of postmodern life and floods through postmodern writing itself. "Very likely I have lost my senses", says one of Barth's narrators; "the carnage at our setting out; or decimation by whirlpool, poisoned cataract, sea-convulsion; the panic stampedes, mutinies, slaughters, mass suicides". To remain in life, says the narrator of a novel by Saviane, "is to walk the smog-streets … it is the cyclone, the torrent, the cancer that wastes the blood…. Is there a way to stem this whirlpool of facts?" In a Borges story, "the present was almost intolerable…. Funes remembered not only every leaf of every tree of every wood, but also every one of the times he had perceived or imagined it. He decided to reduce each of his past days to some seventy thousand memories" only to surrender to his "awareness that the task was interminable" and useless; Funes succumbs to the "heat and pressure" of this "teeming" reality. In a Calvino story "now events come flowing down without interruption, like cement being poured … a doughy mass of events without form or direction, which surrounds, submerges, crushes all reasoning". Postmoderns persistently write of a swarming world of 'junk', 'muck', 'drek', 'excrement', 'waste' in a frenetic barrage. It's not the plenum of data but the anarchy of data that haunts the scene, the lack of *connection* that might turn information into something like knowledge. Here is a universe (in Calvino's fiction a 'gurduluvian soup') that is as if smelted into some 'fourth state' – to borrow the physicist's metaphor – of plasmic in-difference; a chaos of unreasoned sensation. Theorists concerned with postmodern actualities (such as Baudrillard and Lyotard) – and with the very illogicality of choosing among options (such as Deleuze and Guattari) – meanwhile repeatedly found their arguments on an insistence on the glut of sensations of contemporary life that no philosophical or narrative 'big picture' can satisfactorily contain.

For many, the postmodern in this way must spell a universe of desperation. Magnitude, it seems, bites back. In the period of decades coinciding with the emergence of postmodern thought, what physicists and mathematicians call the 'order of magnitude effect' has changed our perspective in major respects. (Because a sorting of information never seriously thought possible can now be achieved in hours or even seconds by means of digital technology, large sections of what had been regarded throughout history as unknowable – for example, about the astronomical universe and the biological 'structure of life' – have been reduced.) Now we hear the protest that the process isn't selective enough – we don't seem able to know *only* what we wanted to know; we are deluged, we say, with information calling on us immediately to decide issues the expanse and implications of which is of such a magnitude that we seem, in another way, back where we started. We are as hypnotized or paralysed by our potential as before we were by our helplessness. This theme – a 'surfeit motif' – is a topos that haunts us. Yet all we know of past cultures makes it plain that the surfeit motif has always been with us. A difference was that what we didn't and couldn't know, someone up there did and could; the gods could contain it, and we – with occasional interruptions – could manage by keeping in touch with them. *The plurality* of existence, then, has never been *intrinsically* the problem. The problem is a contingent one – contingent on how we regard it; and specifically, on what strategies we have for negotiating with it.

As it happens, in psychology, a common perception is that having a philosophically (theologically, say, or morally) satisfying big picture on hand may help us less than we thought, if we're uncertain about where we as individuals are 'coming from'; if we don't have a clear sense of who we are and what (therefore) we need. The crisis arises, in other words, when our *self-picture* is a troubled or fractured or incomplete one. (This coincides compactly with the postmodern theoretical understanding that indeterminacy in general is inextricable from the indeterminacy of the 'subject'.) In this perspective, we are more sensible of our being bombarded by information, by sensations – and are more vulnerable to these – because we feel (and actually *are*, mentally) *more exposed*.

This places the matter of the contemporary sensation of 'bombardment' within a now readily recognizable sphere of experience. The constellation of sensations of overload, of living in a chaotic 'welter', is something experienced chronically by those in a condition of narcissance. Where one is perpetually engaged in a struggle to maintain a rigid self-image, "many needs will instead be distorted, retroflected, projected, or otherwise not dealt with directly, and left as unfinished business", as psychologists often say. "These will *clutter the background of the person's awareness* with ongoing tension".[39]

In fact, the problem is central to the formation of narcissance itself. A clue is to be found in the vastly influential results of the experiments conducted with non-human primates by Harry Harlow and many others,[40] where the observable outcome of maternal deprivation was an array of stereotyped patterns in the offspring of which the most important were their withdrawal from social contact and from the material environment, depressive apathy, context-disproportionate fear reactions, and intensive attention to themselves – self-clasping, huddling, rocking, curling into a ball, self-mouthing, and tendencies toward self-mutilation. What the experiments strikingly reveal is that often the loss most powerfully felt by an animal deprived early of its mother appears to be not so much the nourishment she would provide as its being held; her warmth, and the shelter she gives from – in fact the periodic restraint she imposes on its contact with – the environment, until it's 'ready'. The processes by which its experience of the world is introduced – 'staged', step by step, made by the mother to seem manageable – appear to be indispensable to its future wellbeing and crucial to the way it brings up its own offspring. There is rich experimental evidence that a fundamental function of mothering is not merely a nourishing one but a 'buffering' one, shielding the child from overwhelming stimulation. Children exposed beyond a certain degree and in an 'unaccompanied', 'unbuffered' way, to the deluge of sensory experience – to the flood of sensations that rain over them as they meet the world – have a monumental task ahead. Having been reared without the assurance – by the acts, gestures, and very emotional tone of those who have 'been there' and 'know the way'— that it can be done and is worth doing, children tend subsequently to feel unusually unready for more information. They often find the handling of even the simplest new data beyond their ability, and may seek alternative 'shelters' of any sort, where no more reckonings and decisions seem required.

What in postmodern theory we call 'hyperdetermination', an

'overload' whose ultimate effect is the experience of *in*determinacy, is an elemental experience in narcissance.[41] For children feeling 'unheld' in this way, their sensations uncontained, every experience can seem a 'flood', beyond control, and irresoluble. Not only is narcissant field-dependence thus in the making, it is the very process by which the sensation of overload will now be perpetuated. For such a mind-style, the inexorable outcome can be the conscious belief that every sensation, every idea, is 'unbearably' overdetermined, literally 'insupportable'. Existence seems a world of unanswerable demands and of 'objectively' undecidable, insoluble issues.

When they come to be able to 'support' themselves (which does not mean 'to solve all the problems' but, quite differently, to be able to *live with* problems, some of which they can't solve) – narcissants' feeling of flood subsides.

What goes widely unnoticed is that institutions other than the parent–child relationship can play a vital containing role. It is not simply from material danger but from sensory deluge that the family, as a whole, is often taken as shelter, as are peer groups, school, religion, the job, and close-knit interest groups. All these in-this-respect 'conservative' sites are certainly places where the individual accumulates a store of information, for good or ill, of ideological sorts. In twentieth-century democratic culture a great deal of our energy and thought was devoted to the critical scrutiny of that 'content', and rightly. It became increasingly a lemma of social and political life that such 'sheltering' institutions imposed on us more 'instructions' – that is, injunctions – than were good for us. But there is another vital process whose role is both concealed and as powerful as any *ideological, cognitive 'content'* arising in such environments, *whatever* the information's rightness or wrongness for individuals' intellectual and moral growth.[42] In our attention to our formative environments' 'content', we often failed to observe the in-formative, affective, psychological impact on us of their 'form'. We were worried about the introjects – the ideas, values, illusions – we had been obliged to 'swallow'. Yet we may have missed what else was at stake.

It is in narcissance, above all, that we are most vulnerable, most prone to the swallowing-whole of introjected beliefs. The less narcissant we are, the less others' 'subjects' we are; we know – in a way that leaves us far more able to take action – what we as individuals need and want and what we need to reject. What gives us an edge against the invasion of narcissance can often be the form of those very 'holding' environments whose content we're anxious to repulse. In contemporary society, tangles like these have scarcely been addressed. Postmodern culture shows more often at best a 'desperate' enactment than an aware and reasoned understanding of them, and we'll need to return to some of them in a later chapter.

* * *

To inquire into the postmodern's aspirations must in the end be to ask what their limits are. How pluralistic are its aims, and how free of all metaphysics?

We couldn't conduct what we call 'thinking' if we were to assign equal value to all possible meanings, even in principle. Yet the effect of the 'deferral', the 'de-differentiation' associated with postmodernism is that, insofar as value can have meaning, all values – for want of definitive difference – merge into one. By this postmodern gesture – perhaps unexpectedly for some – what many would call a primitive state of mind is invoked. Whether or not we accept its long association among historians of ideas, anthropologists and psychologists with what they've liked to call 'primitive mentality', it is certainly one whose links with narcissance are clear. That is, a '*participation mystique*' or 'oceanic thinking', where there are no boundaries between persons, between persons and nature or the material world, or between persons and whatever transcendent forces might be thought in operation. In the very idea of the dissolution of 'person', what remains is a belief in the All of the universe as a dynamic, fluid and continuous infinity. The obsessional postmodern motif – borrowed from a classic Greek notion recirculated by Pascal and resurrected by Borges – of a sphere whose centre is everywhere and whose circumference is nowhere, discloses a perpetual postmodern phantasy (and one with which, in its consequent consuming confusion of ego with subject, as we've observed, it must inevitably in its oscillation angrily wrestle). What was a desideratum in Romantic theory – where an *esemplastic* way of thinking was cultivated, by which the Whole of the universe might be experienced as One – becomes a 'reality' of sorts.

This – the conception of an esemplastic impulse at work in human thought – has an important place in the general understanding of 'narcissistic' thinking.[43] The extraordinary recurrence in recent everyday discourse – in the media, in public discussion, even in popular political rhetoric – of E. M. Forster's injunction, 'Only connect', now becomes more comprehensible. It is one of contemporary culture's responses – just as it was Forster's – to the experience of 'fragmentation' lamented by the Modernist that Forster was. If we can only find 'the connections', if we think we've got things into place, it can feel like a remarkably good stand-in for meaningfulness. The phrases 'feels like' and 'stand-in' are essential. Meaning, we say, is about the relatedness of things (ideas, images, sensations); about connections. An observation concerning human mental processes that has proved valuable, at least since Hume made an issue of it, is that we tend to derive from the experience of continuity, of connectedness, sensations of satisfaction and 'rightness' that are markedly similar to those that come with a sense of meaningfulness and reason – whether the connection found is actually, rationally, a meaningful one or a mere accident. The feeling of *fit* can bring with it the sometimes profound mental composure and sense of resolution that's also described, for example, in forms of mysticism (such as those embodied in many major oriental religious systems) where the belief is held that all things in the universe are interconnected even in the face of the failure of reason.

The implications of this for our understanding of indeterminist thought are powerful. If there was a time when people said – in academe and on the street – that it was intelligent 'not to confuse X with Y', postmodern thinking suggests that it's intelligent to say that we 'can't separate X from Y'; in place of 'differentiating', we 'defer'. But if pathos (or as Lacan and Derrida say, tragedy) comes with this new meaning for the word 'coherence' – where everything's 'stuck' to everything else, but now the more 'coherence' the less 'meaning' – there can be compensations. As not only postmodern theorists but post-industrial economists and information technologists say, speaking of a new integrated global web, everything becomes a matter of 'flows' – where All, we're invited to feel, may indeed merge into One.

It might be seductive to see implicit in these observations an occultist inclination 'behind' postmodern thought. But we'll be missing the point if we think of it as having supernaturalist intent. This is not about God or even about what people presently speak of when they say 'I'm not a religious person but I believe there's something out there that influences our lives'. In the postmodern what is at stake is a human mind-style, evolved out of, by, and for humans in the here and now.

The diction in which this perspective is framed is itself more urgent and apocalyptically oracular – to the extent of the rhapsodic – than anywhere else in postmodern discourse. Often it's expressed, in the end, in a specifically metaphysical way. It has become unproblematic among critics to observe Baudrillard's definitive turning in this direction.[44] Baudrillard came gradually to conceive of an 'ecstasy' of history "in the primal sense of that word – a passage at the same time into the dissolution and the transcendence of a form", having its echo in a "transaesthetics" and an "ecstasy of value", "a general metastasis of value" transcending all limits "without bearing reference to anything whatsoever except by way of mere continuity". 'Continuity' alone, and 'the ecstasy of communication', give worth to his entire enterprise.[45]

The revolutionary vision of Deleuze and Guattari – and perhaps their most creative contribution as well as one of the most appealing to post-Nietzschean postmoderns – rests in part on the conception of an organization of experience that is both anti-systematic (it can never be 'whole' in the sense: finite, complete) on one hand and, on the other hand, *continuous*, an infinite rhizomic web of desiring-production. At the centre of this is their emergent notion of a 'body without organs', an organism without the limitation of specific parts. "An infant ... experiences a drive to make a body without organs", an entity that is "the model of completeness". "Autoeroticism, in its most primitive form, concerns the constitution of a pure body of pleasure, a body without organs ... that appears to produce itself as its own quasi-cause." It is this phenomenal organism's drive that produces infinite desire whose force transcends the discrete data of 'material' life.[46] Here the writers' affinity is clear with broader contemporary indeterminism's categorical refusal to identify the 'subject' with a finite body, indicating a form of aspiration via etherealization (if not of shame and denial) that calls for honest inspection.

It would seem at first glance that Lacan must certainly differ from Deleuze and Guattari, since while for them desire is the source of a positive fullness, a plenum, he appears to represent it as productive of a vacuum, a void. The initiating material event for the emergence of the individual psyche is for Lacan the separation from the mother, and the unfulfillable desire for a merger, a blissful universal union in a transcendent whole (for which a physical mother only represents a 'wHole'). But with Lacan there is an essential infinite 'beyond', an aspect of the real, that envelops the subject, that takes form in *jouissance*. This is an experience associated with the rapt (carried away but also enwrapped) bliss of a (lost) phallus. A desired selfless and ecstatic wholeness and oneness can seem surplus to Lacan's programme for psychoanalysis (once the wHole is gone it's gone – if it ever 'existed' in the first place; let's get on with dealing with what's 'left'). Yet, quite apart from the fact that it has left its mark in some form throughout the history of philosophy since Plato (a history of 'traces' that Lacan is content to contest wherever it appears right to do so), this dream of oneness in fact haunts the body of Lacan's writing. It finds its most vivid enactment in Lacan's closing years' 'obsession' with the idea of monstration – a means of communication of an absolute beyond language. By way of verbal silence and the ceaseless fabrication – to which he devoted vast time and energy – of intricate knots in string (which he carried with him everywhere), and the complex mathematical notation by which he formulated their topology, is no radical departure; it was entirely in keeping with his essential vision or, as he would say, his eternal desire.

The theme recurs throughout postmodern literature and is finely foreshadowed by Beckett in his character Molloy, whose compulsive grave play with his 'sucking stones' (where he moves one pebble after another in an unending cycle from ground to mouth to pocket and back) is bound to the view that "to restore silence is the role of objects"; silence is, as Molloy's counterpart Moran says, what is "beyond the fatuous clamor, the silence of which the universe is made. I desired this advantage for my son". That Lacan saw his unifying vision as not merely an aspiration in the face of desperation but as a thing achieved is frequently revealed in his writing, as one of his most effective exegetes recalls in citing Lacan's "grandiose" claim (as Borch-Jacobsen calls it) that his conception of the mirror stage is an "ontological structure of the human world".[47]

A similar way of 'processing' the dilemma that 'we have the idea of the world (the totality of what is), but we do not have the capacity to show an example of it', is Lyotard's. Charged with having chosen to think in categories that always refer to something transcendent,[48] in his definition of 'What is the postmodern' Lyotard proclaims an intuition of a potential space – this time found in an 'aesthetic of the sublime' modelled on but transforming Kant's vision – independent of our construction of it. The intimation of the sublime together with the articulation of its very unattainability is the role of works of the imagination, where this irreconcilable pair – the 'conceivable' and the 'presentable' – may be confronted and retained together. We may ask why any unitary term such as 'sublime', let alone a so conventionally lofty one, should be bestowed on what might at face value seem after all only to be a failure to get things to fit. The word's history is so immutably linked to doctrines of transcendence that we may feel at a loss as to why Lyotard would even think of it, let alone insist on it.[49] Once more a fuller, more open and less facilely presumptive understanding is needed of how 'postmodern thinking thinks'.

Of all writers from whom postmoderns draw inspiration, those associated with deconstruction would seem the most fiercely resistant to an esemplastic impulse.[50] A case in point can clarify how reliable this assumption is. For many of his followers, the deconstructionist Paul de Man's intuition that mental oscillation in itself – the "void" that it articulates in language between the force of our desire for a transcendent logos and our knowledge of its impossibility – provides the leverage by which we can take hold of our fate. Through activities such as deconstruction, we are empowered to create ourselves (since we have no essential nature) and (by means of the social critique that its insights enables) to forge justice. For de Man though, as has often been argued, this constitutes an overarching synthetic truth. Pragmatist philosophers such as Richard Rorty, for instance, have seen in de Man's work a "hypostatization of language", "a natural result of trying to bring everything together – one's most private emotional needs and one's public responsibilities, one's secret self-image and one's shame ...". This "is to hypostatize the central term of one's newly created vocabulary, to treat this term ('Reason,' 'the movement of History,' 'Language') as the One True Name of God". For Rorty, de Man's initial insight regarding the experience of oscillation "does not seem to us to entail that we face an abyss, but merely that we face a range of choices", and that de Man turned "essentialist at the last moment" (1991b: 136–7, 132).[51]

It is not necessary to agree with Rorty any more than with anyone arguing against him, here, on de Man's position. What matters is the difference between the patterns of their views – how Rorty *disagrees* with de Man, and how the possibility of a *choice, an option*, reveals the difference, then, in the dispositions of the choosers. An illuminating distinction between the ways in which oscillation is experienced in narcissance, for example, and in other mental predispositions, is that in narcissance one may feel happy – may even feel it imperative – to relinquish wherever possible the radical pluralism to which others believe its oscillation must lead it. Resembling the narcissant's, de Man's choice entrains an 'instability about its uncertainty', as Rorty might say, of a sort for which the 'merely philosophical' pluralist (such as Rorty) has no use.

In what I've said there is no question of whether postmodern or poststructuralist writers are right or wrong. Nor is it to imply that in their minds is an achieved or 'proved' oneness beyond that of the infinite connectedness of all things uttered, thought or desired. Quite differently, it's to point out that alongside the heralding of the indeterminacy of meaning, an impulse toward esemplastic imagining is an active and vigorous process for the establishment of an *affective pattern of thinking* by which the *feeling* of connectedness amounting to a sensation of unity can be secured. It is a wish among many postmodern thinkers, and a wish that they allow to inform – to colour or 'shadow' – their propositions.

In postmodern fiction, where (for example in Nabokov and Sollers) we may have thought we had found consistently the most radical images of plurality and fragmentation, this further process is widely evident. As we already know, this is a literature seemingly obsessed with the dream of a mathematical or an aesthetic formliness (syntax) that specifically and precisely transcends meaning (semantics).[52] As the narrator says in Sollers' *The Park*, "one could live for ever between that plate and that vase, or simply between these two formless areas of colour: a concerted interval that *links* them, a luminous place without thickness or depth, liberated from space and time...". (1961 [1968]: 72), "I walk among varied and contradictory essences, where one passes without transition ... a whole has been organized here, in spite of everything, in one complicated design.... I at last see what I wish to see ..." (1961 [1968]: 90, 43). Sollers in even his most radical phase says of the 'subject' that it should be seen to achieve the state of the Pascalian sphere (1981: 126–7). In Nabokov's *Pale Fire*, the poet is described as impelled to "plunge back into chaos and drag out of it, with all its wet stars, his cosmos", "the Daedalian plan ... that made the whole involuted, boggling thing one beautiful straight line" (1962 [1973]: 204, 206). Nabokov himself writes of an "aesthetic bliss, that is a sense of being somehow, somewhere, connected with other states of being" (1955: 286). But the dream extends beyond the bounds of 'pure art'. In Fuentes' *Terra nostra* the prophet Ludovico declares that

> We will ... transform this place into a space that truly contains all spaces, into a time which truly embodies all time.... All things being converted into all men, all men into all things, external multiplicity nourishing eternal unity, which in turn simultaneously and eternally nourishes multiplicity. (1975: 705–6)

If there is no supernaturalist motive here, it remains to be considered whether there is no metaphysical one. Hearing the popular postmodern assertion that there is nothing outside language (and recognizing that the speaker is not equally willing to replace the word 'language' with say 'God' or 'the mind' or 'nature' or 'Honey') we are also witnessing something else going on: the assignment of priority to language. We need to know on what grounds other than metaphysical ones this privilege – this 'rule of language' – is meant to rest. Postmodern writers in fact regularly affirm that the 'real' – the outside-of-language that people commonly call 'reality' – is there. It's worth noting that linguistic indeterminists don't trouble to say that they 'hypothesize' the existence of a 'real' world – they typically state categorically that it exists. They simply haven't much confidence that language can be shown to have a lot to do with it.[53] Reality then is like the dark matter – untouched by the light of language – that astrophysicists currently say may make up the majority of the universe. But here – with the conception that we take our *thinkable* form in a species of counter-nature, a kind of 'anti-matter', separate from and parallel to the matterworld – comes an unforetold development. We inhabit a notional 'space' encompassing two universes, neither one capable of supporting a belief that either in any way reflects the other.

This idea of some 'reality's' genuinely existing apart from the world we construct in language troubles postmodern indeterminism, and indeterminists don't like to talk about it much. One of the reasons is not simply that there's not much they can 'say about it', but because there is a hazard in broaching it since it's impossible to conceive of an idea that isn't *metaphysical* that includes a physical universe and some universe alternative to it. We'd be misunderstanding such perspectives if we allowed ourselves to think merely 'No, they believe as they often say, that language is the infinite play of signification'. Language *is* the constant play of signification but it's *not infinite*; it stands separate from something very important, something that in postmodern thought it literally doesn't encompass: that is, whatever class of things there is that allows language to be regarded as a distinct category, and at the very least everything that is 'real'. Any belief in an 'infinity', then, such as that invoked by the aspiring Unqle Sim, includes both this 'matter' and 'anti-matter' or 'language', and is quite literally a metaphysical notion.

Any number of riddles may now arise. Indeterminists may like to ask, for instance: can Derrida die? In answer to this tasteful question it appears both that he can't (linguistically) and that he can (really), and that someone occupies a sufficiently elevated 'meta' position to envelop and knit the worlds in which he does and doesn't die into a flowing fabric, to embroider it as s/he will.[54] An Unqle Trim might take delight in adding that the visionary observation of this double universe, we were being told, was possible only to the intelligent, oracular Subject, the postmodern thinker. That's as it may be. The vision intimates a degree of grandiosity that may not be inapt; but what is more important is that along with it comes an equivalently modest, self-embarrassed aspect that we regularly observe in the discourse of sophisticated theorists such as Derrida: an acknowledgement of a materialist belief that one doesn't feel up to talking about, and that – like many perplexed materialisms – can't let go of a metaphysic it can't accept.

But there is more import here, of another kind. For this discussion, the 'double-universe-metaphysic' argument as an objection to the rule-of-language idea is ultimately of little interest. The greater value it adds is a perception that such a model of existence, the axiom on which much of postmodern thought is grounded – that all that is thinkable and actionable is contained within language – is always only one among competing *desired beliefs* and not an 'established' truth; it is an esemplastic phantasy. In this, and in its oscillation, its inability at the same time to let go of the metaphysic (or the 'ideal'), postmodern thinking's response to the human condition profoundly mirrors narcissance. In a sense, Lyotard's assertion at the close of his most famous argument for the postmodern, that "we have paid a high enough price for the nostalgia of the whole and the one",[55] not only expresses a profound wish but in fact performs it. In postmodern thinking we catch ourselves in the act of *paying* that price.

* * *

We've considered how a kind of desperation may arise in postmodern thinking's confrontation with the seemingly infinite plurality of possibilities, and how the possibility of *deciding* may be paralysed. Actually when we are in a narcissant state we are the people, above all, who cannot decide things. 'Who am I to decide?' Feeling unprepared to 'commit' (to a relationship, to a mission), in narcissance we can't bring ourselves to separate firmly from the imagined state where, as the best evidence we're cared for, decisions are made *for* us. The demand that one decide is a form of separation; narcissants feel rushed, physically grown up too soon, everything is going too fast – getting out of hand – there are too many imponderables to assess and hazards to skirt. And people in narcissance are in revolt, of a special order; the demand that one decide is a form of oppression.

In postmodern thinking, then, is the shadow of the narcissant who 'defers'. Differences are erased – by oscillation, and by denial. The parallel is made vividly clear in one of the diagnostic features by which the analyst Arnold M. Cooper identifies narcissism: the "denigration of all therapeutic gain or effort, and destruction of all meaning" (1986: 141).

In recent pages, in speaking of postmodern '*différance*', I've imported – it's not mine – the unsightly term 'de-differentiation'.

My reason was that while this word has an intent notably similar to deconstructionists' conception of *'différance'* it actually has a much longer and more widespread history in modern thought dating back at least a century and extending well beyond the concern with the deferral of meaning in language, and this history helps greatly to put what has been thought to be a deconstructionist discovery into perspective. For some writers on contemporary culture, such as Scott Lash, "de-differentiation" is the central feature of postmodernism, and we've seen every reason for their saying it. What Lash, for example, doesn't mention (and though he seems unaware of it, it's more likely that he regards it as so well known as not to bear repeating) are the motives associated with processes of de-differentiation and the narratives and images they produce. As Anton Ehrenzweig put it from the standpoint of psychoanalysis, in de-differentiation are "phantasies" that are "narcissistic". "There is the same withdrawal from external reality, the same limitless expression of the self to embrace the whole world". In 'narcissism', "dedifferentiation suspends many kinds of boundaries and distinctions; at an extreme limit it may remove the boundaries of individual existence and so produce a mystic oceanic feeling".[56]

Recent radical thought has never left the esemplastic urge far behind. When Deleuze and Guattari say that "in its most primitive form [their idea of 'auto-eroticism'] concerns the constitution of a pure body of pleasure, a body without organs ... that appears to produce itself as its own quasi-cause", we can recognize what the psychoanalyst Bursten announces in saying that the "main task of the narcissistic personality is to achieve the bliss and contentment characteristic of the primary narcissistic state".[57] It is what Fenichel decribes as "the narcissistic *unio mystica* of the deepest oral reunion of the subject with the universe". When we hear in Fuentes' novel *Terra Nostra* "We will ... transform this place into a space that truly contains all spaces ... [a]ll things being converted into all men, all men into all things, external multiplicity nourishing eternal unity", we are overhearing the "narcissistic feelings of well-being" that Fenichel reports "as a reunion with an omnipotent force in the external world, brought about either by incorporating parts of this world or by the fantasy of being incorporated by it".[58]

It can be helpful now to return to a piece of writing we looked at in Chapter 1, one purposely chosen because on purely chronological grounds we should expect it to be free of any suggestion of a relation between 'postmodern' and 'narcissant' thinking. When I quoted from an article in the 1946 edition of the *Encyclopaedia Britannica* entitled 'Scepticism', a passage that I omitted may strike a now familiar chord. It begins: "the result to be attained by cultivating such a frame of mind" was "mental imperturbability".

> The happiness or satisfaction of the individual was the end which dominated this scepticism ... and ... it consists in tranquillity or self-centred indifference. It is men's opinions or unwarranted judgments about things, say the sceptics, which betray them into desire, and painful effort and disappointment. From all this a man is delivered who abstains from judging one state to be preferable to another.... To be beyond reach of fear or doubt or other disturbance, a man must retire into himself. (20: 57)

Once again, this discussion has not been about the relative merits of philosophical positions, but about specific sensations of need, and how we act out and seek to manage them. About the forms in which (through images and abstract concepts) we alternately articulate and divert attention from them, and about how it arises that even the appearance of need is felt as something to conceal.

In narcissance, desperation is not solved by aspiration. We may be closer now to seeing how, instead, the two are enmeshed and resonate with one another, as they do in postmodern thinking, in constant oscillation.

Emotional Resources: Depression, Mania, Paranoia, Apathy

Emotions that we commonly understand to be 'good, positive' resources as we meet the trials of living – native feelings of courage and 'determination', the sensations of pleasure and energetic desire – need no recounting here, in part because our observing their defeat by narcissance highlights them at every turn. But I'd like to suggest now that in some of those very articulations of defeat there can be crucial, positive functions at work. In what follows I want to introduce – and it must be only in an extremely over-simplified, summary fashion – examples of the relations between actual emotional states regarded as characteristic of narcissance (or 'narcissism') and some of the ways of speaking that these can foster in a postmodern world.[59]

In doing this, I would like – *for a time* – to hold ideas of 'good feelings' and 'bad feelings' in suspension ('in brackets'), not only because it's in keeping with postmodern thinking ('what is good, what is bad?') but because approaching emotions from this unexpected angle can reveal matters that are concealed when, for example, we're inclined simply and unproblematically to 'feel sorry' for people who are depressed or angry. (We'll talk about feeling sorry for people later.) Certainly we may say that a narcissant experiencing events A, B and C *ends up* feeling X, Y and Z. But – as both postmodern theories and current psychological understandings comprehend particularly well – feelings aren't *end products*; they don't bring processes to an end any more than any other mental event does. They are part of the overall process in which a life's experiencing goes on. What happens when we think of feelings not as the 'bad/good outcomes of bad/good events' but, first, in just this way, as functions or processes?

In fact, the supreme emotional resources of the human mind for dealing with disturbances of the self are the states of depression, mania, paranoia and apathy. They are not much as solutions, but they are powerful ways of handling what is at stake. Perhaps their ultimate achievement in this respect – that is, in a final 'decentring of the subject' – is that at least some can lead to suicide. The topic of this brief discussion is, however, about what it can be like not to die but to live with them.

I've spoken a great deal in the preceding pages about fear. This has been largely because when narcissants do 'allow' feelings that they sense to be hazardous, one they may feel safest to reveal – and that we're consequently often most aware of in them – is fear. Fear, after all, except insofar as it elicits contempt, seems little threat to one's relations with others. Indeed, displaying it may even induce something resembling the care narcissants most desire. The truly *dangerous* sentiment is *anger*. How *can* anger, a narcissant instinct says, do anything but raise the threat of others' anger in response – and the direct and irreparable destruction of just that union with others one longs for? Still more, what of the damage to those desired-others that one's own anger might cause? The anxiety of the omnipotence of thoughts rarely exerts more repressive force than it can where in narcissance one catches sight, however fleeting, of anger in oneself. Here is one reason why in cases of narcissance, anger *seems* to be at the 'bottom' of all else. *Not* because it's at the root of all else, but because, instead, it's the last to 'come up', to be seen, to be allowed. A narcissant response to anger is to 'swallow' it, to be revealed instead in forms of shame, self-persecution, exhaustion, depression and psychosomatic illness.

But it's a hard thing to swallow, anger. Indeed, what greater *source* of anger can there be than the rage inspired by just that self-imposed (and socially endorsed) repression of such intense visceral feelings as anger? Feelings, in fact, that are all the more inflated in the imagination to what can seem volcanically ominous proportions by the numinous – diabolical? – qualities we attach to any feelings hidden from view, out of the light of reality where their actual limits might be seen. Here, then, is another narcissant circle. The *circle of unspeakable rage*.

But how is a narcissant, so bound to suppress his or her aggression, to make way in a world in which there are so many competing forces and voices? A most powerful mechanism is, of course, *the indeterminist attitude*. 'What I do has no effect; what you do is of indifference to me.' A narcissant becomes compulsively *determined* to *defer*. To defer to others' wishes; to defer into infinity wishes of his/her own ('Who am I, to be angry?'). And thus more anger is stored, together with fear; fear of his or her anger. In this way, even with no specific, circumstantial reason for anger, a narcissant can feel *anger – and fear – because s/he narcissizes*.

Here then is a special relationship between narcissant anger and postmodern ways of dealing with things. The matter extends to the clear possibility that an indeterminist impulse may articulate some form of 'passive aggression', so commonly found among narcissants.[60] One of the features distinguishing the discourse of postmodern culture is that, unlike virtually every other tradition celebrating itself as a model of 'revolt', while it often displays gravity (and may resemble that of someone in depression) it rarely shows aggression or anger. It is remarkably similar to the ever alert, sleekly intricate, often eloquent if involute, seemingly finely responsive, often 'deferential' speech that we meet in people when they are narcissants.

With this, the matter of *depression* returns. Since Freud it has consistently been held that depression comes about with 'narcissistic identification', where "the object to which the super-ego's wrath applies has been taken into the ego" (Mancia 1993: 10). As a feature of narcissance, depression is *not* the same as pain, anger or grief;[61] a fundamental function of it is to block or shroud such elemental feelings as too threatening to the precarious sense of self. As we've noted, people in depression frequently feel that living things around them seem artificial, flat, unreal – *separate, dissociated* from them. Both the beauty of a sunfilled morning and the sorrow of anyone near are equally 'hollow, empty'. Humans in depression may feel 'beyond anger', 'beyond pain'. Depression generalizes the experience of trouble. It is an aid to the *suppression* of specific emotions. It can damp down mourning over an unspeakable inadequacy or loss and can still those furies that may not be uttered. Depression in narcissance, as has been widely observed, can often be usefully understood as aggression or anger generalized and inverted, *a rage against the self*; an anger obscured and globalized into a pervasive self-crushing darkness.

* * *

But there is another side to this. Depression *frequently* discloses itself not in gloom but in outward excitement, in hilarity even. Unobserved by those encountering it only in its theoretical mode, in art and in popular culture, as we'll see, postmoderns laugh a lot. In her study of contemporary depression, *Black Sun*, Julia Kristeva – like Guattari a professional psychoanalyst – goes so far as to say that the postmodern is a comic-manic mode (1989). And in this conception we discover that most famous of narcissant patterns of oscillation, the manic-depressive cycle. It's what Terry Eagleton refers to in speaking of 'the characteristic post-structuralist blend of pessimism and euphoria'. Manic thinking, as we'll see in the next chapter, is the most direct and vivacious defence brought into play by postmodern culture to meet its psychic dilemmas.

As it's described by Heinz Kohut, the "narcissistic personality disorder ... fits well the psychodynamics of manic-depressive illness.... [S]hame is a central affect for the manic-depressive, which the manic flight attempts to hide through fantasied merger with the ideal self" (Morrison 1986: 359). 'Pseudovitality' is brought to bear as a 'manic-defence' to hide low self-esteem. It rarely enters narcissants' awareness that to others their manic behaviour may seem artificial, lacking in spontaneity, inappropriate to the situation and sometimes strangely angry.

We need to tread lightly here – because mania is not just a defence against depression. It's also a way – albeit a shifty one, like treading on quicksand – by which in narcissance we may touch our natural capacity for joy. What makes the manic experience unique, and different from other kinds of pleasure and enthusiasm, is how mercurially its gleam alternates with, collapses into, dark 'empty' despondency. When – whether in the guise of a postmodern or a narcissant – one is 'on a high', literally 'everything feels *intense*', and 'everything feels *connected*'. When Lyotard speaks of the postmodern, he speaks of it in terms of "the increase of being and the jubilation which result from the invention of new rules of the game".[62] Lyotard finely articulates exactly the double excitement that so typifies narcissant mania – for 'increase' here alludes to both the intensification and the expansion (by connection) of experience.

But in writing of the postmodern's 'jubilation' Lyotard introduces another of its most quintessential features. Jubilation is not merely exultation. It is specifically about shouting (*jubilare*) – about joy not merely as it is felt but as it is *uttered, voiced*. Often the most consistent feature of postmodern writing, both in its theoretical and its fictional expressions, is not its complexity, its so-called 'obscurity', but in fact its verbal fluency and expansiveness, its prolixity. (We've noted this in passing, in a number of ways – in terms of texture, where a trait of the writing is its so-called 'interminable' run-on sentences and paragraphs, where words and images flow on by association as if into infinity – and in terms of volume, where texts appear to far exceed their 'pre-texts'; a seeming 'doggedness', an unwillingness to 'let go'.) There is a curious resemblance between 'postmodern-speak' and the behaviour of a narcissant who, when you think the argument between you is over, follows you from room to room with ever more to exclaim in more ways, and who, alone, will not let go of the 'injury', cannot stop worrying the wound. (It's often from this above all that the notion of narcissists as 'self-centred', 'self-indulgent' arises.) Here is the matter of 'orality'.

Analysts remark it consistently in narcissance. A child whose emotional hungers have not been 'full-filled' can become notable for an 'aggressive orality', not only in insatiable appetites and a tendency toward eating disorders, but in *volubility*.[63] It is as though here were a mechanism specialized in narcissance to fend off silence and 'aimlessness'. Making connections that are literally ceaseless can confer the sensation that one is a living active agent – as if one's whole identity were at risk of collapsing should the 'song' ever end. The "*unio mystica* of the deepest oral reunion of the subject with the universe", toward which Fenichel says narcissist desire leans, becomes 'real' in the process of unending uttering.[64] But narcissants aren't alone in this. Scheherezade, fending off death with her tales, leads the way among postmodern fictionalists' favoured familiar spirits. Postmodern writers actually tell of finding the compulsive power of language not merely in the utterance but in the uttering. For Lacan, speaking is "in and of itself a jouissance" (Ragland-Sullivan 1986: 86). For Deleuze and Guattari a goal of 'schizophrenic thinking' is "a question of attaining the primary process of 'orality', where there is no longer any distinction between eating and speaking, or thinking and being" – where the 'autoerotic' body-without-organs may "produce itself".[65] "No degree of knowledge can ever stop this madness, for it is the madness of words" (Bloom et al. 1979: 68). In the course of Sherry Turkle's study of French working-class attitudes, when interviewees were asked to comment on Lacan, Deleuze and Guattari and other theorists who aimed to speak as their *porte-paroles* (and with whom Turkle herself was in sympathy) – a not unrepresentative response was "They want to talk, talk, talk" (1992: 161).

But surely we know that in postmodern theory, closure is impossible; isn't interminable uttering merely an effective example of a *theory's 'speaking its mind'*? Here we may find help in a celebrated quotation to which postmodern thought continually returns for its inspiration, Samuel Beckett's reply to a question put to him by Georges Duthuit about the project of writing (1949):

> I speak of an art ... weary of pretending to be able, of being able, of doing a little better the same old thing, of going a little further along a dreary road [and preferring] the expression that there is nothing to express, nothing with which to express, nothing from which to express, together with the obligation to express.

In this statement, 'philosophical' indeterminism seems to have come and gone, leaving something new in its wake. Somehow, *utterance is its own warrant*. But what does that mean? The answer is that it doesn't *mean anything*. It responds to a convulsive obligation, a compulsion. And this 'obligation' to speak *may* – at the very instant where it seems most pointless, aimless – achieve something. Humans do actually engage in 'meaningless uttering', and in narcissance – and perhaps in the postmodern – more than usual. When, and why?

Here, 'secondary processing' assumes a crucial role. In everyday life we produce information out of systems of thought, of protocols, formulae for sorting things, that we've learned till they seem to be part of us: making and remaking lists, calculating and recalculating sums and times and distances, charting and revising itineraries, ransacking our brains for better ways of saying what we've said, practising and refining moves, mentally replaying and reinterpreting others' utterances and inflections. But sometimes these 'secondary processing' routines go on when they've fallen out of touch with our immediate practical realities. Particularly, this can happen in the generalized but profound anxiety and depression that comes when we're exhausted by the complex and arduous ordeal of simply living, of keeping up appearances, of performing – where the old answers don't seem to work, and we're stymied. In times of extreme fatigue or stress or in illness, and most vividly when we're falling into a restless sleep and in certain 'maddeningly' endless dreams – our minds are somehow feverishly active, feeling even superhumanly acute: now we cannot stop interminably calculating 'solutions' – adding up numbers, making lists, imaging schemas, analysing others' words, formulating responses, producing what *seem* like 'answers' and more 'answers', connecting and constructing new meanings, meanings upon meanings – chains of meanings, torrents of meanings, whose material *significance* is more and more pressingly *unintelligible* and *empty*.

In actuality, this – that it is meaningless – is often *why we do it*. We have managed to forget what it was for, what *dilemma* had started it up. By a form of secondary processing – by a torrential connecting and chaining of thoughts, a proliferating of ideas whose good is that they are 'new ideas' – we have effaced what was 'primary', primary and intolerable, in our life. Our normative, critical judgement – the way we usually have of seeing the 'crisis', gauging our priorities and making decisions in relation to what is actually going on – has been overwhelmed, suppressed by this ritualistic and incantative form of 'thinking'. Our ostensible 'critical faculty' is vibrantly active, while our actual critical awareness of what purpose it was to serve is smothered, put to sleep.

In the midst of this process of torrential overdetermination – a process by which more 'answers' are produced than we can possibly use or make sense of – what is often most difficult to recognize is that we are not solving a problem but *interfering with the problem* that has been interfering with us. (Psychologists sometimes speak of the whole process as one of reciprocal 'interference'.) Like Beckett's Molloy, passing pebbles in and out of his mouth to restore some form of silence, we place the very act of uttering between ourselves and a reality that's too much for us. Recognizing that this is what is happening is hard and meant to be so, because now, at last and at least, we feel something resembling power; the capacity to create – our power to produce ideas, to spawn a seamless, unstoppable word-stuff.

Such routines, the sedulous manic application of our energy to the business of 'only connecting', where everything's 'stuck' to everything else, will have many effects. They can remodel our philosophical outlook. Language itself may seem to be all, and the utter indeterminacy of utterances may rule; but we've released ourselves from the punishing hard prison of fixed meanings where life is real, life is earnest and time is of the essence. And the narcissant's ambivalent fear-and-rejoicing, the jubilation, in the 'omnipotence of thought' may actually at moments resolve itself into a value-free sensation of – as we'll see in the next chapter – ecstasy.

What is more, if the process of merging meanings fails to 'fix' (settle) one's identity, it may certainly seem to help fix (manage) many things in the fields of relations where a narcissant's problems of self arise. Manic uttering can promote confluence, literally a 'flowing together'. It can be a gesture toward never-closing the conversation, a way of maintaining the appearance of contact, of the yearned-for fusion, a communion in the mere act of communication.

Postmodern theoretical writers are often accused of 'manic logorrhea'. As Susan Sontag put it early, we are "in an era" where "an increasing number of works of art babble. Verbosity and repetitiveness are particularly noticeable in the temporal arts of prose fiction, music, film and dance" (1969: 26–7); Annette Lavers spoke of a "new torrential style of writing" (1982: 23). Ihab Hassan heralded postmodern fiction as "a form of writing that is incessant sound" (1975: 13). One of the useful questions always to ask – when a linguistic indeterminist says (as for example Derrida does) that the outcome of utterance is 'always the same' – is the one we might ask of the narcissant who follows us from room to room, endlessly speaking. 'Why don't you stop?' The ultimate answer of both the postmodern indeterminist and the narcissant is almost invariably to be 'I can't'. As Derrida would say, 'from the moment I open my mouth, even if I decide to be silent, this silence yet remains a modality of speech'. But as an answer to 'Why don't you stop?', this confuses *stopping meaning* with *stopping speaking*. And the supplement, the leftover difference, where both postmodern indeterminists and narcissants insist on continuing to *speak*, has a further effect: it defers difference. It is as though, in a terror of 'stopping', by dissolving differences it can dispel the threat of separation.

That here is a need that narcissance and postmodern indeterminism share becomes clear when the latter, for example, seems to be 'determined' to *differ* – when confronted in a debate, say, with a realist. How can an indeterminist 'win', given that s/he can't 'definitively determine' his or her terms and can't bring an argument 'to term'? Deconstructionists, for instance, entirely rightly insist that they do *not intend* the *'destruction'* of the other. Deconstruction's procedures are precisely suited to the project of the dissolution of the other by means of a manic *fusion*, by dispelling the very differentiation of otherness – by a *suppression of difference*.[66] The more this process continues the more it demonstrates not only that one can but that one must go on speaking 'indefinitely'.

An intriguing similarity between narcissance and postmodern thinking is thus the manner they share of behaving as if impelled into what appears to be productivity by an anxiety of separation. As Mollon says in speaking of a narcissant patient's "non-stop chatter", the patient "found a way of insisting that he was listened to, thereby avoiding his own fear of psychological 'obliteration', but at the same time effectively obliterating others" (1993: 72). Unlike other forms of revolt: for the narcissant, where 'knowing' the otherness of the other is *both* terrible (because it means separation) *and* indispensable (because it means the sole chance of discerning one's own identity), the other's destruction is intolerable, since it must entail not the release but the destruction of the struggling self. Similarly, for linguistic indeterminism, deferring difference isn't merely its 'message', but its wish.

What is more significant, it's a wish that is far from confined in postmodern culture only to language-centred movements such as deconstructionism. In the vitalism of Deleuze and Guattari, heralded by their conception of the infinite rhizomic network of desire, there is what some critics have insightfully recognized as a connection-making "synthetic mania".[67] To Baudrillard, for humans throughout the contemporary world "Things have found a way to elude the dialectic of meaning ... by infinite proliferation, by potentializing themselves, by outmatching their essence" (Baudrillard 1988a: 185). A "fractal multiplication", a "general metastasis of value" (like that of a cancer) in postmodern times, now becomes the prescription for his own work, by which he breathlessly hoards and pastes a universe of disparate cultural images, ever gathering and feverishly linking by virtue of an aleatory, 'vertiginous', "delirious point of view" whatever he considers not yet already linked by a civilization that is itself, in his opinion, "a delirious state of things".[68] Manic assembling and uttering, the ceaseless chaining and proliferation of connections, where *meaning must not be achieved*, is not only the gift of narcissance but an identifying mark of postmodern thinking.

It would be wrong to underestimate the intense attraction of stereotyped strategems of logomania for the postmodern in the face of the devouring darkness, the abyss, the void that de Man and Lacan speak of, where even the active mouth that gives some faltering sense of volition, of self, would be stilled. The haunting image comes to mind of Beckett's play *Not I*, where in the theatre's total darkness (on which Beckett insisted) there floats an interminably breathlessly speaking, shouting mouth. For there are two voids before which the indeterminist, like the narcissant, stands: that of the meaninglessness of the universe, against which the voice saying 'All is meaningless' stands speaking, and that of the vanquished very self against whose dissolution it raises its filibustering voice. The postmodern insistence on the effacement of historical origins and endings – coupled with the narcissant desire "to have created oneself ... to go on forever" – now has new meaning. Writers as diverse as Blanchot, Beckett, Sontag, Barth and de Man, have animatedly argued that what was needed, what was ahead, was a literature of exhaustion, of silence – a literature *speaking the void*. This is the theme that declares the world of language to be a Babel (a topos brilliantly explored by Derrida); a universe where the more that's said in favour of not speaking, the more will be spoken, and where the building of a 'tower of babble' is language-users' own retributive solution for the confusion they have inaugurated in using it.[69] Clinging to this 'tower of their own making', postmoderns (like narcissants) seem to bespeak – in however inchoate and naive a form – the urgency of being heard, if only by themselves, as the producers of their own sound.

* * *

The critical affective force of *paranoia* in the postmodern cultural tradition scarcely needs explication now. We haven't far to go to see why what we recognize to be narcissant behaviour is so often confused in postmodern writing with paranoid psychosis. As psychologists point out, "the narcissistic pathology forms a substantial part of the core of paranoia", and narcissance, in tandem with this, is alive with paranoid signs.[70] The mordantly potent activity of persecutory feelings in narcissance becomes clear when we understand how they enact 'helpless grandiosity'. 'I am the centre, all that happens is addressed to me, I am the victim of all.' This is the ever-swivelling Janus regard and unrest of narcissance. Someone is ever watching; but who? That anyone might feel this implacable 'watcher' to be inescapable, forever there wherever one goes, becomes finally comprehensible when we grasp that in narcissance, the first persecution is self-persecution. So unremitting a sensation of one's own inadequacy and shame must – if it's to be survived – be projected outward; one is a victim, then, of *someone else's* mad hatred, contempt and will to destroy.

Here, spoiling rules; the obsessive-compulsive 'perfectionism' of narcissance makes the individual its slave; fantasies, dreams, relentless flashes may present the narcissant with visions of catastrophic events to ensue from the slightest material misstep or error of judgement. The 'critical mode of thinking' – affiliated with hypochondria and the anxiety that lies in wait with each anticipated move, each fleeting thought – is hypostatized into a 'positive' way of life. (Effective scepticism, and critical activity more generally, find their most reliable and potent motives in paranoia. It hasn't escaped public notice that not only virtually all postmodern theorists but the vast majority of postmodern fictionalists are by profession university professors employed specifically for their expertise in searching textual analysis.)[71]

The sweeping currency of what has come to be called 'paranoid fiction' in contemporary literature resumes many of postmodern thinking's most persistent motifs and processes. Writers markedly divergent in other respects – as far back as Burroughs, Borges, and Flann O'Brien, and from Robbe-Grillet, Butor, Márquez, Fuentes and Sarraute to Pynchon, Heller, Eco, Sciascia, Nabokov, Federman and Barth – have drawn a wide and diverse readership into the web of explicitly paranoid fantasy. Characters stray through labyrinths in search of clues not merely to resolve mysteries but to explain why they are obsessed with the search for clues, and with the sense of being watched and pursued. In the name of the ultimate 'informational paradox', we are lured into a mystery – the vision of threat, of conspiracy and deception, with all the trappings of secrecy, disguise and delusion – not now, as in traditional realist thinking and writing, in order to solve it but to find that we cannot.

It is no accident that as a 'postmodern enterprise' the process of deconstruction is sometimes called "a hermeneutics of suspicion".[72] Just as deconstructionist procedures were adopted in late twentieth-century political writing to uncover social and economic sites of betrayal by teasing out strands of covertly oppressive hegemonous discourse, postmodern 'paranoid' fictions lure us into the tenebrous worlds of betrayers and the betrayed, only to leave us incapable of deciding who is which. As in the case of deconstruction, the process installs a 'virus' in our reading of the text (like a software virus, infecting the very program in which the document is read) that cannot be arrested when it comes to the deconstructionist's own text or the 'text' of the reader's own analysis. In a fashion identical to that of 'the narcissant spin', we are caught in the ultimately interminable vortex of paranoid thinking.

Of all narcissant affective states, the paranoid is the most potent positive force for hyperdetermination – that is, for the concerted production of indecision and uncertainty. Like the manic proliferation of meanings, it succumbs to the mind's compulsion, in fact its wish – like that of the lover (child) obsessively hunting for clues of love and/or betrayal in every detail of others' behaviour – to 'lose itself in the knitting', where the perception of any larger 'figure in the carpet' of circumstance or of its own unfulfilled desire may be interminably deferred. It will play an important role when we come to the matter of whether narcissance – or postmodern thinking itself – has any limits, or can be brought to a close.

* * *

Which of these – depression, mania, paranoia – promises the best defence against problems of the self? In narcissance, depression has special ways of suppressing the specificities of pain, anger, fear that paranoia is so formidable at picking out. Mania achieves much the same as depression but it makes room for the sensations of potency and excitement and includes patches of real fun, which are not to be knocked, though on the downside they can get us into real life trouble that depression generally hasn't the appetite for. Narcissant paranoia unceasingly churns up all kinds of fresh ways of thinking, of new things to distract us from the real problem, but since it can't tell the difference between real trouble and no trouble, it makes life hell. If you had your choice, it would be hard to decide which one to go for – on the flat in the dry with no wind, they're all good for the course. The drawback is, you don't have a choice. If you want to get out of any of these three, you have to get out of narcissance.

In the tone of that last paragraph lies the issue ahead. I don't seem to have got my feelings to join up properly with what I was speaking about. Postmodern literature is full of writing like this, and often we like to say that it's because postmodern thinking asks, 'who is to say what's proper?' – and there's much to that idea. A classic case appears in Beckett's *Molloy*, of which it's customary for readers to say that 'nothing much happens' in it, that it's 'really just two characters' wandering monologues'. It commonly takes a great deal of prompting before readers realize – if they're able to recall at all – that, among other things, each of these characters actually bludgeons someone to a pulp. Why don't we notice? It's because, we say, the decorum of 'serious' sentiment is missing, as postmodern logics so often require. It's not that (as often happens in Modernist writing) Molloy or Moran feels something *unorthodox* in killing – such as joy or pleasure; they feel none of these things. The events are depicted without the affective colouring that 'normally' goes with the telling of such remarkable events. But there is – as we know from what we've seen of Beckett, for example – more to it than this. The 'decorum of sentiment' doesn't 'just disappear' from where it's expected; someone removes it. Who?

An attribute of postmodernity that many have observed is what Jameson has called 'the waning of affect'. Feelings "are now free-floating and impersonal and tend to be dominated by a peculiar kind of euphoria" (1991: 14–16). Not unsurprisingly, it's not uncommon in Jameson and others to speak of the waning of affect as an outcome of the decentring of the subject (there's no one there to feel). But, once again, the impulse to produce a generic description of human experience or of a period in history conceals the fundamental problem: where does this 'waning' take place? Everywhere, at the same time, equally? Wherever experiencing (such as feeling, not feeling) can be imagined to take place? Is it something in the ether, that somehow creates a simulacrum of people, all (not) feeling the same way? Probably not. It happens where people are thinking in a postmodern way. What way, more precisely in this case of the 'waning of affect', is that?

Here is a peculiar observation common among psychotherapists: in the determination to be 'autarkic', to 'do it him- or herself', to conceal any feeling of dependency or need, a narcissant may display "omnipotence, omniscience, envy, greed, jealousy, massive splitting, and projective identification, which tend to denigrate the work of analysis and make the analyst feel helpless, inadequate, humiliated, and *often bored and mentally paralysed*" (Mancia 1993: 28).

Given the first part of this quotation, with all its allusions to an aggressive narcissance, the last phrase concerning boredom and paralysis, which I've highlighted, might come as a great surprise – if we hadn't seen something like it before. It's part of the package of narcissance. The person sitting opposite the narcissant is mastered, put in his place. But what 'place' is that? It seems to be one in which *nothing can happen*. The analyst, in his or her boredom and paralysis, is responding to what is in fact a flattening, an occultation – often out of the patient's awareness – of what is actually happening in the room. Until the patient is able to 'take back', to own his or her postures and projections and make *genuine contact* with the analyst in terms of the *actual feelings and needs* that *produce* this performance, the analyst is obliged to play out a rigid (rigorous, dead) fiction, having nothing to do with who either of them really is, and that – if the patient has his/her way – threatens to go on forever. The analyst, the listener (or indeed the 'reader'), facing this mask, *becomes* the bored one that the patient feared s/he would. The hollowness, meaninglessness of discourse so powerfully intimated by the postmodern indeterminist emerges as a human social reality.

But why must the patient do this? The answer has always been nearby. An essential urge in narcissance is to cling to sameness ('identity') – to hold alterations of one's inner state at bay.[73] Yet if depression serves to handle anxiety, fear, pain, it has its limits. If it's true that one can sink one's specific fears and angers into the darkness of depression, beyond that lies the worse terror: in the morass, the void of depression, 'I, my very being', may sink altogether without trace. With a deadly certainty, for those for whom the margins of their reality feel fragile and ever susceptible to dissolution, the perils of the very intensity of sensations (with their threat to the tenuously felt stability and continuity of one's being) can threaten to be overwhelming. While it will be hard for many to appreciate this, it must be said before we go any further that the threat is equally immanent in depression's intimate counterparts: in enthusiasm and excitement, extreme pleasure, joy and desire.

The work of anaesthesis begun in depression, then, is carried on in full in narcissance by the distinctive process of the *flattening of emotional affect*. Spoiling or wasting comes into play – as an active form of apathy (*a-pathis*, 'without feeling') whose postmodern counterparts are the practice of abstraction and the theme of aporia. The suppression, the extinction and the apparent draining away of feeling is one of the most common and fundamental ways in which a narcissant may manage every possibility of invasion by feelings that might engulf what remains of the sense of self. It is one reason why narcissants may often "describe themselves as encased in a 'plastic bubble' or feel that they are really not 'in the world'", and unable to support the excitement – in themselves *or* in others – of naive believing.[74]

As we'll see in the next chapter, there can be satisfactions here. Mastery, self-control to the point of what may appear self-assured tranquility, irony, sardonic composure, self-complacency and boredom or even utter 'woodenness', 'blankness', can assume for not only the narcissant but to observers the semblance of the most supreme arrogance, intellectual authority and emotional omnipotence. An understanding of this process will have important implications for our apprehension not only of postmodern theories' accent on aporia but of trends in postmodern culture as a whole.[75] *Indifference*, literally, is the rule. I suggest we let this shapeshifting word 'indifference' stand alone for the present, as the emblem we know it to be for the many rich and suggestive features of postmodern thinking that it invokes. We'll return to it.

THE AMBIVALENCE THRESHOLD

It may well seem that so far a great deal more has been devoted to postmodern 'theories' than is humanly decent. The fact is that as soon as we set out to observe postmodern thinking in the ways it is 'spoken' we were obliged to engage with a culture whose manner of speaking has been dedicated, more than any, to speaking theoretically. That is, to cultivating processes of abstraction in the name of a search for the 'general rule', for a meta-view, if only to prove that that was also a contradiction. As we've begun to grasp, this practice has real significance for our understanding of how the postmodern likes to think of itself and how it meets and reveals its needs.

Everyday experience can help to shed light on this. Probably everyone has spent time with someone who was easy, chatty, even loquacious company yet who invariably left us feeling somehow depressed. Seen in retrospect, here was someone whose manner of speaking was what we might call 'philosophical'; people in the condition I have in mind don't speak about how they're feeling, but about 'how things are'. Not only when they may seem cheerful ('things will improve') or just moderate and 'realistic' ('take the rough with the smooth'), or even when they seem pessimistic ('life is a bitch'), we feel no distress during the encounter, because everything *seems 'under control'*. In our average daily lives this process, by which a person persistently converts points of distress into points of third-person philosophical observation, particularly during encounters with others, may be a narcissant one. In fact, when the topic centres on matters that might usually be expected to stir up emotions, but fails to: the more that someone says, without the use of 'I' – where, in other words, 'the subject is decentred' – the more likely it is that narcissance may be involved. The individual's trouble – and this may be either depression or something like paranoid aggression or manic 'flight' – has been *diffused* (defused) by means of abstraction.

This does not mean that thinking and speaking in abstractions can't be among humans' leading achievements. It's simply that when the outcome is depressive feelings whatever the gist of what's said aloud, something else is happening. Contact with us has been repelled – we've been (as Mallory Nash has nicely put it) consuming 'a polystyrene meal' coloured to look like the real thing. In going along with what's said instead of saying, for example, 'Wait, what do *you feel* about this? What do you want to happen when you speak this way?' we've inwardly ingested, 'swallowed' (introjected) the other's covert depression or aggression or manic turmoil. It bears observing that we ourselves have more than likely been colluding by reason of our own narcissance. Looking ahead to the next chapters, this is a reminder of the very reality of narcissance in our 'normal' lives and how easily it may be 'touched' or triggered.

But there's a deeper dimension to this. Abstraction as a process is essential for the survival of life in the style that humans (with our particular physical limitations) need to live. (Without it we could never have conceived, for instance, of making and keeping tools.) Two features emerge here. First, that in this respect abstraction is essentially a response to the *need to predict and manage*. And second, that where prediction and management as objectives radically predominate over other ones (such as the experiencing of the intensity and fullness of the moment), survival seems to be at issue; an anxiety for the surety and continuity of the self. But while this is poignantly relevant when we consider the impulses of narcissance, it appears to fly in the face of postmodern thinking about the decentred subject, where in theory the latter doesn't even come close to anything like surviving; that's the point about the decentred subject, that the self's survival isn't on offer. Perhaps we need once more to think again.

One of the most revealing features of subject-decentring theories is their frequent implicit assumption that every sensation of 'being a subject' must be a positive and indeed a blithe one (whence the merit of the argument that it's a treacherously idealistic delusion). Theories like this are unready to absorb that the experience of self must on balance be pleasant only about as much of the time, at best, as life's vicissitudes are good-feeling ones, and that a self is not destroyed by ambivalence but is simply more 'realized' or 'full' when it allows its ambivalence. Who is it, then, that thinks that the subject, the self, is so magical, so illusory, and so endangered?

Postmodern subject-decentring theories' prepossession with ideas of the sensation of self as a euphoric experience – *and* their determination singlehandedly to expose these ideas forever as snares and delusions – disclose the force of narcissant fantasies driving them. Some psychologists themselves have expressed misgivings about "a unidimensional view of human nature … in which self-cohesion is the highest aim and loss of self the greatest danger".[76] (We can share these misgivings; psychology should *comprehend* narcissance and not merely mimic its preoccupations.) Where – whether to confirm or deny its cohesion – the concern regarding the self 'is in the foreground of awareness instead of being comfortably in the background', narcissance and postmodern thinking are unmistakably mirror images of one another, caught up in the same unique obsessional configuration.

The wider spectrum of postmodern indeterminist thinking is braided up in this. Failing to find a fixed system of values and an unaltering identity entails the utter breakdown of identity and determinable meaning *only for those who must have that extreme ideal as a primary object of desire.*[77] Constructing an overarching principle of thought upon the failure of this ideal marks a narcissant way of processing experience. 'Ontologizing the personal' – treating a distinct psychological process as the pre-condition of all human being, making a (universal) drama out of a (personal) crisis – is not only a particular way of dealing with personal crisis, it's one bound to appeal most to those of us whose crisis is specifically one of separation, of feeling altogether alone.

Over the past century in which it has been an issue, on balance, no pragmatic (social, political, economic) development has emerged from propositions for the decentring of the subject proportionate to the shock-value of its statement. We could by other means have taken the same decisions we've taken, without it. The residue (or 'excess') of shock is what it has had to offer, and that shock, in shock's senses of trauma, emotional dismay and paralysis, is the shock of the narcissant. Theories of the decentring of the subject register – and *keep in play* by means of abstraction – the very real psychological processes of narcissance, whose impact is far from abstract.[78]

Even when we've grasped that narcissance is nothing like the only possible pattern of contemporary thinking, as I've been keen to illustrate by contrasting narcissance with other styles of thinking, the power of the narcissance model is sizable and complex enough that we need continually to take care as, with it in mind, we take in the events around us.[79] In what follows, in broaching again a notion psychologists often advance as essential for the resolution of 'narcissistic disorders', I don't do so in order to 'establish what must be done'. Rather, I offer it as an aspect of the model of narcissance taken as a whole – where narcissance can be more fully understood when one considers its 'outer limits', what 'coming out of narcissance' might look like. It's mentioned, in other words, as a way of *speculating* about what might approach the 'outer limits' of postmodern thinking.

Paul Hoggett, writing about the postmodern topos that "all that is left is to imitate dead styles", calls this "the phantasy of an exhausted breast with nothing left to give".

> This is not pessimism, but hatred and despair. Having been caught once in an embrace with something which was good but then failed, one resolves firmly never to be caught again. The only future for culture lies in 'debunking' and pastiche.... This is a pre-depressive attitude, one without the grace or courage to acknowledge past dependencies. (1989: 31–2)

We hear in this the intonations of Unqle Trim. But the passage does invoke an important issue in the relations between narcissance and postmodern thinking. I'm not going to pursue this at length here, but I suggest it for its conjectural value. In speaking of postmoderns as minds in a state of 'hatred and despair', Hoggett is actually describing depression, and in saying that this is 'pre-depressive' he means that it stands on the edge of the 'depressive position'. This is the matter I had in mind – the 'ambivalence threshold' or 'depressive position' – when I said a few paragraphs ago that self-decentring theories don't take into account that "a self is not destroyed by ambivalence but is simply more 'realized' or 'full' when it allows its ambivalence".

In the face of radically incompatible values – for example both a fantasy of harmonious unity and the seemingly crushing unattainability of it – an alternative way of thinking is to decline either to split and oscillate endlessly between them or to obliviate them by merging them into a universal one, but instead to allow them to share the space of our attention. Taking a stand at the ambivalence threshold, as I've mentioned before, one no longer takes either separation or dividedness – or a realistically measured dependence on others – 'personally' as one does in narcissance. It is not a defect in oneself but a feature of the reality of daily conscious being. ('I am neither all things, nor nothing. I am ordinary, but I am something.') At this juncture, there is the possibility of feeling – of being – no longer driven, dispersed and dissipated by the interminable struggle to elude the dilemma, and of being free to be oneself. That is, one may own one's personal, ever-modifying boundaries – experiencing contradictions but (finding no need to cling to their idealized opposed forms) compelled no longer to feel utterly nullified by their irreconcilable opposition. The chance arises to move '*as* one' through the world.[80]

To be able to do this, however, one must let go of those extreme 'yearnings'; *freely mourning* their passing, one must let them, as fantasies, fall away. Here lies the ('depressive') grief that is inevitable at the ambivalence threshold, and whose contemplation is so frightening to a narcissant. At the ambivalence threshold one refuses to pose as affectively neutral. The condition identifies and *contains* grief without the indulgence of philosophical obliviation – a metaphysical extra that is pointless and potentially damaging to both the experiencing individual and others in the 'field'. Not only must one *separate* from the last hope of what has in the past been desired, but – even more anguish-laden – one must *abandon* the old *structure of desiring* around which one has built one's life, one's ('false') sense of oneself. Ingrained processes of thinking and ways of presenting oneself to the world – and, it may seem, bonds to those patterns of human relationship that have been enlisted to sustain them – are let go. We know intuitively that we can always lose our footing at the 'threshold', and that there must be defeats. That it's no more than a condition of mind, and an ephemeral, liminal one from which we may always fall back and – returning to narcissance – may never find again.

We can perceive now why it is that psychologists often observe in practice that the state of mind of patients reaching the depressive position chronically alternates between the depressive position and – specifically – paranoia. It is as though a desperate recurrent need is there to say, 'It's not me – I don't perpetrate this terrible pain of tearing and loss – I cannot, I *do not* do this to *myself* – it's the fault of the *others*!'

A limit of postmodern thinking discloses itself here. A constant theme among Derrida, Lacan and others is that of 'impossibility' and 'impasse'. The discovery of indeterminacy is in a profound sense 'an end of discourse' (even while the discoursing will return, be interminably repeated); one *cannot pass*. Writers we've considered often cleave to a 'structure of desiring' that forestalls the kind of movement toward the depressive position I've just described. While each writes to portray in depth and often elaborate and moving detail one or another affective state of the sorts we've considered in the previous section ('depressive', 'paranoid', 'manic'), and their accounts in fact oscillate among these, they consistently stop short of the articulation of any conception analogous to the ambivalence threshold. This is *not* to say that they *should* 'go there'. It's simply to say that they don't. As narcissance refuses, falls back in fear or dismay from the possibility of a limit to its own reassuringly habitual processes (and their well-established aura of heroism) – with the cataclysmic sensation of loss that such a limit inherently forbodes – so does postmodern thinking.[81] Hesitation, 'aporia' – if the contrasting conception of moving to the ambivalence threshold has any validity – assumes a formidable new meaning.

This 'hesitation' can of course be thought to reflect a philosophical desire to continue to 'play' – in the infinite play of signification. In view of the 'signs' pointing toward emptiness, delusion, unquenchable desire, impossibility, anguish, death and the void that haunt so much of what it says, some might gasp with relief that postmodern discourse doesn't hold with 'getting serious'. But as we glance at a few examples of things people *do*, in keeping with postmodern ways of thinking, we may gain a different impression. New lifestyles are heralded here, and it all has a lot more visibly to do with play.

5 Ways of Acting

In contemporary material life, postmodern thinking plays a part in fields of experience so far-flung and diverse as to exceed the effective analytical scope of any one book. We enter a realm of sheer experiment, and the caveat that this essay is not exhaustive but suggestive should be emblazoned on every page now. To keep this chapter's speculative nature always in the foreground – to hint at a *kind* of inquiry that might be useful, rather than an achieved one – I'm going to confine it to a very few examples and am determined to let the gaps show; these are samples, 'starters', which others may take up or replace as their own evidence and experience indicates they should. Moreover, I deliberately 'randomize' the selection, to communicate something of the range and diversity of cases worth looking into, and to forestall any anticipation that what's proposed at this stage might be systematic.

The problems are numerous. We can't really 'quote' actions; it is one thing to hazard the interpretation of others' public discourse and another to claim to analyse what they often don't even begin to say aloud. I wouldn't write this chapter if I didn't believe that how we act gives clues as to how we think. (In fact, as before, I'll suggest examples of occasions where what people do seems significantly to belie what they say.) But it would be daft to pretend that the conclusions we draw have the same status as those we base on reading or listening to people seeming to 'speak their own minds'. We can only at best give weight to what seem to be the most accurate descriptions of people's behaviour, and read these in turn as signs with the best sign-reading skills we have.

For another thing, it is impossible to encompass in an orderly fashion a whole culture – especially when its impulse is to disrupt orderly systems – in the way that we may seem, at least, to speak perspicuously about a pattern of thought underlying it. (The Bibliography offers examples of a variety of recent reconstructions of the array and direction of contemporary lifestyles.) Coherence connecting examples given here, then, is not put forward as that of a sequence of activities and interests in some one individual's life or of some discrete social or economic scheme. Those are projects for other studies. Instead, my hope is that it derives from the web of relationships that were described in the model offered in Chapters 3 and 4. (Most simplistically, if in the last chapter we found attitudes 'a' and 'b' linked to an attitude 'x', and if in this chapter we find an attitude with some resonance of 'a' and of 'b', it may be that there is here what I've called a 'family relationship' – that we'll find here too an adjoining attitude resembling 'x' that might otherwise have gone unobserved.) The value I hope this lends is – like a *speculative tool* – that of *a way of looking and seeing*.

It's possible to expect outcomes here that are far from my mind. 'Locating postmodern persons' isn't this discussion's objective. The culture of postmodernity, as I've said, is *not* something everyone in the contemporary world endorses or that anyone subscribes uniformly to, but is only one of a number of cultures individuals simultaneously adopt in their own divergent ways. In actuality, we rarely if ever identify people by the names of the cultures they endorse. Thinking of the hundreds of millions whose experiences, actions and beliefs are more deeply and controllingly informed by the culture of capitalism than any other, we don't call them all 'capitalists'. No person considering him- or herself a Christian does or can do all the many conflicting things that the diverse Christian denominations say a Christian should do. In just the way that I've spoken of narcissants in terms not of personal types but of mental processes, in speaking of 'postmoderns' I mean people engaging, in some significant context, in a given process of mind, one we now recognize as postmodern; people 'postmodernizing'. I hope that readers will be prepared to let stand this rather modestly realistic open-weave notion of the relations between living humans and their cultures, and that the thoughts broached may be seen not as forming a scheme completed and wrong but as a project just beginning and yet to prove itself.

* * *

The way that this chapter is divided into two main sections is meant to reflect that 'two-facedness' of postmodernity – its inclinations (described in the first part) toward the liberation that might be found or sought in *pluralism* and (in the second part) the aspiration toward the dissipation of constraints through *indeterminism*. They *are different*. Paradoxical as it may seem, in the practices of the postmodern the actual relations between these impulses are always a matter for decision, however out of awareness this may be. How can the apparent conflict be resolved between indeterminism (where no foundation holds) and pluralism (where the very existence of a local constituency or value in its difference from others must seem somehow to rest on its intrinsic *raison d'être*, its immediate 'foundational' rights and/or its accompanying sensation of elemental 'rightness')? The separation of them in this chapter is artificial. I say this not because any conceptual differences seen between them are mistaken but because in actuality they oscillate, each juggling for ascendency. The fact that postmoderns regularly confuse them is one of the signs that narcissant processes are involved. Just as indeterminism may call on the plurality of experience as evidence of its rigour, within each special cultus calling on pluralism for its defence it shouldn't be forgotten that radical indeterminism may be stirring and can be expected to speak at any time. The two are in continual tension with one another, and invariably need their difference from one another. If in the following pages I don't always pause to show their oscillation in action, it will help our understanding of the postmodern if we keep in mind – just as we need to do in thinking about narcissance – that wherever processes described in one part seem in play, ones described in its 'counter-part' may not be far behind, rising to challenge it.

A still further-reaching peculiarity of the postmodern, reenacted in the shape of this book, is the very doubleness of the 'feel' of postmodernity, which we can now address. There seems to be a 'world of difference' between the stark, often dark, introspective theoretical postmodernism discussed in the previous chapters and the vivacious clamour, the never-resting multifariously inventive, the sleek and swank razzle-dazzle – the often intoxicatedly idealistic and sometimes outrageously exhibitionist and defiant bustle and welter – of contemporary activity as it's feverishly and exuberantly displayed in the behaviour of people living a life called 'postmodern' in the news, online, in the media, in the shopwindows and on the streets around us. As the presenter said at the start of a recent BBC two-hour documentary study of current British art, "The individuality of their work makes it impossible to brand this generation of young artists as a movement because their work is so varied; anything goes".[1] That phrase (as I promised) has returned – 'anything goes' – and with it the vibrant pacy 'carnival' of extroverted experiments in human lifestyles with which the postmodern is represented in the popular imagination.

It is a theme of this essay that in fact the processes that engender both – what we've seen people bespeaking 'postmodernism' say, and how we'll see people mark out their actual lives as 'postmodern'— are the same. But the surface differences are unmistakable. Why so?

For a start, the very mode of abandonment that ripples through the fabric of popular postmodernity (as I'll suggest later) expresses in a different form the same yearning for oblivion that haunts postmodern theory. But this difference has an ironic effect; the one form must suppress the other. The 'fit' of the postmodern and of the narcissant is clear here. As we've seen, a large proportion of narcissant energies are dedicated to 'burying' the narcissant's own uncertainty and self-consciousness – of which postmodern theories themselves are often the most powerful and explicit expression. The traces of personal self-absorption and 'self-indulgent' angsts that narcissance can entail, and that *theory dramatizes*, must be concealed – concealed by and from the narcissant's own self, not infrequently out of shame, and in self-contempt for entertaining feelings of shame – and from the world, at the world's behest, for the world's own pressing social reasons. Even while it persistently calls on theory by name, a lived postmodern culture must inevitably also sweep much of it into a corner, if not efface it altogether.

The causes for this apparent fissure between theory and the more expansive culture that contains it may run deeper still. I've spoken from the outset of disparities between what postmodern theories 'think' and what postmodern culture thinks they think. We've seen that, for example, postmodern theories are more sceptical about scepticism than popular postmodern-speak allows; they simply won't go so far as to say, for instance, that 'anything goes'. Should we believe that this is because, intellectually, theorists are more circumspect, that they're simply too savvy to 'jump to conclusions'? There's a certain logic (as well as a whiff of elitist arrogance) to this. But the concerted vigour of the *material activity*, of *things done* in the name of postmodernity, by contrast, suggests some more vital process at work. It has something to do with the status of action itself, and with *the status of experience*. It goes like this.

One of the most striking lapses in postmodernist theories is a more than occasional unreadiness to inquire into the realms of affect, and of the physical senses. 'Paying so much mind' to objects of attention as 'simulacra', they are disinclined to observe that whatever the 'reality-status' of objects of experience, *experience goes on*. And it often goes on in characteristic ways that may seem virtually independent of the relative degrees of apparent objects' reality. (Many of our most telling human insights spring from the recognition that we frequently act on the basis not of things-as-they-are but of our experience of things-as-they-seem. The experience, whatever we may say about its connections with any material world, has the force of reality.) This is never more the case than in – it is of course a defining feature of – narcissance. But who then is looking after the realms of feeling and sensation while theorists take a vacation from them?

The effect of this lopsided way of prioritizing concepts and letting experience fall by the wayside is significant. It will strike some readers as strange to find so much attention, under the heading of the postmodern, devoted to language and the processes of abstraction, when we are surrounded by a culture calling itself 'postmodern' whose accent is so candidly and floridly (as we'll review but as we have already been repeatedly reminded by social historians) devoted to material sensation. Knowing something about how narcissance works can help us to understand this. Minds enduring the unrelenting struggle to maintain something like equilibrium for the self as a whole cannot rest with abstraction. They swing between the urge to produce synthetic theories (with all the poignant perceptions these yield) and a counter-impulse to be swept away by the effervescent tide of 'objects (felt to be) outside' themselves. Thus in narcissance one may in one moment strive toward self-organization by means of some abstraction (such as an ego-ideal) – and in another instant feel insatiably drawn toward the self-consciousness-liberating chaos that an 'abandonment to the senses' may fleetingly but potently afford. In tandem with this comes the urge – again, in *apparent* contradiction to the theorist's negation of the possibility of subjects as positive agents, but in no way incoherent once one understands the oscillation inherent in narcissance – to move from a contemplative to a vibrantly active mode of life, where the experience of impotence might be overturned by the experience of omnipotent performance.

Apparent *disparities*, then, between postmodern culture as it's materially lived and as it's introspectively thought and felt-through spring from the very same ambivalent process in which they are both rooted and that unites them. It is no accident that the same term, 'postmodern', is given to both; we are not confusing different 'personality types', with different motives and needs. (Narcissance has no particular cachet, for example, with either introversion or extraversion, with theory or sensation, contemplation or action.) They are two oscillating faces – to some degree the depressive and the manic – of a particular condition of mind.

If the previous chapter – devoted to the express utterances of postmoderns largely alone in their own studies, pressing their indeterminist meditations to the limit – seemed to limn above all something more of the depressive face of the postmodern (which we may feel tempted to think correct, given the affective state we might expect of the solitary narcissant), certainly in this chapter we'll find more instances of the postmodern as it moves toward the pluralistic and the manic (which, again, may allure us with resonances of narcissants acting and thinking of themselves as in harmony with others in the world). But I suggest we stand ready to see them as conditional; in the postmodern, oscillation will always be in play. This provisionality becomes especially vital as we keep in mind that if, in the examples that follow, the sentiment of impotence slides ever more recurrently toward grandiosity and the manic side of narcissance, while it may indeed encompass enthusiasm it is never the same as optimism.

I would like us to *revisit* the sites most popularly associated with postmodern life, and reiterate what is claimed about them – to the point of the cliché – just to make sure I'm not reinventing the postmodern world for my own evil purposes. In fact, if there is validity in what I've said in the preceding chapters, we'll feel that we've returned to places we've already glimpsed. All that I hope to add is a slight shift in perspective.

TRYING PROMISCUITY

The popular association of postmodernism with promiscuity is no mere coincidence. Leaving behind the era that Freud treated as an 'age of repression', we are *not* 'Victorian'; many among us *call* ours 'a promiscuous society'. This has a much wider truth about it than any confined merely to matters of morality. Promiscuity, as its etymology makes clear (*pro+miscere* – to mix), is an innocent word. The '*mixing*' of standards, of values, which is all that promiscuity means, becomes a bad thing only in a culture in which one order hopes to rule – an order dependent for its validity and its material survival on the rationalized 'splitting' we find in discriminations between say 'good' and 'evil'— and regards the multiplication and merging of 'orders' as an intolerable threat to 'order'. Whether or not a society can live without such distinctions, one thing we know is that postmodern thinking cannot live at ease *with* them. Postmodernity is inseparable from promiscuity.

What distinguishes attitudes and activities under this heading ('Trying Promiscuity') from those under the one that follows ('Trying Ecstasy'), then, is essentially that – rather than seeking to 'dissolve' distinctions – postmodern behaviour as reflected in this first part endeavours to work 'analytically', and aims toward the production, rather than the reduction, of irony. It carries always with it that it 'knows' the divisions, the differences; it contains them, maintains them side-by-side, and celebrates their clash. The transcendent pleasure, the jouissance, in the postmodern seen from this prospect is in the *frisson*, the thrill, the chilling friction between contradictory states – analogous to the conjuncture of pleasure and pain, the sentiment of conflictual ambivalence that is central to the experience of narcissance.

A few general remarks are wanted here, about the practical world in which postmodernity moves. One of the most common apparent anomalies in popular discussion of 'the postmodern world' is the identification of it with the growing dominance of science and technology. Judging by postmodernist theories' persistent repudiation of the positivistic quest for 'truth' that we associate with the concerns of science and technology, this should seem unintelligible. Yet, for reasons to be seen, a deepseated feature of contemporary culture is that, while technology seems able and determined to dissociate itself from postmodernist scepticism, postmodernity has never wished to dissociate itself from technology. A fundamental way in which postmodern culture distinguishes itself from preceding movements (from Romanticism to Naturalism) in this regard is its tendency in fact to be so absorbed in current technologies that it surrenders any capacity for their critique. (Indeed, in recent forms postmodernist theory often displays a powerful welcome to the advance of technology – in writers from Deleuze to De Landa and Nick Land.) This seemingly profound enigma illustrates again a difference between postmodernism and postmodernity. But if we consider it from the standpoint of the psychology, the *processes of mind* that both share, it seems that the anomaly vanishes. Can it be that an explanation for this unforetold habit of the postmodern, its ready and exhilarated convergence with technology, is to be found in its prepossession with *tekhne* – in the troubled grandiose dream of omnipotent performance that characterizes narcissance?

Detachment

Here is where I need to talk about abandonment. It's a word often associated with postmodernity's 'Dionysian' guise – an aspect that we've come to expect of postmodern living (which Deleuze and Guattari call 'social abandonism') and that may seem to have been 'strangely absent' from the previous chapters. A spirit of release, of the casting off of categories and rules, of meanings, of constraints of every kind. Yet abandonment has always been another Janus-faced word, looking in different directions at once. To be abandoned is both to be free and without constraint and to be separated, to be cut off, to be left at a loss and alone. We know both those themes from what we've seen of the postmodern so far – *and* we recognize how close they are to the core of narcissance. But there's more.

Abandonment is actually about *control*. In its earliest use, and for centuries, the verb 'to abandon' meant: to subjugate, to rule. To be abandoned – 'to be left *à son bandon*' – was to be left, reduced, to *one's own absolute jurisdiction, authority, and will,* for all it was worth. Here we can grasp the ambivalence inherent in the notion of abandonment as postmodernism inherits it. It is the very name of what happens, the liberating and the terrible, *at the moment of felt separation* as it's experienced in the shaping of the narcissant mind. Abandonment comes when the structure and 'holding' medium – the embrace that gives sheltering authority and control to nascent life – is withdrawn. In the anguish where both freedom and unbelonging are imposed, the mind feels itself left at the lawless mercy of all winds. Yet it has one last recourse. In the very 'pitch and swing' between polar extremes lie pre-emptive remedies. In desperation we can seize just what remains to us, what survives to define us – we may claim our own *'bandon'*, our control of ourselves and, in feral defiance of the desert chaos about us, *declare our volition* to *be abandoned.* In fast-and-loose play with the body, with the world, with its own meanings, by its ambivalent seizure of its own 'self-determination', a mind may assert the retaliatory and desolate freedom that is no one's but its own, to do with its freedom as it may, to *make* of existence what it *will.* [2]

We can look now into some of the ways in which, by means of a continual oscillation between the poles of self-consciousness and abandonment, the postmodern manages the experience of living.

Two of the 'hot', assiduously documented general propositions offered today about the special nature of our times say that we've moved into a *consumer* culture and into a *style*-centred culture. Both ideas are of course in important ways restatements of the Unqle Trim view that this is a 'me' society, a culture of 'narcissism'. But as I've indicated, that is not my thesis; to have noted the currency of narcissance is only the beginning; everything of importance is yet to be understood and negotiated. In keeping with that, it pays to look briefly at those two generalities.

There are numerous definitions of a 'consumer culture', but a sense of the way the idea works and its relevance for us can be gleaned by a brief illustration or two. In contemporary affluent societies where on average only one third of the population's expenditure is on 'essentials', two thirds is optative, and consumers can exercise much more widely than in the past certain liberties in determining (in terms of demand and endorsement) what commodities are sold. But radical developments in technology contribute further to this picture. In manufacturing, tailored/customized production tends to overturn an ethos of mass production that had induced buyers' relatively passive acceptance of the conformity of goods and services. Moreover, by virtue of developments in information technology and communications, where – as compared with past conditions in which information (including entertainment) had always been served to a public 'waiting at the table', grateful for what was on offer – now by what are commonly though inaccurately called 'interactive' services managed electronically, we will be increasingly in a position to *send messages back, asking*. For example, the archive of all the cultural products that have ever been 'recorded' can now or in the foreseeable future be tapped at the point of need rather than at the point of production. (Obvious illustrations are our ability already by means of video and digital recording to retrieve visual and sound images for private consumption as we desire them.) A society is promised where politicians can be interrogated and their worth can be polled by the public at will. Not only industry but government can now generate 'just in time' variants of products and services, tailored to the individual desires of local outlets and customers.

We'll consider important dimensions of these later, but we can see that where the *apparent* balance of power is imagined to shift from the supply side to the user side, from (in quasi-Kleinian terms) from the suckler to the suckling – adumbrates a marked resemblance between a 'consumer society' and a culture whose orientation is narcissant. The orphan asking 'Please sir may I have some more' now believes he is heard. (We may have many questions to ask about this. Is the apparent power shift real? are these developments 'neutrally generated' by 'pure' science and technology or might we have discovered and invented a different technology had we desired something different? are we – for example, economically and politically – beneficiaries or victims? are we seeing things as they are or only as we wish to see them?) But no interrogation of the extent to which there is fantasy here can hope to be coherent, let alone complete, until it includes questions that this resemblance raises.

In a similar way, it would be easy to end our considerations with the observation that the postmodern seeks 'self-realization' in '*style*'. The individual is understood to shape his or her own manner of living – with special attention to its 'feel in the moment' (since foundational beliefs beyond this are without substance) – and secures his or her own identity by means of the outward display of some '*lifestyle*' or other (since how others construe us constructs us, as the narcissant is the first among us to feel). We could stop here, as I say, if all that we wished to do were to establish the simple fact that the concerns of narcissance are active in our lives. But a couple of initial illustrations, taken more or less at random from among contemporary attitudes, of the way that consumerism and lifestyle-thinking merge can intimate something of the dimensions and the complexity of the convergence of postmodernity and narcissance before us.

The first example comes in the work of a popular theorist of consumer culture, Ted Polhemus, the author of *Style Surfing: What To Wear In The 3rd Millennium*. Polhemus declares that we have entered "a dawn of individual expression". The new consumer culture creates a new social order unstructured by class, political beliefs or religion. A world constrained by fashion is about to be replaced by one shaped by style, expressing human choice by the 'iconography' of the products individuals choose.

> You buy things to show what an interesting person you are, you buy things to explain yourself, you construct your own identity through these bits and pieces of the consumer society. Because we don't have significant social structures to provide meaning and segmentation of our life, what we do is we start from style, and we build from this stuff an identity and a capacity to express ourselves and to link up with other people.

People find "meanings in their lives through this visual code", through their purchase essentially of the "meanings" associated with what they choose to buy (such as the meanings linked to The Body Shop). In the new generation, youths read one anothers' styles specifically for degrees of "authenticity"; that is, as expressions of who they 'really are' ("Shopping on Top").[3] My point in citing Polhemus' proposition is neither to endorse nor to dispute it, but to bring into focus an example among many now current of what is actually an analysis based on a species of what may best be called 'a theory of positive narcissance'. In *Lead Us into Temptation*, a study of "The Triumph of American Materialism" (1999), James B. Twitchell (devoting an important section to the well-known theme 'You are What You Buy') reveals – in part apparently unwittingly – the extent to which figures in public life not only display but ground their seductions in explicit narcissance.

As we've already noticed, only the postmodern's most blinkered opponents will conceive the idea of postmodernity's accent on 'style' and the search for a 'lifestyle' as a trivialization of its thinking. The force of the very refusal of 'integrity', 'authenticity', 'sincerity', 'seriousness', of all 'bottom lines' – of 'depth' – is never more evident than in the famous fascination in contemporary culture with 'surface'. Postmodern literature, art and architecture and their associated criticisms accord this all the attention of a 'prime idea'; in the pop-tech world of information and communications it's celebrated with the verb 'to surf'. Detached from what one sees, one glides and gathers. Cultural studies abound with accounts and analyses of the materially most explicit and quantifiable form of this gliding and gathering – in 'the culture of shopping' that so distinguishes contemporary lifestyles in the 'developed' world from those of other societies. As an English prime-time television commentator has remarked, "we have shopping addicts, shopping consultants, shopping sociologists" ("Shopping on Top").

One contributing factor has been the extraordinary expansion in the 'buying of things we don't need'. Is it the mere fact that this is something that 'we can do' that makes us do it? In view of the extent to which this buying is – more than ever in history – done 'on time', with money we don't have, there are inklings of risk involved that seem not to fit with traditional notions of the ethic so long associated with the comfortable but careful middle classes. What makes the gamble worthwhile seems unclear until we take into our reckonings the likelihood that a *questing for things*, which shopping is, takes up more time and energy of more people than ever since the time of our hunter-gatherer ancestors, and can be understood – as has often been remarked – to *fill some gap, some void*. What kind of need is this? Traders themselves are ready with an answer so thoroughly accepted that it's treated as a truism (which sociologists widely endorse). In the words of Eric Kuhne, the architect of Bluewater, the largest shopping centre in Europe (opened in England in the Spring of 1999), the motive for the mall's construction and the public's need for it is that "people realize that they have the capacity to determine and perfect their own identity in the world"; shopping is a way of "personalizing one's life" ("Shopping on Top").

Writers have compiled vast inventories of the ways in which how we dress, what we eat, how we furnish and decorate our homes, what vehicles we drive, how we choose our leisure activities and entertainments, how we identify ourselves with the figures with which products are labelled and indeed with certain brand names, how "the relationship the package establishes with the consumer ... replaces, or at least supplements any relationship that the buyer might have had with the storekeeper or even the farmer" (Twitchell 1999: 131). The vastness of 'Seinfeld's' public around the world, undiminished since the programme's cessation of production – the 'understanding' between the character 'Seinfeld' and his public – becomes clear, where it can be said of 'Seinfeld'-as-possible-narcissant that "He is this stuff. It is his persona" (88). As cultural historian John Storey phrases it, shopping is "the use of consumption to articulate identity" (1996: 117). When Twitchell and others espouse the view that shopping is a powerful natural human impulse, they cite as the causes of compulsive shopping what we understand to be the motives of narcissance.[4]

In keeping with this, a leading feature of the postmodern world that has further seized scholars' attention is not only how hungrily we consume commodities but how we *watch ourselves* consuming. In commerce, fortunes are made in the marketing not merely of goods and services but of vantage points (reflected, say, in all-glass, chrome and multi-mirrored malls) from which consumers watch others and themselves eating, dressing, furnishing and equipping, conversing, gazing, seeing and displaying themselves asserting their power to take possession of things and more things, fancying themselves as the objects of dealers' hungry desire and of non-buyers' admir(ror)ation. As Urry (1990) magisterially shows, tourist industries calculatedly organize sites in such a way that 'sight-seers' alternately forget themselves and observe their own presence with pleasure. 'This is *me* (in front of – dancing with – eating a – –)!' In art, literature and film the self-conscious artist/*auteur* and the reader/spectator observe each other observing the 'text', and the ('reflexive', 'self-conscious') text is regarded as regarding itself.

Something we commonly fail to register – perhaps owing to the relics of standards of decorum long-since formally relinquished in postmodern thought – is that mirror-within-mirror processes can reach into areas of experience well beyond those of the merely aesthetic and contemplatively 'reflective', just as do the mirror-anxieties of the characters in Nabokov, Calvino and Fuentes. They can set into turbulence regions of what we think to be our moral and political selves. In search of a caring society we watch ourselves caring; we form watch groups for the surveillance of products, services, industries, neighbourhoods, the earth's surfaces and the sea and the sky, and we institute ombudsmen and organize vigil-ant(e) leagues to oversee our watchers. A market is growing for media documentaries where the courses of people's births and deaths are observed; via webcam and mass-audience television shows around the world such as *Big Brother*, each month millions more watch increasing numbers of others eating, dressing and undressing, playing, quarrelling, masturbating, sleeping; AIDS victims film themselves dying, and suicide is videoed for mass consumption.

Yet at the heart of these activities are both care and curiosity (whose root – *cura* – is 'care'). Curiosity thus emerges in the interstices between anxiety and diversion (from anxiety). The narcissant thrill of pleasure mixed with pain enlists oscillation in the interests of aesthetic release. Something we saw unfold as we considered the narcissant mind-style has caught up with us – for example in Jools Holland's exhilarated presentation to his watching audience of the office he's built for himself not as a place in which he will live or work but as a structure watching and being watched by other structures, and in Bill Gates' house with its stunning stress on its visitors' *surveillance*. A culture begins to imagine itself creating a public satisfaction out of paranoia. As we're aware now, often in narcissance we load others with care that we yearn for for ourselves; many times we think to see in our physical environment menaces to our psychic stability that we can't attend to ('look at') in ourselves. By spreading ever wider our attention to take in more things to care about – and by inciting the same order of care for what was previously 'urgent' and for what was 'inessential' – we 'flatten out' the 'carefulness', the priorities of 'care' and thus of our 'cares'. The 'pluralization' of things to watch out for merges with the indeterminacy of our decisions as to which ones to watch out for most, and why, or how to watch out for them all.

There seems little doubt that there can be pleasure in that attenuation of difference and distance; the question 'Who am I, to care?' brings feelings of both helplessness and liberation. Postmodernity can only assent to – if not celebrate – this dissolution of priorities. What may be worth 'watching' is not only how the high-anxiety sense of welter may match that experienced by the narcissant, but how close it can bring narcissant thinking to that other pole, aporia and the abandonment – the blissful oblivion – of utter 'carelessness'. (Shall we call it 'carefreedom'?) We'll come back to this.

* * *

I need to suggest a notion rather different from the one on which thinking has tended to rest over the past two hundred years – particularly under the powerful suasion of Realist thought – about the relations between how we think and how we act.[5] Many of the postmodern activities described in the following pages may actually serve the function not of representing the experiences of the people who carry them out, but of quite fundamentally *enacting* them. Let me put this in concrete terms.

Until not long ago, it wasn't uncommon in Britain and the United States for parents, when carrying on a conversation with other adults (and particularly when arguing between themselves), sometimes to say of their children – for example, when the children were being noisy, seemingly aimlessly overactive, or crying 'beyond reason' – that they were 'acting out' or 'creating'. Such expressions were frequently used in a mixed tone of ostensible tolerance and of amused dismissal. Very often a child was accused of acting out or creating who was actually in want of personal warmth and attention, and frequently parents on such occasions in fact revealed (when engaged more carefully) that their own feelings were the very same as the child's. Because there seemed to be no room (or right) for a 'grown-up' to act on such desires, crowded together as they were in the same space as the *child's* demands, the only remaining instinct was to 'shut out' what was happening on both sides. Compulsively the situation was simply 'managed'; the child's behaviour was bracketed and dismissed with the phrase 'Oh, s/he's creating'. It was 'kinder' than a slap and surely (it seemed) not abusive. Often when in such a situation a child filled the space with what seemed a welter of incomprehensible chaotic bustle and noise, it was actually *putting back into the room* the welter that it was *feeling* as its parents 'carried on', without regard for it, in their voluble and perhaps frighteningly home-shattering way. Even to say that the child was 'crying for attention' – as parents not infrequently did to justify their own narcissant 'wall-building' ('– just ignore him!', 'he's spoiled with too much love') – could well be incorrect by the time it was observed. The child might by this time be moving into the psychic realm where relationships were no longer trusted and must be repelled – a shift of which the very act of (repellently) 'creating' might be the first sign and step. The complex dynamics within this practical example, where artificial performance and deep-felt needs intertangle, will be with us as we go along.

The rational Enlightenment made an explicit doctrine of the assumption as 'natural' that actions, even bad ones, are done to *achieve/bring about substantive change*, and Realism formally added that actions are based on somebody's idea of a good *representation of the material world*. But the postmodern cannot be expected to act in accord with these rationalistic and referential end-directed principles. In fact, historically they have always formed a very special and complex cocktail of rules and demands to ask humans to swallow in any case, and it's far from clear that all good human psychological motives for action have ever been covered by them. To say that narcissance (or postmodernity) might be a troubled condition doesn't in any way mean that actions taken by narcissants or postmoderns – however revolutionary their cultural manifestations may seem – will always be directed toward anything more than *repeating the processes of narcissance and postmodern thinking*. I want to indicate another human motive, therefore, to which narcissance and postmodernity may be especially prone.

It would be outlandish (though an Unqle Trim mightn't think so) to suggest that postmodernity is a culture stamping its foot. I've introduced that earthy image – our 'acting out' from our earliest years – simply to call to mind, by way of an experience familiar to all, a human process so fundamental that our theoretical traditions, so shadowed by end-(product)-directed thinking even when they most decry it, tend to ignore it altogether.

Very often in postmodern culture the activity we observe is 'creating', in several senses. It quite definitely puts something new into the world. But it may not be an attempt to tell anything about the world – *or* about itself. This is *not a theory of mimesis*, any more than postmodernist thinking (which continually questions the suggestion of representing reality) would say it should be. It is about acting out – enacting – feeling, and not about reproducing or changing.

Sometimes – and often, in narcissance – this process may well carry with it the effect of radical revolt. But we should *not* anticipate that the need filled by even the most seemingly aggressive postmodern (or narcissant) activity is directly to report *or* controvert *or* give a solution to current conditions. In the West, we chronically indulge in a grandiose (and intrinsically exploitative) conception of ourselves as the elected indirect objects, the designated recipients, of subjects (artists, scientists, historians) striving to give us objects – specifically representations of life and above all of our own lives – when in fact the subjects are often *doing nothing but being (or trying to be) themselves*. Humans have other projects besides the making of representations (whether of the world or of themselves) for others' benefit. When, for instance, postmodern culture behaves as if it is watching itself, it is acting out – is *performing* – a self-watching that narcissance does. It gives no promise that it will *find* or *reveal* anything. The culture is simply doing in the world what the narcissant mind is doing inside.

Propagation

If postmodern culture, like narcissance, is so devoted to detachment, to self-conscious 'watching' and 'reflection', how does it ever get anything done? How does it *produce* things, for a start, that we might call 'postmodern'? It happens in two leading ways, and in this part we look at one of these.

Postmodern production can proceed by '*propagation*'. That is, producing – breeding – not by 'starting from scratch', from seed, from any 'natural point of origin' in which it could have, but by severing a thing from one place and grafting it to another.

As surfers in the world of information on the Internet, for instance, many among us relish the pleasures of gathering and collecting data independent of its 'origin' or 'root', often altogether ignorant of its immediate personal and geographical provenance, and collocating it, 'bundling' it with other data. Copying, downloading, 'cutting and pasting', millions more on line each week are building stocks of text, sound and images to suit their taste, growing archives of information that have all the appearance of 'learning', of a storehouse of knowledge – yet that often fail to attain the conventional status of knowledge, since part of the process' very function is to accumulate data without pretending to 'integrate' it with a coordinated system of understanding and without particular concern as to whether it is in touch with where it 'naturally grew' or ultimately belongs. ('I read somewhere –', is a formula one repeatedly hears among surfers; 'scientists have decided –', 'it's said that –'.) In 'cyberspace' culture we call information, revealingly, just plain 'stuff'.

Postmodern writers have from the beginning acclaimed an unreserved affinity with the uses of electronic ('e-') media in this way. Much of what looks to be 'fixed information' on second glance turns out to be *e-formation*; a rising tide of 'givens', raw data, 'extracted' – pulled out, sliced off – from its context, and re-broadcast by the collector (often by splicing it onto other contributors' data) into contexts (other surfers' screen-images) that, because they have yet to be constituted, are utterly unknowable. Though this process is popularly associated with the World Wide Web, the same dynamic shapes the circulation of e-mail as well, as users know who have engaged in any of the countless interest forums, news groups and list-services that constitute so voluminous a part of the world of electronic communications. A token of the propagational qualities of computer technology can be glimpsed in its own jargon, where new terms must be coined each year for rapidly rising degrees of informational magnitude (kilo-, mega- and giga- and tera- have now by formal international agreement been hastily supplemented with peta-, exa-, zetta- and yotta-) – yet where bodies of data and instructions are envisioned rarely as unified wholes but instead as 'stacks', 'heaps', 'bundles', 'piles' and 'compilers'.

The postmodern attraction to the uses of cyberspace in this way is far from always naive. For postmodern theory, in a certain sense little can be more inimical than to build information into 'knowledge' – whether by integrating it into a system of meaning *or* by seeming to do so by investing it with signs of personal care and commitment. Nor is it merely bloodymindedly negative. 'Fact' is not required, to achieve what is often felt most needed: new ways of seeing.

But more, this version of 'only connect' is resonant of postmodernism's (and narcissance's) manic-proliferative processes of thinking. Growth is rhapsodic (literally 'stitching songs together'); *connecting* 'creates'. Energies are harnessed to the often visibly arbitrary propagation of new combinations. What grows is (as postmoderns often say in speaking of their creations) explicitly 'hybrid', heterogeneous and polyvalent. The phenomenon of 'splitting' returns, alongside postmoderns' fascination with 'poly-semy', 'heteroglossia', collage, *bricolage* and pastiche. The experience welcomed *in the propagation-mode* resembles what we see when we look at light through a kaleidoscope, and watch the patterns form and re-form as the mirrored fragments of coloured glass shift. The intrinsic nature of each of the bits assembled is explicitly left intact, separate, disjoined, uninfluenced by the pressure of meaning or intention. Where what had been thought to be 'known' is thus 'shattered' into fragments and forms new patterns of ostensible 'knowledge' as soon as one 'turns' or 'takes another look'.

We may often feel, in the examples that follow, that here is a spirit of revolt. Certainly much of the vigour of postmodern creation by propagation may arise as a 'pre-emptive remedy' or a retaliation. In the way that objects are 'grafted' in postmodern art, for example, critics are quick to see the free association of theoretical revolt with material revulsion. In what may sometimes appear to be a frenetically assembled accretion of 'stuff' – the 'spray of phenomena', often in the form of the 'junk' or 'drek' of diverse cultures – we meet the welter not only of current material civilization's sensations but of a particular kind of mind. One that, unable to fix a footing in itself on which it might ground a way of sorting – feeling awash and ever about to float away in the flood – anchors itself to 'creation', to acting out its own state. With, conceivably, the spare hope that by naming itself collector, connector (if you can't fight them, 'join' them) it may in-form if not finally identify itself as finder (*trobador*) and 'pro-creator'.

By its very nature, actual postmodern propagation can't be represented comprehensively; one might try organizing examples by categories, but the fastening-together of stuff across categorial boundaries is what makes the production of the new by propagation 'tick'. As in narcissance, the identity of what is produced is no longer satisfactorily confirmed ('identified') by conventional roles, by the 'sameness' or continuity implicit in identity. The narcissant can only aspire to 'be all things to all men', and so will postmodern artifacts.

We experience 'propagation' first-hand in the developed world throughout our daily lives. How grafting goes on in the way people dress isn't merely an expression of 'youth in revolt' – in the mix of jeans, studded leathers, saris, platforms, tights, backworn baseball caps, vinyl, latex, underwear as outerwear, army fatigues, jellabahs, track suits, Lycra, gold lamé, headlined T-shirts, spiked rainbow hair, Mohawks, black lipstick and nails, Doc Martens and jackboots; the mode is appropriated by the bestselling designers of the day, from Calvin Klein, Ralph Lauren, Tommy Hilfiger and Donna Karan to Versace, Gucci and Armani. In Westernized cities and suburbs, in personal- and home-style statements around the world, mix-and-match, pick-it-and-stick-it strategies prevail. The fashion inspires our cuisine; it's not only in Los Angeles, now, that you can eat a pastrami burrito (a greasebomb made of fried pastrami, fried peppers, fried cabbage, guava jelly, pickles, onions, wrapped in a burrito), a comestible first born there of Chinese, Mexican, Jewish and LA chili traditions, made by Japanese for a predominantly African-American clientele. The vogue of multicultural 'cross-over' or 'fusion foods' (like 'cross-over' or 'fusion' music) has spread not merely to the hot-eating-spots of Rome, London, Berlin, Tokyo and even Paris, but is now native to supermarkets throughout the English-speaking world. In the United Kingdom before 1960 few retailers had heard the word 'pizza'; shrinkwrapped cheese-and-tomato pizzas are now sold by the hundreds of millions adorned with carrots, dill pickles and Hawaiian pineapple chunks; the sale of curries is worth more to the economy annually than that of coal, iron and steel combined. If this inclination among the British to put their money where their mouth is reveals a new orality befitting narcissance, it suggests also that people want to put their mouths where they've never been before; the savour of once illicit *mixing* elicits a new jouissance of its own.

Not only in popular music and film from McLaren to Glass and the Kronos Quartet and from Greenaway and Egoyan to Lynch and Cronenberg (and a fast-growing number of indies, facilitated by the vast economies of digital technology), but in their social contexts, the propagational impulse displays itself at large. The 'rule' of juxtaposition and proliferation of tastes becomes apparent as soon as we think of some of the favoured 'labels' of genres in the club scene – where hip-hop, retro pop, drum'n'bass (techstep, 'coffeetable') and loungecore clash and connect with trance (Euro, Goa), progressive breakbeat and hard progressive house, speed garage, big beat, Asian underground, Música Latina, Basic Channel, Goth and Gabba. As disco customers we famously make explicit play of how we 'mark out our identities' by our choices, and often assert the extent of our individuality by swiftly abandoning clubs we had avidly frequented a month before and by protesting among ourselves about the inadequacy of the mix on offer. Most revealing about such individualistic 'assertions of value' is that the names of the favoured mixes I've just mentioned will have changed by the time you read this. What is wanted is often less the object than the experience (so turbulently fought for in narcissance) of seeming able to choose.

One of the highest compliments critics in the fields of contemporary art, architecture, literature, film and music feel they can bestow on their favoured works is to applaud the ways in which they 'quote' other works. In rock and disco culture, the *compiler*, the '*mixer*', making use of ever-more-fluent sampler technologies to manipulate readymade audio and visual images, has taken on the status of the full-fledged public star.[6] Rock video, together with its MTV and commercial advertising heirs, make intimate extravaganzas of the cut-and-splice of traditional surrealist montage, jigsaw-cutting in split seconds among neon signs, singers' lips, castle walls, road accidents, pumping thighs, revolving gears, roaring crowds. The sheer raw pace and quantity of cuts-per-minute lionize as much the form, the prowess of cutting and grafting, as any 'contents' on show. Volume and assembled profusion become goods in themselves – making not only aesthetic but now also good marketing sense.

Propagation isn't the province only of those buying and selling in the explicit marketplace. Public interest groups seek to amplify our inventory of the natural world. Calls for the preservation of species are far from always justified on the grounds of ecological equilibrium and seem puzzling to many until it's perceived that a further wish tacitly invoked is for the expansion of the reservoir of 'natural' experiences into which we may not only dip our appetites but refresh and reclaim the entitlement of our imaginations. If there are economic and culinary appeals in the breeding of Arabian ostriches in the Cotswolds for steaks, projects are in hand to restart the population of Europe's vanished wolves and restore the world's extinct moa pool by propagating from chickens injected with museums' dusted-off moa genes. We know of the dinosaur dream. There is talk of kickstarting the cells of Pharoahs.

In the arts and architecture – the traditional heartlands and arch-sites for the radical abutting of signs and senses – the volume of current writing about the effects of 'grafting' already abounds. (It finds classic expression not only in Derrida's famous assessment of the power of 'grafting' in language but in his architect-collaborator Bernard Tschumi's assertion that 'it is where two ruthless architectural logics collide that architecture begins to happen'.) A few literally 'superficial' recent examples may serve to illustrate the process at work.

In 1998 in London the Albert Memorial – a collossal, elaborately ornate monument erected by Queen Victoria to her deceased consort – was re-presented to the public, regilded in all its original and now frankly garish Imperial splendour. The same month, a tall building of uncertain use (and instantly deplored in some quarters as the 'shed of the Midlands') was completed near the castle in Nottingham; resembling a lighthouse it casts its beams desultorily over the modern inland industrial city. (In the same half year, after centuries of use, the last 'real' historic working lighthouse on an English coast – a sentimental popular treasure – was 'switched off'.) Both items in the public landscape were greeted by currently esteemed art and cultural critics with the same characteristically postmodern honorific: as brilliant "follies". Pleasure, regard and reward are associated with objects by imbedding (or resurrecting) these in contexts where they are *detached* from utility and ostensible symbolic meaning and serve as pastiches of such uses and meanings. (New public and domestic structures are planned bearing embellishments appropriated from the Albert Memorial, styled to highlight the 'anti-structural', ornamental emblems of the 'folly' tradition.) The leap of 'madness' ('*folie*') of which deconstructionists speak – whereby the subject is conceived and at once mocks itself – is self-consciously vested with material form. In this way, postmodern architectural culture 'renews' itself by explicitly propagating images recycled from traditions in which it renounces faith, making of its loss of 'trust' the prime principle of its innovation.

Meanwhile, the first public project of the Wysing Gallery (of art) in Cambridgeshire was the erection in a field of a small building called "Tree Keep". Eerily recapturing the organic arabesque/grotesque fairytale dwellings represented in children's book illustrations and in New Age art, a three-storey play-house was constructed. In what appears to be a flowing, dream-creature-like free-form design, unmorticed segments of tree-limbs are merely interlaced or end-butted and side-tacked to one another, producing a fabric of loosely bundled heteromorphic strands, arcing and weaving. It seems to have 'grown', without inner foundation, out of its own image of itself. Coherence of surface, the superficial picking and sticking of amorphous fragments, replaces internal structure, and – much in the way in which the narcissant hollowly assembles a public self-image – it is less erected than embroidered, appliquéd around the space it's chosen to darken.

As is the case in a capitalist economy, where survival requires the ceaseless production of the new, in postmodern culture propagation and the obsolescent or ephemeral go hand-in-hand. In Vienna, in a positive gesture to bring art out of the studio and into the hands of the people, the poet Helmut Seethaler hangs out his voluminous verses on scraps of paper along many-metres-long clotheslines strung from lampposts and anything else that stands still long enough in streets, alleys and malls. In the public jostle, passersby read, take down and walk off with whatever poems they like. As Seethaler is not unaware – and local shopkeepers and police remind him with ire – by this activity he creates what is itself a 'happening' that accents the rigidity of traditional genres and frames of reference, and features the troubled dynamic of the linking, the cross-over between them.

In the world of the contemporary art museum, emblems of the cheap and disposable, of wear and irrevocable waste, of transience, absence and loss – like the 'lost self' the narcissant laments and the synthetic fantasies s/he recycles, feeling ever more 'cheap' – are compulsively recombined and recycled, sometimes deliberately (in spectators' view) 'ad nauseum'. Exhibits in diverse galleries recently summarized in one issue of New York's *Time Out* magazine, for example, were of sculptures made of rubber tires; objects covered with a fecal-brown crust; forms cast from the negative spaces the artist finds in plumbing fixtures and flotation devices; an installation incorporating lots of wallpaper and the recorded sounds of turkey calls; forthcoming were large-scale works based on the undetectable (black holes, stellar birth and molecular structures), and a sperm bank made possible by contemporary artists' donations. Rachel Whiteread, the creator of what have been called some of the greatest English public sculptures of this century, and recently offered a membership by the prestigious and erstwhile infamously traditionalist Royal Academy of Art, transmutes the oscillations between permanence and permanent loss, inside and outside, presence and absence, into a prime topos. She exhibits within a gallery room a plaster cast made of the interior of an entire room, or places in a vacant lot a 'building' that is the inverse or 'negative' of the interior surfaces of the building she has used as its mould. By each she thus makes 'negative space' an object; "fundamentally, these sculptures", as one reviewer has put it, "attempt to describe absence ... how to make a mark that says 'I am not here'."[7]

Damien Hirst – often hailed in the contemporary British art world as (and explicitly calling himself, with candidly narcissant overtones) an '*enfant terrible*' – is a propagator par excellence, and few contemporaries have won such notoriety as 'promiscuous' in the violation of taboos. In his "hope to make the world richer",[8] Hirst's most famous works to date stitch into the world of gallery art the organic objects of nature, and (while much heart has been given to their Modernist symbolic interpretation by him and others), their impact in public discussion has turned virtually entirely on precisely this fact (do you bring animals into the museum? do you kill them there?). In "The Physical Impossibility of Death in the Mind of Someone Living" he presents a fourteen-foot shark (deceased) floating suspended in a glass tank filled with formaldehyde; and in "A Thousand Years", in a pair of joined glass cases, generations of flies are born and feed from the carrion of a cow's head in one case, proceed to mate in the adjoining space, and are zapped dead on contact with an electrified insectocuter. For Hirst, the project is to create "an object to describe a feeling or a contradiction". Above all, by means of the irony latent in his juxtapositions, but also in the structure of his works themselves, he produces separation as an overarching theme. In the object exhibited in his famous debut at the Venice Biennale – "Mother and Child Divided" – two once-living animals stand in separate formaldehyde-filled glass cabinets. These are a full-grown cow and a calf – only, there are not two cases but four: one pair containing the two halves of the cow, cut cleanly lengthwise, internal organs on full display, and in the other pair the two halves of the calf. Of this postmodern Madonna and Child the intimation (confirmed by Hirst) is that the division of each of the figures in itself is implicit in the figures' division from one another. "I think it's about being divided two ways", Hirst says, "about being separated from the people around you, and about being cut in half ... about trying to hold yourself together".[9]

* * *

In postmodern life the rate of our cargo-cult-like uptake of objects and ideas is radical. The most forceful postmodernist arguments for 'rigour', however – for switching off our 'uptake inhibitions' – fail to explain the wish, made explicit by contemporary artists, to *shock*. Here a chronic objection raised by conservatives face-to-face with advocates of postmodern 'promiscuity' may contain an insight: 'How can you be human, and the person you are, and still expose us to this?' We may find such polemics blinkered. But it may not be enough to say that 'What I think/desire is acceptable' is problematic in the mere generalized sense, for example, that 'anything goes' is. We need the further understanding that inhibitions rooted in the so-called 'normal' *sense of self* are 'disabled', as they are in the extreme field-dependence of narcissance. What is put into question by the promiscuous gesture is precisely 'Who I am' – and, with this, 'what I need (or value, believe, desire)'.

At this level of concern even the use of shock to '*make a name for oneself*' takes on a poignant new meaning. With the 'propagational attitude' claims to 'originality' are renounced; there is only recombination. The will to create is as irresistible as ever; what is expunged is the presence of the 'originator'. Might there be in this an articulation of the burden of self-consciousness in contemporary thinking? That we might seek release from the very issue of personal being? Yet such an idea becomes all the more puzzling given what seems frequently to be an equally aggressive *assertion* of self (for instance in the celebration of '*enfants terribles*') in 'recombinant' postmodern activity. (The phenomenon is solemnized in the commonplace that in their radicalism postmodern artists are 'creating new identities, new selves'.) How can this work?

An answer to this riddle may be revealed in what we know of narcissance. Therapists in our times hear client after client protest that the values they've held are imposed upon them by others, that the 'meanings' to which they've attached themselves are false – and who cry out, often in rage, with the desire for something to 'speak' from within them, for some true inner 'nature' or enduringly vital 'will to live' to issue forth, to take over and animate their lives. In such a state of mind, the denial even of 'personal values' in the name of a literally meaningless assemblage of 'raw materials' can enact a reaching after what might override all 'constructions' – a longing for an intuitive raw inchoate and irrepressible *élan vital* to bespeak itself. Seen in this way, where the Romantic in its 'involuntary' poetic invention sang the divinity that inspired it – and the Surreal in its unexpected juxtapositions of objects and images, its play with free association and chance, sought a transcendent plane of being *(point suprême)* – the postmodern would release, by the medium of uninhibited propagation, the force of an unnameable, unchallengeable spontaneous authentic inner *being*, free of (even and above all) its very consciousness of itself.

Postmodern living is incessantly accused of being an obsession with innovation – a compulsion to assemble and consume the news and things new. There's no use pretending it's not so. (Often as much as 50 per cent of 'the news' that's reported in the United States is made up not of accounts of events but of people's anticipations of events – new products, new leaders, new hazards, recreations, diseases, scores, disasters, new lifestyles, new crimes.) Surprising as it may seem, not everyone goes to the news and new experiences for the same things and with the same thirst. Many people regard them as worth attending to with a view to locating specific ways they may improve their lives – helping them to understand, and to prepare. Others have difficulty in determining what such ways might be, for the very reason that they're not certain what their needs are, what the qualities of improvement might consist of – of who, in other words, *they* are. In narcissance, one is like that. One may – when not immured in depression – hunger for news and new stuff 'promiscuously'. This isn't to say that people don't find 'pure entertainment' in news and new stuff. But actually entertainment isn't 'pure', and it has at least one profound function; it is literally what 'holds' or 'fills the space between'; it fills the sense of void. Among those who are 'indiscriminately ravenous' for the kinds of entertainment that the new provides ('event freaks', as we sometimes call ourselves), then, narcissance can be a unique and potent stimulant to that hunger. This is not about 'escapism'; the anticipation of the new promises more than just the rainbow's end for which an unresolved and restive narcissant continually scans the horizon. As creators and designers of daily media-content know (and count on), it is continually conceived that some new turning may – as in a dream, a revelation, out of an idol's or an idyll's image or a song or a scene, even if it gives a new shape to *fear, anger or grief – provide the horizon* for one's 'true' values and lifestyle. Again, this isn't everyone's way. But if there is among us some 'innovation-madness', it can help, in each case, to ask why.

Transgression

Postmodernity can be thrilling. If its culture has a perplexed relationship to feeling, to say that it looks to surfaces and seeks strategies of detachment doesn't mean that it's without what feels like feeling and the vigorous activity that comes with feeling. One of the myths perpetuated by many of us engaged in the past in the debates of a narrowly conceived theory-orientated intellectual cadre, too far removed from what was happening on the ground, has been that the experience of contradiction and of indeterminacy leads inevitably to aporia, to hesitation – as though 'the frustration of expectations' were finally little other than an all-paralysing puzzle whose outcome must be passivity, hebetude and inertia. As with narcissance, in postmodern life's mixed rush toward and flight from 'knowledge', there is all the fever of both the languishing to enter (to step into the state of believing, the convincing illusion, the meaning-full life) and the rage to stand clear. But in its 'promiscuous' form, the charge, the buzz, literally the '*rush*' is in the oscillation and the collision between states. A quintessentially postmodern sensation of pleasure lies in the 'thrill' (from a word meaning 'pierce') where pleasure and pain meet. We can understand better the roots of the popular intuition that postmodern life is 'sensationalist' when we grasp that a 'life of the senses' can often be a life in which sensation stands in for feeling. And that the postmodern ethos of thrill is the aesthetic counterpart of ambivalence.

In social terms then, along with the propagation of the divided-and-disparate new and the aesthetic of thrill, there comes the vital urge toward *transgression*. Narcissance is about boundaries, and boundary games are a postmodern obsession. Impelled to repulse the experience of dependency – dependency on conventional systems and objects of belief and value whose failure had by accident or design engendered ambivalence and the sentiment of betrayal – in postmodern culture there is scarcely a field of experience where an impulse isn't articulated to shatter common codes, to break out and break away. Psychologists have helped considerably to gain a purchase on this in the accent that many (from Winnicott and Kohut to Ehrenzweig, Grunberger and Alford) have placed on the ways in which the 'narcissistic' proliferation of mould-breaking self-images has special potency both in allowing for local ambivalence (and the avoidance or displacement of pain associated with it), and in the creatively productive discharge of energies it can enable. In practice, postmodern living – in a fashion that is no more 'decisive' than aporia, but far more dramatic and actively transgressive in its manifestations and material outcomes, in a way that theories of aporia were never equipped to explain – often vigorously displays itself in an aggressive flood of 'omnivalent' bustle, or in a volatile (and sometimes seemingly desperate) discharge of ambivalent outrage.

Being Individual

While common-code sufferers will see the transgressive 'violation' of norms as the remedy, this doesn't always take the form of explicit violence. In the lives of individuals and with the indispensable support of new technologies, postmodernity frequently reveals its dissident, mutinous impulse in 'quiet' ways. Often it appears in the private culture of what some have called the do-it-yourself, 'self-help cascade', so widely mocked as evidence of the 'narcissistic self-centredness' of people today.[10] In social life it shows up (often in the name of health, personal wholeness and self-realization) in the rapid-fire spread, for example, of new modes of conception and birth, of models of parenting, of family models, of patterns of work, of patterns of community, and of new manners of – and reasons for – contraception, sterilization and death (for the unborn, the ill and aged, and the otherwise unwanted).

Let us consider the first mentioned, birth, as just one example: a child may be conceived by the eventual 'parents', but may on the other hand be conceived by other parents, known or unknown, in or outside the womb, before or after the biological parents' death. It may be carried to term by the eventual mother or by another or, in the near future, may be borne by no person but in an artificial environment. With benefit of cloning or genetic modification, the child may or may not be the product of all or some of the genes of one or both of the eventual parents. Where adoption is concerned, the child, as ever, may never know its biological parents, but as never before, a right to this knowledge is increasingly presumed, and the legal age at which this is given may decrease. The potential effects of the multiplication of parent–child relationships merely illustrate the formidable implications of postmodern 'ways-of-processing-life' for society in the twenty-first century.[11]

Issues of the self seem to echo everywhere in developments like these. Not far away are the fantasy haunting so many narcissant lives that 'I'm not (really) my parents' child'– that one is riven from and bound to seek forever one's 'real' (meaning 'ideal') parents – and the pressing vow that '*I* will *not* be with *my* children as mine were with me'. The culture's driving intent to *control* and *manipulate* the conditions of parenting and of child development – to set new conditions shaped by the vision of a family ideal – is richly creative and holds enormous potential for society as a whole as well as for the many individuals wishing they could 'start life all over again'. But there are signs that the will to exercise 'freedom' and 'choice' in the design of new biological and social relationships within the formative family may be coloured by narcissant aspirations – just as the disinclination to look too deeply into the psychodynamics of the issues (as reason would suggest) has equally the earmarks of narcissance. An intelligent look might be given in particular to those assertions of 'freedom', since narcissant decisions are rarely as choiceful as they seem.

The propagation of new community and work styles needs no rehearsal here. It can be worthwhile, though, to consider an example that has preoccupied many: the great increase, over the generation coinciding with the development of postmodernity, of the splitting of families into separate households and of individuals living alone. This is costly to governments but enormously in the interest of business, and we could blame it on the building trades (controversial); but might there be postmodern reasons? Possibly. More than most other human social issues, the business of living with others calls up the matter of how well one lives with oneself – and this brings narcissance to mind. But if the incidence of narcissance has increased, how – with its awesome anxieties of separation – could more people seek to live separate lives?

This isn't the paradox it seems; it involves the precarious balance among peoples' felt needs. The 'collapse of traditional family values', so often linked to postmodern attitudes, can help to explain why families may feel less obliged to live together; but not why they'd want to live apart. Again we need to notice the difference between well-known (and well-worn) platitudes about 'What postmodernists think' and what postmoderns may feel. The testimony of people who live alone after having been married shows a feature widely overlooked, and one that is nothing so simple as mere conventional loss and grief. It is hard to miss ambivalence there. When we feel sorry for those living alone, and try to help them to *make more contact with others*, this often comes nowhere near the problem, or indeed what people living alone feel a need for. The truth of this surfaces when we hear individuals say 'I could never live with someone again' and 'I've learned too much the value of living and running my own life'.

This is a radical development. We have little record of people alone feeling this way in great numbers in previous ages. The process becomes evident when we hear how now many couples, often in even the early years of marriage and describing themselves still as loving and respecting one another 'as much as ever', speak of feeling 'suffocated' and/or 'hopeless' and 'exhausted': exhausted, we learn, with 'coping' with – attending to, satisfying, organizing and 'bending' their feelings around – others. The urgency – or the burden – of 'coping' in these ways isn't felt by everyone, as we know. We have no difficulty in recognizing the particular mind-style at hand. In *some* conditions of mind, solitude actually brings with it the feeling of relief – a release from the trial of the ever-defeated desire for unbroken intimacy with an ideal other, and the accompanying endless (self-)demand to earn this with an equally perfect 'performance' of one's own. That for increasing numbers separation appears to be the only way out, the only acceptable option, makes clear the specific force of narcissance in this postmodern social development. What we know of the anguish of separation here reveals just how vital for survival a *relinquishment* of intimacy is felt to be. It seems likely that so long as narcissance prevails, increased living apart will never be only a temporary glitch.

As we come to recognize with unease that many current developments (for example, in the workplace, and in housing) are actually fiercely imposed as makeshifts by commercial, industrial, educational, medical and state institutions in the interests of economy or profit, it's revealing to find that the *last* to protest are those who endorse postmodernity. It may prove difficult to deny the charge laid at postmodern culture's door that such changes place greater and greater emphasis on the search for self-realization and the accommodation and assertion of personal individuality (of 'private self-interest') at the expense of community in its conventional, wider sense – at least at present. (The instinct of those calling this the product of something like 'narcissism' are intuitively apt, though their having little purchase on the dynamics that make it so can lead to serious trouble, as we'll see.) If 'transgressions', deviations from traditional norms seem often in contemporary society to 'come down from the top', a feature that postmoderns will have increasingly to confront face-on is the extent to which, for both ideological and psychological reasons, they are logically caught having to live with offers they can't refuse.

Being Cool

'Transgression' itself is thus two-edged. It raises questions about exactly whose interest it serves. Partly because 'who' and 'interest' and 'serve' are all (for the expressly postmodern) thoroughly questionable and (for the narcissant) fraught with dilemmas, a postmodern culture calls upon a distinctive and striking – and now foreseeable – resource: *the culture of cool*. What differentiates postmodernity's sensationalism from other varieties (such as those foregrounded in the Baroque, the Gothic and the Romantic traditions) is that it is cool about it. 'Feeling' of the sort associated (in Romantic culture, for example) with a *commitment to desire* is deflated, emptied. In a universe missing a stable 'I', it adopts the perplexed essential insight of narcissance: '*Who am I to complain?*' The End of

Desire is the end of desire. Transgression thus develops special skills. It manages the toss and turn between the languishing to enter and the rage to stand back, and calls above all on that elemental defence against engulfment: the suppression of affect. 'Disinterest' and 'indifference' are made manifest. 'I'm not bothered' 'I'm cool'.

* * *

The posture of transgressive cool operates in many ways. *'Being ugly'* is one; in the adoption of radical ('indecorous') clothing modes, for example. Cross-dressing in the spirit of postmodernity is carefully managed *not* merely to cross gender codes (and especially in its logic it can never be simply transvestism, to conceal one gender in favour of another); commonly, one individual explicitly combines what had formerly been the clothing styles of both sexes. Dress is chosen to invoke periods and lifestyles associated with poverty and with the loss of 'grace' – ostentatiously in 'bad taste', 'cheap', meant to seem uncomfortable, 'shocking', 'gauche'. The wardrobe of 'the Slump', 'the Depression', is a revealing favourite. As Twitchell says, listing the products of one currently popular cosmetics manufacturer, Urban Decay,

> has lipstick, nail polish, and rouge with names like Plague, Bruise, Rat, Roach, Pigeon, and Apshyxia for young ladies – and Uzi and Asphalt for their young escorts.... The height of chic is cool, and nothing is more cool than to look poor, downtrodden, and beyond style. (1999: 222–3)

Cool attacks glamour – both the false glamour of Hollywood idols and of 'class'; it yearns to expel forever the demands of the *ideal* in which in narcissance one must endlessly clothe both oneself and others, to the point of exhaustion, in order to carry on. In this assault, we can sense the persecutory angst regarding the 'narcissist's' own "painful self-consciousness, pre-occupation with grooming and remaining youthful" so often noted by psychologists (Cooper 1986: 128). There is a grain of truth in the mixture of liberation and of self-contempt that people often somehow feel in the presence of the cool assumption of ugliness.

* * *

The culture of cool also operates by *'making noise'*. This isn't about just the decibels of rock – one of Unqle Trim's favourite whipping boys – though that, as we'll see, is a vital feature of it. It's about noise in a far-ranging sense, and one immediately recognizable as we think back to the matter of white noise and of postmodern torrential utterance and its implications. We recall Beckett's Molloy – "the noise of things bursting, merging, avoiding one another, assails me on all sides ... each pinpoint of skin screams a different message, I drown in the spray of phenomena", and the 'overload' of emotionally unsupported sensation of overdeterminacy whose ultimate effect is an elemental part of the formation of narcissance. Often consciously informed by modern theories of noise (drawn, for instance, from physics, neuroscience and information technology), in dress, in literature, music and the arts – in the deliberate choice of clashing sounds, colours, images, themes – noise is made not only audible but visible. In the media, in images of idyllic pastures, supermarket shelves, sexual intercourse, intergalactic space, religious icons, orgiastic feeding, car chases, classical art, laser duels, organ grafts, kitchen-sink romance, famine-heaped bodies, lipstick ads, animal slaughter, children playing hopscotch – signs flow forth without judgement, meticulously arranged to display the glittering detritus of culture as a mosaic, a history-broken-to-bits. The witness, as creator and as spectator, is both orphaned from any specific 'past' or 'home' and – left convulsively 'hungering' for these – made to believe in no one place, object or time, but rather to 'swallow' all.

In this 'cool noise' project, whatever its immediate context, whether for High or Low Art or the sale of a fizzy drink, an appeal is made to a sensuality torn out of the pages of conventional meaning, belief, feeling and aspiration. This is philosophically in keeping with postmodernism. Anyone acquainted with the calculatedly 'noisy' collision of the motifs of the romantic and the diurnal banal in the music of Captain Beefheart, Queen, Bowie, Beck and Mercury Rev will know the rasp of gears where the mundane and the sensational mesh and ironic sparks fly – and it's tempting to conceive of those 'sparks' as the 'natural' outcome of the philosophical attack on the 'original' and 'authentic' in favour of the 'synthetic' ('stuff artificially stuck together').

But it's not quite as simple as that. To ignore its experiential effect would be only to reenact the performance of cool, without regard for the turbulent psychological resonances it bears. In the cool-as-noise, the witness is in one breath imaginationally 'wrenched from the womb', hurled into the weltering street to relive the ordeal of 'fending for itself', and bathed in an ironic silence serving as a warranty that this is but a carnivalesque spectacle, a potion distilled for 'heady' consumer pleasure.[12] Cool noise both acts out the experience of inner dis-integration and operates to off-fend and drown out external authority. It asserts the rights and exclusivity of the individual's own sensibilities, of our discrete sensational states as against the state of affairs at large.

One of the great contradictions in postmodern life, for outsiders, is this combination of the cool, laid back posture and the cult of noise. To understand it, we should always scan the personal choice of noise – loud music, loud dress[13] – it for the possibility of *deflection*. The 'ordinariness' so poignantly resisted by narcissants (the unamplified, 'unplugged', banal detail of our everyday being) is here 'ghetto-blasted' away. What is 'given' is the vibrancy of surface; potentially emotionally testing encounters are buried in the background and superficial sensation is made figural in the field. Against the classic sociological image of 'conspicuous consumption' proclaiming personal identity, the postmodern seeks to disperse *claims* on that identity. Where we can't vouchsafe what we 'mean', we may feel safer sending mixed signals, shattering into fragments others' chances to sum(mon) up what we are and the responsibilities that this might entail.

By staying cool, chilling out, disabling the interplay of feeling ('I'm not ready to get involved'), maintaining indifference in the face of the world's material Babel and the mind's inward babble – and by taking a dynamically active part in the effervescent creation of interminable 'pointless' difference – postmoderns often say in one way or another, 'If not peace, I can produce my own brands of pleasure, free of rules'. Here, neither the catharsis nor the release-in-laughter that Western tragi-comic traditions would have accorded such dramas – and which depended on some doctrine of definitive personal transformation that neither postmodern nor narcissant thinking can sustain – is an option. Postmoderns love to watch spectacles like *Dallas* – but 'from the side'.[14] Pain may instead be drowned out in the anaesthesis of torrential imag(in)ing. As Vonnegut's narrator says in *Slaughterhouse-5* whenever someone or something dies, 'So it goes".

With this, we can be cool by *'being automatic'*. Both in public represention of life and in personal performance come the frissons accompanying 'cold, unfeeling' simulations of humans as mechanical automatons. In film, video and digital imagery, eerily 'smooth' featureless, characterless 'characters' have become standard icons.[15] Observers frequently comment on the 'robotic' appearance of rave-dancing. The Modernist revulsion in literature and the arts against technology and the machine now thus 'turns', to take on in the cult of automatism the aura of *schadenfreude*, of the pre-emptive psychic remedy that is an identifying feature of narcissance. 'Automatic cool' mimics with remarkable accuracy the freezing of feeling and the periodically self-contempt-laden sensations of artificiality, hollowness and 'deadness' that often overtake narcissants (and that, as often as profound depression, is what leads them to call for professional help). It acts out narcissance's ambivalence toward its own *tekhne*, the power and anxiety narcissants feel regarding the false faces by which they manipulate their encounters with others.

In postmodernity, where gestures toward mastery must always be problematic, this 'management' by 'automatic' processes comes in unexpected ways. George Cockcroft, a writer of the 1970s with a more recent cult-following, in a book called *The Dice Man*, gives voice to 'Luke Reinhart' who decides his life's actions by throwing dice. In his typical relish for paradox, gambling lends him the sensation of *control*. By detaching his acts from feelings that are, he believes, always a trap determined by his introjected sentiments and preconceptions, dicing is an act of positive will. This peculiar application of chance as a means of control is (as it was among Surrealists) a favoured notion among postmoderns with now familiar narcissant echoes. As a variant of the processes of 'abandonment and propagation', the relinquishment of the world's constraints is hoped to release something more true of one's self. As the very conception of 'gambling' suggests, the principle at work is the 'rule of apparent indifference' – a species of cool control that is the special forte of postmodern thinking as it contemplates the mystery and ordeal of living.

* * *

When they're not theorizing uncertainty, postmoderns laugh a lot. We may often feel that it's a complicated laughter, more consistently tinctured with a sense of the importance of 'being indifferent' than we associate with easy humour. We've seen complex uses of laughter before – in satire, for instance. But in the eyes of the radical postmodern, the tradition of satire is a bygone thing, an instrument of cultures giving faith to the possibility of 'positionality', of implying what was 'good' and what 'evil'. Typically, postmodern cool instead commends being 'Bad', and invokes the laughter – or rather, the grin, sometimes not unlike a grimace – of 'parody' and its frequent companion, 'camp'. As theorists have frequently highlighted by allusion to its etymology, parody needn't be normative in intent. In its postmodern uses, it's not the revelation of its evil or inferiority that undermines a thing, but merely the fact that there is, 'parallel' to it – an alternative.

In this respect, then, yes 'Otherness' is embraced. The difference now is that the *significance* of the other, of otherness itself, dissolves. Everything brings its other with it, and further disperses the obligation to choose. (This contrasts, for example, with the otherness accentuated by political movements, and with the otherness that brings laughter in Chaucer, Dickens and Shakespeare, where a kind of openness and sympathy invites us to accord value to others.) Otherness that – in the view of psychological as well as political praxis – is contactfully frictive is elided, evaded, erased. Each 'other' is offered in brackets. Postmodern 'play' works hard to maintain the 'insignificance' of difference. We grin because we are (or make as if to be) indifferent.[16]

Still, a feeling can persist that here is indifference with a vengeance. In the same vast population centres where postmodernity thrives, *violence* flourishes as entertainment and, alongside it, a fascination with stories of people violated that's impressively documented by the receipts ringing in the market's tills; the study of it has itself become a serious growth area. In the news, drama, blockbuster films, rock videos, general information, infotainment and infomercials we consume, in producers' finely tested knowledge that we wish to, scenes of so-called 'pointless' ('indifferent') brutality. As moral traditionalists tirelessly point out, the day's screens are occupied with images of mugging, mutilation, rape, serial and opportunist killing, public execution, accident- and disaster-fetishism, occasional cannibalism, and frequent internecine massacre. Traditions descending from punk and grunge – movements that emerged simultaneously with the popular appearance of the word 'postmodern' – continue in new ways to cultivate images of social and personal 'sleaze' and sado-masochistic play, but consistently and fluently mastered by the sardonic mask and gesture of self-mockery, self-contempt and overriding postures of ultimate 'cool' indifference. Asked why he made *Natural Born Killers* 'so violent a film', Quentin Tarantino is reported to have answered "Because it looks cool." Cruelty and brutalism are expressly converted, transmuted into sophisticated icons of 'anomie', brought to a promising head in, for example, imported Japanese television's torture-game-shows. It has become a traditionalists' commonplace to protest that daily new configurations of these show ever-diminishing 'cause' – 'unwarranted' violence, untroubled violence, violence with a poker face.

In individual human terms this has important dimensions. There are signs of an increasing attraction to – and in commercially articulated youth culture an identification with – transgressive charismatic public figures articulating precisely those forms of ambivalence that possess the more sardonic postmodern mind. The play of 'indifferent badness' extends well beyond whatever complex effect a Michael Jackson (an icon of the 'I'm cool, I'm bad' theme) is conceived to have had with his child audience. In the cool of female characters developed in films from *Play Misty for Me* to the vogue reflected by *Fatal Attraction*, and in male characters cut early by Jack Palance, Clint Eastwood, James Woods, Tommy Lee Jones, Christopher Walken, John Malkevitch, figures catch the eye with a new charismatic trait: the ability to be the master of oscillation. Equivocal, volatile, twisting inner ambivalence is contained within a persona displaying the impassive surface 'nerve' previously associated with the hero of 'integrity'. In recent times the intense, all-absorbing and self-effacing emotional investment in charismatic role models – commonly regarded as a classic index of narcissance – has often fastened on just such figures. It's a high-tension, high-risk mix winning the ultimate badge of 'cool', and seems evolved consummately to meet the fantasies of a narcissant life.[17]

A puzzle for readers of postmodern theory will be the social aspects of 'indifferent cool'. In spite of theory's high-profile rejection of social codes and distinctions, when we're 'cool' we follow very distinct behavioural protocols. When and where you 'rock' and don't 'rock' is an example. 'Outsiders' are sometimes discomfitted to find that when they exhibit strong feeling or go 'over the top' with laughter or are so excessively stirred by 'cool' music as to move to it elsewhere than in the right venue for dance – instead of listening deadpan, (e)motionless – they will be treated to forms of cool indifference that seem palpably elitist or 'superior'.[18] Reading this 'purely sociologically', 'from the outside', in terms of social hierarchy, we'd be obliged to revise all we had heard, and consider postmodern lifestyles stunningly classist.

It's when we recognize the underlying play of narcissance that we see that to be a misreading. Superiority is not the issue. What is excluded is not 'socially inferior people' but people challenging the emotions. Face to face with potentially provocative events, cool is a form of withdrawal. Far from being an expression of *authentic* indifference, its ethos is a rule of differentiation and in fact of suppression, and one of the more austerely enforced codes in contemporary culture. It's an alternative mode of decorum, of suppression, that is simply unfamiliar to many, because it must not be formalized, stated. In postmodernity, at the level of its lived performance – that is, where human beings actually make contact – differentiation is not simply readmitted, it is *urgent*. And this urgency needs to be understood as the urgency not to be (or appear) overwhelmed.[19] Inasmuch as narcissance is involved, the conventional socio-political forms for the redress of suppression can have no effect here.

This isn't because the fabric of the inner life is intrinsically more delicate, but because – as against the various weaves of social and political control – the warp and weft of its processes are different.

Expansion – toward Heterogeneity

'Promiscuous, propagational' living has an outcome with features of its own – an expansiveness of scale. Is it only a side-effect – or can it be that it's something we seek in itself – that so widely in postmodern life we're invited to take part in the creation and use of 'hypermarkets', 'hyperspace', 'hypertext', of 'hyper-isms' of all sorts? One of the special features of 'postmodern' industry's and commerce's combination of globalization of communications and distribution with particularization of production can in theory be universal pluralization; wherever in the world we are in material terms, as individuals we're invited in previously unforetold ways to construct our own lives. The pivotal aspect of this within the constellation of postmodernity I speak of here (the 'promiscuous' dimension of the postmodern) is in fact what some prefer to call – however awkwardly – 'glocalization'. By way of the networking – in the broadest and most multiform sense – of special-interest communities, world culture takes on a different contour, and one that in its very constitution leaves behind personal notions of national or geographic identity. New human connections are made not only along conventional lines such as those of ethnic, economic, sexual, gender, vocational and recreational investment, but in further ways scarcely yet considered. By means of 'trans-societal flows', fresh kinds of 'locality' proliferate. Following new 'link-lines' and joined by new varieties of bonds, *worldwide* particularist communities or 'virtual communities' take shape. An ever more heterogeneous population of individuals unfolds, individuals with dispersed multiple identities of affiliation, and with multiplied 'identity spaces' – together with new ways of feeling 'betwixt and between'. The world becomes diversified, 'hybridized', 'creolized' and potentially fractured in heretofore unimagined and presently incalculable ways. The disintegration of relatively unified notions of time, space and person bids to become a universal precondition for living. That's promiscuous postmodernity for you. What is crucial is not simply that many of these developments mimic hopes and anxieties inherent in narcissance. It's that more than a few of them are thus likely to carry with them – cannot be prevented from bringing with them – narcissant processes of thinking and desiring, with all of the profits and liabilities that that must imply.

That there are 'profits' here is unmistakable. Individuals in the most isolated physical and social settings can within instants form connections with others with some like interest or attitude on the other side of the world whom they would never in a lifetime have otherwise known. The chance is there for people to confirm values in themselves that their native geographical communities might have unremittingly condemned or ignored. The anxieties of (postmodern) context-boundness or (narcissant) field dependency may, we think, be reduced. The experience of 'contact' and of reassuringly focused and concentrated satisfaction sought in narcissance seems at hand, and one can legitimately feel that one has styled one's life to one's taste. A peculiarity of such contacts is that the '*whole* person' is confirmed only to the degree that he or she is disposed to fasten his or her whole being upon the interest that brings him or her together with someone of 'like mind' – someone more likely than ever to be at a great distance and never physically known.

Questions may arise. For instance, might this highly *stylized* life come to resemble that of the 'honeycomb' variety whose liabilities we've seen in narcissance? where the individual – with his or her diverse values and feelings safely but potentially antiseptically hived off from one another in a way suited to each context – enters new forms of isolation? An analogy is the case of our experience in the contemporary mall, which has sometimes been enthusiastically compared with the great institution of the agora, the forum or the town marketplace. As sociologists often observe, what the mall-shopper experiences is 'reflection rather than interaction', where commercial, product-orientated exchange is vigorous but where – since no mutual responsibility inheres in each encounter beyond that immediately relevant to the particular commodity involved – the forum's rich processes of social exchange among diverse personal beings tend to disappear. Not personal wholeness but increased personal diffraction and dispersal becomes the key to a new superficial mental ease.

But perhaps there's something further to be gained – something desired – in the explosively expansive worlds of the mall, the hypermarket, and hyperspace that outweighs such qualms. In contemporary life, like any other, of course shopping isn't only about watching and seeing oneself reflected – it's about buying. The extraordinary explosion and extravagance of choice in the 'consumer society' – of objects and services we can purchase – is one of today's favourite topics, as the Sunday colour supplements and the media in general endlessly herald[20] and sociologists assess. Conventional accounts of the time, energy and money committed to hyper-shopping call on such notions as conspicuous consumption and keeping-up-with-the-Joneses; but these applied as much to eighteenth-century shopping among the affluent as they do to a far wider population today. They often fail to touch what most vitally typifies the postmodern marketplace, which is not how many more people can exert choice (the vast majority are still excluded) but how many more choices they can exert, and the commercial and psychological culture built around – above all – the proliferation (propagation) of *opportunities to choose*.

One of the fundamental themes we've seen linking postmodern and narcissant thinking is the sensation of the impossibility of deciding. A feature of shopping is that it allows the repeated, regular and definitive choosing of *things* where the definitive choosing of social, moral and psychological positions, values and actions seems beyond reach as it does in narcissance. It's difficult to overstate the gratification often felt by narcissants in being able to anticipate pointing to an *object* and saying with comparative ease – for what one's giving up is 'only money' after all, and not oneself – *'I'll have that', 'that's what I want'*. The very experience of committing in this way, and being immediately rewarded by the receipt of what's been asked for, can be an enormously potent balm. What one's been led to believe to be the best one can expect – material 'belongings' – is instantly fulfilled. Even the ordeal of choosing among products is anticipated with pleasure, for 'at the end of the day', a narcissant knows that a deal can be *closed*, with a containable degree of loss; the quest/ordeal will have *a quantified end*. The phenomenon of the 'shopaholic' speaks for itself; for a narcissant, few pleasures can be more addictive. But more: each time a product is purchased, a fragment of reality is cornered and possessed, taken in and integrated into one's own 'system'; a bit more of the material substance – the *hyle* – of 'reality' is added to one's sense of one's being; one feels more anchored in the world. The frail diaphonous envelope of what one imagines oneself potentially to be is 'stocked', con-solidated, filled in, filled out. 'I am substantiated.' Or at least that would be the dream.

Here again, postmodernist theories often fail to grasp the experiential side of postmodern living. Choosing can enact an often aggressive reaching for the stuff lying outside the infinite and interminable process of narcissant thinking.[21] (For psychologists there can be another resonance in this of what some analysts – such as Bursten – call the orality of a narcissistic 'craving personality'.) The generation coinciding with the first wave of postmodernity, in giving itself a name, didn't call itself a 'user society' or a 'supply-side' or 'buyer' society but a 'consumer society'; it speaks of itself as one that stuffs its stuff – puts its goods – in its mouth. 'Hyperistic marketing' can be one unexpected and vital form of 'body-building'. It appeals to a desire literally to amass 'goods', to give bulk and mass to one's reality, to amass one's identity. Postmodern culture isn't only a hungry culture, as its opponents like to say; it's hungry for assimilable, 'soluble' choices. Perhaps in recent years we've all sometime, when we've been disappointed, hurt, frustrated or felt lonely or empty, gone shopping for something we seemed not to need. Implicit in this is that in more lives than we generally acknowledge there may be something like a nameless wound which, when for any reason it's reopened, only some new possession can stop up or staunch. There are good reasons for seeing contemporary 'hyperistic' culture as a means for the *repetition* of an urgently pleasing experience, where the radical expansion of variety conceals that it is a repetition – multiplying not simply choices but the act of choosing.

Revolt

We're invited to blame a spirit of revolt in contemporary life on something called 'youth culture'. It's not my ambition to describe here, let alone account for, all of what that means. One overarching thing that it implies, however, is a culture of revolt that youths define and now have economic power to promote – and that 'grown-ups', effectively their parents, seem hungrily to envy, appropriate and maintain. What's going on?

We often hear that – in competitive capitalist society where living at the growing edge and the appearance of vigour are essential for survival – it is by their 'narcissistic' efforts to appear and feel *young* that people today convince themselves of their viability. That otherwise, they feel, they'll be left behind. But why should the 'mature' – unlike previous generations throughout history – believe they must emulate the *currently* young in order not to be 'left behind'? Why, for example, can't they feel in themselves the nous and power (social, economic, political) that they've gained only in their maturity?

One reason may lie in the anxiety expressed in the phrase 'left behind'. A trait of narcissants' thinking, as we've noted, is an inclination to attribute to their children the roles and the powers of parents. Not only do narcissants *solicit* this in and yield it up to their children, but often – having done so – they fear it in them. Above all, there is the threat of abandonment, and of betrayal. Ironically, the generation in which postmodern thinking has evolved – that of today's youths' parents – has laid itself a multiple trap. That is, *both* an anxiety that they'll be betrayed by their children (as up-and-coming parent-surrogates), *and* an acceptance of the attitude which they themselves had elaborated that parents are the betrayers whom the children *must* expose, deconstruct, regard with contempt and 'leave behind'. (When young rock culture says, for instance, 'You betrayed us', adults recognize themselves in the young's cry, even while they resent – and dread hearing – it.)

This complex system, bearing the idiosyncratic marks of narcissant oscillation, is further articulated and complicated when it shows up in explicitly material, 'real-life' terms. In the distribution of power – with regard to money, for example: it has long been an *idée reçue* that the power of 'today's youth' comes from the fact that for the first time they're given money to spend and the freedom to spend it as they like. Let's follow this logic where it leads. Populations in developed countries actually have in real terms a lower per capita income than they had a decade ago. More importantly, in traditional societies affluent parents have conventionally been far more close-fisted in this regard except where children's expenditure was carefully managed to display the family's (the parents') values. What needs to be asked, then, is why are children currently 'indulged' in this new way? Without shrinking from the patent rationality of facilitating the young's chances to explore their own potential, it makes sense to ask what are the feelings that go into this change?

One answer worth considering is that at least one group of parents who have in particular given extensive monetary power to their children – and who are often ones who express resentment in doing so – are those who have done so *because* they resented them. Often we say that it happens when parents have less time for their young; where the mother is a lone parent and/or is free or obliged to pursue her own career, or where both parents aim to be left freer to respond to increasingly complex and distressing work demands and/or to explore their more far-ranging avocational and recreational potentials. What is frequently missed is that whether the reasons are or are not because the mothers as well as fathers have desires that compete with their desires to be with their children, the effect is *likely* to be that the child – with scarce experience in the distribution of desires – *sees* things in this way. For children, then, being given money to spend as they like is being 'bought off'. This is not simply a question of the parents' giving their children 'stuff' to forestall or occlude their sense of being uncared for, or, put coarsely, to keep them 'out of trouble', out of the wavering and restive realm of parents' own identity formation. Far more significantly for the dynamics of a culture seeming to foster postures of revolt is that the 'stuff' they feel they're being 'bribed' with often carries the implication (the 'information') that goods – and the quality of goods – and not 'quality time' is what life is all about, what they have to look forward to, what there is to hope for. And that as their way of reflexive redress, they build into the commodities they promote the emblems and gestures of the anger and anguish that this 'bribery' excites.

I've spoken of the according of 'power to the young' here not merely because it's something that contemporary commerce and industry 'bank on' but because it illustrates in the briefest and crudest shorthand a large-scale and intricate cluster of relations in which inversions, contradictions, oscillations and processes of transgression and revolt often associated with the postmodern culture are foreseeably coloured by constellations with distinctly narcissant preoccupations and processes such as these. The famous commodification of contemporary 'youth-culture' seems able to pattern itself only by means of this nest of forces – and will always need to be interrogated in the light of it.

Numerous other manifestations of a spirit of revolt are associated with postmodern life and deserve looking into in this light. A now old puzzle is the way in which postmodern architecture and urban planning have been received as forms in which to 'house' our domestic and public life. An endlessly discussed example has been Los Angeles' Bonaventure Hotel, a site that "reflects the very nature of the postmodern experience", as Edward M. Soja (following Jameson) has said; a "postmodern hyperspace ... a landscape that's highly fragmented, a space that decenters you, makes you feel lost ... dislocated", where "you feel that your only recourse is to submit to authority" which "you can't find". "Made helpless, you're peripheralised, you're lost".[22]

Who wants to live or carry on business in an ambiance that deliberately problematizes our sense of inside and outside, of location and direction, of origin and destination? We recognize its theoretical allusions to displacement, *dépaysement*, and we think it's conceived to loosen the straps of authority, of 'structure' and the structures we're harnessed to. But here is either an extreme example of the detachment between theory and practice, or – as visitors instantly suspect – a dedicated display of monetary power and of the manipulation of witnesses' sensations, where scarcely anything is asserted more vigorously than authority. Back to square one, then; by what authority, what motive, are we installed in such a precinct? Is it possible that in this is an 'acting out', of 'creating' that calls on our paranoid resource, engaging us at the boundaries of risk, and always with the ambiguous guaranteed consolation that the world (the environment) is to blame?

A form of cool transgression that has in more recent years been heatedly debated and is likely to gain still greater attention is the 'ungoverned', so-called 'wanton' dissemination of the 'illicit' in the form of information. A growth area is the 'unrestrained' (and often openly autographed) distribution of How-Tos over the Internet – on the home-manufacture of drugs and bombs, on modes of suicide, of civil disobedience and of terrorism, on hackers' tactics for industrial, economic and governmental espionage and 'systems meltdown', and on the strategies of transnational CyberWar. Can this be – as outcry in certain quarters has explicitly labelled it – a 'potentially catastrophic' enactment of promiscuous indifference?

However this may be, if indeterminist thinking sometimes seems inexplicably a kind of celebration of – a revelling in – impotence, it is easy to forget that once the narcissant sensation arises of others' endlessly demanding desire and expectation, impotence can often be a powerful instrument of withholding, of revolt and of passive aggression.

A stunning aspect of the examples touched on so far in this chapter has been that, however informationally radical, they suggest a postmodern 'transgression' that is materially – by contrast with some forms of 'revolution' in the past – 'non-aggressive'. That is, transgression is performed in a backhanded, 'I don't mind' fashion – ungrounded and shifting. Impulses, seemingly individualist and on the verge of suggesting withdrawal into isolation, show at the same time a shifting self-conscious eye to 'what others think' – calling for life-in-the-particular-and-in-the-moment, yet ever fluent and ready to seduce us with a general ontological theory of their behaviour, swinging between the extremes of an exclusionism verging on contempt and a markedly self-effacing compulsion toward 'to-each-his-own' compliance. This coruscating chiaroscuro play of apparent waywardness and ludic elation seems 'beyond reason'. How did a culture of humans alive in the world ever arrive at such an eddying, equivocal, catch-me-if-you-can style of 'revolt'? Perhaps one of the things that need to be learned is that while there are reasons, they are not all motivated by 'rational' principles or grounded on dedicated theory. To get a handle on it, it's hard to do without some conception of the mind-style of narcissance.

The examples from the Internet just mentioned dramatize well a hazard in generalization about the postmodern. The impulses behind the 'illicit' Net communications from, say, those giving Ecstasy recipes and those calling Zapatistas to action have been, by even the most modest accounts, somewhat different. Neither impulse is postmodern on its own any more than grandiosity or paranoia on its own is narcissant. The issue of the Internet – or indeed of 'consumer culture' or 'lifestyle culture' – as a postmodern phenomenon is joined only when, with its myriad readings and uses, like narcissance, it's observed as pluralistic in its totality. In the remainder of this chapter, however, we'll see that postmodern culture doesn't rest as easy with pluralism as we're often invited to believe, any more than narcissance docs.

TRYING ECSTASY

As happens in narcissance, if an idea, an event, an act in life is to be postmodern, it brings its contradiction with it. It exists in its ensemble, the ensemble is complex, and we can't encompass it by simply practising a piercing stare. In what follows we'll need always to remember that there aren't two postmodern 'camps', those that are 'promiscuous' and those that are 'ecstatic'; they are the same postmodernity, living out its inescapable contradictions. As when people 'speak postmodern', people's 'postmodern lifestyles' oscillate between polar extremes in their meaning and function. While (to make matters at least provisionally clear) I want to single out examples of the 'ecstatic' distinct enough from examples I gave of the 'promiscuous', they should always be imagined as 'shunting' or 'shimmering' as each meaning and function changes place with its counterpart in real life – like the duck/rabbit or the solarized portrait. From time to time I'll point out an obvious case of this oscillation itself, but only by way of illustration of a far more widespread phenomenon.

The popular association of postmodern life with narcotics and above all in recent times with a drug bearing the name Ecstasy is no accident.[23] We've seen that in its 'promiscuous' perspective the postmodern is impelled to pluralize experience. In its ecstatic aspect it acts out its equally native indeterminist impulse. Infinitude (literally, borderlessness, limitlessness and not merely the aggravated awareness of the *ambiguity* of limits) becomes identified with All and – by extension – with Unity or Oneness. Here the loss of or escape from identity becomes the 'ground' or harbinger not of anguish but of some form of *bliss*. Where there is diversity in experience it's not fractured, splintered, but is felt instead as iridescent – the shimmer of the rainbow, as if observed not now in the kaleidoscope but through the prism of unceasing creation. Here is an aspiration where – contrary to that of the 'promiscuous' impulse, where the point is to lay bare the stitching – to make 'seamless' is to make good. Fluidity is all, and at the centre of the vortex may be the dream of ones' flowing and unbounded self.

Our glimpse of the nexus between postmodern and narcissant thinking has prepared us well for this. Its historical background becomes palpably evident when we recall the obvious resemblance between postmoderns' siren desire for 'release from self' and the more perennial aspiration of mysticism echoed in the West in Romantic literature.[24]

It won't be enough merely to say that in this perspective 'difference' becomes unimportant. More, it is *important* that *irony* be *reduced*, and *difference be dissolved*. In the ecstatic mode, the injunction 'Only connect' takes on the status of an eleventh – or rather, a first and last, since the others are formally abandoned – commandment. The processes of 'analysis' and of 'propagation' – the 'breaking down', the severing of received connections and the 'splicing' of new ones – are replaced by a common fascination with the contrary idea of 'growing and multiplying organically', 'from the inside', out of some single *élan* or 'seed'. Terms 'taken from nature' abound; the self is to (e)merge in the 'matrix' (mother) of Nature. A fundamental distinction between differing recent theories of process is exhibited here between ideas of fracturing, of rupture, and ideas rooted in biological and psychoanalytic metaphors (such as Deleuze and Guattari's), where the production of the new is not by grafting but by a continuous, branching rhizomic growth. (Contemporary information and communications technology frequently articulates an analogous vision in its language in terms such as 'flows', 'tracking', 'threading', 'looping' and 'streaming'.) In ceaseless competition with the pluralist impulse of the 'promiscuous postmodern' there is that alternative, seemingly paradoxical, *esemplastic* thrust underlying postmodernity's enactment of the narcissant condition. A '*merging*' mode – with its associated delirium, its ceaseless swerving, turning and returning – comes into its own.

Displacement

Where in the perspective of promiscuity a fundamental pattern of thinking is that of detachment, in the perspective of ecstasy there is *displacement*. Hovering in the background, behind the impulse to transgress, is that other, dynamically opposed sensation – one of the most common, persistent and life-shaping of narcissant experiences

– that we call *separation anxiety*. We have all sometime had the perplexing experience, on making a change that in every way seems a good one – setting out on a long deserved and desired holiday, going to a party where we know we may make good friends, moving from a bleak house to a bright new one, quitting a mean job for a better one, giving up a possession or a pattern of behaviour that we know has long been bound to values we no longer hold, leaving a pain-laden and destructive relationship, even simply getting out of bed in the morning – everyone on some such occasion has, for all that the change promises pleasure, had a sensation of anxiety, melancholy or even fear. One feels 'I don't want to (let) go!' Separation anxiety can, more than any rational reservations we may entertain, be one of the most powerful forces behind our failing to leave behind what we're in disaccord with, are ashamed of, and even detest most in our daily lives and in ourselves. In narcissance, this is not a chance anxiety but relentless – an experience that makes growth impossible and further narcissance inevitable. And with that, an apparent alternative to the quandary of separation anxiety steps forward: let go of nothing. Find some way of clinging to – even of being – all things at once.

Perhaps more than anything else, this affects narcissants' – and now postmoderns' – relationship to the past.[25] People not equally familiar with both postmodern and narcissant thinking can be struck by this apparent oddity, that they happen to share an almost obsessive *nostalgia*. Coincidence isn't in it. Separation anxiety haunts both. We've seen the seeds of nostalgia in postmodern discourse.[26] In contemporary life it has become one of the essential forces fuelling both developed and developing national economies. The media provide a vivid example, in the immense commercial success of film and television productions devoted not only to stories set in the period of the youth of baby-boomer's parents (the 1950s) but in the more distant past (not only in such popular media series as "Upstairs/Downstairs" but in adaptations by Merchant-Ivory and others of the novels of Forster, Hardy, Dickens, Austen). Probably never in history have "retro" fashions not only in clothing but in the shaping of the environment – architecture, landscaping, furnishings, décor – and in the collection of objects (classic cars, *objets d'art*, bric-a-brac, the trove of myriad hobbies) so occupied people's time, space and energy.

Is this, as the press likes to declare, a hankering to 'return to traditional values'? One thing we know is that actually there is no such tidily unitary thing as 'traditional values' (which? whose?) to which our 'collecting of the past' could easily return us. What has meaning in the phrase is not 'values' but 'tradition'; that is, the eidolon of a continuous and stable (generically 'traditional') world in which our needs and dreams might be welcome and safely contained. Few, given the option, would choose comprehensively to exchange in reality their values, possessions and lifestyle with those of the 'real world' of past generations. What does have use-value finally is the notion of psychic *return*; 'nostalgia' means literally 'homesickness'. The nostalgic activity we find seesawing in oscillation in the post-modern with its counterpart, the spirit of transgressive revolt, invokes a *displacement* with which narcissants are deeply familiar. The shift into a mode of feeling in which separation is defeated, where neither the past (with its '*mistaken*' traditions so lucidly illustrated by say Austen and Forster) nor the present (with its – and the narcissant's – tumultuous clashing uncertainties) exists, but both are merged and dissolved in an imaginary, equipoised and somehow 'warm' timeless condition of animated tranquility.

There is a species of control, of mastery here. As postmoderns would happily say (and the operations of pastiche illustrate), tradition and indeed the artifacts of time are made 'toys'. Postmodern displacement takes still further steps along this path, as people physically displace themselves as tourists. Alongside information technology (where we displace ourselves in 'hyperspace') tourism is the largest growth industry in the world. The extreme dependency of 'developing' nations (among which those of the former Soviet bloc are in this context included) on tourist trade for their leading source of annual revenue is well known. But for even an established 'First World' industrial nation such as the United Kingdom (while one out of every three Britons each year visits a foreign country), tourism is the largest invisible-export industry. That Americans have special reasons for feeling they're 'coming home' to the British Isles isn't the whole story. Here as elsewhere around the world they jostle alongside camera-porting Japanese, Germans and Chinese, and temporal 'displacement' is the project in hand at every turn. The sites/sights meticulously organized for their gaze are of a past that Britons have by-and-large long-since forgotten: Madame Tussaud's, the Tower of London and further castles everywhere (animated, for example at Warwick, with automated human figures and the sounds and smells of 'the past '– the incense and the picturesque dung, the lutes, the ring of anvils and swords). Tourists throng dreaming – or as close to dream as they and the organizers can collude to produce – in cottage, cathedral, pub and shop – 'Dickens' London', 'Shakespeare's Stratford', 'Hardy's Wessex', 'the Brontës' moorlands', 'Joyce's Dublin','the Highlands of Scott'. Further afield, we feel it in our power to revisit the 'deeper' ages laid before us in famed whole 'museum-cities' (Venice, Pompei, Prague, San Gimignano, Carcassonne) and in the 'reconstructed real worlds' of the comfortably caricaturesque and thus 'hyper-familiar' Disneylands and their many imitations. 'Authentic primitive' Edenic sites await us (Bali, Madagascar, Tahiti) where we may 'actually go native' in some desert-oasis or oceanic paradise. Inspired by Thomas Cook's group-organizational strategies, raised in the postwar period to the level of a major interactive performance art by Club Méditerranée and its successors, now more and increasingly more powerful conglomerate transnational event-management industries (whose relationship to tourism is ever more concealed and remote) – literally reorganizing our sight – 'take us away' in manufactured worlds.[27]

Featured further in postmodern life is that this revisiting can happen at home – or in the holiday homes-from-home we make for ourselves by an increasingly widespread form of transhumance. More and more typically we make our own homes our museums, our castles, turn our own backyards into Tahiti. What the house-designers of Beverly Hills built for the stars (those icons of simulation) in the 'Golden Age' of the Hollywood 'dream factory' – the mock-Tudor mansions, castles and mock-thatch cottages – now many build for themselves in the suburbs of every major city in the developed world. In seeming contrast, the drift of the liberal and thoughtful elite to the American Northwest, building forest 'cabins' for their moral and emotional retreat, may be yet another case in point. Like Jools Holland, Christopher Morahan, Bill Gates, by means of a kind of 'sincere' pastiche, we can organize creative 'vacation', if not vacuity, from the pressing tests of the diurnal urban grind; we may take absence with leave and commingle our reality with the more exotic reaches of past cultures' and our own self-imagination.

But in the 'psycho-logic' of displacement as these examples disclose, in the end it's less the place that counts than the retreat into experiences beyond place. 'City-ships', the largest buildings in the world, are now on the water. Mega-cruisers like those of the Carnival Line set out not for weeks but for months. Regarded as the first step in 'a revolution in the use of water' (presently each over 100,000 tons, and with vessels planned in the next few years to reach 250,000 tons, the largest buildings in history, great self-sufficient cities on the move, each a glitter of glass, chrome, plastic, overflowing with foods, music, games, shows and dance), built not to stand high seas but of metals light and soft, made for peacetime and cash – they sail the oceans like vast welcome Ships of Fools in search not so much of geographical places (for few ports can receive them) but of ways to create in each timeless moment the ultimate release. In the 'shipboard romance' the resemblance to the fusion and separation fantasies of narcissance is striking. The seemingly most intimate connections are formed, free of dependency, of 'commitment', built on conveniently simulated (or at least unassimilated and uncontested) identities, yet with the intensity of 'all-consuming passion', designed by pre-agreement to dissolve without blame or excess lamentation in the steamy dawn of some mutually accorded day as the final sun rises to the accompaniment of just-suitably plangent horns, and in the wharf-bustle disappearing figures leave their traces (un)stained in the memory forever. For the pricey but psychologically wound-free cost of a ticket, again postmodern culture finds a way of re-enacting and polishing to a numinous shine, if not purging, its latent psychic drama.

To be sure of our footing here: we don't need to be narcissant to want these things. But there are signs that one needs not to be narcissant to elude their mesmerically potent allure.

Delirium

The impulse to merge the givens of experience into an all-embracing whole by means of science and technology has captured the imagination and become integral to the systems of power in our times. The bulk of the literature and media attention devoted to the matter is immense. Front pages and prime-time television announce the imminence of a unified theory of the universe and of the origins of life. This in itself is to be brought about by the rapid communication and *coalescence* of the observations and the associated technologies of the new world order's once diverse intellectual disciplines. Not only is contemporary language charged with slogans advertising the *mediation* of our knowledge and experience via 'the Web', 'the Net' – the very words announce the theme – but we engage in 'networking', using 'linking' protocols, are pressed to get 'online' and 'wired' and are now regularly sociologically assessed and commercially polled with regard to whether or not we are 'connected'. In the trade literature of communications, IT and the media, 'convergence' and 'globalization' are viewed as the inevitable desiderata and destiny of the technologies for all our information as well as our pleasure. In the new world economy of 'cyberspace' or 'hyperspace', "convergence is becoming the basis of all sectors" (Tapscott 1996: 59). This is unquestionably the central metaphor in which the society giving rise to postmodern culture is currently investing more of its faith and resources than any other, and there would be no sense in thinking that any metaphor receiving such concerted investment is not an indicator of a profound and equally overarching psychological investment.

The word 'hypertext' (the medium in which, among other things, the World Wide Web currently operates) – with its unmistakable resonance of the postmodern indeterminist's conception that every articulated thought is merely a node in the overarching 'network' or 'archtext' of language – articulates as richly as any utterance could the junction between postmodernism as a constellation of ideas and the world as an evolving material environment. By means of HyperText Mark-up Language (the ubiquitous 'html', a universal computer-language protocol) or some augmented form of it, any utterance or graphic or audial sign, once electronically registered in digitized form, may be 'hyperlinked' with any other utterance or sign, anywhere within whatever whole hypertext 'book', 'picture' or digital video or 'soundtext' in which it's been imbedded, *or* – by a further simple software routine and the most modest hardware (such as a modem connected to a phone line) – with any text in any other place that can be reached by electronic, digital communication, anywhere on the planet.

The power and wonder of hypertext needs no selling here. Knowing that by 'clicking' on a highlighted onscreen word or image we can move 'transparently' to any of billions of other images generated by millions of other persons in millions of invisible and geographically unknown other places, we're brought closer than ever imagined to the dream of the world where we can go where we wish, apprehend things as we like, activate or withdraw our commitment at whatever point we desire. We can 'seamlessly' add our own utterances or signs to those we see before us, embedding our ideas among those floating in the world's fast-expanding hypertextual space. Scientists, international economists, leaders of government and of transnational industries as well as political and social activists now speak of their affairs as taking place in a virtually timeless exchange, second by nanosecond. Already literally unquantifiable volumes of information (including the instantaneous movement of trillions of dollars, pounds, deutschmarks, yen, each day) change hands – *power* flows from hand to hand and mind to mind – so rapidly that users are often compelled to decide and take action as if, as we commonly now say, specific geographic localities have effectively melted into a vast generic, oceanic 'cyberspace'. In a hypertext medium, the possibility of 'merging' can seem unlimited; one becomes at last 'one with' the 'others', in the world of signs. Here there are the blended seductions of a 'union of minds', of a perpetual indeterminacy, of an artificially induced clarity, and of a kind of anonymity and human disengagement, approaching those of the most complex and ambiguous narcissant fantasies.

This is where 'delirium' comes in. Hyperlinking doesn't merely allow selection, it invites *veering, swerving*, in a fashion determined not by the rationale of the 'sender' but according to the inclination of the mind of the receiver. For those seeking information via the Web (or reading a hypertext novel), an extraordinarily invaluable feature is the refinement – and hence the speed and ease – it provides for the searcher to *bypass* apparently irrelevant text and go straight to material of immediate interest. The process is steered by the associations and desires of the user (what is relevant to me, to my conception of the topic, what *I* want to hear and see). It begins to seem possible that, surprisingly perhaps to some, hypertextuality is about plurality with simplicity – as though a covert motto sustaining it were 'Multiplicity Yes, Complexity No'.[28] That is, that when the postmodern is drawn to something like hypertext (and hyperspace), it keeps utter faith with multiplicity, but may choose *clarity* against complexity, in the name of the unperturbed experience of the power of a seemingly 'important' (if not meaningful) connectedness, where the importance is constructed by the individual who *imports* it. This is no mere play on words. In increasingly widespread ways in postmodern culture, first: 'import' (such as value or meaning) is constituted by *importing*, where the individual decides what to 'read' or experience and in what context, and what to leave unseen. And second: what grows in 'importance' is the experience of importing/ not importing; that is, of optimizing the pleasure of 'confluence'.[29]

Superficially this freedom to choose one's links would seem to accord with postmodern notions of how texts are determined by their readers, and encourage belief in the freedom and power of the individual, the user. How free is s/he? This has several dimensions. For one, what such notions don't take into account is the effects of the psychological constraint placed on the reading of *conventional linear* texts – which tend to invoke end-directed thinking. Invited to believe that the point of reading is to consume the *entire* text, to see 'how it all comes out', we're compelled to *work our way* page-by-page *through* the text, engaging with all the traps and ambiguities the writer may have inscribed there; complexity (of the sort Modernists insist we negotiate with) is part of the 'signification' of the work. The fundamental difference, the 'value added', in hypertext is the opportunity to choose to seek (and, as hyperspace expands, to expect) no end, to avoid seeing what one doesn't want to see, and to immerse oneself in the feeling that – with or without reason – all things are connected, and in something like the way we *want* them to be. For the arch Net operator, the hacker, a vital motive is the passion to overcome all separations, together with the aesthetics of the tactics of self-determined, self-willed convergence.[30] Here is a rare and precious phenomenon, for the narcissant most of all. The sensation of unbroken, infinite 'confluence' is enhanced, and the feeling is simultaneously induced that one is – in the very act of 'making connections' – free of dependency and, with regard to the data (the chaos of 'givens') of the world, in control to the point of a heretofore unattainable omnipotence. By tapping *as we like* into the continuous and uninterrupted flow – the torrential proliferation – of information we may conceive that the world is our oyster.

Another dimension of the question 'How free is the user?' arises here. The steps by which information can be made to lead to re-formation of the world may be complex but they are swiftly growing more 'real'. The data (bits) of 'factual' events, digitally registered, can be manipulated in the interests of profit. (In a television commercial seen by millions Steve McQueen may appear enthusiastically driving a car – a Cary Grant may pour a beverage – that never existed when he died.) This extends far beyond the 'funny bits'. The potential political yield of such reinformings of history can be formidable. Knowing the organization of 'information' in the DNA of particular species, we can now reorganize that data in a given material chain of DNA and produce an altered – 're(in)formed' – species (and individuals or corporations can own the rights to these). Of special satisfaction for postmodernists, the distinction here between what's 'natural' and what's 'artificial' or 'synthetic' loses much of its meaning. Most salient of all, few can take so deepseated an interest in entering into the 'ecstatic flow' of information as those engaged in the shapeshifting processes of narcissance, whose very sense of being is most threatened by disorder, and for whom not only flexuous responsiveness but the strategies for the manipulation of material events to bring them in line with inner fantasies are 'second nature'.

The question of 'ends' arises. Postmodernist theory consistently implies that there can be 'no end' to the flows of information. It consequently can offer no redress wherever anyone – for example, a narcissant glossing his or her actions with the promise of innocuity (indeed, of helplessness) – acts in such a way as to bring about inadvertently what others regard as very tangible and conceivably terrible material effects or 'ends'. The user's 'freedom' can be a fairly critical matter, then – do postmoderns want so much freedom? are we really free when we're in a condition of narcissance ...? We'll want to look a little further into this later.

Incorporation

New communications technologies such as those driving the move toward globalization aren't just about data, they involve people. A widespread belief is that 'the global network' is 'full of people hiding from full relationships in the real world'. Engaging epithets like 'nerd' and 'geek' have been adopted as euphemisms for what's often secretly thought to be something more unspeakable – the Net narcissist. Sheltered under the aegis of this widespread 'understanding' it would seem easy to go on to say that never has there been so explicit a fulfilment specifically of narcissant fantasy as the world of the Internet. In cyberspace the reader creates the world in which s/he reads and is empowered to spin away without inhibition in her/his solitary narcissant vortex forever.

But this notion of the individual as solipsist misapprehends 'Net people', postmoderns, and narcissants in one fell swoop. It is true that arguments and 'research evidence' against this idea – typically assembled by, and polling, pro-high-tech enthusiasts (such as the editors and readers of *Wired*) and showing 'connected' individuals to be not 'passive, retreating, anti-social' but highly motivated community-active types – have so far been extremely unconvincing. And uniform withdrawal is, as we know, not narcissance; it's at most only half the story; a signature of narcissance is oscillation. But I want to pursue this popular theme, since – as with many persistent misunderstandings of material fact – it contains a valuable psychological intuition.

What does distinguish many users of electronic communications ('comms') today is that they seize with both hands the opportunities that the nature of comms creates, allowing their oscillation (the agon within themselves) – rather than the rules-of-engagement of more conventional social 'fields' – to determine the conditions of social exchange. To appreciate this we need to recall some of the features of the experience of communicating and playing in a digital environment.

Anyone who has played a computer game or read a few messages in any of the thousands of special formats in which communications go on here – in commercial services (such as America Online), Internet forums, list services or news groups, or in conferencing – will have seen a unique pattern of 'self-identifying' at work (or rather, in play). In online comms generally, when a message or 'posting' from one of us to others in a group appears on screen, it shows up under a 'nickname' – one we may have chosen for ourselves when we 'joined', but one that, because we can choose it, may be anything (and often is); John P. Smith, Jack, Darling, Mr Magic, P Kabu,

Avenger from Hell. In games, we're commonly invited to create for each of ourselves an 'avatar' – an object (like a piece on a gameboard) with which our movements through the character-crowded game-space may be 'identified'. You become a green man, a teradactyl, an earth goddess, a laser gun, a penis, according to taste. Thus we organize and '*incorporate*' (embody) ourselves in explicitly fictional signs – the 'real person' is by common accord no longer at issue. The effect is strikingly like what's achieved when commercial corporations are formed – 'organizations', that is, with '*limited liability*' ('Ltd') or '*anonymous* societies' (*sociétés anonymes*), as the British and the French significantly call them – where living individuals are no longer held fully personally responsible.[31]

Further, in e-mail communications and on the Net, where from the earliest days a special anxiety emerged that the very spirit of the words used might often be misread (since here verbal exchange is unaccompanied by our physical presence, and the Net was never to be confined to people regarded as 'writers' with 'special verbal skills'), down to the present moment we have commonly smoothed the way by a vast set of conventional symbols expressively called 'smileys' or (depending on the degree of our ambition) 'emoticons'. We follow a potentially ambiguous phrase with a symbol like ;-) or <G> to represent the harmless 'Grin', or 'ROFL' for the cordial 'Rolling On the Floor Laughing'. The level of sophistication of such alternative texts (taking the technology of communication back to the age of the wooden club and the catspray on the wall) discloses a fantasy in which personal complexity and otherness, the frictive differences between discrete identities, may be dissipated with a keystroke; that by melting ourselves as subjects into convivial simple giggles and grunts we may forever forestall confrontation, and achieve some earnestly desired confluence with the world. It is linked to a fantasy familiar to us now.

We might think that by these 'supplementary texts' we thus 'recreate' standard sociable contexts to the best of our ability, given the limited 'bandwidth'. That is, lacking the capacity to move sufficiently numerous bits of data through circuits sufficiently fast to convey along with our words our facial expressions and body language, we've found a shorthand for the job. We might say 'Just wait till we can all *see* one another on the Net!' But in fact things don't seem to work quite that way; it's not about bandwidth. As telephone corporations around the world have long had to recognize, the public has turned out to be notoriously unresponsive to the offer of visual phone technology. Though commercial pressures for innovation must ultimately compel consumers' acceptance of such technologies, like the failure of early crude blank-featured automaton figures to disappear from film and video when the technology had caught up, this seeming rejection of the refinement of our detailed exposure of ourselves does not appear to go away. The number of people calling out for visual contact online is vastly outweighed by those investing in technological means by which anonymity can be *preserved* at will, or moulded or concealed behind alternative, invented images.

This resonates with something very like the fantasy in which the intricate and exhausting acrobatic *performance* (self-assertive yet bringing confluent harmony) might be *reduced* to the slightest gesture, the way a child may wish its simplest tear might bring immediate care. And it may suggest to some that the desire to be personally known is not unmixed with a desire to be personally unknown. As if we might merge, dissolve ourselves into the post-modern's network of signs.

Perhaps that is too generalized, too extreme. To qualify and sharpen the details, it can help to think briefly about some of the qualities of online exchange. Whatever the site we visit – whether it's devoted to the day's news, plane bookings, the life and times of Charlemagne, NFL football, Kreuzfeld-Jacob disease, refrigerators, the philosophy of Heidegger, dolphin-empowered consciousness, or how to build a rocket – here is a 'space' where connections are swift to form, since the venue (the 'field') inherently and instantly determines the participants' shared interest. 'Connectivity', as Bill Gates – the last quarter of the twentieth century's 'most successful (and certainly richest) man in the world' – long insisted, is what the world wants and will pay most for. Again, we put our money where our mouth is.

But if communication is what is wanted, it has a distinct new disposition. From the outset, the conceivable range of the user's *control of connections* – and the value placed on control – is greater than ever before. While electronic messages travel with lightning rapidity, they can be *dealt* with as *slowly* as the 'communicant' desires; one may respond this minute, tomorrow, or never. This has, in online exchanges, marked side-effects. Misunderstandings are rife and volatile, and scarcely in fact because of the inadequacies of smileys: more because of the parameters now set for each 'relationship' itself. Most of the constraints that applied in the past in the choice of interlocutors – such as timeliness, geographical amenability of meeting, even physical appearance – are simply missing. One can steer clear of (de)selected others with ease. In online groups elite clusters form and the balance of power shifts swiftly; an 'other' who's the centre of the group's attention one month is likely to be totally unknown to virtually all those meeting in the same 'place' the next; persons are identified in speed-of-light semi-fictional stereotypes, are assessed in terms of their information, and often when the desired 'data' has been secured, 'partnerships' may dissolve overnight. The implications of what can be called a new, socially volatile 'Net effect' stemming from this conflux of a plurality of voices are potentially vast.[32]

A representation of the 'information superhighway' much in circulation in recent times has been that to an unprecedented degree we can now extend ourselves into something resembling 'infinite space', and not only go where we wish and when, but 'lurk' (as surfers say) in what shape we may wish, take and leave what we wish, read/apprehend things as we wish, and withdraw, never seen. We've found pungent reasons to interrogate this hope and ask who hopes it. Communications are both increasingly *expansive* in imaginable scope and increasingly *'narrow-band'* in practical character. The traits of the developing forms of exchange to which postmodern culture responds are typically shaped of course by the technological, but even more by the *human* 'bandwidth' that postmoderns desire for their contact with others – and the favoured objective is not that this 'human bandwidth' be increased but that it be decreased. What is most striking about this phenomenon is how it enacts a tacitly guarded wish for the sensation of confluence and universal accord.

Few developments in the way people 'relate' to one another can better dramatize the restive flux and reflux of the hunger for union with the hunger for space. The quest, that is, for infinite connection (and for situations in which one may be attended to with approbation or not at all), coupled with a hypersensitive (if not paranoid) self-concealment – with the shallowness of emotional/interpersonal engagement that this unique combination entails. It seems just possible that some of the most urgent fantasies of omnipotence that can fleetingly sweeten the anguishes of the narcissant are enacted here.

There is yet another dimension to the human project of creating smoothly confluent but highly selective, reassuringly field-sensitive self-identities in the coming communications world. The potential in cyberspace for the multiple representation of our selves – the incorporation of ourselves in many 'virtual' forms in ways that digital communications make easy – is one that has been powerfully advocated in recent times.

As it's put by Sherry Turkle in one of the most thoughtful arguments to date, *Life on the Screen*, advancing a view in (ambiguous) support of a postmodern decentring of the subject, "the culture of simulation may help us achieve a vision of a multiple but integrated identity whose flexibility, resilience, and capacity for joy comes from having access to our many selves" (1995: 268). By means of a variety of multi-user software programmes (most often called MUDs), individuals on line are invited to allow to come to the surface, or to invent, widely different persons for themselves with different names and thus, in the shelter of anonymity that the Internet makes possible, live out different personal relations with the other 'persons' they encounter there. The spreading popularity of MUDs in increasingly numerous communications and games contexts is significant. By sharp definitions of their selves to suit different occasions, the constraints of reality with which narcissants struggle are radically reduced. Inventing roles and inventing roles to support or replace those roles, to the extent of chasing after fantasied lifestyles (and lovers) through digital dreamscapes, the individual is encouraged to "redefine healthy identity not in terms of a core identity – of a one, of the integration of self into a one – but as someone who is comfortable with the many aspects of self, the many roles that we play".[33]

Anonymity, self-concealment and self-construction have still more materially telling new effects. On the Internet, for example with regard to commercial pornography and gambling, the enormous increase in numbers of people participating – as recent British statistics have shown concerning the historic rapid growth via the Net in women's gambling – are clearly owing in large part to users' being able to control the conditions in which they represent themselves and where their experiences take place. Instead of going into a (traditionally macho) booking shop or a brothel and physically handing over cash, in online gambling and cybererotic exchange those who are 'wired' can deal in invisible electronic cash any time, any day or night according to choice, with what seems like total anonymity, in the comfort of their own homes. The individual extends him- or herself around the entire world of material and imaginational environments according to desire and with 'total' plasticity of self-presentation.

Most people who've spent a reasonable amount of time on line will have been 'accosted' there by at least one 'person' posing as 'someone else' (a man as a woman, for example), with one or another of the conceivable, often dramatic and even legally (not to say ethically) significant effects. That is not what writers like Turkle have in mind as ideal (though it is an ever-increasing reality of which they're aware). What raises their vision above this level is their aim, which is precisely to address the coalescence they intuitively perceive between postmodern theory and the dilemmas of contemporary narcissance. The MUD solution is a thing to which we'll need to return.

* * *

We come now – as contemporary culture has – to that juncture where the eidolon of 'incorporation' becomes a literal, material project, where the *description* of our selves as 'constructs' oscillates with a *prescription* for the reconstruction of ourselves. As never before, the human physique is treated as a proper object for engineering, and the fusion of postmodern technological and narcissant fantasies here has become explicit, profusely illustrated, and one of the most ardently discussed topics of daily life.

It requires no special savoir to observe – since it's a cliché of everyday parlance – that self-image management is one of the fundamental activities (and one of the most lucrative industries) among humans in the 'developed' world. The time and money spent on the manipulation of our appearance and sense of wellbeing through exercise and diet alone is now proverbial. In this the collaboration of the medical establishment and commerce (from the marketing of media idols to foodstuffs) – and indeed, of the solemn pronouncements of government – with what has been widely called our personal 'narcissism' has achieved fame and notoriety. The transition from weight-control (with its psychosomatic accompaniments in, for example, anorexia and bulimia) to cosmetically manipulated shape and colour control has been an easy, almost unnoticeable step. What lifestyle can't fix, we feel cutting and pasting will. The rapidly developing strategies of medical engineering, designed to keep us going and keep us well, have tended to merge with those addressed to the repair of our appearance; we not only slim certain parts but inflate the bulk and outline of others – our eyes, cheekbones, lips, chins, calves, buttocks, breasts and penises – and inscribe and pierce our skins' surfaces with ritual tatoos and stud-glinting mutilant glamour. More bodies every day are laden with foams, jellies, rubbers, rare metals, gases, silicon, glass and other sand by-products, polyvinyls, jewels – both internally and built into our eyelids, teeth, tongues, genitals and navels – and with springs, motors, computer chips, clocks, radios, loudspeakers, and considerable portions of other peoples' – and animals' – bodies. Of chemicals, beyond those designed to control the pace of our organs and the flow of our fluids and to pacify and excite our self-attitudes and our imaginations (including our attention, our mania and depression, our apathy and our paranoias), we ingest and inject 'lifestyle drugs' meant to manage our hands' shaking, bleach and darken our complexions, thin and thicken our muscles and hair and swell our breasts and our erections. We change our sex, our apparent size, age and race. Increasingly, leading our lives as a people whose psychic survival feels ever more uncertain, we are assured that a swift attention to preserving and strengthening the fabric of our physical being by artificial means will hasten to our ultimate rescue. We must each 'get a new life'.

As a companion to these developments, there is scarcely better evidence of self-preoccupation in contemporary society than the outrage of moral conservatives against the surrounding culture's investment, particularly in America, in psychotherapy. In his grandiose resentment – '*I* have to do it / I can do it myself / I don't need anybody caring for *me* ' – Unqle Trim gives himself away. America's psychotherapeutic culture – the most unregulated as well as the most diversified in the world (where everything from psychoanalysis to daily submersion in a light box may be treated with the same degree of regard) – at once lays itself open to just such objections and defers the possibility of its intelligent critical assessment. In the name of self-improvement we adventure into the often simultaneously anxious and ecstatic project of redesigning (as we often declare) our 'identities'.

In our attitudes toward our own mortality, the impulse may well have extraordinary material effects in the future, through the public's steadily growing investment in the technologies, for instance, of cryogenics and human part-replacement by cloning. I regard my true self as yet-to-be-realized – as disabled or neglected and stunted by circumstance – and I dream I can be reborn into a world that knows how to attend to me, into a time when medical assistance can take hold of my fate and bestow on me the condition and fortune I deserve. Here in popular culture the *tekhne* of the postmodern and that of the narcissant *tekhne* converge. The hope that a recovery of the self by a return to the body as the original, native site of the sense of being – where the 'firm, restored' body confirms in its integrity our inborn whole(some)ness – leans relentlessly toward the fantasy that by 'reconstituting' our bodies we can 'reinvent' our very selves.

But the 're-conception' of self actually oscillates between two quite different dreams. According to one, the self is to be recovered as unique, as distinct and separate from others and their portents. But according to the second, the subject comes to 'know itself' as an entity more thoroughly *merged* with the world of other bodies and minds. Where – both as postmoderns and in our potential narcissance – we're endlessly reminded of the contingent and evanescent nature of the boundaries marking out our identities, we convert their fearsome dissolution into a positive aspiration. One of the most enthusiastically and volubly represented of contemporary themes is the revival of rationalist mechanistic conceptions of the human organism, and of the merger of 'man and machine'.

The 'human-machine paradigm' is a flourishing motif in, for example, the manifold musical forms of techno, psychedelia, space and electronica. But this is not 'mere child's play', nor is it only 'a game artists play' (where, as happened in England in 1998, for instance, an artist came to public attention when he was jailed for stealing human body parts for use in his sculpture). With cybernetics – the ensemble of theories and systems relating to the interface between human and technological activity – in vigorous visions of *virtual reality* and of the *cyborg* (cyberorganism), humans not only play with machines and play like machines but are to become machines and integrate with their counterparts, machines becoming human. (The postmodern fascination with the automaton and with the 'humanoid' – whose implications in narcissance we've seen – enter the realm of the 'practically real'.) In virtual reality, by means of computer-linked sensory-activation equipment the individual is 'plugged' into an artificial environment where the physical sensations of an alternative verisimilar world are induced; what reality can't be, virtual reality promises to be.

The 'hitch' is the human body we hitch to those virtual surfaces; for postmoderns as for narcissants it will never be enough until the body itself can conform and merge with those promises. On information technology's wishlist, the ultimate transformations must be those involving the cyborg. That is, where a "seamless boundary between the body and technology" is developed (Tomas 1995: 39). The distinguishing central objective of cyborg operations as opposed to VR experiences is that what's at stake is not merely "transport[ing] our nervous systems into the electronic environment" (Heim 1995: 75), but that the material, physical properties of existence including human bodies (which in a cybernetic perspective are, after all, only 'a matter of information') may be subjected to potentially infinite electronic manipulation. Matter – where the machinic and organic merge – is massaged into new effectively 'real' forms and behaviours.[34] As numerous recent writers have said, in a cyberworld the "'subject' constantly revises its identity through a sampling process: 'wrapping itself in the changing fashions of the mediascape, mutating to the mood of its environment'"; we "retune the body's signifying surfaces from one moment to the next: this is the burden of a corporeality brought up to the speed of the fashion industry. 'The mix and match body, therefore, as [sic] the new body type for the age of recombinant culture'".[35]

There is no reason for surprise now in our finding this an exact dramatization of the attitude of interminable field-dependency. As we are always to understand from the very project of cybernetics as a whole (whose sphere of activity, finely analogous to that of narcissance, has from its inception been precisely the development of communications and control systems), the motive, far from finding the subject indeterminate, is to render it more *controlledly plastic and responsively determinate*.

Early experiments have been dour. In one of the most widely publicized examples a subject stands on a stage or is suspended naked from a wire above the observing audience, his facial and bodily muscles wired by electrodes to equipment the spectators remotely control; his body/machine is made to twist, wriggle, jump and grimace at the crowd's button-punching pleasure. There are few ways to stage better the heroic ordeal of the narcissant's everyday performance. It may be no accident that, further, in the name of pushing the envelope, human/machine experiments with striking frequency involve events entailing what would normally be called pain. Significantly, in its so-far modest triumphs, the undertaking reenacts ecstatic postmodernity's special mode for the management of ambivalence. By means of its 'electrifying' acts, the two, pleasure and pain, seethe down into a molten unified thrill, in a manner that unmistakably acts out the narcissant's turbulent psychological – and the postmodern's similarly turbulent theoretical – ordeal in which the ambivalent/contradictory relations between subjective experience and material performance are suffered and celebrated.

A feature not to be missed is that, at variance with much poststructuralist and postmodern theoretical thinking, in this oscillant ecstatic mode there is a positive effort to *deny surface and refuse superficiality*. What is wanted is not to expunge the illusion but, to the contrary, to bring the illusion *into the body*, to bring into coalescence the artificial and the organic. In alternation with the accentuation of irony there is an effort to *reduce* irony. (The Deleuzian body-without-organs bids fair to return in material form.)

On a website dedicated to the work of Stelarc (the most internationally famous and among the most articulate of high(ly) wire(d) cyborg performers – as opposed to 'pure theoreticians') appears this slogan as its logo:

CONSIDER a body of Fractal Flesh, a body whose agency can be

> electronically extruded on the Net – from one body to another body elsewhere. Not a kind of cyber-voodoo; not merely of remote control but of displacing motions from one physical body to another Net-connected. Such a body's awareness would neither be 'all-here nor all-there'. Agency could be shared in the one body or in a multiplicity of bodies in an electronic space of distributed intelligence. . . .[36]

Meantime, as another has put it, contrasting life on the Net with life in 'meatspace' (the 'real' or 'natural' biological world), "we are all just bits and bytes blowing in the phosphor stream".[37] Wherever in postmodernity (as in narcissance) there is an impulse toward some intensified sensation of a sharply defined unified personal identity it is accompanied, in oscillation, by an equally extreme impulse to dissolve and disperse – to release – the sense of finite personal being in the medium of some cosmic totality. It is a fantasy whose oceanic aspiration we know well, and whose narcissant echoes we'd be mistaken to miss, particularly since here they aim to prepare a future to which we're all warmly invited.

Expansion – toward Homogeneity

The brevity of this section reflects more than the fact that the preceding lengthy passages on recent technological developments will already have intimated much of the expansionist ('hyperistic') quality of postmodern activity in its ecstatic aspect (where we find an equally powerful impulse toward expansive homogeneity in oscillation with the impulse toward heterogeneity explored in part one). It signals still more my hesitation in speaking of another, *counter*-technological urge toward unity calling upon us today. This hesitation stems from my unease in applying this essay's model to a constellation of movements whose energy is unquestionably devoted to the matter of our very survival on earth. But – to be consistent – try it and apply it I must.

As in narcissance, where categories of identity (what's dead is dead, what's past is past, what I am is me) dissolve in the churning wake of contradictions, what is often in postmodern discourse said to be left – and to be defended at all costs – is the uninterrupted and eternal continuity and flow of nature. Extinct moas, like all those flora and fauna now living and threatened with extinction, can't be classed and sorted as noxious or nice and reproduced or erased according to taste. They are nodes in the web, elements in the whole on whose very unity and coherence our survival depends. *Separation*, in this view, *destroys*.

Here then is a new meaning – or rather, another role – for the conception of globalization. Alongside our schemes for an ever-expanding hyperspace come visions of our physical world as a drop in the continuous sea of the universe. An organic holism is called for; movements gather for the restoration of the dreams of one language, a Whole Earth, the planet as Mother, the universe as Gaia. Our battle to save all species is to save ourselves, for they're all part of us, and the waters we fight to purge of pollution are the same as those out of which we were born and that run through us still as life itself.[38] As I've mentioned, we sit before light-boxes simulating the psychic-curative powers of the sun, Feng Shui our homes, give 'hug' time to the embracing of the boles of trees, swim and sing with dolphins, we dream of a fruitful engulfment in the sea (the mother?) of supply, in the iridescent many-splendoured prism of Creation, in the continuous universal One.

I've no wish to argue with this, any more than with the vision of a utopian world where hyperspace is to become our 'natural' medium. Yet not everyone has the same dream, and this oceanic order of dreaming has about it some traces of a familiar process of thinking.

It is rare, in fact, that arguments for the fostering of the environment aren't ultimately framed by or rooted in the proposition that a fragmentation of nature means a fragmentation of our *selves*. Here it can be sensible to refer back to a few of the features of narcissance. One that we know of is the insistent anxiety of *doing damage to the other* like the damage to oneself that one fears; I must be gentle, tactful, tender even, or I will destroy you. In a fantasy of omnipotence that is the other side of helplessness in a world felt to be in chaos, merely a word, a gesture may be lethal. In narcissance the *suffering and destruction of the others* is our suffering and destruction. A species of identification, of magical thinking, prevails – and with this, there is a measure of slippage into grandiosity. In view of the sheer immensity and power of the forces of the actual natural universe, in our more extreme forms of New Age anxiety to preserve the environment we may be thinking along rather unique and exceptional lines. That, for instance, if we don't stop feeling for Nature, She will stop feeling for us.

Contemporary environmentalist and ecological thought – which I mean to defend elsewhere against certain postmodern effects – is associated with a genuine and profound love for nature. (This is so even when it may be felt that some of its representations of 'nature' seem not to include all of what humankind is, and that here actual humans are not infrequently treated to manifestations of rage peculiarly resembling ones directed at grossly negligent parents). And it is true that we are in grave danger of damaging our species' chances of survival. Yet 'Nature' will go on, even if humanity is destroyed, just as human life will go on even if the individual infant is (in someone's mind) left infinitely vulnerable. Are we sure that in our most radical gestures we're not projecting onto 'nature' something that belongs to the human child-mind? Might it be useful, even wise, to distinguish among these?

A feature of narcissance is a predisposition to hypochondria, and with it its obverse, paranoia. Is it possible that, in our concern for the environment we make increasing (and not infrequently beneficial) use not only of the hypochondria but of the paranoia – that is, the sense not only that 'my body threatens me with its mortality' but that the world outside does the same – that narcissant processes put at our disposal? A landmark in history is the degree to which, in a time when in health and longevity we have never been so 'well', fears of epidemic infection, toxic pollution, and pandemic genetic damage appear to shape so much of our thinking. Here public and private preoccupations converge; we appear to feel ourselves both collectively and personally to be inadequately bonded and bounded, just as a narcissant may. That is, the bonds joining us as humans seem insufficiently strong, and the delicate barrier between us and our environment (the 'field' in which we live and act) seems insufficiently impermeable, to withstand invasion and annihilation. Can there be connections between this cluster of sensations and those of narcissance? Wherever we experience intense and growing anxiety, to the point where we believe we have no 'natural' defences to save us from the effects of our own 'artificial' and manipulative actions, we may be mistaken not to ask regularly 'What *precisely – and in full, in all its dimensions* – are we afraid of?' When these combine with what may sometimes seem an inclination to stretch compulsively for an infinite Eden, it can help to give a thought, without prejudice, to this unusual constellation's implications.

Oblivion

An experience on which everyone seems to agree about postmodern life is that it makes things disappear. Noteworthy among the things it 'disappears', we like to say, are space, time and human identity. This act – strangely recalling magical thinking – is a hard one to follow, if only because it seems hard to 'follow' where it comes from. It should seem obvious that if we didn't want 'real' space, time and identity to go away, we wouldn't put so much energy into making it happen. Who would want the 'usual stuff of reality' to go away?

Certainly we do this partly in a spirit of play – and there's every evidence that we'll pay a great deal today for the chance to play. Computer games, worldwide, now gross more profit than the film industry does. Half of the entire revenue of the vast Sony Corporation, whose practical appliances fill millions of homes, is from the sale of playstations. As we flash to an infinite array of other-wheres, through *worlds in our control* – whether in videogames or in cyberspace communications or in virtual reality – it appears that those we converse or play with across space, *in order to function* in these contexts, tend to 'fade' into semi-fictions for us, bearing just as much reality as we feel inclined to confer on them. And we're not uncommonly heard afterward to say that we'd 'lost all sense of time', 'I totally forgot where I was' – and, perhaps most revealingly, 'I *lost myself* in what I was doing'. To which those who 'don't understand us' sometimes reply that we were 'just killing time', if not 'spaced out'.

Whether or not we do kill time and space when we play, a kind of 'hard reality' does enter here. Throughout his monumental and richly documented work *The Information Age* the world economist Manuel Castells argues that we have in the most material terms and with immense material consequences moved irreversibly into a "spaceless space" and a "timeless time" (1996, 1997, 1998). One of the things that bankers and military tacticians as well as sociologists and moralists point out about crime and war in the electronic age is that there is a significant decrease in what in life before may have been an important crime-deterrent; the intended victim is no longer 'material'. This was the point made when what NATO did in Iraq and in Kosovo was in the 1990s called "postmodern warfare".[39] Here was another ideal (and no doubt sumptuously significant for the future) way of getting rid of the subject as agent. If there's no (visible) victim, there's no (visible) criminal, no 'perp'.

It is not difficult to find a certain *frisson*, another thrill, in these developments. We can feel the mix of excitement and anxiety – two sides of the same coin (as psychology reminds us) in narcissance.[40] We feel anxious about what is potentially exciting, and by our consuming excitement with the new we (in narcissance) may extinguish our consuming 'old, inveterate' anxieties. By a kind of 'elective mania' we may hope to obliterate by the sheer *fascination* with things not only other persons and their apparent needs and demands but the exigent contingencies of the field, of time and place themselves.[41] We may blot out the perplex of self-demands (life is real life is earnest, I must be lovable, I know my place, time is of the essence) in the magical phantasm of a finally unselfconscious, virtually childlike spontaneity.

It shouldn't be left ignored how such beliefs in involuntary desire – notions of an ineluctable impulsion beyond consciousness and beyond self that are also characteristic of the vitalistic strands of postmodern thought from Lacan and Deleuze to De Landa – often prove to be essential in 'rescuing' narcissants from the impulse to suicide.[42] Postmodern enthusiasm-without-optimism may to a considerable extent reflect 'positive' instincts of this sort – though it's worth considering that without narcissance the most urgent call for them would fall away. On a less encouraging side, it is 'elective mania' and the impulse toward oblivion that finds postmodern lifestyles vulnerable to the popular conservative charge that they invite intellectual vacuity.

This brings into the foreground a force in contemporary life discussed by many with varying degrees of animation and concern, depending on their particular preoccupations, but whose reach is rarely remarked. We've noted it so far only in relation to consumer culture, where observations of 'shopaholicism' and its implications have gained prominence. This is the matter of *addiction*. What is significant is the ever-widening range of objects and activities to which people are reported to be addicted. The extent of so-called 'Net addiction' is now such that there have been academic studies of "non-obsessive Internet users".[43] "Greater use of the Internet", one of these states, "was associated with declines in participants' communication with family members ... declines in the size of their social circle and increases in their depression and loneliness". Accounts provided by 'self-described "dependent" users' featured a particular 'dependency' on MUD games. (Alongside this, the term 'teknosis' has come into circulation to describe more widespread addictive behaviour among not only 'administrators and industrialists' but a growing proportion of the broader public induced into 'compulsive technologistic' thinking and activity.)[44] Where here we may be inclined to laugh (or hope to, soon), there are further forms of addiction – including drug addiction – about which some laugh more than others, and of which more in the 'social mainstream' today than ever in the history of Western culture have some personal experience.

It is often difficult to perceive the symptomatic nature and pervasive implications of individuals' fascination with what to others may seem merely quirky and occasionally irritatingly 'all-absorbing', 'hobbies' or 'habits'. This is in part because addiction virtually invariably entails secrecy – not merely because (as it's commonly believed) it leads to shame but because it can arise out of shame and, in any case, often evolves with a wish precisely for the 'cut-off', circumscribed, 'isolated' experience that is an *objective* of addiction. Some single drug or some intensely localized, discrete activity around which mind and body may finally find a focus becomes a powerfully attractive 'good', as if it might bring rescue from the anxiety of engulfment by the world that so harrows field-dependent lives. Except in cases of iatrogenically induced addictions, it is not addiction that creates an addictive psychology but the individual's psychological disposition that makes way for addiction. It is crucial to comprehend that *'socially induced'* addictions are *not* excepted here, the vital event being that they exhibit all the features of a wish for confluence and extreme social compliance.

It is in narcissance that experiences like these take seed and multiply. Here, any dependency may seem 'ideal' that seems to fill a hunger or a void by its 'consumption' and its surrounding ever-reliable rituals, and that can at the same time yield a sense of autonomy, of control of one's own life. Of being in charge, that is, of one's *sensation* of the world or of some single 'personally owned' area of it, split off and secret as it is.

The root of the word 'narcosis' – *narki*, numbness, deadening – is the root of 'Narcissus'.[45] This connection affects more than simply the insistent anaesthetic impulse we've noted in narcissance. Of all generalized so-called 'abnormal' mental conditions (as opposed to specific compulsions), narcissance may be the one most commonly predisposing individuals to addiction.[46] Narcissance *centres* on issues of dependency, and on the urgent substitution of alternatives in place of a lost 'primary object'. The search seems unrelenting for alternatives that will leave one feeling *independent* of other human beings, that can subdue sensations of loss, loneliness and pain. As psychologists, social workers and addictives' families know, failing *psychological* development, when one addiction is blocked a new dependency almost invariably follows. In this respect, the range of extraordinary, ever newer and more arcane 'addictive substances and objects' to which people turn cannot be cause for wonder. Given narcissance and its quest, it is essential and inevitable.

An illustration of 'today's addictive mentality' that seems to swamp the daily media and public debate is the amount of time devoted by the populations of the regions of the world where post-modern attitudes are most widespread – one third of people's waking hours in English-speaking nations – to watching television. Videogame-playing takes further time now, and it's not yet clear that it replaces hours given to television; studies suggest that these combined with the wildfire increase of time dedicated, in a similar spirit, to surfing and gaming on the Internet – each activity frequently avowed by users to yield hours that are gratifyingly 'mindless' – often actually replace not only (home)work- but inter-personal-contact time.[47] Problems arising may increase steadily without notice since – because it would appear to involve no economic loss – there are no institutions disposed to take concern (except of course the traditional ones of community and the family, whose future is in any case in question).

About the uses of narcotics themselves, *in this context* addiction is not the ultimate issue. Rather, their *effects at the time of use* are still more significant. We return to the word Ecstasy and the drug-of-choice at raves. As it's frequently described, the narcotic Ecstasy (as Sheila Henderson records)

> makes you feel happy, confident, loving towards others, exhilarated, sexy even.... You ... enter a sensual pleasure landscape much bigger and so much longer-lasting than any club you've ever set foot in before. Complete strangers, often from a completely different social group than your own, become your instant friends. Anxiety and self-conciousness are out the window. Ecstasy is something that allows you to ... feel like you belong with hundreds or thousands of other people more than you ever did before. (1997: 47–8)

Rave-dancers express feelings of rapture and of 'oneness' with the 'whole environment'. The dynamic, the drama, of narcissance is acted out here. The finely ambiguous words 'rave' and 'ecstasy' describe both what makes one wish to go to a rave (the complex array of chaotically ambivalent 'raving' emotions felt in narcissance), and the kind of excitement (the pain/pleasure thrill) one seeks in the quest for the obliviation of narcissance.[48]

It seems to me very important – here as elsewhere in this essay – not to attack out of hand what is felt to be a solution for some people, solely because it's felt to be a problem by some others. This is all the more crucial when – as a society, for example – we can't presently claim to have offered to apply any serious alternative solutions to the problem. I'll set out very briefly, then, by way of conclusion to this section, what some people feel to be symptoms in different patterns of contemporary behaviour, and note their possibly unexpected convergence, and leave it at that.

Something else happens at raves. There is music, and dance, and spectacle, and all of these are of a particular variety. Few objections to contemporary ('youth') culture are more common than those lodged against its music and dance and the settings and machinery of presentation and behaviour associated with them. People say that the music's 'relentless and overwhelmingly deafening volume and "monotonous" machine-like beat, its words' "meaninglessness", the dancers' close-crowded unceasing "expressionless robotic gyrations", enveloped in darkness and fake "smoke" and the blinding light of laser sweeps and flashing strobes' – that these 'numb the brain', and that the traditional lyric, *personal* embrace and personal *emotions* have gone out of music and dance, to be replaced by sheer *'demented', 'mindless' motion.*

They are in fact stating not what is a 'bad side effect' but the primary effect. These aren't signs of an inevitably deteriorated, uncreative quality of music in our times, but an altogether different conception of music's purpose. The conception's starting point is, what is music for? And the answer is, what always distinguishes music from all other forms of expression: it touches vital, elemental, visceral rhythms and chords directly, immediately, unmediatedly. Not only is its value incommunicable in abstractions, in words, which are only obstructions to music's intrinsic effect and function (says this answer); it is actually an error to think that *emotions* – love, desire, sorrow – specific relations between individuals – weren't also obstructions in exactly the same way. They produced conceptualized, themed situations and settings, from which music ideally should untrammel itself as rapidly and thoroughly as possible, so that those 'vital, elemental, visceral rhythms and chords' can be broached – so that the body itself can be directly 'moved' (not in emotion but in motion) into dance. In this context, music and dance and setting – especially combined with narcotics and the neurochemical secretions known to be released in the body (and which narcotics simulate) by prolonged unaltering repetitive motion and anaerobic exertion – achieves exactly that. Here is a culture acclaiming its 'cool' that – perplexing to outsiders but entirely coherent from the standpoint of narcissance – calls on the resources of sensory welter to anaesthetize intellection and circumspection. Self-consciousness and its defences are 'broken down'. Dancers at raves appear 'demented'? The word – 'out of one's mind' (de-mentia) – coincides not only with Romanticism's but with the postmodern's key desiderata of rapture, abandon, entrancement, transport, ecstasy. There are few terms for which there are more synonyms popular today. Dancers at raves look 'trancelike', like 'zombies', 'automatons', 'robots'? Again, this is not an unfortunate side-effect – it is the *design.*[49]

Like many current designer drugs, to express it crudely, this is part of a sophisticated technology of oblivion. Seen in terms of narcissance, it works to reduce the demands of personality-representation and personal engagement, to produce a sensation of undifferentiated confluence and solidarity among individuals otherwise interminably self-conscious of their separateness, and to induce liberation from the toils of personal affect and the menacing challenges of context and contingency. As it's frequently put in psychological studies with regard specifically to narcotics and their relationship to 'narcissism', an individual's turning to drugs can often express "part of his efforts to throw off a false identity, to destroy … a psychic structure based upon accommodation to the other, and to recover a more authentic self" (Mollon 1993: 58).

The significance of this – I suggest, again tentatively – sharpens when we let our view range more broadly over current culture. In recent evidence accumulated in neuropsychology there appears to be a marked similarity between the effects on the central nervous system of: (1) the specific heavily rhythmic kinetic movement and the high-contrast visual and auditory-nerve stimulus experienced at 'raves'; (2) the independent effects deriving from the consumption of narcotics such as Ecstasy; (3) the effects of video-transmitted images experienced with television (as compared with reading and film-watching) – where, in ways related to differences between 'left-brain' and 'right-brain' processing, the eye/brain activity required seems physiologically to suppress analytic consciousness. Motor sensation is enhanced (or, where video/television is concerned, the energy given to conceptual processing is displaced by the neural cost of image-processing), critical thinking and self-awareness are repressed, and intellectual obtundity and a generalized, expansive feeling of sensual euphoria is induced. There may be some evidence of similarities between these modes of suppression of (self)consciousness and ones thought – at the time of the emergence of postmodernism – to be achieved by 'brainwashing' by means of 'white sound'.

There are signs that the decentring of the subject that postmodernists sought finds its fullest expression in narcissance's flights into ecstasy. It is here more than anywhere that personal being and self-identity seek their own dissolution. Postmodernist theories' common declaration that the end (goal) of desire is the end (termination) of desire may be only a rehearsal of the feedback-loop that we call addiction. The contemporary popular and sometimes compulsive seductions and addictions of narcotic confluence merge with postmodernism's delirious torrential 'esemplastic' thrust toward indeterminacy. And both, it's difficult to deny, may actually be engendered in the narcissant longing for oblivion.

But this needn't be the same as to be bound to live fixed in a state of theoretical aporia, of apathic paralysis where – like the experimental primate sensorily bombarded with an excess of options and retreating into a corner as though it is 'not itself' – the individual is unable to eat, sleep, choose, decide, act, care enough to live. Nor could we ever hope to contribute anything useful to any culture-to-come by giving-over such notions into the hands of postmodernity's rabid detractors. In postmodern culture, we can't forget, there's another side. Along with the 'out-of-mind' abandon of 'raves' there is something else that traditionalists equally decry there: a cool and promiscuous self-conscious irony. In the postmodern, the urge toward a seamless ecstatic communion – like one of the two coiling strands of the double-helix that's so captured the world's imagination, ever twisting and dividing – will always be gyring in a spiral side-by-side with its antithesis: the dividing and expanding, pullulating multiplicity with which it also aspires to fill and blow wide the world or – failing that – 'blow its mind'.

6 Living through Postmodernity

Not since the last century of the Roman empire has a Western culture been so vibrantly and concertedly committed to the pluralization, expansion and diversification of value-codes, tastes and lifestyles. The postmodern not only lightens and enlivens the senses by the variety of experiences it cultivates but – by its deliberate philosophical appeal to the uncustomary – it raises the public consciousness of alternative options as to how personal and social life may be patterned and lived. Sustained by new technologies it encourages unforeseen possibilities in private individual enterprise and invention in commerce and the arts. Rarely has so summer-styled an outlook been shaped in the face – and perhaps by the grace – of such wintry intellectual and psychological conditions.

An extraordinary gift to contemporary society made possible by postmodernity is its reconstruction of innocence. By throwing into doubt the boundaries that allow for the perception of guilt, it has been inclined to liberate many from conventional mores, and people are enheartened to act out desire and 'play' more freely. By assailing foundational thinking it has eased the way for the dismantling of class, national and gender chauvinism and ethnic bigotry, has tended to erode some traditional socio-economic hierarchies and encouraged multicultural tastes and values to flourish. It has been especially effective in attacking the slick glamour-shielded-and-wielded 'clean' sentimental middle-class conformism that first inspired a generation growing up in the 1950s and 1960s to postmodern revolt. Moreover, it makes room on a wide scale for alternative social groupings and a pluralization of modes of social connection. In theory, the perennial difficulty of making oneself heard in any but the violent manner of open rebellion, or by the brutal wielding of hierarchical power, should wane under the pressure of postmodernity. We don't have to be violent nor brutally rich to give vent to our ideas. A postmodern ethos would legitimate, as technology enables, the relatively free universal circulation of our 'intellectual goods', and we should find ourselves freer to 'circulate', to 'put ourselves about', as well, as physical beings. Perhaps never has there been so explicit an invitation to each to be him- or herself in all his or her unique way, yet free of the more concerted forms of the savage '*cult* of the individual' with its sometimes historically devastating consequences.

The key to this is postmodernity's supreme, often powerfully uncompromising and luminous emphasis on *process rather than product*. 'There is no complete truth, no total understanding, no final answer or interpretation – the best thing we can achieve is a rich awareness of the creative *processes* by which we seek to construct these. To devote ourselves to *finishing* is to lose sight of the conditions of meaning and to miss the wondrous dynamics of the *experience* – of sensing, imagining and reasoning. Get a life. Let us celebrate the processes of the moment, of living, of making, instead of obliterating them in the blind fixation on ends, on products.' Where the 'end' is not an issue, one is not required to prove one's right-to-be in some agonistic, survival-of-the-fittest contest. Who says that thinking of a life as a unitary trajectory toward 'the right target' is a good idea? At last we can relax. The postmodern says 'If you wait for legitimation (a meaning, a kept promise) you'll wait forever.' The individual adopts openness, an apparent *disponibilité*. 'I'm not who I am but what I am doing.' Experience is a *mélange* of hungers, and being is a basket of fruit; you seize it – now an apple, later a pear; you are what you eat. Come to the mall. Rather than having your choices defined by your identity and the story you hold in mind for yourself, what you choose defines your identity, and your story unfolds.

Some people may expect trouble here. Questions arise (such as Who has access to the basket?). But with society's resources increasingly on the postmodern's side, we're on a roll. No culture could be more prepared than the postmodern to concur with the technological revolution, sharing as they do in the active promotion of lateral thinking, optimization-via-randomization, anti-normative experiment, an attraction to the proliferation and pluralization of options, and to unmediated, middle-man(agement)-free, local, situation-specific action for the communication and implementation of choice. Where, increasingly, the individual case no longer requires to be argued-through on a metaphilosophical 'macro' level, micro-management multiplied by as many humans as there are *becomes* macro-management. Instead of seeing ourselves as parts of a unitary system, each of us *is* a system of his or her own making – and instead of *conforming*, we *link* as we *like*, with perhaps the proviso only that we make sure that the links between us are operating in mutually harmless or beneficial ways.

We're not, by the way, misled regarding the postmodern's fascination with technology. The postmodern is not futurism. It doesn't make promises it can't keep – which is only what we'd expect of an ethos built on the experience of broken promises. It is simply caught in a tangle with technology – another of those 'offers the postmodern can't (either logically or psychologically) refuse' – and aims to make the most of it.

With this hope burst free all the verve and élan that are released where – when they seem founded in abstraction, eschew complacent personal assertion, and insist on meaning many things at once – they appear socially inoffensive. Scarcely ever has a radical movement so successfully diversified and dispersed its image as to leave the public so safely untroubled to ask exactly what its nominated and intellectually inspired spokesmen had to say. When we're onto a good thing, hearsay will suffice; by the sceptical cracking of the 'atom' of false optimism, the explosive energies of literally unbounded enthusiasm are let fly. And something else is added. In postmodernity there are signs of the heroic. It displays the earmarks of an invitation to *make a difference* and to *change*, even while difference and change are the stigmata of separation. The postmodern seems at the last moment to face up to separation, with all the hard bits – dependency, loss, fear, anger – that it contains.

THE PROBLEM OF CHANGE

Or have we missed something? Nothing is so easy to miss – because it seems so contradictory – as how difficult it actually is for the postmodern to *make a change*. From its earliest days, this has been one of the most popular topics in the discussion of postmodernity and it – the problem of whether postmodernity can actively make a difference – is the subject of the next few pages. I don't mean to resurrect questions here of the validity of assertions about uncertainty, about the decidability or undecidability of value, truth or meaning. As I've said, that is not this book's subject. My interest in mentioning such matters at this essay's start was to call attention to their persistence in people's minds, and in subsequent chapters it was to examine, among other things, what was behind that. If in what follows I summon up the topic once more it's because it has a bearing on what we need to explore now. That is, the extent to which postmodern beliefs can bring about change in our existence in the way that we hope it can and as other beliefs (whether logically valid or not) seem to do.

How We Speak

One of the greatest benefits on which postmodernity stakes its worth is that it releases us from the traps of rigid ideology and from social, economic, moral and political domination. We become more circumspect, we look at all sides, and – revealingly by now – we look over our shoulder. This can make us more open and more tolerant (let us put aside for the moment our perception that paranoia as a rule does the opposite). And most all, we think it can provide us with the most powerful tools for critical judgement by which we can at last hope to prise ourselves free. Well, of course that's not quite right; it is by engaging in the infinite play of meaning-creation – by *relinquishing* 'judgement' – that this postmodern critical freedom is engendered. But now what of that word 'critical', whose root (*krinein*), we recall, is 'to choose, to decide'?

It is most important to keep in mind that whatever I say here, it is not meant to raise doubt as to whether postmodern thinking shapes our lives. The question at hand is whether it does so when and how it 'means' to.

As we saw early, unqualified linguistic indeterminism – if it actually occurs, as many speaking for postmodernity have thought it did – isn't actually 'usable' as a critical analytical practice, since it cannot name a 'crisis', a boundary, a limit or turning point at which it will 'make a difference' what is said, and it can't defend its assertions against opponent assertions. Thus as Derrida has unceasingly maintained,

> deconstruction is not a critical operation, the critical is its object; deconstruction always bears, at one moment or another, on the confidence given the critical, critico-theoretical, that is to say, deciding authority, the ultimate possibility of the decidable; deconstruction is deconstruction of critical dogmatics....[1]

This would seem to give reason for fundamental anxiety about the effective force of practices whose aim is thought to be to problematize the assertive capacity of discourse. Here is a case in point. It has been argued that deconstruction could show that propositions for the 'limited, selective use' of military nuclear power as a deterrent against war are unworkable.[2] That sounds encouraging; but before going ahead to deconstruct nuclear-deterrent propositions, it is sensible to ask, do we believe in the limited, selective use of deconstruction? What 'meta-proposition' (and it must by definition be that) can a consistent deconstructionism offer as the basis for the pre-specification of target-discourses (e.g. pro-deterrence discourse) to which deconstruction would be 'pertinent'? It would be too much to ask for a deconstructionist discourse that could argue in any self-consistent language *for* an *anti*-deterrence programme. But can deconstruction, without interfering with the processes of exposing semantic undecidability that are fundamental to it, name a body of discourse not subject to the same critique? What rules can it allow itself, for instance, to prevent deconstruction from spreading to the *deconstructive* ('critical') text, even where this had been hoped only to propose deconstruction?

This is the postmodern *virus problem*, where – once set in motion – indeterminist thinking, like a computer virus, disintegrates every system it touches in a way that is, by the very definition of indeterminacy, unable to exclude its own system. A sensible response to suggestions that the virus of radical indeterminist thinking can be useful for the selective undermining of abuses of power would seem to be, 'If you like forest fires, let a forest fire do what it does best and forget trying to endear it to civilization by saying it'll also make tea. With a friend like deconstruction, who needs enemies?' I'm afraid we'll find this thought returning soon in other contexts.

Postmodernism in its paranoid mode, its anxiety of betrayal, offers good techniques for discourse analysis. But criticism and practical action, on one hand, and postmodern thinking inspired by radical indeterminism on the other, may actually be destined for an unhappy marriage. As we recall the extremely widespread recommendation of 'postmodern criticism' among recent social movements advocating change (for example, in gender, sex-preference, civil rights and cross-cultural politics), we become aware that this problem is only the tip of the iceberg. It raises an issue of a far more primary and elemental sort. This is the problem of change itself; how we recognize it – or the need for it – when we see it, and how we actively bring it about.

While we know that things are continually changing (we must abandon the fantasy that anyone – some hegemonous group, for example, however 'rigid' – doesn't in fact know and act according to this knowledge), we are continually, moment by moment, through every day of our lives, called upon to act in a way as best suited as possible to a decision-line – a 'crisis' – that is both 'nominal' (nominated, constructed by us) and at the same time has all the force of 'reality' that we can conceive reality might possess. Now I must decide whether to brush my teeth or not; now I must utter the right word for what I want or I will receive something else or nothing; now I must move or that bus will kill me; now my eye is dry and I must blink. 'Crisis points' don't have to feel crucial; but it's by virtue of them that we 'sense the difference', and that change can take place. Instead of a desired change, what we're left with when someone has been engaged in obliterating crisis lines – when we'd thought the agenda was a critical one, to 'see things new' (that is, differently) and 'make some changes' – is the residue: someone desiring to prove that concerted change is essentially 'undo-able'. But why should anyone wish to undo 'signs of crisis'? I'm going to suggest now that it's because they hurt; and I'll suggest in a while that they hurt more than narcissance and the postmodern can bear.

It would be blinkered if not foolish and even dangerous not to take in the impressive range of pleasures that postmodern 'crisis-undoing' carries with it. Bringing at long last the possibility of forgetting history, and the abolition of a delusory anthropocentric humanism, the postmodern can turn into aesthetic objects the furniture of our most painful past. As we know, concentration camps can be converted to low income housing projects, and disused artillery bunkers and gas-chambers made places for public entertainment (theatres, discos); not only Gestapo uniforms, weapons and torture instruments (all special favourites) but the salvaged clothing, gold toothfillings and bones of holocaust participants can be collectors' items; the shadowmarks of Hiroshima victims are featured museum and tourist items for the sensationally and celebratorily as well as the guiltily inclined, and settings of mass graves can provide inexpensive, already often well-maintained and attractive Woodstock-style sites for international concerts, yielding special frissons for the descendants of inmates.

In mentioning these developments – and in this style (where is the pain?) – I've broached an issue I've contrived so far to treat as immaterial, but that is far from that. A reader of postmodernist texts may sometimes wonder what it may actually *feel* like to live as they propose – for example, when writers from Hassan to Deleuze recommend 'schizophrenic thinking'. It can be hard not to ask, 'Mightn't it hurt?' This the matter of *distress*.

It isn't easy, bringing this up. My approach is not that of a therapist; if nothing else, I have strenuously declined to make free with determinations of 'abnormality' and 'illness'. Deeply cognizant of how positive forms of resistance can be abusively suppressed in the name of the public management of mental illness, I feel that, at the very least, all such terms must be vigorously scrutinized for resonances of authoritarianism. In speaking of narcissance itself, wherever possible I've resisted reference to terms – fundamental to psychological theory and practice – such as 'disturbance' and 'disorder', feeling that these too readily presumed norms of mental arrangement and order. But it must be recognized that this practice is always itself at best a polemic deception, partly because it actually entails the deliberate *concealment* of essential aspects of experience which it's our burden in life to acknowledge, and partly because it is impossible to conceive how any argument against oppression is not itself founded entirely on some outstanding presumption of distress.

In the end, then, the enormous problem of personal human suffering cannot be indefinitely brushed under the carpet, and will have to constitute a part of every future assessment of postmodernity. Articulations of suffering are an important part of human experience and discourse. (Indeed, we could not manage to survive danger without sensibility to pain.) For reasons I hope to have made clear, a feature of postmodern discourse is its inclination to 'bracket' if not suppress or extinguish these. In so doing, postmodern culture is disposed to avert its gaze – in a way that is incompatible with its claims to openness and all-inclusiveness – from a major and not only poignant but pregnant aspect of human existence.[3] And most important for the present, no account of any form of the mind-style that's the particular subject of this essay is not inextricably associated with clear expressions of distress.

As it happens, if there is any identifying point above all others at which postmodern thinkers and narcissants meet – and differ from thinkers of the previous two hundred years – it is that they cannot write, cannot speak, about the fullness of distress or argue-through the relative merits of different ways of responding to it. The implications of this are momentous for any idea we may have of active change – of *change*, that is, *by choice*. The issue at hand is conflict, and how we feel about it. We cannot bring ourselves to a point of change without perceiving conflict – the difference, the line of crisis, between what is and what's wanted.[4] And with this there must be distress – the letting go, the daring to enter, the pain of what is, the pain of what may be. By this I don't mean the sentimental/philosophical 'Ah life! it always – incidentally, along the way – includes pain.' I mean that *for there to be change* – of any sort we might call chosen, and might regard as growth – the experience of stress is integral with it. *Distress is met at the growth edge*, and is a primary way in which the possibility (or necessity) of change and growth is *experienced and joined*.[5]

Put in banal terms: as the trainers of those 'body-builders' of the last chapter will know, the exercise that stimulates growth – for example, of muscle and bone – entails the triggering of neurochemical signals of stress and in fact of moderate injury. This mention of injury will have resonance for us, and also makes way for some clarification of the problem. As the conception was developed by Lacan, the grief of separation and loss leaves an inexpungible wound, a scar. We've seen this at work in the broader perspective of narcissant injury as a whole. But this wound, this 'lack' is also the cicatrix – in plant biology the mark of separation – that is the mark of the *essential* event *that makes the sense of self possible*. 'I' can't see another until I see 'myself' as separate – nor can I see my self until I see that separateness. The cicatrix is not only part of me, one may say; it *is the mark of me*. (The dignity that in earlier heroic traditions was confirmed by the cicatrix of initiation bore with it an important psychological intuition.) It is the mark of *where I became me*. The anguish of difference, otherness, separation, loss, is where I *begin*, where *you begin*. It's not only the destruction, carried with us in every moment, of the possibility of *fixed* identity (since it *is* the emblem of change, of flux, as Lacan was saying); it's also the *start* of identity. It is when you look at the lack as your defining part, that you begin to be yourself.

The conception of our *dissolution* (instead of our 'self-discovery') in that lack, that injury, is the evidence of a narcissant arrest, precisely. The point where a narcissant says 'If I can't be fused with the Other then I'm nothing', is also the point where, instead, one has the *chance* to see that this – the place where one separates from the other – is where one begins to *be something*. (Lacan – sometimes explicitly, often covertly – represented the maintenance of awareness of separation as heroic; but we have no chance of becoming a hero until we begin to see that it marks out who we are, who this person is that could be a hero.) The difference between being a narcissant and becoming something more like a whole (though forever changing) person is exactly that the narcissant's stopping point is also the 'person's' starting point. The moment of loss – exemplified not merely at the moment of separation at birth but at the first instant of cell-division – is the moment of beginning, of formation, of growth. It is here, in naming the crisis, in the confrontation with what is 'other', and in the powerful affective properties springing from full contact, that one can commence – if one dares – to 'be' oneself.

The evidence that narcissance underlies a hesitation to take such steps seems irresistible. But the question for the moment is postmodernism's own explicit position.

It would be perverse to say that postmodernity in its 'openness' is ultimately the expression of a desire for a much-needed holiday – retreat, a rest from conflict, from all that stress. But there are acute signs that by virtue of (and not 'in spite of') its radical perspectival openings and its anti-critical uncertainty, it lacks the daring often assigned to it. It risks narrowing and stultifying our experience by skirting the boundaries, since it is there that 'the real action' takes place. In its 'rigorous' rejection of closure, by foreclosing *investment*, it fore-closes the *only way we can test* the relevance of a sensation or the workability of a belief or a dream.

So far as 'real action' is concerned, a place where it is a capital event in our material lives is the realm of social action. Whenever we encounter radical hesitation – an unwillingness positively to confront one view with another (instead of merely 'grafting' views without reserve), an inability to name a crisis (to identify something as wrong and offer a concerted critique), and an unpreparedness to propose (to advance a coherent alternative with dedication) – we are face-to-face with a phenomenon of the greatest importance for anyone interested in bringing about social change. There is no room here even to begin to detail its potential impact, but a few brief remarks may suggest something of the quality of it.

It's not unusual for scholars – on the 'right', 'left' and 'centre' and including those arguing for deconstruction – to say that postmodern thinking will be politically indeterminate. "You could either see a Lacanian position as being ultra-left ... or conservative" (Richards 1989: 28). "Postmodernism" is "both radical and conservative together" (Eagleton 1996: 132). Beardsworth closes his long and meticulous study *Derrida and the Political* by saying that one can, equally and without a way of deciding, imagine a political deconstructionism of the left or of the right (1996), and Paul Smith says that "Derrida's view of human agency is limited in such a way that it could not be adapted to *any* oppositional politics" (1988: 50–1).[6] Indeed, to attempt to assess the postmodern in 'right/left' terms is to be entangled in old habits that are its very target. In a period when communism came to be popularly associated with dictatorship and the collapse of communism in the Soviet Union was celebrated as an 'overthrow of the right', and when the association of Reaganism/Thatcherism with freedom and the 'rights of the individual' against centralized government constituted a radical revolution, the very meanings of the words reveal their inadequacy. If a banner is required to assemble positive forces for change or for conservation, what it must have inscribed on it is not a shibboleth such as 'Right' or 'Left', 'Change!' or 'Don't Change!' but the name of the condition or value one wants to keep or change.

A trait of postmodernism is that this is something it cannot coherently do. We might say that it is up to postmoderns to decide whether that's a problem or not. But this is complicated by the fact that for postmoderns, deciding what is a problem is a problem. (We're obliged now to acknowledge how authentically narcissant such an imbroglio is.)

From experience we recognize that the active use of what we might call constructive 'anti-alignment strategies' – such as the strategies of promiscuous propagation we've seen, of grafting and collage, with their appeals to carnival and to deconstructive polysemy – may disable the organization and commitment of rigidly reactionary hegemonies, for our political liberation. But the outcomes will inevitably be as unfocused and indeterminate as their performance. In this regard, a postmodern politics literally *can't concentrate*. Practical analogues in social and political terms are the emergence of an ostensibly indeterminate 'Generation X' (or, recently, 'Y'), and of a society increasingly disposed to treat elections as occasions for aesthetic diversion at best.[7]

Observations such as this should not be taken automatically as lamentations, but rather simply to point out that the promise of postmodernism is inclined to misstate the case. The overdetermination of values may never be the same as successfully resistant heterogeneity. 'Disintegrative politics' – the overthrow of hegemony by the disintegration of its discourses – infects the 'disintegrator's' discourse by a process that cannot be arrested, and its inability to name responsible agents or their precise dispositions, in relation to any specific effective action, hampers its style.[8] In seeking change of a desired sort it may not be a particularly useful formula, in the long run, to say 'I can't decide'.

Postmodernism as a body of theoretical expressions, inasmuch as it distinguishes itself from other contemporary forms, is incapable of constructing, for example, an open society, of exerting a concerted critique within or upon society for its betterment, or of maintaining and choosing to defend society or itself against assault from without. In its radical indeterminist aspect it cannot selectively 'overthrow' anything without overthrowing everything, and – if it had – would be unable to choose to put anything specific in its place. Insofar as this is a problem to some people, reactions to it range from the uneasy to the inflammatory. They most often take vague and generalized visceral, kneejerk forms that are not productive, and must be subjected to much closer scrutiny in every field in which they arise, as we'll see.

What postmodern culture can do with great power is transmit – among those disposed to listen – the sense that societies are without foundation deserving a differentiated and committed engagement, and imparts an envigorating, searching sense of inquiry for which it knows there can be no rest. At the same time it trails in its wake the trace of a mind-style desiring uncommitment, disengagement and indifference – a style of mind to whose further, unencompassed desires it leaves society entirely exposed. It is to these that we must turn now.

How We Act

For all the encouragement that postmodern life promises for the more spontaneous, uncalculated, in fact incalculable movements of our minds and bodies, we're in the end free only as far as our awareness reaches. An opportunity to think with more clarity – and effect – about how much the postmodern may liberate us to create the world we seek arrives when we consider its connection with narcissance.

It turns out to be delusory to imagine that progress can be made so long as seeing this connection is taken as the end of the discussion. Little can be achieved by declaring the desultory and righteous conclusion that postmodern culture is 'simply marvellous', or that it is 'narcissistic' and that this merely means it is an unhygienic culture of 'selfishness' that must quite simply be crushed. Even the most conservative must realize that they will not make postmodernity go away by calling it names. And because its forms of resistance rest on the principle that it offers no dogmatic resistance, it is not something that can be 'crushed'; whether one's for or against it, it must be negotiated with. This is difficult not just because explicit postmodernist attitudes *propose* 'all kinds of thinking' too indeterminate to bargain with; it is so because they leave us open to quite distinct, further-reaching impulses active in the very process of mind that spawned them and that they *don't* propose, accommodate or 'own'.

I have in mind the potential effects of narcissant processes in several regards: in terms of their role in matters of social contact, social motivation and social practice. Scarcely any style of mind is so potently equipped as narcissance is with the flexibility, fluid mobility, subtlety and range of imaginative resources and physical interactive finesse in language and behaviour needed for meaningful *social contact*. The question is, as with all technologies, how does narcissance actually use them? In fact, with them come ways of managing relations with others that can serve both to *defer* true interaction and to *conceal* that they are doing so. An extraordinary spectrum of powerful strategies for deflection may always be in play.

By projection, by delusory identification, by retroflection, by transference, by introjection, by projective identification, by reaction formation, when genuine exchange is called for – not only in personal connections but on the plane of collective communication and action – social exchange may be distorted or displaced, if not at crucial moments altogether obstructed and suppressed. Mechanisms for withdrawal and the defeat of contact can flourish. Intense forms of self-consciousness can force an unresting attention to and manipulation – both open and covert – of appearances in place of actual feelings and beliefs. The intricate habits of self-doubt and irony can quarantine meanings and decisions to the point where they fail to be 'seriously actionable', where they cannot be lived and traded in 'the real moment' and where, drained of belief, they collapse and wither at the point of exchange. With the extreme impulsion toward confluence with others, and the disinclination to acknowledge difference not only between things and ideas but between people and how they see, say and do things – both as individuals and as groups – the reality of situations can be obscured and even obliterated. This distanciation may be redoubled by the ceaseless oscillation that arises between compliant self-effacement and grandiose disdain.[9] Contempt for others (from whom it's believed nothing is to be gained) and for otherness (from whence critical insights and new ideas of value might be gained), can inhibit human connectedness and authentic change, and forestall the opportunities of individual growth and of collective development.

While the conservative tradition in raising the cry against 'narcissism in our time' is to play up the easy conception that this means the cultivation of personal penchants and private fantasies, that is *not the theme here*. Narcissance entails not mere 'self-centredness' but more complex, dynamic and far-reaching whole patterns of perceiving, feeling and reasoning – including not simply selfish *desire* but, for example, its contrapuntal opposite, *indifference* – that may do more than hedge individuals from one another and individuals from groups. They can serve to cordon off, sanitize and depotentiate interactive relations between groups, and disintegrate the investment in modes of desire themselves – not only individuals' desires but those motivating collective decision and action.

Social motivation itself, then, may be affected in a variety of ways. The de-differentiation of the codes and the conceptions of value and their limits that are essential to a sensation of the need for change ceases to be a 'merely intellectual exercise' of the sort frequently associated with postmodern theory. It may be put into palpable and dramatic action by the narcissant obliviation of boundaries such as those between the real and the fantasied ideal. Postmodern hypotheses of the decentring of the subject may be promoted to powerful psychological reality by narcissant self-uncertainty to the point where the experience of personal agency and responsibility ('who am I to decide, to do –?') is dissolved. Narcissant habits of inextinguishable distrust and of self-and-other-contempt can disclose postmodern theoretical anti-humanism and anti-meliorism to be a potentially toxic reality. The postmodern cultivation of surface, its dedicated repulsion of 'seriousness', its accent on reality as simulacrum, and its 'promiscuous' aestheticization of experience – when impelled by the psychological urgency of a narcissant withdrawal from engagement and committment and the narcissant compulsion to dwell for sheer survival on appearances and on the *tekhne* of dissimulation – can vitiate the belief in the substantive 'real' effects of action. Narcissant parity routines, treating all judgements as having equal latent power, can induce an understanding of the social and political world as a place where 'anything goes' is indistinguishable from 'nothing goes'. Postmodern thinking's fixation upon the particular, the local event to the exclusion of general 'understandings', imbued with the force of narcissant habits of 'splitting', can preclude constructive confrontations. The inexorable oscillation between this and the postmodern's ever-returning alternative inclination to etherealize actualities into ontological meta-theory, and its recurrent leaning toward the esemplastic, can launch the narcissant pursuit of oblivious abandonment in an oceanic all-is-one universe, where the very conception of decision and action loses all meaning. And the narcissant annihilation of affect may silence the very sensation of the need for change, and induce a consuming condition of social and political anomie.

But there is another side. All of these are concerned with the disabling of social contact, interaction and change. Yet as we've seen, except in the most profound depression, in narcissance we don't *do nothing*. Its routines can shape patterns among us of florid activity. We do a lot of stuff; and it's right to ask whether in our actual *social practices* as postmoderns we may not in fact – without principled planning – 'achieve' a great deal. The difficulty is not that postmodernism as a body of thought – of already existing *logics* and *propositions* – throws into question what we mean by 'achievement'. That is so all-encompassing as a conception as to be impracticably empty when it comes to examining social uses. The real trouble – commonly concealed by the flurried popular citation of relativity as the cause of all our troubles – is much less vague. Even before or without questions of what is 'true' or what is 'good' or 'right', *specific narcissant processes of mind* can generate *specific* interventionist mechanisms forestalling the achievement of significant or reliable social ends.

These can best be seen in terms of a relational modality, of social *positioning* – of where people stand in relation to one another. A few examples may illustrate how they function. One is that when narcissance is operating, the rush to uncover sites of betrayal ('But you said—') makes improbable if not impossible the occasion for a confident agreement as to what is happening at a given time. In our treatment of others, chronic narcissant oscillation makes it unlikely that people (or groups of people) can arrive at a conclusion as to who is what in relation to whom. Under the sway of oscillations between idealization and contempt, grandiosity and helplessness, and between descriptive and prescriptive routines – by narcissant pre-emptive remedy or retaliatory or passive-aggressive cross-dressing – we confuse what we think we and others are doing with what we think we and they should be doing, and can confound what we think *is* with what we say *should be*. In a field-dependent, compliant state, by strategies of suitable vacillation – where, uncertain about the relations between proven truth and approbation, we make shift to provide the latter (not proof, but grounds for approval) – we may leave one another never certain what we stand *for*. And in the narcissance that produces this condition, equally inevitable swings toward withdrawal lead us to adopt omnipotent individualist postures of defiance ('I'll do it myself', 'I need nobody', 'everyone interferes with the real me') that place the very possibility of transaction beyond reach. Further, by confusing sincere 'meaning seriously' and ironic 'using seriously', we dissipate the terms and conditions on which we might agree, disagree or compromise.[10]

Beyond these liabilities where direct interaction between people is concerned, narcissance propagates patterns of psychic behaviour that trammel the medium in which exchange might take place. Fantasies of impotence and omnipotence, as well as the oscillation between them, can produce notions of reality and what can be achieved within it that breed sometimes altogether unmanageable problems both between people trying to work together and between those striving to present each other with credible opposition. In addition, obsessional patterns may develop that can cloud and choke communication itself. Narcissant paranoid thinking throws up conspiracy theories that may become irresistible and impenetrable. Pseudo-critical, end-deferring practices can lead participants and their interlocutors to lose themselves in the knitting, and may evolve imperceptibly into torrential uttering or babble. And narcissant spoiling routines, where 'there's always another answer', can leave proffered solutions and resolutions never 'good enough' and lay waste the energy and motivation required not only for the perception of achievement but for any meeting of minds.

None of these outcomes is guaranteed by any postmodern theory. But *all* of them may lie in the offing where the galvanizing force of narcissant processes in the culture – perhaps both beneath postmodern theory and beyond its grasp – are at work. The potential practical implications are far too vast to be expounded within the constraints of this essay. Their urgency in the caring professions – that is, not only in educational environments but crucially in health and welfare – where narcissance plays an understandably vital and volatile if largely concealed role, has never been more critical. Here the otherwise 'inexplicable' nexus between supreme self-effacing altruism and the growing efflorescence of cases of neglect, abuse and violence in the treatment of those in institutional and domestic care are likely to call for increasing attention that postmodern thought is inherently unable to sustain. It may require 'thinking the unthinkable'.[11]

Meanwhile, a few remarks may be worth a moment. One of these has to do with the very 'immeasurable' nature of many of narcissance's effects. Examples are the roles of this in the matters of pain and desire. While it's impossible to quantify different peoples' suffering, the pain a narcissant may feel for others has dimensions of which others may have no experience. It has no limit; no treatment given those for whom the narcissant 'suffers' can ever have enduring effect; the distress s/he feels in them can never be ended. Since its real untreated source is in the eyes of the narcissant beholder, it can colour with anguish all that the narcissant sees; the world itself aches, literally beyond measure. At the same time, while he or she may perform as the most caring of carers, the attention bestowed may have no bearing on the real needs of those afflicted.

With this obliteration of boundaries another matter arises. The complex, contradictory nature of the mind-style reveals itself; the nonspecificity of desire keenly described and not infrequently *advocated* in postmodern discourse reproduces the nonspecificity of desire we've found in narcissance. Not only in theory (from Lacan to Deleuze, Guattari and De Landa) but in common popular speech, a striking development has been a shift from 'We want to do X' to 'We can (and therefore) do X'. The issue is of the shift into the foreground of what might be called 'aimless power'. An important part of the story is the possibility adumbrated in narcissance of an inclination, with the dispersal of identity, to diffuse the explicit desires associated with an explicit identity. Trying different desires arising with different roles, aiming to be a 'man-for-all-seasons', to 'have something for everybody' and to draw on the energies of all, narcissance can inaugurate a quest for something like raw power in the place of directed power.

The phrase 'aimless power' is not to be confused with ones taken from the age-old lexicon of traditional discourse full of catchwords like 'pure greed' and 'unadultered evil'. ('Greed' isn't far away, as we now know – as a generalized orality, an omnivalent and omnivorous hunger; but there is more to it.) It is concerned with a quite precise psychological condition in which issues of dependency and omnipotence are in operation, and where the very sensation of generalized, infinite desire is quintessential, keeping out of the subject's awareness the dilemmas and distresses from which they spring. In narcissance, as we know (and as Unqle Trims highlight by their clamour against 'narcissistic' self-indulgent lust), among one's options a high profile may be accorded to the urge to control. But an obsession with power can be a primary index of feelings of powerlessness. Understanding narcissance, we can grasp how in contemporary culture these unnervingly emerge together in constant oscillation – in the widespread and growing protests (evincing a kind of melancholy grandiosity or tragic omnipotence) that, along with our enormous growing potency in the material world, we have been *'cut off from the sources'* of power.

The future implications of this heady, potentially vertiginous mix of feelings of both powerlessness and of aimless power in postmodern life are impossible to gauge accurately at this point. But certainly some of the most vital issues that they must engage are the relations between postmodern culture and *fundamentalism* and *corporatism* with their branching and spreading strategies and technologies.

THINGS WE CAN DO

It is estimated that some two billion people in the world today lack access to basic health, nutrition and education, and that – according to the same report (by the United Nations Human Development Programme) – the cost to provide this for everyone on earth is less than the amount spent annually in the United States and Europe on perfume and cosmetics. Alongside this, in the past decade of world peace more than 2 million children have been killed, 8 million have been wounded, well more than 12 million have been left homeless, and 1 million have fought, in armed conflicts.[12] It appears that there is room for improvement. In fact, it seems that (with regard to perfume and cosmetics) narcissance plays no small role both in the differentials and potentially (with respect to children's future) in the forthcoming effects of our behaviour on the planet. How, in view of the tendencies I've been describing, can we better our chances for effective decision and action for change and growth in response to existing conditions and to conditions that may arise?[13]

When I use the word 'we' here I don't intend it in a unitary sense, except insofar as, as I'm well aware, many entertain no prospect of effective decision and action of such sorts and needn't regard themselves as suitably addressed in the following remarks. The first evidence that I mean to keep an open-mind about who 'we' are is that I want for a start to name things that we can do that some may decide they don't in the end fancy doing. Several of our present popular concerns and efforts for change may be problematic, and I would like to mention a few examples. These are in the areas of our responses to 'Unqle Sim' (which you'll recall is a kind of acronym for unqualified linguistic indeterminism), to 'Unqle Trim' (a posture affirming unqualified truth in support of a foundationalist moral conservatism), to technology, and to the pragmatics of social action.

Wasting

Though I've mentioned only one, there are at least two different ways we can waste our assets and energies. Blindly, we can spoil them, throw them away without looking into how they might benefit us. We've seen how narcissant wasting can work very much in this way. Or, thinking to be smarter than that, we can use them, but in ways that can't do us much good. Now I'd like to explore a few examples of this second; how we can fall into something like the narcissant whirl.

* * *

'Unqle Sim', as I've said, doesn't really exist, since nothing we say or do achieves unqualified linguistic indeterminacy; but it is an emblem for an aspiration that guides much postmodern thinking and practice. What I want to suggest is that *wrestling with it* will not be helpful if what one seeks is effective change. I've mentioned a 'funny peculiar' but not so 'funny ha-ha' phenomenon that psychologists sometimes experience in dealing with narcissants – that is, the experience of feeling 'bored and mentally paralysed'. This is remarkably close to peoples' descriptions of their experience as they attempt to maintain 'rational, analytical' distance – rather than bringing full empathic curiosity about 'the other' into play – when they strive to negotiate their way through extended indeterminist argument. They feel 'sucked in', in a labyrinth of circular uttering. The feeling one experiences is a clue to what's in play in the situation: a process is at work in the room (the field) assuring that 'nothing can happen'.

What is important here is that, though the narcissant (or the indeterminist) may have set this wrestling in train, nothing can happen because now parties are entangled in the process and neither can break out of its hold, its vortex. This is a way of illustrating what I mean when I suggest that the rejection of postmodern indeterminism on the grounds of some illogicality in it, for example, will not be the most useful way to proceed, even if postmodern theory allowed unproblematically for such tests. In dealing with radical postmodernism one is not dealing with, for example, anarchism, which must name and oppose establishments 'outside' itself. No one discontented with radical indeterminism can reduce or erase it by countervailing theoretical arguments. While certainly we deal in provisional (in)determinacy every day of our lives, the best way that we can do full justice to Unqle Sim is to agree that – quite exactly as linguistic indeterminism forcefully instructs us – we *can't take it seriously*. For example, put in practical terms: fractures or oscillations within the 'subject' may perform a species of resistance to any stable idea of the subject that might be interpellated in a given (for example, hegemonic) ideology; but it is in the constitution of postmodern oscillation as it is of narcissant oscillation, that it cannot *name any specific* transformation, other than unpredictable and continuous oscillation itself, which it might hope or be imagined to inaugurate. It is only if one declines casuistic *wrestling* – but instead insists on *engaging at the contact boundary* – that a way of negotiating may be found. We'll return to this notion.

* * *

It's in the language of Unqle Trim that the most vociferous and popular body of public objections to postmodernity has been heard. It insists that postmodern indeterminism and pluralism may or may not be logically wrong but they are ugly and bad.[14] To understand accurately this movement's assault on both postmodernity and 'the culture of narcissism' (Lasch's famous term, still animatedly in use today)[15] we need to consider not only its unpreparedness to address postmodern theories themselves but its misapprehension of the precise features of narcissance.

Few in the late twentieth century were so finely observant of certain social trends as Christopher Lasch. When he wrote that contemporary writers' 'narcissistic' irony, for instance, was a kind of renunciation of 'seriousness' and 'truth', aiming to "charm the reader instead of trying to convince him" – "escaping the responsibilities that go with being taken seriously", asking "the reader not for understanding but for indulgence" (1979: 20) – we know well what he meant. But in these words at the start of his most famous work and that flood through his pages – 'responsibility', 'indulgence' – there are further resonances we also recognize. (Lasch's diction will become progressively more vehement as the book progresses, speaking of narcissism as "the blight of our society", "exploitation", "thriving on ... adulation", "manufactured fantasies of total gratification"; 50, 51, 231.) Something is peculiar about it. When we observe a pattern in someone's behaviour – even when we see in it signs of 'self-indulgence' and a wish to avoid responsibility – must it immediately and exclusively arouse in us *contempt*? Where have we heard – or might we imagine to hear – this kind of speech? For it is itself a classic illustration of a certain stereotyped behaviour. 'I have to strive day-in-day-out for self-discipline, some kind of self-respect, why should they get away with this?' 'Who do they think they are?!' Who is it that speaks this way?

Here is a language that is familiar to no one so much as to a narcissant child of narcissant parents; the tones by which parents induce shame and an unqualifiedly attentive self-disciplined parenting *from their children*. The person who is most likely to broadcast these injunctions – an individual feeling s/he has enough to cope with, and has least room for others' problems ('pull your socks up!' 'get hold of yourself!' 'straighten out!') – is another narcissant. The voice of an Unqle Trim was always the voice of the put-upon narcissant parent, projecting onto others his neediness, and treating with the profound contempt he feels it would deserve should he glimpse it in himself.

What I say here is not to be taken as a reconstruction of the psyche of any writer. If there can be a culture of postmodernity establishing processes of thinking and stereotypes of discourse, as we've seen, that may be adopted by many with only loose (and certainly diverse) personal biographical causes for their adoption, there can be – and every sign suggests that there is – a culture of anti-postmodern thinking and discourse with the same open relationship to the biographies of its adherents. And with this, if there is a 'culture of narcissism', as Christopher Lasch put it, we need to recognize (as perhaps Lasch didn't) that one of the first things it will do (as individual narcissants consistently do) is display grandiose contempt for – and apply aggressive shaming epithets to – those who show narcissant 'self-indulgence'.

This is the tangle of indulgence and contempt. Clues of its entrance on the scene appear in phrases whose message is 'Stop begging off!' 'Get hold of yourself!' 'You think you've got troubles, you should hear what I have to live with!' It indicates the presence of a narcissant ('A') thinking that s/he sees a narcissant ('B'), and who accuses 'B' of self-indulgence. It doesn't happen only in the kitchen and the hall; it appears readily in people's response to radical indeterminist theorizing, when *for them* the *figure* in the field is 'I've got to go to work/eat/get some rest/check to see if my daughter is drowning/clean the sink'. For them, indeterminist discourse can seem a noise in the street, in the '(back)ground' – a supreme *indulgence*. A self-indulgent mental activity made possible by 'my going to work' – by the grace of '*my* paying the bills'.

The problem is that, as we've seen, no definition of 'indulgence' with its associations with reckless insouciance and abiding pleasure can be made to coincide with the narcissant mind-style we've been considering. It scarcely bears repeating that the 'narcissist' is not the last but the first among us to hear with acute sensibilities the demand that s/he 'get hold of him- herself', 'pull his/her socks up', stop complaining, and the readiest – not to cry noisily for 'indulgence' but – to withdraw into utter silence. This withdrawal suits well the needs of someone (narcissant 'A') caught in the 'indulgence/contempt tangle', for whom it is not possible to let narcissant 'B' be. Whatever s/he's doing, 'B' *must be stopped*. That this process, this tangle, is out of the 'headmasterly' moral conservative's awareness is revealed by how out of touch s/he is with the effects it will in fact have.

There are many useful articulations of how things actually work in this regard. Here is one given by Kohut and Wolf:

> overtly expressed excessive narcissistic demands ... are not the manifestations of an archaic narcissism that had not been tamed in early life and that must now be tamed belatedly. On the contrary, it is the essence of the disease of these patients that the access to their childhood is barred.... If, on the basis of a therapeutic maturity- or reality-morality [one] concentrates on censuring the patient's manifest narcissism, he will drive the repressed narcissistic needs more deeply into repression – or he will increase the depth of the split in the personality that separates the sector of the psyche that contains the unresponded-to autonomous self

> from the noisily assertive one that lacks autonomy ... (1986: 193–4)

The history of how people speak who are involved in this tangle is enlightening. During the 1970s and 1980s when it became part of popular discourse for one person to say to another 'Do you want to talk about it?' or 'Is it something you can share?' or simply 'I'm here' – or to speak of talking to or caring for or holding one's 'inner child' – it swiftly became equally popular to cite this as evidence of the insidious spread of narcissism in our times that must be brought to a quick and efficient end. The naiveté of this as a remedy is apparent to anyone not in the tangle. We know the effect of trying to get a man weeping in grief to buck up and get hold of himself, or to bring a rapist to his senses by keeping mum about his desires and telling him to pull his socks up. But is narcissism 'talking about yourself'? What is difficult but valuable to perceive is that speaking out private angers, fears, feelings of need is actually one of the things that those most deeply caught in narcissant processes are the last to do; and that – for narcissants – *responding* to freely given invitations of this kind to 'let go' may be a courageous act running against the very grain of their deepest impulse. Speaking one's feelings, for a narcissant, may be not the problem but one dimension of the effort to make way for the problem's solution.[16]

Something not encompassed in contemporary expressions of contempt for discourse invoking the 'inner child', for instance, is that feeling one's way through or 'owning' childlike impulses in oneself is *not the same as becoming* a child (and hence contemptible and the last thing a sane adult would want to do). *That* fear is a *narcissant* fear. It unveils an incapacity to acknowledge boundaries and difference, to 'own up' to the inevitable *separation* from childhood and from the fantasy that 'remaining a child' (whether as an ideal or as nightmare) is. It acts out a belief that one can easily sink back into 'being an infant', and it leads to our projecting onto others this fearful – and blissful – fantasy. No one who reads this, for instance, is ever going to be a child again, and the function of inviting the child into the room is to uncover precisely that insight and make room for its implications.[17]

Either submitting to *or* wrestling with Unqle Trim, then, where postmodernity is concerned, isn't something to do without thinking about it. Contempt expressed for narcissants invariably needs investigation. This is not merely because wherever there's contempt there is quite possibly self-contempt that calls for examination, but because – with one exception – contempt, unlike anger, has no positive social function. The exception is that in certain limited situations contempt may suppress fear; and that can occasionally prove handy. But where there's fear there are certainly further questions to be asked.

* * *

Should we throw ourselves into the scuffle between Unqle Sim and Unqle Trim, the outcome is fairly clear. It would be bloodyminded to say that narcissance is just a bell to Unqle Trim's clapper – his own narcissance stirred into gonging action. But in the clash between them, the rights and wrongs in the matter become a matter of indifference. The result – foreseen in that favourite motif of Derrida's – must be 'impasse', so long as the missing element remains unconfessed, suppressed. What is suppressed is that here is an encounter between mind-styles bound (by the identity between them) never to listen to each other – narcissance *projecting* ill-disguised self-defences *versus* narcissance hearing and rejecting that charge, in defence of its own narcissance. It can be no more useful to engage in moralistic rant against postmodernity than it is to rage at it logically, and for very similar if not identical reasons. The outcome will be the same as that for those caught in the indeterminist maze; radical postmoderns and their radical conservative opponents will rave in an interminable vortex. This doesn't mean they're not nice persons.

Why, if there is narcissance latent in Unqle Trim's responses, is there an Unqle Trim – why hasn't narcissance made *all* postmoderns and *no* moral conservatives? Narcissance is not ethos-specific, so far as people's everyday specific normative attitudes are concerned.[18] It will only make sure, in its unique fashion, that – whether under the aegis of postmodern indeterminism and pluralism or of aggressive conservatism – each positive attitude is also negated. It's in this way – not merely because of the well-theorized logical contradictions inherent in political action but because of the nature of narcissance – that *radical* 'right' and 'left' must be locked in a mutually paralysing embrace.

* * *

Should we wrestle with technology? It's not a coincidence that the Frankenstein motif is among Romanticism's most vibrantly active legacies in public discussion today. Many regard technology's power in our lives – technology as a *general fact* independent of its specific products – as a universal menace to be 'wrestled with'. Echoes of an earlier 'narcissant (Romantic) culture' in this area give an invaluable clue that we might do well to scrutinize our more heated reactions to technology-as-a-generic fact. In our debates we may fail to take into account the weight we assign *tekhne* in our mental life when our narcissant processes are engaged. Should technology be endowed in our minds with the complex psychological force that *tekhne* – the eidolon of *performance* – carries in the life of a narcissant, with its full ambivalent burden of grandiose idealization, libidinal investment, shame and raging condemnation?

Technology is one of the fundamental mechanisms by which *Homo sapiens* survives. (For centuries many have liked to say 'by which we "identify" ourselves as "human"', for what that's worth.) No one alive today is not inextricably implicated in that particular 'fold' of human life. The question to answer can never be 'Whether' but 'Which'? It's when we fail to think of technology as *job*-filling that we're in trouble, just as we are whenever we think of art and science as *only* job-filling. In our coming lives, what functions, what jobs shall we assign – or surrender to – technology?

One of our most common habits – encouraged by commerce and industry – is to think we've assigned such specified jobs when we haven't. An example is in the province of 'communications'. Communications in 'the digital age' has as much bearing on the sharing of thoughts as has the expression 'the bathroom communicates with the livingroom'. We may do ourselves considerable mischief when we inflate the value of 'comms' by conflating the sharing of bits, of electrical impulses, with the sharing of meaning. There is nothing intrinsic to our improving 'comms' that says it entails anything like 'improved relations', any more than breaking a hole through the wall between the bathroom and the livingroom is going to enhance relations between the people in the two rooms, especially when one of them is a narcissant. With increased electronic communications all the work, the job-assignment, remains to be done.

The same misapprehension comes with our enthusiasm about the globalization of our lives. One of the more embarrassing habits of contemporary thought is the fantasy that there can and will be only one kind of 'globalization'. Anyone who seeks to advance globalization espouses some globalist ideology for which there are categorically different globalist counter-ideologies.[19] Globalization is never to be a uniform and all-uniting event. In the first wave we have found it convenient to think of it as such – partly because the posture of innocence suits any narcissant (ecstatic) fantasies we may have, and partly because the alternatives are too complex and multiplex in their possibilities and awesome in their implications. Who, acting in keeping with what belief as to what is important, decides what gets 'globalized', at what pace, having what effects on whom?

In the postmodern nexus of 'communications' and linguistic indeterminacy a similarly problematic pattern affects our thinking about 'information'. At a moment when humans are more widely worried than ever about the degree to which 'knowledge' and language are to be trusted, we have also developed the most grandiose fantasies in history about the power of information. No belief in our technological omnipotence in 'comms' will not be in part a deflective fantasy in a culture that from the outset regards as bleak the prospect of individuals' ('subjects'') effectively 'communicating themselves to one another'. We've glimpsed openings, ways toward our coming to grips with this apparent anomaly. One is the observation that it *is* an extreme, oscillating, bi-polar contradiction. And second, that it expresses the central anxiety, and the very process, of narcissant ambivalence with regard to communication, and may deeply inform the array of complex and equally ambiguous 'computerist' impulses around which we increasingly organize our mental and practical lives.[20]

A still more dour problem with technology is that jobs, powers, are already assigned it that we don't observe without intense and steady application. The foundations and public (often formidably covert) uses of corporate power in technology are an issue of ever-increasing material importance – perhaps the most urgent and mordant ahead. The trouble will often be that we feel worried, but don't know which kind of anxiety is involved, or even that there are worries of at least three different sorts. 'Worry One' is that we increasingly collect information without noticing that it's not knowledge (that is, we act on it as though it were organized into some meaningful system, and one that we would naturally endorse, when it's not) and, thus oblivious, we let our actions be driven by some other, psychologically determined routine such as narcissance. 'Worry Two' is that when we think that the 'information' before us is 'neutral, pure' information, when it reaches us it is actually already organized as 'knowledge' and our actions on it are thus in fact not only shaped by someone else's political or commercial interests but may be driven by someone else's still more volatile and pressing psychological routine, of which narcissance is one particularly likely candidate. If any of this is true, a still more fateful event might be that we *didn't* worry about these possibilities. This leaves 'Worry Three' exposed to view. *We* choose what technology does, and where we think it chooses what we do, the case should be scanned for signs of narcissance. Technology does not create these hazards. People do, and how people think is something to think about.

* * *

My continual sense in regarding this essay's abiding resistance to the temptation to consider partisan social and political questions – such as those affecting issues of gender, sexual preference, ethnicity, class and the environment – is not merely that it is 'justified' by the practical impossibility of addressing each of them in this space with the precision they deserve. In leaving these spaces blank I earnestly hope others may feel invited to test and explore unsparingly what's said here about the postmodern in the context of their own fields' concerns.

But it can't have escaped notice that political refuge (or support) is something that postmodern thinking-practices cannot offer. Superficially, some of the most influential traditional terms of political revolt must inevitably be vitiated by postmodern praxis. Many of the negative coordinates that gave sense to Modernist dissent are dissolved – such as *'fragmentation'* (there is no whole to be fragmented); *'alienation'* (there is no essential being from which one might be alienated); *'disorientation'* (there is no absolute 'Orient' or 'magnetic North', no grid of 'true direction'); *'estrangement'* (there is no 'home' or native/natural land from which one might be made '*étrange*, foreign'); and so forth. A further feature severely handicaps movements for radical social reform in some of their more popular forms – where it is often hard to discern motives for adopting 'postmodernism' beyond a paradoxical (narcissant?) longing for cultural connectedness and an eagerness to seem fresh and to accrue charismatic force by a general association with the innovatively dynamic. This handicap is their frequent failure to appreciate the impact of important postmodern themes and habits. (Striking for its absence at crucial times is the necessary awareness of the possible effects, for example, of accepting postmodernism's rupture with the past and with notions of solidarity, and of its irony at moments where political action requires intense affective engagement.) If political action is to be associated with postmodernity, and escape the appearance of mere pastiche of itself (if not the plain blank stares of postmoderns whom activists expect to spring to their side), it must behave in a postmodern way and for postmodern reasons; but this may cost more than activists feel it worth.[21] In 'appropriating postmodern strategies', political actions may easily become appropriated *by* them; narcissant processes can become theirs.[22]

As we know, divergences from cultural norms, far from acting to overthrow a dominant ideology, often effectively conceal ('divert' from) the true force of the established order.[23] Postmodern deconstructive strategies can trenchantly expose such otherwise 'invisible' counter-revolutionary trends; but they are never so intrinsically radical, politically, as is sometimes popularly assumed. They do what they can to dissipate the belief that political action in traditional, partisan terms is workable. Yet this is not anti-political; it favours the political disruption of confrontational, adversarial politics. Those working for a 'cause' (a term that the postmodern would have difficulty swallowing until it had ironized it) are extremely vulnerable until they have met the implications of this.

In fact, it is not unusual for contemporary social critics apparently fiercely dedicated to the overthrow of established systems to deplore the confrontationality traditionally associated with effective political practice. In warmly adopting the strategies of deconstruction, we say not 'I disagree with you' but, instead, 'You disagree with you'. In this tendency to see in the 'ideal (most readily undermined) enemy' the 'divided other' – one who is both despotically grandiose and covertly in conflict with him- herself and who is unready to speak from a committed, dedicated centre – there can be signs of the projections and uncertainties of postmodern narcissance. The refusal to 'speak with certainty', in a broad society where refusing to speak assertively is not the done-thing, can be taken as compliance if not collusion. This is all the more so when others – for example, fundamentalists in the same society though not within the same culture – can be found who show no difficulty in doing so, and who bring arms to bear to prove their ease with it.

Contemporary militants – as well as postmoderns – often readily acknowledge that a species of paranoia must be cultivated if oppression is to be discovered in time. And the paranoia of those with a sense of self can sometimes produce dazzling effects in the political arena; successful leadership often carries strong traces of it. With the paranoiac moments of postmodern narcissance, that is not the case.[24] In narcissance, as in the explicit postmodern, embattled continually by the self-esteem-destroying vicissitudes of social struggle, one may not be expected to maintain the fight for sustainable change for longer than the space of time between seemingly irrational oscillations (a year, a month, a chance morning?) Can there be a distinction we can make use of between narcissant paranoia and aware, 'reality-grounded', socially effective scepticism? It seems that postmodern thinking on its own allows for none. Are there any alternatives? I'd like to return to that in the next section.

We may believe that in a postmodern plural society, traditional monolithic (and megalithic) adversarial party politics of the geographically broad and demographically numerous kind can be replaced by a consumerist model of a less confrontational sort in which individuals – and individual groups – work effectively for their own local interests. The specific features and general quality of our lives are conceived as a matter of 'elective' taste, producing a society whose 'style' is determined by the sheer cumulative effect of the agglomeration of styles of self-regarding individuals as consumers, voting with their wallets (some of whom can afford to 'elect' more decisions, some less). Once again, the variety of models for a plural society are so divergent and each so complex that this matter can't hope to be adequately addressed here.[25] But we can see how such visions of culture are regarded as abandoning ethics for 'aesthetics' – and it's easy to recognize here the vocabulary not only of postmodernity (and its preoccupation with 'surface' and 'sensation') but of narcissance (and its preoccupation with the self). Strange as it may seem, it is not necessary to test this vision by aesthetic or moral standards to see that it's wanting. The question to answer is, should the taste run sour – whether for a community or for any individual – does a postmodern ethos make provision for its alteration – for its improvement, its 'sweetening', say? Postmodernism often proposes quite reasonably that unsavoury power systems are always subject to disintegration by the active deconstruction of the language in which power is enacted. But to imagine that in such a regime some asymmetry will step in to aid the individual, or the individual interest group – that the disintegration of individual self-determination isn't thus equally entailed – is itself an unmistakable narcissant fantasy.

A consistent and often eloquent facet of postmodern thinking is its celebration of the plurality of 'others' of diverse political persuasions. But the special *nature* of each as other is something to which the postmodern can give no critical assessment or empathic concern, and individuals' social and economic vulnerability is something that postmodern thinking cannot 'fix' or address. It warmly accords sympathy to the pluralist spirit that might logically allow them to live side-by-side, but it can neither provide any way to assist in the task of resolving the competition and often treacherous conflict among them, nor defend the body of them against aggressive anti-pluralist forces in the same society or in the world at large. In a sense, within postmodern culture activists haven't a leg to stand on. Once more, with a friend like this, who needs enemies? Members of society seeking to bring about some specific determinate change in a socio-political formation without coming to terms with narcissant postmodern processes, then (even if only to institute the 'right conditions' for continuous change), may as well leave their guns on the wall.

Investing

The ideas expressed here should be seen in the most modest light possible. One of the problems with studies of postmodernity intimating that it has liabilities has often been that, failing or declining to identify processes underlying these, they may be left incapable of suggesting what might be done – beyond pulling our socks up or stuffing our fingers in our ears and screaming – to deal with any dilemmas it presents. What follows is not about ranting or retreating but about listening and negotiating. Without presuming to set out solutions, I can best simply seek to describe things people experiencing narcissance do to deal with it when they feel that its benefits are outweighed by its limitations. If I occasionally speak here of things we can do as though we 'ought' to do them, this is only to give some rhetorical focus and clarity in a few pages to some conceivably useful alternatives to ways of thinking-and-doing that I've described at considerable length through a number of chapters. Above all, even if a positive relation between postmodern and narcissant thinking is acknowledged, narcissance's evolutionary course and rhythms must by definition be unique in every human case. I mean to finish as I began, then, by describing patterns of thinking, and of ways of addressing them, in only the most general way. Some might think, for instance, that here I must recommend psychotherapy. Again, this essay's project is something different. I wish to indicate certain ways of mind that may lay a context, for people of diverse inclinations, in which decisions might be intelligently reached about the appropriateness of any of a number of approaches to the postmodern experience.

* * *

The effects of the postmodern – like the narcissant – inclination toward stereotyped processes of thought are more significant than has been so far suggested. By its displacement of awareness in favour of self-consciousness, generating stock routines for managing appearances, throwing up 'safe' walls around our 'false selves', it forestalls our essential engagement with others and with ourselves. Its oscillation, like its radical conceptual indeterminism, is a protocol for a mobility of thought that feels busy but that obliterates what is figural, stalls choice and freezes positive action. Its cultivation of deflection and (dis)simulation markedly resemble the manoeuvres by which the narcissant inhibits authentic contact with what is new and the assimilation ('metabolisis') of experience, to the extent that – as psychologists often describe – it can forestall developing thought and the ability to learn. Out of awareness, the multiplication of the faces we present to the world in the spirit of compliant response, like the philosophical posture of flexibility and openness, can flatter (us) to deceive (us).

If this seems to be a straightforward criticism of the postmodern, it needs to be considered with care. There can be no advantage in replacing one form of rigidity with another. As is clear in psychotherapeutic work with 'narcissists', if the

> "temporal stability, structural integrity and positive affective colouring of the self-representation" were preserved too well, this would not be adaptive. It would mean at least some denial of reality, and at worst ... a psychotic state of grandiosity. Growth and adaptation to reality mean giving up illusions, allowing change and development and a continual processing of information about self in relation to others.[26]

Alluding to narcissance as 'abnormal', as pathological, needs to be resisted not merely out of sympathy with postmodern anti-normative thinking but because a genuine understanding of the psychological background to postmodernity requires it. The reasons for this are well expressed by Stephen A. Mitchell:

> The concept of psycho*pathology* implies a normative human mind, analogous to the normative physical functioning of the human body, with psychoanalysis as a treatment for deviations. But if each person is a specifically self-designed creation, styled to fit within a particular interpersonal context, there is no generic standard against which deviations can be measured. Rather, difficulties in living would be regarded with respect to the degree of "adhesion" to one's early relational matrix and, conversely, the relative freedom for new experience which that fixity allows. How rigid is the self-organization forged in early interactions? How much range of experience of oneself does it allow? How adhesive are the attachments to archaic objects? How exclusive are the loyalties demanded by them? How compulsive are the transactional patterns learned in these relationships? How tightly do they delimit actions within a narrow border fringed with anxiety? ... [T]he analytic process is not so much a treatment for psychopathology, but, more broadly, a uniquely structured experience which allows the possibility of loosening the inevitable restraints generated by the residues of early experience. (1988: 277–8)

Much of what I say now is meant to focus on the difference between a stereotyped mind-style that brings with it such liabilities as Mitchell mentions, and a style that allows for a loosening of restraints, an extension of the range of experience of oneself, and an authentic freedom for new experience that many might have expected the postmodern to welcome.

* * *

Face to face with postmodernity, some people appear to feel that we need to try a good stiff Heimlich manoeuvre – grab our culture from behind and give it a quick heavy hug to expel certain obstructions (false selves, idealized others, specious fantasies, 'bad thinking habits') that it may otherwise choke to death on. Whatever our aims, in dealing with our minds we can't really do this – we need to be somewhat more resourceful. I'll mention just a few examples of some resources we might turn to.

When we feel that every experience brings with it its contradiction, can we ever do more than 'defer'? One potent answer is the observation that we can let go of the confusion between *ambivalence* and *contradiction*, where contradiction is taken to mean not merely *counter-saying but* – in addition – *reciprocal refutation* or *mutual exclusion*. Rarely in life is there ever, in this sense (anything so simple as), a contradiction. (I cannot think of an example.) Every case for decision comes marked by values that aren't even on the same plane, let alone in opposition. For example, we may think: 'I feel I should go – I feel I should stay'. But the reasons and values attaching to each of these two choices are typically *rich, and not in opposition*. Poised between going and staying, I may be torn not 'between' but 'among': I need money, I'm in love, I want to paint, I'm angry, I can't stop gambling, I'm sexually hungry, I'm allergic to cats, my best friend's death haunts me, I'm scared to say 'come with me', I want a certain job, I'm tired, I want to forget the whole problem. It's on the basis of the *balance* of these that my decision to stay or go is reached. The fact that I feel there is a 'contradiction' in my wishing both to go and stay is interesting (and may indeed feel dreadful). But here the contradiction ends – for it is fundamentally unimportant. It's in the array of other feelings (my love, hunger, scariness, itchiness, fatigue et cetera) that the field is fully constituted and that the issue *begins* to be joined.

Postmodern thinking tends either to insist on sticking to its 'contradiction'/'reciprocal refutation' story (indeterminism) or to let all these many feelings stand (pluralism) – and, in either case, declines to *negotiate* the conflicts it apprehends. In so doing, it perpetuates the narcissant condition. It is in narcissance that the mind can focus only on the *fact* of contradiction or of infinite multiplicity, and on routines of oscillation between extremes or among options in ways rarely having much if anything to do with the situation at hand. It can only stop at the go/stay nexus, evading dimensions of reality that it finds too messily irreconcilable with an awesome phantasy it entertains of completeness, singlemindedness and perfect order. In narcissance, prepossessed with watching the boundary disintegrate under the pressure of confusion, we miss seeing the *formation* of 'contact boundaries' and what is occurring there. But that is where the dynamics of relations and change take place.

If it were never the case before (which is hard to imagine), ours is a symbol-driven culture, and we don't wish to rigidify our symbols. But to keep symbols pliable, we need to know what we mean in each situation, and positively negotiate it. This means seeing and negotiating with narcissance itself in its field. Any time we insist on ruling out (in the name of 'openness', say) the differentiation of our thoughts and behaviour – of their specific shape and character – we obstruct the possibility of 'breaking the moulds', the occasion for just that continual 'transformation' invoked in postmodern culture. What is at issue is a difference between 'openness' as a readiness to respond at the point of encounter, allowing difference to disclose itself and be met, and as a mechanism to pre-empt and dissolve criticism, exchange, negotiation, engagement. Otherness is in all our contacts, and it seems that we need to deal with it, deal *in* it with full awareness, rather than defer it. It's a fearsome project, since here our vulnerabilities, our limits become exposed. But little threatens more our freedom to act effectively than concealing these from ourselves, and little eases our relations with others more than our unveiling them. To be able to say 'I don't think I can do that' or 'I can't help this anger' or 'I don't understand' or 'I'm afraid.' There are few acts we can perform that are more capable of easing the burden of our existence than, for example, to relinquish our grandiosity and our shame.

* * *

I've now allowed the matter of 'feeling' to 'enter the room'. We've noticed that missing from the discourse of postmodernism – all the more striking for the lexicon's enormous richness otherwise – are some of the most fundamental and insistent terms in the human vocabulary: words such as 'happiness', 'sadness', 'pain', 'sympathy', 'passion', 'anger'. Is it enough that we now understand why? It's time to acknowledge that one of the most prevalent and powerful tools we have for registering difference in human life is our sensation of emotion, of the affective qualities of our experiences.

My initial concern in mentioning this chasm in postmodern discourse – where there are gaps in what the postmodern wishes actually to *experience*, in its indisposition to allow an active and intelligent confrontation with some of the most prevalent of human experiences – is not to point out its theoretical inconsistency, though that is serious. It's rather a concern with the practice of living and of the 'languages' in which we do it. Our expressions of feeling are vital significations of the ways that we experience others and ourselves, and around which we construct our actions. Our emotional responses – however 'reasonable' or 'unreasoning' they may be – are among the most significant events telling us literally that something makes a difference. They constitute an essential medium of *contact* – for interaction, exchange, negotiation, and for what possibility there may be for growth and change. To shunt aside transaction with them is not simply an abandonment of 'rigorous analysis', a radical form of (fore)closure, but the furthest possible thing from the promotion of openness that we wish to believe is the spirit of the postmodern.

It's impossible to overstate the practical aspect of this. For example: it can be extremely helpful for ourselves and our relationships to sort out the difference between depression and sorrow. The ways of dealing with someone's existential depression and with his or her sadness over some specific event are quite different; to dismiss the former as a feeling that will (as the latter may) 'pass with time' can be as perilous as to treat the latter as something to be met with the main force of long-term therapy. Still more important, depression is catching; when our narcissance is engaged (as it easily is when depression comes near), the defensive boundaries between us and others soften and may be quickly infiltrated. To be able to feel sad for someone who is depressed can be much more helpful to both – and more realistic – than to hold feeling altogether at bay or collapse compliantly into ('go confluent with') another's depression. Further, it is reasonable to be sad for someone who is ironic (or who is manically euphoric), since the roots are the same and depression may well be in the air.

In actual situations it is the possibility not of delivering an instruction or of stating a belief but of saying 'I' – 'I feel' – that allows for rapprochements that make life together not merely poignant and exhilarating but manageable. Much of the disruptive rage in social life comes from not doing so – as well as the sense of deception felt by one in another's not doing so. Asking 'How do you feel about that?' can be pampering chic. When its thrust is understood it can also be intensely practical. 'I want to know how you feel about that because I want to know what you're going to do, and I want us both to think about it before you do it. I want things to be real. I have become disappointed with what happens when people feel one thing and think another – and with people's holding opinions without knowing why they hold them – and most of all because when this happens what they eventually do has little to do with either.' To avoid a morass of personal, social – and philosophical – confusion and paralysis, few skills can be of better service than our asking questions that bring out what feelings are actually alive in a situation.

* * *

Narcissance should not be expected to lead anywhere but to more narcissance. We have seen this eternal round eloquently described (and indeed we can see it enacted) by Lacan as an endless search for an ideal, a self that doesn't exist. This book has been arguing that that process need not be in theory – and is never in practice – humans' only option. A difference between narcissance and non-narcissance is a difference between not owning and the possibility of owning what one experiences in a given field and in the passage from field to field.

Here our practical experience is pivotal. Ideas of 'owning' and of 'decentring' the self represent two quite different visions of living. As it happens, while theoretical postmodernists highlight the 'decentring of the subject', many people in postmodern culture 'on the ground' speak actively both of what it feels like to be 'uncentred' and to be 'centred'. Their descriptions of an 'uncentred' feeling are of sensations of confusion, vulnerability, anxiety, ineffectuality and pointlessness. What they describe when they say that in a given situation they've felt 'centred' is quite different.

We've most of us experienced it, some time or another. We feel in place, 'focused'. (Athletes aren't alone in saying of the day 'when it all came right' that they felt '*within*' themselves.) We're at our most fully open to the world – we 'see the ball' in flight, we 'have all the time in the world' to prepare as it approaches – we 'have our wits about us'; our sensibilities, our responses and our intellectual and physical abilities are ready for anything, *disponible*. And, strikingly, it's on these occasions when (as observers remark at the time) we are furthest from being 'self-centred'. Our feelings are *our own*, no one else's, yet simultaneously they're at their most open and at others' disposal; we have room, 'all the time in the world', for others. Feeling no need to embattle ourselves with masks and ploys, we're at ease and seem in some significant sense 'at one' – not with some transcendant and evanescent cosmic principle, but with our own existence. We're without nostalgia; we are at home, we feel wc bclong. It's not a feeling that draws us to narcosis, either physical or social; enslavement to what's outside has no allure. We don't hang helplessly on others' approval, and can feel content even when utterly alone. Relationships with others are the object neither of terror nor of manic obsession, they are simply part of, and contribute some essential fullness to, our sense of being. We meet encounters with spontaneous welcome and buoyant anticipation; within them we feel vital, alive – yet free, when need be, to go.

This experience is never permanent. But – 'centred' or 'decentred' (these terms have both been red herrings from the start[27]) – it appears we have some choice as to the vision we elect for our lives: which experience seems most apt for a world and a being we're ready, able and glad enough to inhabit. The 'owned' or the 'disowned' self are not things we can simply put on, like masks. They are bases for kinds of praxis, of process, the latter with narcissance as its motive and end, the former with an end of narcissance as its aim. Both require a life's continuous work, each involving different tools and practices, different emotional and intellectual investments, different measures of success and failure.

The most difficult task is in 'figuring things out'. In narcissance, as in a postmodern mind-style, no image, idea, perception, feeling – where I am, who I am, what I mean, what I want – is allowed to become dominant, figural. Getting the project of abandoning narcissance to work means not 'creating oneself' but creating the conditions for the figure in the field to emerge. A measure of trust becomes essential – but of a particular sort. It begins with the acknowledgement that 'the world hasn't crushed me', that 'survivability is in me – is proven and is mine'. (People who trust aren't actually saying 'I know you'll never let me down' – no one can know that – but rather, 'I trust myself with you.' They know from their historical acquaintance with themselves that whatever the other does, they do survive, and that thus they can accept the risk of the relationship – and of its possible loss.) Such 'simple' observations – easily missed, never actually simple, and repeatedly hard to 'credit' – are where a move out of narcissance begins; in trust for oneself – a kind that rests not on a hope but, unexpectedly, on established, personally encountered fact.

But in narcissance, as in the postmodern, this may seem all too easy. There are too many often anguish-laden intervening doubts – about one's own very nature. 'Owning up' is involved; acknowledging not merely the possibility of survival but what stymies the wholehearted desire to survive. Here one of the most central perceptions in psychology must be taken on board: "The paradoxical theory of change says that by identifying with your current existence growth and change occur."[28] The difference is vital, at this point, between postmodern and narcissant self-consciousness (knowing *about* oneself as if someone other) and awareness ('living in the moment of feeling' – however burdened with distress – where growth actually takes place). If it's true that where there is anguish there ought to be compassion, compassion must begin where anguish starts, 'at home'. In the process of a clear-eyed self-recognition and an acceptance of what one has been disposed to disown, a different relationship forms with what one cannot 'bear' of oneself, with affects that have led one to split and disown – with seemingly interminable sensations of loss, suspicion, envy, anger, fear of separation (from the past, from false self-ideals), long-clung-to sensations of injury, hungers for unneeded forms of power and esteem. Individuals moving out of narcissance often find themselves saying inwardly: 'Let it go.' It's in letting go not only of grandiosity but of shame, for example, that an individual stands a chance of reclaiming his or her own potency,[29] along with a balanced sense of limits and self-responsibility.[30]

In an interview he subsequently entitled "There is No *One* Narcissism", Jacques Derrida has avowed that "It is likely that I have a rather complicated relation to my own image, complicated enough that the force of desire is at the same time checked, contradicted, thwarted ... the right to narcissism has to be rehabilitated". Perplexingly phrased until we grasp Derrida's struggle with an outmoded meaning for 'narcissism' we too have learned to question, the insight he offers is the need to own oneself.[31] In this process, throwing down barriers between provinces of one's mental life, one comes to know better the working boundaries between oneself and others.[32] In owning one's difference – one of whose conceptual roots most certainly lies in Nietzsche's 'forgive yourself your own self' – and in shedding some of the scourges of both false fantasy and nightmare and the longing for a 'home' outside oneself, may reside the possibility of a belonging within and to oneself. In such a perspective, owning up to narcissance is the first step out of narcissance. Disowning it – and the differences that makes – perpetuates it.

This perspective reveals the fundamental weaknesses in a widely acclaimed postmodern response to problems of the self; that is, that a strong solution lies in the cultivation of the variety of 'persons' that we feel to be 'in' us. The conception that we 'contain' discrete 'persons', each of whom should be allowed an autonomous and fulfilled day in the sun untrammelled by interference from 'the others', is a dramatization of the splitting by which we perpetuate narcissance. New cyber technologies designed to facilitate the splitting process, for example, characteristically recapitulate the crisis that their passing sensations of gratification induce us to feel they 'resolve', as the increasing number of reports of 'MUD-addiction' reveals.[33]

Does this at last vindicate the narcissant yearning to merge and melt one's conflicting impulses into some overarching and unaltering personal oneness? For all our dreams, it can't work in that way. The solutions to conflict and the ordeals of change aren't to be found in dissolution but in transaction. Dissolving differences, we must remain unable to negotiate the contradictions within us, respond to alterations around us, grow, or savour the richness of our being. (Postmodern expressions of a wish to 'live in the moment' reflect an instinctual glimpse of this.) It merely brings with it the impedimenta of compulsive regimes and constructions of thought that can obliterate the moment's effect. It *is* here in the moment, stripped as fiercely of those constructions as possible, that – *because* we're in touch instead with the needs that had fashioned them – we may allow and possess what we can of who we are. Sustained by the thread of continuity made possible in part by the persistence of memory, the sense of 'self-as-place' and of expansive self-belonging, we 'figure out' our selves day by day.

Can such a perspective answer the charge that human existence is ultimately without point or meaning? To this it can solely respond by recalling the essential, devastating intuition that the narcissant him- or herself must endure every day: that it is always pointless to live a life that is not one's own. But isn't striving to 'own oneself' just the final enactment of supreme 'selfishness'? The answer to that can be learned only through experience: It's when we feel we've stayed with what's figural and done justice to our own resources that we then feel released and happy to seek out others, to engage with the world and its further voices.

* * *

Acknowledging in each different moment the clash between what one may be and cannot be is the first condition and leading step toward the simultaneous grief and release that constitutes the ambivalence threshold. One of the essential processes on the way out of narcissance is one that sorts the differences between the ambivalence threshold and narcissant and postmodern oscillation. In experiencing 'life at the threshold', the competition among senses of self and their seemingly irreconcilable rival desires ceases to mean a lapse into generalized oblivion. There is no magic room beyond this 'threshold'; it's the floating vantage-point from which one may see both one's realities and one's ideals. The individual knows, contains and owns the incompatibility of desires, holds them unblinkingly in mind at once not as mere contradictions but as interwoven with one another, and moves on with a modicum of freedom (trammelled only by the seductions of depression, paranoia, mania and apathy) to act with intelligence appropriate to the actualities of the moment.

This poignant task can not dissolve the narrative of ourselves as orphans. Ending the 'cause' of our feeling alone, like ending our history, isn't an option. Rather, the game is, again, to *own* the story in full awareness – it is ours, after all – and empty it where we can of the literally extraordinary obsessive fantasies and destructive delusions that its suppression engenders, and from which it draws its groundlessly numinous and nightmarish emotional din. It's a perspective that means looking and imagining back, looking and imagining ahead, open-eyed in the face of loss and change, ready both to mourn and celebrate.[34] In this view, we live with ambivalence rather than inside it; it's not the whole nor the definition of being. In many respects it is irrelevant – even while it's the background – to what we experience and do.

* * *

Exploring alternatives to narcissance can put postmodern living into a fresh light. In order to 'go on', with increased freedom from narcissance, contact at the boundary between self and other has to be engaged. The individual must live with and through the fact that relationship and responsiveness to others means the acceptance of a measure of dependence. This can never mean 'only connecting', nor dreaming superhumanly to 'connect' equally with the entire universe of events and ideas. And it has to mean avoiding the anxious haste to spoil, to turn to waste the intensity of felt moments. While it entails responding directly to the terms in which others articulate themselves, engaging also means refusing to be 'swallowed up' in these, and insisting on fuller, more reciprocal forms of engagement. This requires the relinquishment of the fantasy that all social talk and action are equally contactful, and demands mindfulness that that fantasy is a primary delusion of narcissance. It recalls that zealous intellectual 'debate' or emotive bustle may operate to deflect or collusively to efface difference and dissolve otherness –

that either may be brought glamorously into play precisely to arrest engagement. Understanding this means letting no one sell us an end-to-exchange in the guise of 'leaving things open'.[35] To engage is to recognize what is a problem and what is a symptom of a problem, and to insist on finding out and negotiating what is at issue at all levels rather than only at the level of selective (for example intellectual) performance. Aware and active engagement can have a bearing on every dimension of postmodern life, from how we make use of its new forms of communication to how we might construct a society appropriate to it.[36]

So long as we engage with the other-than-ourselves we are committed to change. How can one do that – happily gamble, invest in decisions and the actions they command? How much are we willing and able to invest?

This question doesn't lead to so vague or indeterminate an answer as it seems. As we've been obliged to recognize, choices are actually always being made. 'Owning' is simply a special form of investment. It's literally about "response-ability", as Yontef says; "an ability to respond, to be the primary agent in determining one's own behaviour"; about the decision to make 'choices' as *choiceful* as one can.

Revolt is a case in point. As we've seen dramatized, revolt is far from always choiceful – it can be compulsive, obsessional, driven. Often in postmodern life it can act out a *submission* to dictates altogether out of our awareness. It's true that much that happens is beyond our choice – and we seem repeatedly called upon, further, to suppress who we are. But there is a kind of experience common among individuals who have confronted their narcissance. Having had something asked of them that they know to be fair in the terms of their relationship and situation, yet that seems a demand to set aside their own vital needs: instead of repulsing the demand out-of-hand (in an exalted spirit of revolt), they express and live through the pain and the loss it would mean – and feel unexpectedly liberated to respond nonetheless. It's as though both needs – to honour the relationship and oneself – are, in the act of acceding, accorded justice and fulfilled. With the grievance integrated as part of the situation and lived out (and in a sense mourned), the deed comes unaccompanied by the shame of refusing what may have been quite reasonably asked, or by that that comes of acceding without due attention to oneself. To live out can be to outlive. The process has been carried to a point where choicefulness has been brought into being.

What happens on such occasions is that, while one may thus

sustain a new loss and its specific hurt, one has purged some portion of that more vast and nameless, seemingly existential pain that belongs with an injury long past, an injury to regions of one's self-esteem that in the present situation are actually not under attack. Asked what at first seemed an intolerable subjection of one's being, far from having passively followed a line of least resistance – the well-worn track of some formulaic chart of revolt, or a mindless mechanical deflection of the issue or an obliteration of it in endless tergiversation – one has initiated the creation of a different, more self-affirming relationship. It's in ways like this that through engaged awareness even acceptance may be choiceful where revolt may not.

We are gifted in our ability, as psychologists sometimes phrase it, to 'go confluent with' our uncertainty, our emotional confusion; this can provide a seductive rationale for flight. But testing as it always is, sometimes uncertainty is one of the most luminous c(l)ues life can present us that we need to look, feel, think and commit again. It can be the liminal condition that's the seedbed of growth.

As I've said, this is not about a 'cure'. In fact, therapists seldom think of curing 'narcissism'. Living with it – and *living through* it – is the aim. It's not uncommon in psychology to speak of an "addiction to despair" (Mitchell 1988: 198). We've seen this in many forms – addiction to contradiction, to concealment, to fantasy and more. The kind of process I'm describing now is not a 'remedy' but *remediation*. To mediate again and continually what narcissance, for its special and addictive reasons, disposes us – often in intellectual and/or emotional and sometimes manic despair – to imagine is beyond determination or negotiation. Postmodernity frequently invites us to do something much like what psychotherapists commend as a way to remedy; to "play at illusion building and relinquishment" (198). But the postmodern solicits this often in the interests of forestalling the anguish that it anticipates we must otherwise eventually experience should we *believe* in the changes we thus bring about. The anticipation is correct – if the test, the expectation we apply, is completeness, perfection and omnipotence. Remediation works instead in the mode of provisional believing, letting go fantasies of omnipotence in favour of competence, of a sense of the possibility to be and do what is (as psychologists say) 'good enough' in the field, for the circumstances at hand, and of 'setting the stage' for effectively adequate change.[37]

* * *

I've suggested throughout this essay that potentially 'wholesome', productive processes fail and give way to narcissance *when support is missing.* It's inconceivable to pretend to provide here a blueprint for the successful provision of support. But it is possible to suggest ways in which we may be misled in thinking we provide it.

Narcissance springs from dilemmas that are universally with us, and from an instinct and a struggle to *solve* them. The ambivalence involved can turn to anger, fear, suspicion, depression and an array of escapes when – for lack of support in crisis – the effort comes to be *expected* to be hopeless. Postmodernism as a body of thought may often simply act out and promote the dilemma's 'eternal return'. The question is whether a culture exists or can be found that might counter such effects.

A critical problem is that society can perpetuate narcissance rather than contain and support the struggle to break free of it, and not merely when it seems to promote an ethos of 'every man for himself'.[38] It can do so, for instance, when – in the spirit of Unqle Trim – it confuses the symptom with the cause. When, that is – like narcissance – it fails to grasp the differences between systems of so-called 'neurotic' dependency and systems of support; when it confuses the issues of guilt with those of shame; when it makes abuse possible in the name of caring; and when it encourages the exploitation of its young in the name of parenting.[39]

How social misunderstandings such as these can 'work against us' can be intimated when we recall the last-mentioned of them as an example. As we now recognize, parents' emotional exploitation of their children is the most common and one of the most damaging forms of child abuse. It comes about, among various ways, by parents' unrealistically requiring young children to 'act like grown-ups'; by not allowing them to express or tolerate grief, fear or depression; by requiring them to make up for their (the parents') own depression, fear, shame, emotional flatness, emptiness, their deficiencies and/or dysfunctions; by covertly/unconsciously obliging them to provide them with constant, unmerited admiration, idealization; by compelling children to supply what courage, positive caring feelings, good humour, optimism, amusement, pleasure in life and cheer that they as parents can't provide for themselves; by inculcating, out of their own fears, habits of anxiety and dependency-thinking under the unbreakable cover of reason. Each of these has its obvious and veiled parallels outside the home, on the social plane and in the lifestyle-ideals promoted not only by government but by industry and commerce, and no society can begin to create a culture of support 'against narcissance' without having scrutinized its institutions in these regards.

A further, particular and unexpected confusion that prevents contemporary culture from overcoming such self-generating obstacles to the management of narcissance and its influence on postmodernity is its misapprehension of what contemporary psychology itself says. The popular notion of psychological help is that it simply aids the individual to deal with her or his 'inner conflicts'. Here the aim of classical (for example, Freudian) analysis misses something crucial. "Resolution of internal conflict is not sufficient" (Mollon 1993: 188). As we've learned, *containment* – by which the fabric, the weave of the self, can be felt to be no longer a hopelessly unstable and meaningless if not hostile *place to live* – is essential before conflict can be addressed. And that can only be provided by outside support. To offer this, a society must be built on a culture that, *at the very minimum,* consistently (1) communicates a sense that the compulsive struggle to live without supportive contact is unneeded, (2) allows the terrors of personal collapse and anti-social anger to be met, (3) contains these within a framework of realistic awareness, so that where there is delusion it can be put into perspective, and thus (4) builds a counter-realization that uncertainty and suffering can be survived.

There are some things of a specific nature that can be done in bringing support. First of all, we would need to observe that certain things we're inclined to do, and that easily seem sustaining, are not supportive in the end. Society is always in fact mobilizing narcissance – and *exploiting* it. We call on people's need for self-esteem in order to achieve things; we summon up their acute communicational and observational skills, invoking their instinct for compliance to make things run smoothly. Trade, industry and government activate narcissant fears, dependency, and narcissants' dreams of finding or buying means to greater esteem. New ways are developed each year for mining the expertise of narcissance. All of these need to be watched and – to make progress – many may have to be at least provisionally *renounced* by both narcissants and those engaging with them.

On the creative side, support means encouraging the engagement of narcissants with themselves and with others – in a way that regularly allows for the suspension of conceptual argument and analysis, permitting individuals to 'get back inside', to experience, with the aid of their uniquely active imagination, the dimensionality and substantiality of their inner environments. Social support can provide room for people to *live through* their sensations of need in a way that lets them find that these are never of themselves overwhelming, that every anguish comes and goes with the larger rhythms of physical and psychological being and may be safely both contained and exhausted. Individuals can be invited to perceive, accept and celebrate their own uniqueness, rather than seeking universally to seem to 'fit in'. In relationships they can be asked to hold onto the feeling of wanting to 'bracket', to ironize their experiences – and bring it into lively engagement with the desires, contempts, griefs and threatening wishes that irony conceals from them. In learning environments they can be encouraged not to cling to the fact of contradiction but to feel safe in contradictions, and see how they're not the end but the beginning. They can be motivated not to be too sure that endless processing and ceaseless talk are doing or saying more. They can be heartened to see what they may be losing touch with when they cling to feelings of multiplexity, uncertainty and pointlessness, and be let know that both the new limitations and the new burdens thus encountered can be borne when shared. In all these, those acting in support stand ready to interrogate their own impulses for signs of narcissance. They know that uniform confluence is not the goal, and give no grandiose soothing without giving of themselves. They address immediately and directly where and how these processes touch their own uncertainties, limitations and wounds – and keep ready to call for help themselves. For the safety of others and themselves, this is never more essential than where the slightest intimation appears that the margin has been reached of what they can manage. They know that trust is a powerful gift and must be held with an open hand and with infinite care.

In a society informed by the postmodern, a supportive practice can produce kinds of engagement that can turn 'intersubjective' uncertainty into something more like 'interactivity'. A characteristic of the discourse of people speaking for postmodernity is the repetition of formulaic bywords ('undecidability', 'simulacrum', 'aporia', 'decentred subject', '*différance*', 'absence' ...) that we've heard seemingly interminably before. The tireless return to stereotyped formulae is always in some sense a masked appeal, to which we are *not* responding when we argue or wrestle or even concur unqualifiedly with that explicit 'content'. To the contrary, we may be feeding the speakers' sense that they are incessantly unheard or that abstract and interminable uttering is the best they have to offer, to 'say for themselves'. Nor should we imagine that by bringing to bear some last-stand argumentational blitz we may induce them to expose 'what is really going inside'; a man who is narcissant will as-soon fight to the death as expose himself to anyone so ruthlessly uncaring. What we *can* do is allow him to see that we are willing to hear his arguments again – *and* that we will value him even when he feels they're at their weakest; that *we are ready to hear what else is there*. This may be no more than the expression, 'I'm tired' or 'You'll be tired of hearing this' or 'Why must I continually repeat myself?'. Taking hold of it, to follow where it leads, we make clear that it will be treated not as discrediting whatever else has been said, but as another part of the person whose concerns, at every level, are respected. A culture of engagement expresses faith in the *situation* and the *contact* and not just the 'content', which – as postmoderns know better than any – may be the least substantial part of an exchange.

I mentioned 'calling for help'. It's one of the last things a narcissant can do simply, and something we may be able to teach; how to seek and accept support in a spirit of freedom, without fear of shame. A 'holding environment', is never as well tuned to serve (and never less wasteful of energy and eventual resentment on all parties' part) as when it's asked for – when it's defined, shaped by the need. There, at that point of difference where desire is openly and reciprocally articulated, engagement and negotiation are renewed; it's where the will for mutual support can arise.

It's passages like those above that Unqle Trim can find hardest to cope with. It can be most difficult, particularly when narcissance may colour the thinking, to appreciate that in the attention that must be devoted to individuals' encounters with themselves in the process of remediation, the outcome might *not* be selfishness but a groundedness from which for the first time they become genuinely – rather than falsely, selfishly – altruistic. But there can be no confusing support with mindless collectivity. The problem is not one of an ailing social body – a body politic – for which there is a compact political cure by means of the celebration of togetherness such as is described in speaking of the rehabilitation of public morale when a nation wins the World Cup, or of the public healing of the wounds following the Vietnam war, or indeed in the oft-repeated slogan that the Falklands war or the bombing of Iraq rescued Westerners' sense of themselves. For all the narcissant craving for confluence and union, the image of a collective solution in speaking of 'narcissistic wounds' begs the question – it may be a contradiction in terms. The apparent strengthening of the sense of self by means of a broad cultural identity (such as patriotism) is more than likely to be merely a reenactment, a perpetuation of the problem – the emptying out of the sense of personal agency and the effacement of self in favour of a borrowed external ideal image.

This is far from meaning that collective action need not be taken, or that in fact a particular collective self-image may not help to galvanize that action. It only means that whatever we do, so long as a social, collective image is offered not as a strategy but *as the solution* – as a substitute for addressing experience at the level of individual subjectivity – it will remain, if not subterfuge, some version of flight. More effective collective action may lie in the development of a firmly sustaining ambiance in which individuals are each helped toward a more subtle and rich relational intelligence of their own and others' processes, to make each their own unique way to a more resilient and creatively evolving transaction with these. The prevention of child-rearing in unhappy domestic environments, for example, by the increasing communal provision (as in Germany) of 'baby-flaps' – where parents may dispose of unwanted children anonymously through a flap in the streetside wall of a care facility – may in the end, however principled and technologically astute, secure limited social gains.

There are unequivocal signs that of the forms of social and psychological support mentioned above, postmodern culture cannot provide the minimum. In further, purely practical terms, it is unlikely to be able or disposed in a concerted way to resist rule by technocracy, oppose abuses of power, resist violence, sustain coherent decisions affecting the management of the environment and its genetic resources, set limits to the manipulation of minds, choose an 'appropriate' pluralism, or make adequate provision for its own future. This is no cause for surprise; *narcissance cannot rescue itself*. It's for this reason that questions useful in dealing with narcissance are ones to which the postmodern needs to respond.[40]

* * *

Greater awareness doesn't guarantee happiness. We can, however, feel less shame about what can't be achieved, and – where grandiose fantasy plays a smaller part – achieve more of what is imagined to be achievable. Fuller engagement with what is and what we are expands the reach of our lives and leaves us with less failure sprung from false ideals, and less fear. This means a *disponibilité* (broached by Modernists and commended by the postmodern though often more as a shelter from engagement than engagement itself) of an affectively more embracing and realistic kind. The "ability to mourn", for example,

> can restore vitality and creativity to the depressive, and ... free the grandiose person from the exertions of and dependence on his Sisyphean task.... The true opposite of depression is not gaiety or absence of pain, but *vitality*, i.e. the *freedom to experience feelings which are spontaneous*.[41]

This is what would be meant by 'living *through* postmodernity' – in the way that one may think of 'living through narcissance'. Not merely to *live* through it (to get through life as an endless shuttle between irreconcilable oppositions) but in the fullness of its ambivalence to live *through* it, by means of it. We can put postmodernity's questions to work – putting them to ourselves and others – but now not without demanding not merely what abstraction but what moment, what relation, what person and what process of mind they serve. Asking themselves such questions a few professors might take early retirement, but postmodernity would approach the fluidity and rigour it proclaims.

Just as indeterminacy in life is always conditional, never absolute, so we never live closer to actuality and to ourselves than when we engage in deciding, however provisional this must be. Decisive engagement, of the human sorts I've indicated, is not simply in the interest of our grounding our thoughts and actions in reality. It is where the experience of support begins, and of the individual's reality in the world. This support is of a kind that – though they can strengthen it – no philosophical positionings or understandings can replace. When, by conventionalized theoretical and procedural protocols of discourse and by personal strategies of posture and escape, we shore our sensibilities against the shock of felt actuality, we may – as we speaking as postmoderns still often avow we do in spite of our established efforts – feel famished for a quality of experience that is more relationally real and self-justifying as well as more potently creative of meaning. It seems that each individual has a chance for this. It may arrive when we let go of the 'But you said!' cry, and instead look and listen. When, inhabiting the shifting middle-ground that we sense to be our 'selves' in each moment, in full awareness and wholly engaged, we lend an ear and hear what and who else – other, different – is there, and are *prepared to be surprised*.

Afterword

TALKING ABOUT THE POSTMODERN

What I've been suggesting as a model carries with it liabilities that must be interrogated with vigour. One I mentioned at the start is that the pattern – as a tool, an 'orienting device', a kind of template exposing the fold in the historical map where the postmodern episteme seems to occupy the same space (or has 'relations of consistency', as Deleuze and Guattari put it) with its experiential and affective shadow, narcissance – is bound to obscure landmarks important to others seeking other ways through the landscape.

My still deeper concern is actually a quite different one. Some may welcome what's said here with greater and less critical enthusiasm than I feel may be helpful. I worry that their sympathy for this book's *reservations* about contemporary culture may 'get the better of them', and that they may discover 'narcissance!' everywhere, in the witch-hunt tradition. To anyone feeling so disposed I can only say (as they must by now expect me to), please examine with utmost care why you wish to do this. (In the same spirit I'm certainly prepared to say what functions it serves me to write this essay – personal as well as theoretical and professional – and refrain only because it would be inapt to presume on listeners with gratuitous discussions of the sort.)

There are more particular gaps as well. While I have noted examples, I've given less attention than I would in other contexts to very important differences between postmodernity's forms in different national cultures. And issues affecting the sheer 'mechanics' of postmodern and narcissant thinking need more exploring.[1] Above all, in my determination to keep to a descriptive account of postmodern patterns and their psychological parallels, I've limited the discussion by offering no more of an etiological account than I could ground on immediate compact evidence. It is one thing to suggest what kind of mind-style might make postmodern ideas and cultural forms 'take', and another to argue through in detail what mechanisms could lead to the development of an individual psychology into forms attaining the status of a culture. This isn't to say that that's not done every day, as the storm of confident pronouncements on all sides shows, from the anxious claims on the 'right' (such as Lasch's) that narcissism has created a 'me society' to enthusiastic ones on the 'left' (such as Gergen's) that the loss of sense of self has yielded an 'anything goes' culture.[2] My own present reticence stems more from the fact that I feel that the case for the connection is still stronger than has been made out, and that the 'connecting' processes involved are more manifold and complex than those so far represented. These call for an intensive study organized and directed in a different way, and need more space to unfold (or 'unravel') than is permitted here.[3]

Readers will find problematical the workability of generalizations about the nature of some of the crises experienced by individuals formed and living their different moments in the world. I concur wholly with this concern. It's for that pressing reason among several that the emphasis here has been on the urgency of the development and support of skills and sensibilities for the direct-most engagement with 'what is in the field', and for the reduction of narcissance's potent generalizing strategies (such as abstraction, deflection, fantasy) for evasion. Beyond this, I've made no attempt to provide a concerted social and political meta-theory to which this might be systematically related, or to describe in detail institutional reforms to bring these about. In view of the problems that emerge as one seeks to free theories currently in circulation from their infection/inflection *by* the mindsets I *have* described (problems with which any such scheme would have to negotiate if it's to be effective), seeking to devise ones we have our work cut out for us. I hope that the space left here will be taken as a warm and positive invitation to respond to that challenge.

I've no illusions about the 'finality' of this discussion's foundations. Arguments from affect (such as ones on which this essay partly rests) have no more philosophical validity than the conception that humans have the right to life, liberty and the pursuit of happiness, and at best can have no more force than these had in the history of people feeling they possessed the right to life etc. Still more, it can be easy for some to see a psychologically orientated reading of a cultural movement as an effort to draw radical action into a discursive web of categories serving, for example, capitalist abuses of power (though my sympathies, it should be clear by now, run quite the other way). It would be unforgiveably glib to dismiss critics holding such a view by saying simply 'this is their problem' (showing possible traces of fear of entrapment and betrayal, outward-projections of struggles with self-definition, and so on). Isn't psychological modelling potentially politically oppressive? Of course it is; all modelling is. We need to refine all our skills to deal with that. One thing we can do is avoid brandishing categories such as normal/abnormal and sane/insane as weapons.[4] But worse still would be to take the political charge as a reason – as such arguments often are when advanced in the name of postmodernism – to retreat from the challenge to seek a paranoia-free *engagement* with new models on all sides.

I regret particularly having to sacrifice consideration here of the place of postmodernity *vis-à-vis* new developments in social, economic and political coercive systems and practices. Among those of most concern are, first, the rapidly growing capacity and will of supragovernmental corporate establishments to appropriate postmodern strategies – and make appeal to narcissant impulsions – for decentralization, dispersal, concealment and seduction in the interest of 'aimless power'. Second is the question of the relative potentials among the intricate array of possible postmodern-endorsed pluralisms (where claims so far have on balance been unusually marked for their lack of critical 'rigour'),[5] together with the questions of postmodernity's logical and temperamental ability actually to sustain them, and of the degree of safety and support it can provide for the individual, on which the validity of a plural society must rest. And third is the psychologically predictable upsurgence alongside postmodernity of its intrinsic rival, fundamentalism (including contemporary militant libertarianism), and the matter of postmodern and narcissant thinking's clear disposition to create decisional vacuums into which totalitarianism can, 'no questions asked', freely plunge without obstruction.

Isn't psychology itself potentially deleterious, in any inclination it may have to maintain "a unidimensional view of human nature … in which self-cohesion is the highest aim and loss of self the greatest danger" (Mollon 1993: 6)? It is. Psychology, I repeat, should comprehend and engage with narcissance and not merely mimic its preoccupations. Compensations are that few psychology workers do fall into this trap, and that without the contribution of those who don't, we should never know of – let alone be able intelligently to manage – the problem. A great deal has to be done on the politics of psychological modelling, and with less jumping to facile, however charismatic, conclusions.

CHOOSING

All of us stand somewhere between Unqle Sim and Unqle Trim, in actuality. Between the 'possessed' and the 'dispossessed'; the narcissant that postmodernity gives voice to, and the materially suffering that the moral conservative wishes to speak for. It's impossible – for me, at least – not to feel equally the pull of both, once their impulses are understood. But when it comes to postmodern life, we're beginners, and we need to get beyond entry-level thinking about it. It's *not* purely and simply everything we can imagine ourselves believing and trying. As we look more closely, a more distinct image of a human mind-style emerges, and, through this, some perhaps more compassionate means of approaching it. In its dynamics – a coherent if volatile drama of separation and ambivalence, of fantasies of catastrophic betrayal and unconstrained attainment – we can see a steady vortex of unique and persistent urges beneath what may seem a chaos of obsessions with language, with surface, with sensation.... The culture's radicalism falls intelligibly into place alongside its irony, its extravagance, its promiscuity, its paranoia, its indifference, its rare mix of apparent aimlessness and obsession, of abstraction and visceral sensationalism, of futurism and nostalgia, of interminable doubt and dreams of utopian power, its explosive imaginational energies, its famed states of aporia and anomie, its yearnings for creation and for oblivion.

If the postmodern seems to be wavering, 'shimmering' – if it appears fugitive, 'uncatchable' – that is exactly because, different from other styles of thinking and being, it is defined by its wanting to be that. It has good *reasons* for this. By vigorously disabling the control and *triage* of cultural objects and 'operators', it makes conceivable a more liberal and prolific dissemination of otherwise marginalized, unorthodox and innovative individual ideas, images and actions in the intimate and vivid process of their vivid generation than totalistic, ideologically driven systems of the past have allowed. A special achievement is its having conferred new dignity on a notion that had lost some of its shine in the period of World War II and its aftermath – that is, the phrase 'Who is to judge?' – one of the most precious and poignant, if also sinister, of human utterances.

Above all, in teaching us to honour process before product, it conveys a vital insight. When people have felt transfixed or paralysed in the face of the postmodern, most frequently it has not been owing to the power of an ideology, now, but often precisely because what they see declines to be apprehended as an ideology, but rather as a process of thinking. We need to accept that that is what the postmodern itself is. Coming with this (is it the opening of a new era? perhaps so, in this sense) is the perception that each process, like any ideology, has its specific character, bringing its own profits and losses, and that *mental processes* can seize, paralyse, coerce and oppress, *just as ideologies* can.

The limitations of formal philosophical reasoning in the face of this are as ample as postmodernist thought expressly means them to appear. If postmodern thinking sometimes seems never exhausted, seems to 'protest too much', is 'never satisfied', no matter how many times it states its case – if it seems sometimes obsessional – it expresses a symptom, a psychological actuality that philosophy can't manage to argue away. The likelihood of this is finely illustrated in the distinctive trait of postmodern scepticism that it does not (as scepticism traditionally seems to promise) in any way demystify our relations with reality. Instead, it preserves and promotes the mythos of the two universes of 'language' and 'reality', with all its resemblance to the oft-recited nightmare of Narcissus for whom 'inside' and 'outside', self and other, may never touch. It is possible to be sceptical about radical scepticism; that is, to hesitate before imagining to sever relations with 'what's out there'.[6] There can be genuine practical value in our loosening what may presently feel to be the dead hand of a now highly conventionalized set of tropes and routines of thought, by allowing ourselves to observe that it is but one set among many, and represents a choice, however unchoicefully out of awareness this may be, and to inquire into the predisposition it enacts.[7]

We may find good cause to do this. If narcissance is implicated in postmodernity, it can be a mistake to think of the postmodern as only a theoretical position. It is one thing to play at playing in the infinite play of signification, but you cannot play around with a narcissant. The stakes are entirely different, they are high, and the response may – without warning – be anything but playful.

Few matters can be more complex than the relationship between personal psychology and positive social action. It seems reasonable to ask 'What does it mean to say "nobody owns me", "I'm a free woman", "I believe in the family of humankind', or to call oneself "conservative", "liberal", "for labour" – and yet to say "psychology doesn't come into it", "nothing personal, you understand"?'. Yet we recognize the view, so well articulated in Marxism, for example, that in narrowly psychologistic perspectives lie the 'morbid' seeds for the destruction of collective action. But a society cannot hope to be coherent that denies the significance and power of private experience, and it appears we must learn to put up with the inconveniences this raises; certainly any postmodern pluralist society must 'put up or shut up'. In a society potentially informed by narcissance, in particular, there are possibilities – too considerable not to be considered – for oscillant mind-styles to engender bizarre and unpredictable manic bonds on one hand, and depressive ruptures, on the other, of aggressive sorts, along with problematic anomic silences (such as those increasingly arising at election time) where a society founded on consensus might have hoped for active critique and negotiation. Politically (even if we dismiss the outside possibility of actual 'brainwashing' to which it may conceivably be prone), narcissance can leave little to choose – or little aware choice – between shopping fatigue in the face of the felt-welter of social options, on one hand, and the artificial hardening of postures associated with both idealistic dependency and grandiosity, on the other. And both are human mental eventualities of just the sorts on which totalitarianism battens.

To strike the stance of overweening moral rectitude, in the hope of resolving such problems, offers little promise. War on 'selfishness' has about it all the feckless naivety that 'war on drugs' often has. Selfishness, like other addictions, is a symptom before it can be a cause. Nor can we legislate against 'promiscuity' that starts not in the sex organs or in greed but in loneliness, desperation, self-uncertainty; it only emerges elsewhere, in addiction, child abuse, physical violence, crime. You don't deal with narcissance by becoming narcissant. As the force of moralistic injunctions to keep-our-troubles-to-ourselves gain sway in the name of a smooth-running and less demanding society, we're likely to see around us not more 'open communication' on moral issues but a deeper silence, sustained by still more steely nerves, with no reduction of the narcissance they've been summoned to suppress.

There are signs that important actual recent developments in human social arrangements – arising without (and often in spite of) deliberate political programmes for change – are being seriously misread. Failing an understanding of narcissant processes, no account of major alterations in lifestyle affecting marriage, partnership, family, child-upbringing, work and recreation can hope to be coherent or actionable.[8]

I've said that it can be a catastrophic mistake to conceive of social revolt and reform as products of pure narcissance. But it begins to appear that there may be equivalent civic hazards in neglecting to be critically aware of the affective forces that may become enmeshed with them. The web of forces in play in a society – given a certain affective culture within it – is far more complex and volatile than we think to encompass when we simply analyse them in terms of power relations such as the distribution of wealth and information.[9] If social action is to have effect it must be harnessed to the impulses that will sustain it, and to hope to drag it by beasts that may be destined to turn on it – and may actually be inimical to it – is to beg for disaster.

The World Health Organization predicts that in twenty years depression will be one of the most pervasive serious illnesses on earth – as widespread as common forms of heart disease and cancer.[10] Many civic and corporate bodies already regard illness due to stress as epidemic. Unfortunately even if we set aside psychogenic illness (and its increasingly observed implications for social and economic life) as uninteresting, the problems don't go away. What is post-modernity ready to do about the other world, where the majority of humanity live and die? Many in the 'developed' nations are fed up with the news-broadcast sight of millions in abject poverty, starvation, physical and mental distress, and with the smells of urban fear and anguish. Some, on the other hand, have grown weary of the sheer expenditure of energy and motivational morale in fighting, through diversion, to screen their senses from these. It's true that systems have to be purged from time to time, and few intellectual activities can achieve this better than radical scepticism. We need to empty the tank and sweep out the sludge, decoke the engine by a high burn, set the oven to 'self-clean'. Regrettably, while this is going on, you can't do anything with the system; can't drive (at a traffic-appropriate rate), can't cook (at least not food).

As happens to hundreds of thousands every year around the world, on a summer afternoon two men in a doorway on East Seventh Street, in search of a livelihood, put knives to my stomach and throat and expressed discontent with the dollar-fifty and bag of fresh cherries I had to offer. I asked these men to defer my death, to entertain with me the spectrum of cognitive frames and uncertain conclusions this might lead to. They failed to see it my way. I came gradually to feel not only that this was a moment in which a difference between *différance* and difference existed, but also that it would make a difference if I deferred – if I didn't 'close' with some distinguishable, hopefully (though only probabilistically, never certainly) appropriate action. It was owing not to indeterminist thinking but to our negotiation separately and together through our sentiments and material circumstances – joint terror, a grain of generosity, inconvenience, the modesty of what remained to be achieved – that we all survived. Actuality carries a knife, and its ultimate uses are decided in the relations within and among people as real living beings.

When we consider figures such as Derrida, Lacan, Deleuze, Baudrillard, Lyotard, we may gain most from them when we think of them as among the great *poets* of the second half of the twentieth century. It may be their articulation of a complex, ambivalent species of nerve-charged autoallergy to our humanity that will be their most potent legacy. In a postmodern perspective, the *richness* of experience gained is not tangential but essential, and we've no need to fear our losing sight of such poets; society's sense of their worth can only be the greater because their styles of mind – and in some cases their lifestyles – differ from others'.[11] The problem, instead, is whether the difference is important in our lives, and if so, what if anything might this mean we should do?

I've said that postmodern thinking has its limits; that for any help in 'deciding what to do about things', we must turn elsewhere. This means: to other rules and processes of understanding – the gritty, forever contentious disciplines we've known, the myriad new ones now forming, and those that we need still to evolve. It must be correct that, as Gregory Bateson (1972) says, the self is not the ultimate unit of good, in the context of the total ecological system. The problem is that it is only the self that can know this and act on it. This, we say, demands continuing courage and needs support. Can society develop processes to provide it?[12]

Can we work our way beyond those generalized observations about our 'loss of the traditional social bond' that are so familiar to us now that they seem often to drift into the realm of the unactionable cliché? The problem is that we can create all manner of beliefs – none are better at that than postmoderns – but we can't create believing. Not only beliefs but degrees and kinds of believing are shaped by our mind-styles, and in our times may much depend on how we deal with our narcissance. We may inculcate in a future generation ways of speaking and behaving that look *something like* believing. The stress placed by governments of recent years on nation, family and 'a return to basics' reflects that ambition. But we detect the incursions of doubt its artificiality evokes. Dealing with narcissance is a *way of facilitating the process of believing*; not what is to be believed, but the sense of self without which believing can't begin.

Few things can be more precarious and difficult than to devise and put into place the relational structures needed to provide an adequate containing environment – one that is unsentimental and that instead aims to strengthen more realistic and deep-felt, engaged modes of attachment. The difficulties *feel* more critical the more we let go of the safety of false images, fantasies and longstanding stereotyped routines of thought and make our way out into the more open space of creatively situation-responsive ways of living. 'Life in the open' can seem frightening – but there seems no other alternative to prolonged and mounting narcissance.

With this in view, it becomes important finally to think about the meaning of 'living in the moment', since there are vitally different ways of understanding it; it is central both to postmodern thought and to ideas for the overcoming of narcissant processes that promote postmodern thinking. One of the most vivid, challenging contributions to contemporary experience has been postmodernity's invitation to a style-of-being free of the constraints of constructed understandings – a style seeming to entail living in the moment; obliviating the past, in essence as though it never happened. (Many traditionalists protest that this is indeed how 'the younger generation behave'.) Yet living without a past isn't actually an option – if only because it's there that virtually all that we can think (including the meaning of 'living in the past') is constituted. This is the right place to point out that "another century's worth of history will always make the last century's attempt to be ahistorical look ridiculous",[13] and that, as a matter of course, where the postmodern fantasy of an end to history is concerned, this is already happening.

But there is something much more central and formidable at stake. A far more fateful constraint than the impossibility of erasing the past is the *desire* to. It binds us to a web of thinking woven from a fantasy of completeness and a myth of loss that must be unravelled and let go. The sense of what I'm going to say now will seem a paradox and isn't easy for everyone to take in at first (though it will be familiar to those who have overheard psychologists saying it, as they so often do).

To be a postmodern, for the most part, one 'lives in the moment' only inasmuch as one does in narcissance – and the narcissant rarely inhabits the moment at all. In narcissance we live in an injured past. And so, as we've seen, does the postmodern. And here is the observation I wish to make: when it comes to our most obsessional anxieties and fears, *what we fear most has already happened*. This is true, most significantly, of the mordant experiences of separation and of the torturous self-dividedness it brings and that can shape our thinking processes for the rest of our lives.[14] It is also true that, in the course of life, separation often comes again. And one of the ways we know that separation is resonant with what has already happened is that it comes so often with a burden of anguish far exceeding what immediate circumstance, common sense and reason would predict; it 'returns' – freight with a myth from the past. What is more, many of the times that it reappears are times when it is *we* who return to *it*. We anticipate it, fore-see it, because in its formative incarnations it has hurt and marked us so, and left its seal on our thoughts.

We have the choice to search it out – regarding everything said, everything thought and done, as an instantiation of that loss, that felt betrayal – and to camp perpetually at the site of that wound. Or we can choose to live, knowing that we must encounter it again, and yet again, and meet it squarely each time. It's a choice we would have to make over and over. Or rather: we would need to find in ourselves a kind of life that lived out that 'choice'; something like a way of being.

It's important to know the modesty of what can be achieved. Personal meaninglessness needn't kill. We have postmodern thinking to thank for the sense that the quality of the life actually lived is what is in question. An unusual feature of life to come is that an increasing number of humans may *survive well without a good reason for living.*[15] What penalties the experience may carry with it can scarcely compare with the interminable hushed anguish of self-punishing – and (as psychologists describe) ultimately impoverishing – expectations of loss. And we may be liberated from such expectations and anguish as we let go of some of our narcissance.[16]

* * *

There may be ways, then, of being both less possessed and dispossessed and becoming, instead, in the must human sense, self-possessed. But psychological awareness does not break forever the processive circle implicit in postmodern thinking. We vitally need the interplay, the checks and balances, made possible by the engagement among diverse frames of reference. We must make our way between the aporias of postmodern narcissance and the most intransigently unresponsive forms of decisiveness of movements in the name of social justice, material welfare, fundamentalist faith (with the purblindness and bigotry that may accompany each of them). Individual psychological awareness is not an *alternative*. It must accompany and negotiate as equal partner with the others. In dealing with mind-styles – because the *field itself* is not simply 'one thing or another' but a mosaic – a mosaic of practices can (as is often said in medicine) hold the most promise. You can't file a class action against postmodernity any more than against narcissance. Every case is a transaction, and must be negotiated in its own field, with the benefit of experience but on its own merits. There are no fixed formulae; what we do have are questions.

This essay's claims, too, are much more limited than might have been expected of one ending up in the quarter in which the wind of its logic has blown it. This is neither a self-help, better-lifestyle book nor a work of social criticism. Suggestions about the provenance or the needs served by a body of activities and beliefs cannot constitute a critique of it – and are not intended to here. Sometimes they can provide a better chance to trade with it in the fullness of its context and thrust. In the end these chapters can at best only hope to yield a resource through which readers may create their own meanings and relations. Narcissance, however, is not the business only of the conspicuously narcissant, and the same goes for the postmodern. We've seen the anger some feel on contemplating 'postmodernity'; we may wonder about that. Whoever we are, our positioning with relation to it is at stake, and we may need to interrogate our own ambivalence. Rationalism, Realism, Modernism – and Postmodernism – they (like any parents) were doing the best they could under what they felt to be the circumstances. I suggest we let rage go; anger, like fear, can be not merely a wall but a gate, but we need to pass through it. Asking questions is the trick.

* * *

To understand the *intellectual* culture contributing to postmodernity we need to examine the unique event that distinguished and made it possible – that is, the loss of trust for the systems of signs sustaining human communication. Inevitably, insofar as it evinces scepticism, it is the thematization of a crisis of trust in the area of human relationship, and its implications. The more closely we observe its flexions and inflections in the context of life as a whole, the more clearly postmodernity springs loose from the ideological constructs that for a brief time seemed to underpin and legitimate it. The unique mechanisms of postmodernity, including its most extravagant turnings, are not parts of some abstract intellectual plot to 'problematize reality'. They have evolved out of a vital struggle – as though by compulsive instinct – to *deal with* a constellation of far more profound dilemmas. They represent an urgent – and quite particular – *strategy for living*, for coping with certain distinct and otherwise intolerable psychological realities, whose shadowy bulk and force we can't fail to see as we look more closely. They are neither solutions to the crises of separation and loss and the ensuing failures of the sense of self and of meaning, nor demonstrations that they can't be dealt with. They strive instead to shatter and disperse in shards, or to dissolve into oblivion, the experience of them.

To live through the postmodern doesn't mean to 'treat' or 'retreat from' but to 'treat with' it – not to live 'without it' or 'lost within it' but to live with it with vigour, intelligence and creatively responsive humanity and humour. It can't hurt to tease out the more hidden and glinting strands of which the culture's own fabric is in part woven and which it itself sometimes compulsively works in the same moment to ravel and unravel. We comprehend that uncertainty, in all its anguish, is the seedbed of growth, and that deciding and testing our decisions is the only way we can engage with and 'grow into' reality. We can see, as we do, that the postmodern deploys churning imaginational energies it hesitates to name, and that it does actually offer many of the things it claims. That it aims for a great deal more than it declares aloud. That it presents problems about which it keeps (and logically must keep) silent. That, above all, it is – in elemental ways that its opponents have missed and which postmodernism itself, by its very nature, can never reveal – *a matter of choice*. And that we've choices to make.

In all this, if it's to be genuinely engaged, postmodernity must be met not only where it likes to be seen, dressed up in public, but where it is when it's at home, where it hungers and eats and paces and plays and sleeps and tends its wounds, and dreams.

Notes

Certain specific issues broached in this essay are more fully discussed in Nash, *Criticism and the End of Desire* and "The Culture of Global Feudalism", forthcoming. These are indicated here as CED and CGF.

* * *

FOREWORD

1. That is, as one particular pattern of thinking and behaviour among numerous overlapping traditions making strong contributions to contemporary life. In this view, it operates in parallel with e.g. Christian, Jewish, Islamic cultures, the vigorous cultures of the many ethnic, women's, gay, environmental and cybernetics movements – each articulating with other ongoing social processes at different points, yet seeking (in the interests of its own integrity and for what it conceives to be the general benefit) to address or 'take in' as much as it can of contemporary life as a whole. It is no less a mistake to conceive that 'postmodern' 'covers' everyone in our time than to say that Jane Austen was a Romantic because she wrote in the heyday of Romanticism, that Zola writing in 1880 was a Symbolist, or that the thirteenth century in Europe was a chivalrous era because the chivalric code was one favoured construct of that time.

   An essential venture of this essay is to disclose the plurality of postmodern ideas and gestures. The tradition that there are as many postmodernisms as there are postmoderns is well rationalized in postmodernist theory, on the grounds that unitary, systematic accounts are problematic. Further, postmodernity's featuring contradiction is one of its defining traits. But as will become apparent, to cite such resistances to the characterization of the postmodern is not the end but the beginning of a description of postmodernity, and constitutes a vital part of a definition of what it aims to achieve, for its own special reasons. This project is markedly different, then, from that of historians disposed to call ours 'the postmodern age'. The matter of contemporary contradictions, for instance, to which leading thinkers have tried to respond, is vital. (When Fredric Jameson writes of 'the mystery' of recent anti-foundationalism's flourishing side-by-side with the recent ecological, feminist and fundamentalist revivals [1994: 46–7], and calls this "a fundamental antinomy of the postmodern", that is because he treats the period as a postmodern or late capitalist era en bloc – that is, as a heterogeneous culture that can be treated, perhaps paradoxically, in a unitary way – while I do not.) In this essay, the emphases placed on contradiction and plurality – to the extent that they are not features of other epochs as well – are considered as manifestations not of the present's 'total character' but of the pragmatic force of the local culture of postmodernity within it.

   The history of the difficulties with the term 'postmodern' is notorious, and I use the conventional generic word for want of a better. The words 'postmodernism' and 'poststructuralism' (a term assigned to a number of schools of theoretical practice cotemporaneous with postmodern culture) present matching problems. Each encompasses a vast variety of positions, and not all of these presented by writers who like to be labelled as 'postmodern'; yet all have been claimed by – and incorporated in the central arguments of – writers who do. (A unique and significant characteristic of postmodern thinking is that its 'brand-name' was never designed to impart the resonant force of a crusade expressing group solidarity.) That this has often been misguided is the focal point of Chapter 2. It is what the misunderstanding tells about the culture (and not about the authors whom the culture 'misreads') that I'm interested in. I rarely apply the term 'poststructuralism', then, purely for the reasons that the distinction it evinces can contribute little to points made in this particular book (though it can pay off in other ones) and to use it in a generic way would only scandalously compound the problems already incurred by the word 'postmodern'. Should I occasionally, for sheer economy, use a term such as 'the postmodern' it should be understood that I mean not a 'postmodern time' or a 'postmodern person' but 'postmodern activity' or someone engaging in it.

2. A 'characterological' reading of postmodernism was proposed in lectures in the mid 1970s and in 1985 in the first draft of the first edition of Nash 1987, as the sequel to a chapter on the decentring of the subject. When, considering it premature, and unhappy with the term 'characterology's' mis-intimation of fixed 'character', I withheld from publication the long closing section of the book, 'The Limits of Anti-Realism', this perspective went with it, surviving only in the occasional note in published editions. With the expansion of postmodern culture, signs that the model must be broached became compelling, and it is that broader 'canvas of evidence' that gives this book its scope and shape.
3. For a comparison of this approach with ones parallel to it – e.g. Dunn (1998) and Turkle (1992) – see CGF.

CHAPTER 1: THE POSTMODERN TRADITION

1. Gergen 1991: 6, quoted in Turkle 1995: 257.
2. Ibid., quoted from Howard Rheingold, The WELL, conference on virtual reality (vr.47.351), 2 February 1993.
3. 'Doug', an Internet interlocutor; Turkle 1995: 13.
4. This translation from Derrida's *L'Ecriture et la différence* is Culler's (1975: 247) and is more liberal than literal. "L'absence de signifié transcendental étend à l'infini le champ et le jeu de la signification" (original 1967: 411). Cf. Bass translation (1978: 280).
5. Doubt as to language's capacity to represent the world absorbed medieval thinking. See e.g. Eco (1979 and 1989). I thank Jonathan Key for recalling the first and informing me outright of the second.
6. *Encyclopaedia Britannica,* 14th edition (1946), Chicago, vol. 20, 56–9; article signed by A. S. Pringle-Pattison and R. M. Wenley, revising Pringle-Pattison's original (see 11th edition, 1911). The allusions to Pascal and Bayle, who grounded quite different conclusions on their sceptical premises, recall the diversity of *functions* these may have, and which it's an aim of this essay to bring into fuller view.
7. The present observations have no issue of historical chronology at heart but, very differently, that a tradition resembling contemporary indeterminism is itself perennial rather than contingent upon contemporary experience.
8. In this essay examples are drawn from many hundreds of postmodern fictions,

for which detailed bibliographical reference, except in the case of extensive or controversial quotations, would create unnecessary clutter and exceed the space limits imposed by immediate publishing constraints. Readers interested in pursuing illustrations of the themes and models outlined below will find further discussion with abundant analytical examples, as well as full bibliographical data affecting all passages cited here, in Nash 1993. Each novel is unique and no one novel could be expected to display all the traits described.

9. Flann O'Brien, from a letter appended as a 'Publisher's Note' to *The Third Policeman* (1974: 173). Cf. e.g. Sollers on reading and on 'human identities' as 'circular'/'ciphers' (1981a: 69–70).
10. Diegesis, from *diegeomai*, to describe, narrate, state.
11. For illustrations and analysis of postmodern diegetic strategies see Nash 1993.
12. For example, *Venus on the Half-Shell*; the 'real author', appropriating Vonnegut's perspective, was Philip José Farmer.
13. See Barthes 1987 (translation mine from the original, 1979: 21).
14. Zavarzadeh 1976: see 17, 30–1, 26.
15. Sarraute 1956: 88; Robbe-Grillet 1965: 62.
16. "Conceiving a character as the representation of a human person, having a consciousness and an identity manifested in its actions, is an ideological, not a scientific concept" (Lavers 1982: 178, paraphrasing Roland Barthes). As a 'speaker' phrases it in Brooke-Rose's novel *Thru*, "The notions of subject and object correspond only to a place in the narrative proposition and not to a difference in nature hence.... the agent is not the one who can accomplish this or that action but the one who can become subject of a predicate" (1974: 69).
17. BBC2, 8:50 pm, 4 January 1996.
18. Cf. e.g. Crosby Hall, completed a few miles from Holland's office (and at the same time) by Christopher J. Morahan. This building excited controversy different from that surrounding postmodern architecture (since it entails positive presumptions about the sequence and significance of history that Holland's, for example, doesn't). Now the largest private residence in London, it is a genuine late medieval building that has been physically moved from the City of London to the Chelsea Embankment. Around it, Morahan has built massive further wings that are carefully modified reproductions of other existing buildings of subsequent Tudor styles. The final structure creates, with meticulous attention to historical detail, the impression of a building that had naturally, organically evolved over a period of 150 years. Morahan plans to be buried there, and to leave the property to a charitable trust. "We're mere dots in the passage of time", he says; "it's a very profound thing to do, is to create this wonderful palace, which should last forever". In this sense of 'profundity' (as against explicit superficiality) in the act of the precise placement of an authentic object back into a confident narrative of a factual and coherent 'natural' history (as against an artificial and unstable fiction), with its permanence and its enduring value for the nation (as against an ephemeral construction without regard for such conceptions as 'nation' and 'value' beyond personal caprice), Morahan manifestly sets his face against the postmodern impulse (see 'One Foot in the Past', BBC2, 20 August 1997).

CHAPTER 2: A FANTASY

1. In what follows, purely for simplicity I speak of unqualified linguistic indeterminacy in the indicative ('Unqle Sim is/does –') rather than the conditional, as a 'real position' rather than a purely theoretical (effectively fictional) one.

2. Such arguments, for all their worth, fail to 'keep up' with the level of sophisticated engagement shown in indeterminists' own early awareness of the 'problem' – for example in Derrida's consistent observation that the problem itself is in fact 'essential' to his mode of discovering indeterminacy (that is, that 'yes, deconstruction can never obliterate the structures it undoes').
3. Most widely associated with linguistic indeterminism, Jacques Derrida repeatedly speaks of himself as a discrete subject, declares that we can never separate our utterances from the metaphysical, and can and should never abandon grand narratives (such as what he calls 'the narrative of emancipation'). On the matter of "anything goes", as he says (though with a characteristic complex abundance of intimation that popularizers of postmodern thought would find welcome though unsuited to mass consumption) "No one is free to read as he or she wants"; 1980: 22.
4. Distinctions of this sort have been essayed before – but drawn along other axes. Cf. e.g. Scott Lash 1990, centring on differences between philosophical outlooks as foundations for different cultures – where 'modern*ity*' and 'modern*ism*' are viewed as different philosophical positions.
5. Cf. e.g. Gerald Edelman's "however grand, the scientific view *derives* from other cultural ingredients and does not compel them" (1989: 270).
6. In a postmodernist perspective, indeterminacy is necessarily *produced* – by someone's introducing a context, a set of rules, for the reading of signifiers in a particlar way. Often when we decide that there is a contradiction (leading, for example, to uncertainty) it is because – as is common in recent postmodern 'criticism' – reading is treated as 'rigorous' only when the rule is adopted of reading an utterance according to two or more sets of rules simultaneously, with these rules assigned equal value and none given 'right of way'. That it is a self-sufficient 'meta-procedure' is a fiction; it is only a reading style, one that *is* given right of way. For e.g. Derrida, "there are ... some general rules, some procedures that can be transposed by analogy.... I]n what I write in particular ... there is idiom [singularity, signature] and there is method, generally" (1995: 200-1). (Students readily play the game of writing down in advance how an unread deconstruction of a read text will develop; they can identify reasonably well in the target text the terms/signifiers that the decontructionist text will particularly fasten onto, and predict the lexicon of the latter's discourse, the special species of patterns it is predisposed to unveil, and its thematic outcome.)

   In the physical sciences, decisions are made as to whether or not to adopt a procedure admitting contradiction. Cf. procedural decisions in chemistry and physics as to whether – and if so, how – to observe quantum events. In information technology, the conventional mode of signification (via binary coding) is specifically designed to be free of invasion by contradiction, and computers' immense power lies exactly in the fact that signifiers (electronic impulses) may be read any number of ways (as texts, images, sounds, etc.), depending on the software (reading rules) employed. Efforts are in train via 'quantum computing' – through what are called 'superposed' stacks – to generate protocols for the production of information in 'indeterminate' form. (Fuzzy logics are deployed similarly.) In other words, one needs to do a certain amount of *work* to produce contradiction. Where we call our enterprise a 'science' (cf. Derrida on deconstruction) it can cause trouble not to declare what procedure is to be adopted, what is likely to be its *kind* of outcome – e.g. that the 'default software' will produce uncertainty – and why it is adopted. (For more detailed discussion see CED.) An aim of this essay is to explore postmodern thinking in the light of these questions.
7. From *de-lira* – away (from the) ridge, furrow.

8. The titles (in literal English translation) of novels and essays published between 1955 and 1957 by Alain Robbe-Grillet (the first two) and Nathalie Sarraute.
9. Rorty 1991b: 136.

CHAPTER 3: AMBIVALENCE

1. Lest this be thought an unwholesome inquiry into intentions, linguistic indeterminists may be misguided to disclaim speculation on (construct possible) intentions of possible agents of utterances and actions. Not only because they actually regularly do so, but because any perception of indeterminacy would be not 'closed' by an examination of intention but prematurely closed by the exclusion of it.
2. Here contemporary linguistic indeterminist tradition reveals one of its weakest points, since it inclines (against its own 'better judgement') to speak of the operation of language as tantamount to a natural law – rules of language engendered by an always implicit nature of mind.
3. Difficulties with this view are evident. The properties of language – e.g. rules about the operation of signs, about difference and *différance* – cannot be understood outside of some notion of mind in which they would be constituted. It is feckless to claim it's more 'rigorous' to halt at that point in this circle (as linguistic indeterminism must), where 'the way *the* mind' processes through language is characterized, than it is to pause to characterize *what kind* of mind processes through language in this way. Or – since language is culturally constructed and since (as postmodernist theories customarily fail to observe) cultures differ – *what culture*, specifically, solicits this kind of procession.
4. The practical need for a variance of focus such as this is clear. An advertisement for a college textbook on the media, published in 1999, said: "Using approaches such as discourse analysis, semiotics and poststructuralism, with which students are likely to be more familiar, the book gently introduces the reader to psychology…" (Macmillan Sociology catalogue February 1999: 14, re: Valerie Walkerdine's *Psychology and the Media*). So – now we know where we stand.
5. For broad-ranging, non-technical surveys of the topic of 'the subject in question' see Carroll (1982) and Smith (1988). Whether the area of concern is philosophy or postmodern anti-philosophy, psychology or anti-psychology, since there's no way of thinking of these as anything constituted anywhere but in human minds, deliberately to sidestep their examination in psychological terms is to guarantee shortsightedness, if not some form of suppression, that must itself be subject to sharp psychological interrogation.
6. See e.g. Derrida (1998). It should be understood that in what follows I am not naming the 'contents' of 'subjects' minds' but offering an inventory of current discourse in which representations of the self and problems of the self are constructed. On balance, it proves wise to spend as little energy as possible in adventuring into anti-psychological argument until one has made sure that it can be purged of psychological models of thought.
7. Drive (or hydraulic) models have been criticized as naively reductionist, theoretically problematical, skewed *vis-à-vis* empirical evidence, and historically vulnerable – i.e. clinically less successful in dealing with the typical spectrum of cases current in present times. On the Oedipal mythos, a typical observation is that therapeutic practices grounded on the Freudian response to what in anglophone countries was conveniently called 'the Victorian ethos' – and on Continental responses (e.g. those inspiring writers such as Foucault, Lacan,

Lyotard, Deleuze and Guattari) to analogous European conditions – having had marked success in the early/mid-twentieth century in the treatment of repression-based neuroses (notably forms of 'hysteria'), simply no longer have the same widespread effect. (See e.g. Stolorow 1986: 197–8, 204; Mitchell 1988 and Mitchell and Black 1995.) In crass terms, among professionals in e.g. the United States it is widely acknowledged that traditional Oedipal and drive-based therapies have lost much of their appeal and income.

8. On the ultimate merger of ego and subject in Lacan, see e.g. Borch-Jacobsen (1991), and on this and the problems related to his having founded his argument on a notion of 'the narcissistic ego', see CED.
9. Cf. Jung's famous dictum – expressing the conception that the ego's depression and inflation arise with its separation from or too-close identification with the self: "Any victory for the Self is a defeat for the Ego." Derrida, correctly asking "is the 'ego' ... the only answer to the question 'Who?'", speaks of "de-simplifying, of 'de-homogenizing' the reference to something like The Subject"; "There has never been The Subject for anyone" (1992 [1995]: 262, 264). Psychology's central project (beginning with Freud) has been to reveal how 'person' was never monolithic in the way that theories of the decentring of the subject presume to have been the universally agreed case until they came along. For a discussion of this and the history of the (largely French/German) European debate on this subject see CED.
10. "There has been a gradual but consistent movement of the mainstream of psychoanalysis in the direction of field theory, and toward the interpersonal context as the medium of both normal maturation and therapeutic change" (Bromberg 1986: 438). For obvious affinities between psychological 'field' thinking and subsequent postmodern theory see Yontef 1993: 297–309.
11. Put in classic Freudian terms of 'horizontal' layers *within* the self: id, ego, superego would each play a role varying in significance and force from moment to moment in response to the 'vertical' divisions in the *relations between* ourselves and others.
12. Schafer (1968, endorsed by Lewis 1971: 30). If "what is *felt as 'belonging, in place'*" seems vague it can be useful to observe infant behaviour. See Lynne Jacobs, referring to evidence compiled by Daniel Stern (1985): "analysis of infant research confirms ... that contacting is extant from birth. He confirms that some degree of boundary discrimination ... occurs even in newborns" (1992: 38). Stern's evidence is further adduced by others; see e.g. Mollon 1993: 11. Postmodern arguments (following e.g. Lacan) that newborns cannot experience self-as-me or self-as-I leave us unable to explain neonate behaviour without some theory such as Schafer's.
13. On the experience of (temporal) continuity, see CED for a discussion – drawing analogies from complementarity in physics; biological events organizing the organism's effective action in time (as performed e.g. by the hippocampus); and, in neuropsychology, the persistence-of-vision-effect, where a motion picture's blurred individual single-frame images appear selectively consolidated to provide the 'moving image' with high-resolution definition. Postmodern thinking uniquely focuses on the 'blurring' (as indeterminate) of 'set' images, resisting as unproblematically delusory the 'clarity' of definition produced in time.
14. A woman may relate to herself and others as professional, child, lover, mother, partner or wife, friend, rival, citizen, natural organism, creature of God. At moments *the problem of choice* among these may seem to shake the foundations of her beliefs and her sense of her place in society, yet her sense of her self may remain intact.
15. Psychologists may place emphasis on 'mother', but make clear that anyone (of

any gender) may fill this role as described, and more commonly in society now than ever.

16. On contemporary obsessions with 'purity' see Baumann 1997. On unsuccessful attempts in psychology to dismiss parental influence see e.g. Mollon 1993: 76–80, 94–8.
17. Dynamic models are narrative models and subject to critique as such, as are those of postmodernists attacking Grand Narratives, who regularly stake arguments on large (often undertheorized) grand narrations of their own – featuring e.g. the overthrow of Enlightenment rationalism, 'archeological' and 'genealogical' understandings of culture, 'postindustrial' and 'cybernetic revolutions', the 'killing of reality' – entailing rhetorics tied to aggressively dramatized diachronic, historicist visions of the disposition of events (see e.g. Kellner 1988: 255–7 on Lyotard). On this issue see Nash 1990.
18. Cf. Jameson's introduction to a discussion of contemporary relativism: "In what follows ... we will collect a few of these paradoxes for examination as symptoms rather than as occasions for demonstrating something about the structural incapacity of the mind itself, or of its languages" (1994: 7–8).
19. Above all, while what's said here is informed by case material and by information from specialists whose work to determine general principles affecting mental activity is orientated quite differently, as analysts in the field of psychology in general will recognize instantly, I could never presume to be undertaking what they do in their practice, not least because theirs can be rightly carried out only in the context of specific cases.
20. I owe the valuable conception of readiness for ambivalence to Mallory Nash, "Narcissistic Journey", unpublished thesis, 1994.
21. First advanced as a central concept by e.g. Melanie Klein, and adopted by many (such as Winnicott) disagreeing otherwise with a number of her tenets.
22. Lasch 1979: 34, 33. Among psychologists, Stephen A. Mitchell devotes considerable space to describing how since Freud "conceptualizations of and technical recommendations for the handling of narcissistic phenomena have had an enormous influence on clinical practice across all diagnostic groupings" of psychoanalysis (1988: 177). For Kohut, problems of the self/narcissism are increasing in current western society, while problems of inner structural conflicts (of the sort Freudian thought concerns itself with) are decreasing (1977). Cooper (1986) cites studies by Glover, Lazar and others indicating "the scarcity of the 'classical' neurotic patient" and "the increasing numbers of patients with characterological disorders of some severity, epecially [sic] the narcissistic character". He notes the claim that "conflictual transference neurosis of primarily oedipal nature is now rare and has been replaced by the patient with narcissistic and even borderline features" and, despite uncertainties, concludes that "changes in the culture ... may have produced more frequent and more severe forms of pathological narcissism" (114, 126–7, 141, 125). For Morrison, "psychoanalysis is accepting more frequently for its specialized treatment patients who suffer disorder narcissism"; "such patients present with" a number of dynamic features "making them resistant to traditional psychoanalytic treatment" (1986: 367–8). Arguments that psychologists 'see this phenomenon now because that's what's on their minds now' of course miss the point; the question regarding the culture is, Why is it on their minds now?
23. For a generally well-received summary of uses of the term 'narcissism' see Pulver 1986.
24. Mahler and Gruneberger, separately, put the most extreme case. "The entire life cycle constitutes a more or less successful process of distancing from and introjection of the lost symbiotic mother, an eternal longing for the actual or

fantasied 'ideal state of self,' with the latter standing for a symbiotic fusion with the 'all good' symbiotic mother, who was at one time part of the self in a blissful state of well being" (Mahler 1986: 148). Gruneberger envisions a 'cosmic narcissism', a state of beatitude, completeness, unqualified omnipotence and elation (e.g. 1971).

25. Quoted phrase from Mollon 1993: 4. Given such broad meanings these terms, I hope, beg none of the questions that some other definitions raise, and provide a rough starting point for this discussion. The Bibliography will indicate writers whose views (while importantly divergent among themselves) have served as the most consistent basis for my own thinking here, and that I've perhaps least abused by synthesizing them with views of mine, for which I am solely responsible.
26. "The transition to the depressive position involves acceptance of separateness of self and other, the giving up of illusions of omnipotence, and an acknowledgement of ambivalence towards the other. This greater acceptance of reality results in depressive feelings to do with loss and guilt...." (Mollon 1993: 99).
27. For an interesting deconstructive reading of the Ovidian version of the myth, see Brenkman 1976. Taking as pre-text a predetermined 'overt' narrative theme that seems oddly unsophisticated (the myth as a neat story of Narcissus' punishment) it is a classic illustration of the procedure; the more widespread view that the myth bears on the indefinition of the self is left largely unaddressed.
28. About 'narcissance': this enallage (via a participial suffix) reflects an understanding perhaps closer to one many psychologists would prefer in any case. (No excuse but a possible consolation is the famous example of Freud's neologism 'Narzissmus' in place of 'Narzissismus'.) 'Narcissist' ('narcissistic personality type', etc.), is often used in clinical diagnosis more to solve legal and administrative problems than psychological ones. The term's frank unorthodoxy is hoped to help avoid misleading caricatural connotations of 'narcissism'; to insist on the dynamic of an ongoing process; to uncouple the argument from easy normative intimations of an illness to be clinically cured; and to leave the discussion more free to include cases not 'narcissist' strictly speaking but where (in e.g. 'borderline disorder') narcissance is nevertheless a significant feature. Among professionals concerned with diagnostic categories, the recurrent theme is often finally '"Narcissist", ok – but narcissist *what*?' Cf. "Borderline: An Adjective in Search of a Noun" (Akiskal 1986). Note e.g. cases of schizophrenia much of whose apparently more successful partial 'cure' in psychoanalysis in recent years may be owing, as some have recognized, to the more alert treatment not of their schizophrenia but of their narcissance.
29. "Oscillatory patterns" are characteristic features of 'narcissistic' and borderline cases, showing "splitting and the maintenance of alternating or often coexistent yet contradictory ego states". "[T]he perception of other people becomes grossly inconsistent and variable, showing a lack of awareness of contradictions from state to state, a rapid fluctuation between contradictory states, and a volatility of behavior" (Meissner 1986: 423–4). "The presence of extreme contradictions in their self-concept is often the first clinical evidence of the severe pathology ... hidden underneath a surface of smooth and effective social functioning" of a 'narcissist personality' (Kernberg 1986a: 215). "Their expectations are inflated, in an all-or-nothing manner.... There is no middle.... It is not a system of continuities, but rather of dichotomies" (Yontef 1993: 438–9).

    Oscillation is not rigidly 'structural', to be globally mapped. Rather, it is *predispositional*. If narcissance periodically recurs it is not because a preexisting psychic structure insists on it but because there is a *predisposition* for it. When certain cues appear in the field, certain *kinds of response* (deployed by mechanisms no more 'structured' than, for instance, local association or conditioning) may arise to meet them.

30. "The Freudian notion of self-esteem as the libidinal investment of the self ... does not fit the clinical facts. Individuals with high self-esteem are precisely those most able to be more interested in others, while those with low self-esteem are most likely to concentrate upon themselves" (Pulver 1986: 105). For expositions of the clinical failure of Freudian analysis due to its incapacity in this regard see e.g. Morrison 1986 and Mollon 1993.
31. Mitchell 1988: 202, echoing Kohut.
32. Thus the most agreeably self-effacing individual – suppressing 'normal' but potentially confrontational anger – may also be the one who seemingly at any time flies into an 'inexplicable cold blind narcissistic rage'.
33. See e.g. Yontef 1993: 208–9.
34. Oscillation is not merely what occurs in the flow of 'selfings', of changing figures in the fields of our experience. When Jack fights with every ounce of strength for his life, we don't assume that he is also fighting to die. But when John, speaking from narcissance, seems to be saying 'I am totally responsible for my life', it is quite possible that he also feels that someone else is totally responsible for John's life. It is by *virtue* of this very precise *activation of extremes in contradiction* that narcissance articulates itself, by much the same means as postmodern thinking articulates and distinguishes itself from other modes of thinking.
35. A *fil conducteur* linking many from Klein to Lacan and Kristeva.
36. When e.g. we find writers speaking of 'loss' of and any desire to 'return to the mother', this is an image for an idea of 'mother' that *the mind makes*; a phantasy, and only rarely a fantasy. For example, for Lacan, few adults desiring a 'return to the breast' would respond with pleasure if asked if they'd like now to suck at their mother's nipple (see Lee 1990: 145).
37. A child's initial existence is in some respects always a response to a parent's need and not the child's need. From the moment it becomes apparent that it has needs of its own, every child is thus potentially well placed to feel unwanted, and the extent to which children don't feel this way will depend largely on how prepared parents are to accord value to (and indeed perceive) the child's intrinsic individual being and wants.

    Thus by a 'holding behaviour' the mother is "the midwife of individuation, of psychological birth" (Mahler, quoted by White 1986: 151). It involves the mother's "capacity to reduce physical and psychological tensions ... (e.g., in soothing the infant to sleep)", a capacity "gradually taken over by the baby through a manageable, bit-by-bit withdrawal of the mother's ministrations" (White 1986: 151). Thus narcissism, for Mollon paraphrasing Kohut, may arise: "if the normal selfobject availability of mother to child is reversed, so that the child is required to be selfobject for mother, required to ensure mother's well-being and mirroring mother's grandiosity, then the child's spontaneous self-development is derailed in favour of the mother's agenda. The child develops a false self" (Mollon 1993: 81), where e.g. the focus of a mother's 'mirroring' of the child is "selected to keep him dependent on her ... to brace up her own, precariously constituted self" (Kohut and Wolf 1986: 189–90). Cf. Alice Miller's popular work, centring on this reversal of parent–child roles.
38. Psychologists seeking to secure therapeutic ends by recovering past events in the history of the patient are in the minority. It is the experience of the parent as an active event in the present field of the patient (and the therapist) that is to be reckoned with.

39. "Highly intelligent patients with this personality structure may appear as quite creative in their fields: narcissistic personalities can often be found as leaders in industrial organizations or academic institutions; they may also be outstanding performers in some artistic domain" (Kernberg 1986a: 215).
40. See e.g. essays in Morrison 1986 – by Kernberg, Pulver, Bursten, Meissner and others – and Cooper 1986 for detailed differential diagnostics contrasting 'narcissism' with other 'disorders'.
41. For a detailed discussion of reasons that the operation of a narcissant mind-style is dedicatedly (and collusively) concealed on both sides – involving e.g. the complex attitudes of both society and narcissant toward (1) oscillatory behaviour, (2) grandiosity and 'healthy self-promotion', (3) shame and modesty, (4) depression, (5) boundary conflicts, (6) self-control and social control, (7) the relations between self-revelation and risks to 'the false self', (8) the relations between individual (private) needs and individual (public) demands – see CGF.
42. As Lasch's works' subtitles reveal; see 1979 and 1984. Cf. Marin 1975, speaking of "The New Narcissism". A sense of this approach, together with the uneven quality of its purchase on the dynamics of narcissance, appears in Lasch's proposal that at bottom narcissism – by its association with "mass consumption", "the emergence of the egalitarian family, so-called", and "the child's increasing exposure to other socializing agencies besides the family" – "makes [people] weak and dependent. It undermines their confidence in their capacity to understand and shape the world and to provide for their own needs". Together, they produce "infantile feelings of helplessness" (1979: 33–4 and 1984: 185). Lasch posits as both historical evidence and prognosis an America in an economic slump, suffering Cold War paranoia and paralysis.
43. Clements (1982) argues that we turn a clinical diagnostic term into a moral judgement when we speak of a culture as 'narcissistic'. As will be seen, the views expressed regarding e.g. Lasch aren't to be supposed to impugn the taking of a moral or political position. Meanwhile, not all socio-historical outlooks stressing 'narcissism' in culture are negative. See e.g. Alford (1988), commending the trend on the grounds that it sustains needed forces for individual creativity. (This can be true, but can miss narcissance's crucial inclination toward confluence and conformity.)
44. For example, a problem for any child is not merely that it wishes its parents/carers to show certain qualities and finds them lacking – it's that often they *possess* those qualities, *and* also qualities that seem to oppose them; and that this is a feature of humans' relationship with reality throughout life.

CHAPTER 4: WAYS OF SPEAKING

1. Paraphrase by Goodchild 1996: 88. On Deleuze and Guattari's active (and logically consistent) repulsion of the label 'postmodern', see CED. Their impact on and their appropriation by postmodern thinking, the concurrence of many of their ideas with it and the energetic uses they made of it, however, makes their regular appearance in this essay's discussion inevitable.
2. "Lacan from the beginning conceived the evolution of the relations between the 'ego' and its 'objects' on the basis of the narcissistic phase alone" (Borch-Jacobsen 1991: 48). "The tragedy of the human condition is implicit in Lacan's theory that both the object and goal and of the drive toward constancy converge in the Desire to be … recognized by the mother so that the infant feels one with her" which constitutes an "early dependency on an external and, therefore, *inconstant* source of 'self'" (Ragland-Sullivan 1986: 73). On Lacan's extraordinary insistence on binding his vision of an always-already-happening

event in language to a material narrative of separation in the development of individual human organisms – perhaps his theory's greatest liability and the least comprehensible without an understanding of narcissance – see CED.

3. Lacan 1977a: 4. Compare psychological accounts of separation as experienced in 'narcissism': A "tearing from the empathic matrix, leaving a frightened self at the centre of a cold and hostile world"; "what is missing is felt to be part of the self". A "failure of the caretaker's empathy ... is felt to be a wrenching away from the orienting framework" (Mollon – concurring with Kohut – 1993: 58, 72, 60).
4. Derrida 1995: 391. 'Narcissists' are commonly reported feeling 'burnt out', 'a shell' or 'shadow of myself'.
5. The narcissant is "fearful of a world which seems ... hateful and revengeful.... The greatest fear ... is to be dependent on anybody else because to depend means to hate, envy [those they most desire], and expose themselves to the danger of being exploited, mistreated, and frustrated" (Kernberg 1975: 233, 235). Life is that of "'a hungry, enraged, empty self, full of impotent anger at being frustrated and fearful of a world which seems as hateful and revengeful as the patient himself'" (Kernberg, quoted in Mollon 1993: 79).
6. For 'narcissists' "a common underlying theme [is] of having been disappointed and betrayed by someone who was not powerful enough or ready enough to give when they needed it" (Bursten 1986: 387). "The theme of exploitation of the child by the parent is implicit in Kohut, Robbins, Schwarz-Salant, Bursten, Gear/Hill/Liendo, Rothstein – even Kernberg hints at it.... [T]he child [is] treated as a pawn in a parental drama" (Mollon 1993: 103).
7. Cf. Alice Miller's comparison of Beckett's famous recollection of his family and their treatment of him as ideal with his writings' thematic bleakness. See note, Morrison 1986: 333.
8. Children are far from being without philosophy, and we know the potential philosophical thrust of their challenge '*But you said* –!' But when this is a persistent refrain, what concerns the child is not always so much the matter of the inconsistent detail (what was said) as it is the aura (what was communicated) of our relations with him or her in terms of *constancy*. 'Can I count on you? are you truly *there* when you speak to me?' In this essay the intimate affinities become important between anxieties about discursive philosophical inconsistency and human, relational inconstancy.
9. Kernberg 1986b, especially 266–7; emphasis mine.
10. Miller 1987: 35; cf. Derrida 1995: 384.
11. Not simply because we would be at a loss to conceive who wouldn't expect fictions to deceive, but because it has the earmarks of a *diversion* from the scrutiny of texts – excluded by followers of de Man as 'ordinary' or 'informative' – where it might more certainly hurt to be deceived.
12. History offers scarce evidence that in societies with more mirrors more people have an active sense of themselves as wholes. The experience of coordination arises not from mirror reflections but with a living organism's inherent need to coordinate its sensations and movements ('organization'—>'organism') in order biologically to survive, and an actual rapid development, precisely at the 'mirror stage', in childrens' own internal neural, muscular and skeletal coordination. In the context of neuropsychological evidence – particularly affecting the neural matrix and the early formation of the body self-image, e.g. in phantom limb studies – Lacan's scenario is unusually naive. That Lacan is unable to assign the responsibility-for-the-promise either to the child's own biological condition or to specified events in an actual human (say, family) relationship, but must 'deflect' it onto the child's interaction with an idealized 'transitional

object', highlights the narcissant nature of his rendering. If so, the process of deflection (or of 'sublimation') has only begun; his most immense achievement was to go on to theorize a towering abstract structure with 'the Symbolic' as the true responsible party, with implications to be examined.

Compare Schafer's conception of 'self-as-place', and the 'true self' of Winnicott (unlike Lacan a lifelong clinical child-psychologist), which "comes from the aliveness of the body tissues and the working body-functions, including the heart's actions and breathing. [It collects] together the details for the experience of aliveness" (1965: 148). Mahler: "the earliest awareness of a sense of being, of entity ... is not a sense of who I am but that I am ... the earliest step in the process of unfolding individuality". Discussing the mirror stage Mahler lays stress precisely on the child's confusing but also "sorting and clarifying the relationship between himself and 'the image'" (1975, cited by White in Morrison 1986: 149, 152).

13. For a more detailed discussion of strategies in recent criticism – e.g. in the application of deconstruction – involving (1) the 'rush to the site of generality/abstraction', (2) the effort to uncover duplicity, contradiction and uncertainty, and (3) the selection of favoured text-sites for this purpose, see CED.
14. In Barthes' seminal discussion of Sollers, the effect of "*l'oscillation*" is that it "attacks the Image", to "forestall the formation and stabilization of each and every Image" (see 1987: 88–9; this translation mine).
15. Leading postmodern writers regularly confuse schizophrenia with 'multiple (or schizoid) personality' and ignore the differences between both and what they themselves advocate. Guattari, having clinical experience, confessed that he had never seen a case of schizophrenia of the sort he commends in his theory. The choice of 'schizophrenia' celebrates it as a condition regarded as relatively intractable to uniform definition or rationalist cure and as socially marginalized/excluded/punished; it has little to do with psychology and is an important socio-political and openly utopian gesture of revolt, treating the dispersal of the subject as a positive social opportunity (an example of the 'description/prescription routine' considered below). For a detailed discussion of the 'postmodernist/schizophrenicist' gesture see CED.
16. See e.g. Robbins 1982.
17. See e.g. Yontef on the urgency for *both* the 'confluent' and the 'isolate' that "the forces that ... might impel awareness of separating or breach (e.g. open anger) must be isolated, disowned, projected" (1993: 208–9).
18. The best known, projection can be most widely misunderstood; to illustrate briefly: A patient "plays out the role of helpless and impotent victim, while at the same time he projects the elements of aggressive destructiveness and powerful persecutory threat onto [another, such as] the therapist" (Meissner 1986: 429).
19. One of the most commanding and intricate of psychological processes bringing boundary confusion with it is *transference*, whose force has been a central preoccupation of dynamic psychology since Freud. The special complexity of its theoretical and practical implications leave it beyond the compass of this introductory essay.
20. Barth 1969: 148.
21. In this essay the word 'irony' is applied in keeping with popular usage, and with serious misgivings. Concerned here is not genuine irony (which – e.g. etymologically, signifying polemically strategic disinvolvement – entails positioning) but hyperdetermination (anti-positioning). A tendency of discourse about postmodern thinking is to confound these radically different conceptions.

22. To learn the conditions of its own production, as postmodern theory often phrases it. "After all there's something narcissistic about this business of exploiting the authorial voice" (Barth quoted in Bellamy 1974: 9).
23. Mollon 1993: 79, 55; the passage Mollon quotes is Kernberg's. A postmodern predilection for schizoid models is revealing insofar as psychologists consider them defensive strategies for *dissociation*, for quarantining or 'anaesthetizing' intolerable emotions and ideas about the self as a whole.
24. Cooper 1986: 132; Kernberg 1986a: 221–2; 1986b: 269–71, 288.
25. Being "'turned off' emotionally" in this way ("narcissistic affect block") "result[s] from the fear of being overwhelmed by the intensity of affects"; Modell 1986: 293–4. Kohut discusses the effect further, 1971.
26. Nabokov 1975 [1926]: 113–14, 118–19, 121.
27. P. Hildebrand's view, paraphrased as a "personal communication", by Mollon 1993: 113.
28. Summarized in Mancia 1993: 4, whence the observation on an 'intellectual' type of narcissism, cited below. Cf. Freud, the "belief in the omnipotence of thoughts.... [T]he overvaluation of psychic acts can be attributed to narcissism and even considered an essential component of it"; cf. Baudrillard: "the omnipotence of thoughts, a magic narcissism" (1976: 219).
29. For detailed analytical examples (in e.g. Lacan, Derrida, de Man, Deleuze and Guattari, and American theoretical writing since Hassan) see CED.
30. E.g. Smith 1988: 51.
31. "One prominent reason why [narcissistic] patients cannot tolerate facing their feelings of hatred and envy is because they fear such feelings will destroy the analyst" (Kernberg 1986b: 267–8).
32. Kohut and others give 'pathological lying' and 'imposture' as leading traits of narcissism. See e.g. Deutsch 1942: 265 and Mollon 1993: 160.
33. See e.g. Mollon 1993: 58.
34. At issue here are *not* matters of fact, to which few are more accurately attentive than narcissants. A narcissant *is* deceived in what s/he 'hears'; what s/he can't see is that s/he is bound to be. Where s/he is 'let down' is in the matter of *feeling*, which can never match the feeling desired, and yet cannot be openly addressed. Recognition that they are *regularly*, and with such highly developed finesse, *finding* others deceptive or deluded would expose more than narcissants could tolerate knowing – a *prepossession* with duplicity and concealment whose root is itself unthinkable.
35. Kohut and Wolf 1986: 187. For Winnicott, Mollon and others, a "common cause of feeling insubstantial is the defensive projection into others in phantasy of parts of the self, especially aggressive parts, leaving the self depleted" and unreal (Mollon 1993: 13).
36. The individual may finally retreat from relationships as literally 'insupportable' – all-the-while working harder to maintain a tolerable self-image of congenial and even cordial social nature. Under the assault of self-punitive perfectionism, what is 'real' or 'ordinary' comes to be both detested and adored. In the context of a species of 'moral masochism', "others are allowed to be 'ordinary' but [the narcissist] is not" (Miller 1986: 333); others' freedom "to be 'average'" is envied and indeed a source of "dammed-up rage" (330). Something *called* 'true Reality', becomes idealized as unattainable. In narcissance (as in postmodern culture) the seemingly unfulfillable yearning to 'get back to nature', to the 'real, elemental reality' of the earth, of the 'primitive' becomes entangled with anxieties of what may 'really' be 'meant'. (Does he really love me? Are the people on this island real natives? Will this new car/toothpaste really give me power/beauty? Do they want me for anything but my money?) The phenomena

of daily existence itself, then – failing to meet the test of and occluded by the Grand (fantasied) Reality – come to be regarded as false, mere shadows. 'Reality', 'the real thing' has been 'lost', 'murdered'.

37. Uncannily like the narcissant, Baudrillard sees 'subjectivities' as the mere objects of simulacra-production processes. Personal reality is dissolved ('assassinated') in endless simulations.
38. For classic cases: Borges' "La busca de Averroes" and Larissa in Brooke-Rose's novel *Thru*.
39. Cahalan 1983: 46; emphasis mine.
40. See e.g. Harlow and Zimmerman 1959: 1971; given the choice between food, on one hand, and contact with a soft warm 'embracing' cloth-covered wire frame, infants regularly chose the latter.
41. Popular when postmodernism was taking root was the idea of brainwashing via sensory deprivation and bombardment (white noise); the essential was *not* merely the presentation of conflicting experiences, but the victim's isolation, deprived of support. Of interest is not its pulp-fictional appeal as a means to ideology-replacement (*Manchurian Candidate*) but the culture's fascination with mechanisms attacking the sense of self. More recent literature on sensory-deluge management in child development is summarized by Bowlby (sharing attachment theory with Harlow) 1988.
42. Twentieth-century communist, fascist, ban-the-bomb, animal rights and anti-abortion rallies, where a strictly political analysis might aim to show internal social structures to be organized by belief systems, actually disclosed not different but, rather, remarkably similar discursive and behavioral traits, with identical acclamations of solidarity, fraternity etc. This point is not an invitation to ignore the socio-political disasters that accompany spurious sharp distinctions between 'form and content'.
43. 'Esemplasm' in Coleridge's English version of *ineinsbildung* "is to convert a *series* into a *Whole*: to make those events, which in real or imagined History move on in a *strait* Line, assume to our Understandings a *circular* motion – the snake with it's Tail in its Mouth"; the worm Ouroboros, the archetypal emblem for Jung and Neumann of the *puer aeternus*, whose mental processes accompany narcissism. McGilchrist 1982: 193, quotes Coleridge.
44. See e.g. Best and Kellner 1991: 129ff.
45. Baudrillard 1987: 68. We have entered a new, fourth, 'viral stage', "without bearing reference to anything whatsoever except by way of mere continuity" (1989, from a lecture, "Transpolitics, Transexuality, and Transaesthetics", quoted by Best and Kellner 1991: 136; see also "The Ecstasy of Communication", in 1988a. On 'ecstasy' see Chapter 5, here.
46. Goodchild 1996: 77–8. This construct is more than just (though it certainly also is) an ambiguous (or ambivalent) pastiche of Enlightenment mechanistic visions of a unified universal system. But the extraordinary gesture of constructing an abstraction and of naming it 'body' – one now of literally infinite potency and creative power free of the attributes (literally free of the limits), of actual (ordinary) bodies – is striking. (Why not call it 'spirit' or '*élan vital*' or 'Honey'?) As Deleuze and Guattari's emphasis on infantile desire prefigures, it markedly resembles the 'narcissist's' (frequently clinically observed) self-shaming 'contempt' for his/her own (limited personal) body and the grandiose idealized (unlimited) bodily image that s/he 'imagines into' its place to draw others' rapt attention and desire. The subject is discussed in more detail in CED.
47. Borch-Jacobsen 1991: 47, citing Lacan 1977a: 2/94. Finally revealing in Lacan's account is that whether the crucial separation were of child from mother or of the child entering the Symbolic, it rests on a phantasy that the *mother herself*

(or some other matrix, or the Symbolic itself) is *not* separated from some imaginary or imagined All.

48. By e.g. Deleuze and Guattari.
49. It would be unrealistic to say that Lyotard was so enthralled in the network of post-Kantian thought not to have seen the polemic need to replace the word with another, had he wished to clear its referent of transcendental connotations. The adumbration of a double-universe intuited by a centred 'injured subject' leaves its trace throughout his work. On Lyotard's ambivalence in this area and its possible sources (philosophical, political, religious, temperamental) and stylistic manifestations see CED.
50. Derrida consistently withstands the seduction of such notions as *jouissance*, sublime, body without organs, transaesthetic. Derrida's case is more complex than can be fairly dealt with here, but as two examples of ways in which he may appear to drift into the pattern of 'aspiration' suggested, see Beardsworth 1996: 156, on Derrida's notion of "the promise as 'pre-arch-originary'", and the closing words of his paper "There Is No *One* Narcissism" (1995) where he intimates a belief in reaching toward a purity exceeding the bounds of material value. There are signs of a subject-centred heroism, as his comparative studies of himself and e.g. Lacan and de Man show in lectures on the occasions of their deaths, and there are questions to ask about the status of the self intimated there. See CED on e.g. his provocative and problematic self-representation in "For the Love of Lacan" (1998).
51. What is more *à propos* than the issue, raised by Rorty, as to whether in his 'essentialism' de Man solicited colleagues' belief that he was a man of the left (as Derrida certainly says of himself) is that it has always been more economical to understand – and easier to correlate with historical events – that it wasn't the 'left' or 'right' qualities of de Man's 'One' that counted most. (Liberals' disappointment on learning of 'right' leanings in de Man's past derived fundamentally from this misunderstanding.) What counted was the very Oneness of what 'one' he chose at a given moment.
52. See Nash 1993, especially 248–76.
53. Parallel to Lacan's grounding his theory on the mind's beginnings in a physical organism is Derrida's prepossession with physical death; see his discussions of his colleagues' demise, where e.g. he speaks of de Man, deceased, as 'no longer there' (thus throwing his problematization of 'presence' into turmoil). Lacan, positing "a grimace of the Real" beyond and indeed behind our subjectivities' constructions of it (1974: 17), worked industriously to differentiate himself from both classic and modern Idealists' insistence that reality is a pure product of mind. Baudrillard founds much of his writing on the distinction between reality and a condition from which it has been stolen. Lyotard's theory of the 'sublime' requires that a 'real' or 'beyond-utterance' be posited. Deleuze and Guattari are avowedly materialist.
54. It's not good enough to say that in this double-universe scheme the real isn't known and that consequently it is merely another word-game to call the schema a metaphysical one. Given every occasion to deny it, Derrida positively and unrelentingly names (and powerfully laments) a terminus, death – and the 'signs' he yields up showing that he believes he may not infinitely defer this terminus can only be read as a rich body of 'knowledge of reality' that he uniquely declines to 'contra-dict' as such. (From the perspective of a thoroughgoing deconstructionism this point would be merely pin-dancing. What are the grounds for empirical inquiry on which it depends? Derrida's 'actual' death would be only a sign of his death, and for life everlasting all he needs to do is give us a sign.)

Lawrence E. Cahoone (1988) considers twentieth-century "radical subjectivism" an artifact of "splitting" by which philosophers see no foundation for arguing for the existence of an objective world, yet live 'as if' it is there. He sees the ensuing oscillation as the source of what he calls "philosophical narcissism". Cahoone's shrewd intuition is an important step; but scepticism (or even splitting) alone doesn't make 'narcissism' or postmodernism (neither of which he considers in detail), and how the reverse can be true needs demonstration. For a discussion of Cahoone's study see CED. This essay is not meant to replace his; having different objectives, they may be taken as complementary.

55. 1984: 80, appendix to the English edition, "Answering the Question: What Is Postmodernism?", tr. R. Durand; from "Réponse à la question: qu'est-ce que le postmoderne?", *Critique*, no. 419 (April 1982).
56. Ehrenzweig 1993: 188, 294.
57. Bursten 1986: 381, citing Rado, Lewin, and Reich in support.
58. Fenichel 1945: 40, 425. On plain biological grounds the conception of the organism's ever having experienced continuous perfect untroubled ease and plenitude, much less every individual's having experienced it in the same way, is fanciful. There is little sign among species that the young seek to remain huddled in an inseparable stationary nursing heap with their parents, let alone permanently at the breast or 'within the mother's womb'. (Cf. e.g. Magarinos et al. 1997 on experiments confining animals as an optimal means for inducing symptoms of distress.) Most appear to crave the freedom – and stand little chance of survival when it's withheld – to move, explore, try skills against obstructions, experience variety and change, and live apart for extended periods with a strong measure of autonomy and independence. It is of the *logic of narcissant thinking* that the *image* of a blissful fetal state will be an essential part of its background, as its 'shadow'. The recent bias toward notions of separation as an unqualified ordeal, and toward the phantasy of 'return' to an omnivalent fetal nescience, reveals the force of a contemporary wish elucidated most cogently in some theory of narcissance.
59. I have so far used 'affect' in a broad informal sense to mean simply 'what is felt' in relation to things we perceive and conceive. But as some psychologists insist, 'feeling' and 'emotion' are different things, and 'affect' in the following pages coincides more precisely with 'emotion'; i.e. with somatic processes and their more immediate psychological correlatives.
60. "[T]he entire defensive effort of these patients [is] to depreciate others, and to avoid dependency" (Cooper 1986: 138, paraphrasing Kernberg). The cognitive deconstruction of discursive positions has notable parallels with narcissant depreciation of other voices and indeed of separateness, otherness. Unlike traditional philosophical acts of revolt, each of these promotes a *generic* hesitation regarding any position as foundational or 'essential', combined uniquely with the inability to assert any essence or foundation for itself. With its ostensibly non-aggressive finesse, the "depreciation and devaluation" of others' constructions of value "permits the denial of dependency on others, protects the individual against narcissistic rage and envy" (Kernberg 1986: 263). Simultaneously, deferral of outright 'difference' gratifyingly allows the sleek seamless assimilation into the narcissant activity itself of the other's apparent power.
61. "[O]ther personalities ... can tolerate the loss of beauty, health, youth, or loved ones, and although they mourn them they do so without depression.... One is free from depression when self-esteem is based on the authenticity of one's own feelings and not on the possession of certain qualities" or on the satisfaction of what are imagined to be others' expectations (Miller 1986: 329).
62. Lyotard 1984: 80, appendix to the English edition, "Answering the Question:

What Is Postmodernism?", tr. R. Durand; from "Réponse à la question: qu'est-ce que le postmoderne?", *Critique*, no. 419 (April 1982).

63. Cf. Kernberg quoted in Mollon 1993: 79.
64. The manic aspect of affirming the self's 'pro-activity' is vital – as an "attempt to turn experiences of helplessness or lack of comprehension into actively repeated, self-initiated action" (Mollon 1993: 20, paraphrasing G. Klein).
65. Goodchild 1996: 77–8, 82–3; on orality, see their *The Logic of Sense* and Guattari's *Chaosmose*.
66. Deconstructionist writing, popularly called 'analysis', is for many difficult to distinguish from analysis' opposite, 'hermeneutic chaining' – a form of secondary processing commonly targeted by analytic critics, who accuse 'hermeneutic criticism' of 'finding connections wherever it likes'.
67. See e.g. Bogue 1989: 107.
68. Lecture, 1989, "Transpolitics, Transexuality, and Transaesthetics", in Best and Kellner 1991: 135. On 'delirium' see Chapter 2. Psychological and musical denotations of 'fugue' (flight) converge here. Cf. Lecercle (1985) on *'délire'*, representing contemporary culture as laden with an irrepressible ("compulsive") "ambiguity" signally resembling, in its ensemble, narcissant oscillation; cf. Derrida (1979) on *delireium* and reading.
69. Cf. Pinget's exquisitely logomanic (and aptly titled) diegetic novel *Graal Flibuste*.
70. Meissner 1986: 413; Kernberg, Bursten and many others are vigorous on this point.
71. "Many paranoid personalities lead active and productive lives – especially in vocations where scepticism, suspiciousness and criticism are important components" (Bursten 1986: 384). Radical scepticism and criticism are however essentially polar opposites; see Chapter 6.
72. For example by Goodchild 1996: 7.
73. For Freud, "in secondary narcissism, libido is withdrawn ... to protect the individual against anxiety and other painful affects connected with objects" (Pulver 1986: 106–7).
74. Modell 1986: 295. To work, flattening must also disable the ambiant feelings of others. Having given pleasure, a narcissant may be unable to resist 'taking it back' ('I won't always be able to – don't count on me –'); the moment is 'ruined' or 'shit on'; experiences are deflated in the name of 'realism' or 'the broader view'. However showy in outward panache, narcissants may find themselves accused of being cold or 'withholding', and skirt situations where – and from people with whom – issues are presented as vital, and dependency might become an issue. 'Meaningfulness' (significant gestures, glances, words) may be averted. Contrasted with *accidie* or *anomie* in religious/ethical contexts, apathy's relational functions reveal narcissance's presence.
75. Patients in depression commonly present rigidly ironic attitudes. Where irony is persistently deployed it can be useful to scan the field for depressive and apathic processes.
76. Mollon 1993: 6, paraphrasing Ticho and Richards.
77. Irresoluble complexity (or 'reflexivity') "does lead to paradox, but this is only a problem if all paradox has to be resolved at a meta-level" (Cilliers 1998: 121).
78. Thus we understand postmodern theory's proliferating unsophisticated attacks on a never psychologically justified notion of the ego as identical with the self. They decoy or deflect attention from crises of the self extending well beyond those of the ego and, ultimately, from the possibility and menace of the depressive position.
79. I must reaffirm vital differences between this essay's approach and that of

practising psychotherapists. Their proper inclination is to ascribe narcissism to specifically personal biographical events, and they invest much in the idea of its cure more than I do here. See Chapter 6 on 'remediation'.

80. In deliberately simple form Winnicott describes a stage in childhood of 'I am', one "very closely allied to" Klein's conception of the depressive position: "At this stage the child can say: 'Here I am. What is inside me is me and what is outside me is not me'" (1971: 130).
81. For a consideration of the relations between the ambivalence threshold and synthesis, sublation, and deconstructive play, see CED.

CHAPTER 5: WAYS OF ACTING

1. "The Greats: Artists", BBC2, 15 July 1999.
2. In deconstructionist theory a part-analogy would be where the 'moment of decision is the moment of madness'; see e.g. in Mouffe (1996) Critchley (35), and Laclau who argues that this leap – mad decision – "is the subject" (52–5). By way of abandon the subjective 'declares itself'. Note the common charge that postmoderns are '(narcissistic) control-freaks', manipulating their own subjective experience.
3. The theme of "Shopping on Top", *Big Ideas*, BBC2, 11 July 1999.
4. "Shopaholics are victims of loveless and/or molested childhoods.... Hence the roots of compulsive shopping lie in unresolved childhood problems. People whose parents withheld attention and affection or set impossible standards may feel driven to purchase power, control, and prestige" (1999: 252). For an analysis of the self-presentation of 'Seinfeld' and other cult-figures starting with an examination of Twitchell's reading of them, see CGF, forthcoming.
5. The perspective put forward here follows on from a view of the operation of works of art introduced in Nash 1987 and 1993: 135–41, on the 'commutative' function, where it is suggested that created works have functional effects as well as referential ones – effects so divergent and of such consequence as to be complementary at best.
6. "The star now" isn't the guitarist but "the disk jockey" (Eric Clapton, "The Frank Skinner Show", BBC1, Thursday, 20 May 1999).
7. Janet Goleas, <http://www.zingmagazine.com/zing3/reviews/023_luhring.html>, June 1996.
8. "The Greats: Artists", BBC2, 15 July 1999; quotations here, transcribed from that broadcast, were originally recorded in 1997.
9. Ibid.
10. See e.g. Mullan (1998), a study of the phenomenon of the self-help book, its motives and effects.
11. For a discussion of recent experiments in community-construction and patterns of work, see CGF. Revealingly, many new domestic lifestyles (including new family forms) provide for living alone or as single parents, or living with others sharing degrees of 'identity' (e.g. sexual 'sameness') previously regarded as socially intolerable. While 'community' (or 'teamwork') is often the slogan, localization and pluralization are publicly stressed. The capacities and desires of the individual are featured (not least in communities where the accent is on sharing) in ways not predicted by influential theories of 'mass culture' of the 1950s (with their famous forecasts of a conformist society dominated by the cult of the 'other-directed', faceless grey-flannel-suited 'Organization Man'), and that often appear to leave in the lurch theoretical assertions about the decentring of the individual subject. A dominant chord is the fantasy of the

unique, independent yet universally approved and integrated, desired individual – the hope that galvanizes the narcissant imagination.

12. A 'cool' theme is that apathy and aporia liberate aesthetic sensibility. Expressions of value may be treated as components of collages appreciated for their constructive heterogeneity. Increasingly critics praise the show of 'feelings' on stage, screen and the page not for their 'depth' but for the vivacity of their clash. The less we engage – e.g. with the feelings of a character in a scene – the better we appreciate the frisson of the ensemble, as represented sensibilities 'rub against one another'.
13. On postmodern 'dressing-down', where attitudes associated with 1950s youth (Cohen 1980; Hebdige 1979) are reversed, see CGF. Notions of solidarity and personal dignity are treated as the spent sentimental outcome of untrustworthy opportunist liberal ideologies.
14. Moving beyond what Peter Brooks calls the modern 'melodramatic imagination' by which in shows like *Dallas* the classic 'tragic structure of feeling' is reorganised to signify the ('real') pathos of everyday life: the postmodern displaces the latter in favour of an 'aesthetic imagination'.
15. Like the crude automota of early science-fiction cinema, significantly they have not disappeared with the refinement of subsequent automation and texturing technology. In postmodern cool, the chilling gesture, the 'robotizing' of humans, parodies the old humanistic assertions of the distance between human and machine. Canons acclaiming the superiority and nobility of the human sensibilities are thrown into question.
16. Cf. the popularity and influence of MTV's iconic effacement of the complexity of interpersonal exchange and its repulsion of psychological nuance. (For example "The Real World" – a series advertised as 'about real people trying to live together' – whose glossy glamorization of colour, contrast, volume and pace casually 'swamps' 'human issues'.)
17. Cf. the long Cagney/Bogart/Widmark tradition, where the 'transgressor pays in the end'. Ethical motivation no longer turns the trick – or the screw – in e.g. Beckett, the theatre of cruelty and of the absurd, and the post-war black humour of Heller, Vonnegut, Nabokov, Southern, Pynchon.
18. In rock culture "there was an esoteric (and often elitist) celebration of the very 'meaninglessness' of the music" where "'straights' were excluded because they lacked access to the 'secret' code" (paraphrase by Storey 1996: 105, of Paul Willis, *Profane Culture*, 1978).
19. Kernberg sees a "splendid isolation" in the "cold, contemptuous attitudes of the narcissistic personality ... a defensive retreat from dreaded object relationships characterized by intense dependency" (paraphrased by Stolorow 1986: 198).
20. See Twitchell's catalogue of the extravagant finds on offer in a day's trip through a mall (1999: 232ff.).
21. Classic conspicuous-consumption economics, grounded on an interpersonal theory of narcissance, didn't foresee this intrapersonal efflorescence. Theorizing goods as mere signs in the network of language further skirts the essential experiential dimension, where consumption reaches specifically for the sensuous assimilation of matter in its apparent stability and solidity. (Again: not all those buying VCRs and gowns and cars seek this to the same degree; it is a measure of postmodernity and of narcissance.) To say that materiality is itself only another sign, that in 'having' we 'still never have', is precisely to narcissize, foregrounding specifically the anxiety of narcissance. Cf. Brooks' survey (2000) of 'bourgeois bohemian' ('Bobo') self-image building via the stylized accumulation of possessions.

22. "LA – City of the Future", BBC2, 'Open University', repeated Autumn 1997.
23. Cf. Lacan, "narcissism is ecstatic" (see Borch-Jacobsen 1991: 49) and Baudrillard's celebration of ecstasy, cited earlier.
24. For a comparative discussion of the centrality of narcissant *extasis* in the Romantic tradition see CED.
25. Postmodernist theories seldom discuss *how* radical severing relations with history is, so long as the 'anxiety of origins' is entangled with narcissance, they are impelled to conceal its full dynamic. Radical ruptures with authority and the past are inevitably stained at the point of severance from the family, or they fail their claims. Like that surrounding the conservative view of e.g. Fukuyama, the acuity of discussion on the postmodern approach to the theme of the death of history is thus predictably uneven; see e.g. Hawthorn 1996; Jenkins 1997; Munslow 1997; Windschuttle 1996.
26. When Jameson (1984) charges postmodern architecture with nostalgia, Charles Jencks responds not that Jameson is wrong but that nostalgia can have more radical uses than Jameson believes (1988).
27. As tourism speedily propagates niche markets, displacement redoubles. In film-tourism: world travellers visit a corner-shop in a run-down industrial estate in Sheffield where *The Full Monty* was filmed, returning to the 'real origins' of favoured fictions; over 250,000 film sites have been published on the Web to date.
28. Inducing the reader to follow links and register the ensemble's complexity is dependent on the strategies of seduction entrained by linear (syntagmatic) thinking. For rich discussions of hypertext see Landow 1994.
29. As can be expected, oscillation arises – e.g. in the connection-hungry user's ambivalent response to 'cookies' and 'spam': Serious Net-users deplore being required to identify themselves on each return to a site and welcome that on their first visit a 'cookie' may have been written to their computer (invisibly marking it as a past visitor and liberating it from having actively to identify itself there), yet may be enraged on being told (their past visits' interests having been recorded) to visit lengthily listed related sites (or, via 'spam' sent now to their address, goaded to buy products of related interest). As in narcissance, extreme confluence – 'connectivity' – is ever locked in perplexed struggle with self-interested withdrawal.
30. For an analysis of public hacker discourse displaying recurrent themes of separation, tyranny, concealment and parents' betrayal of the child, and of online globalistic ventures (such as the SETI project), see CGF. Many in IT feel that 'nothing should be secret' and that all connections should be unqualifiedly and irrevocably open. For cases in the debate see e.g. Brockman 1996; Dixon and Cassidy 1998; Featherstone 1990; Featherstone and Burrows 1995; Featherstone et al. 1995; Loader 1998; Scott 1997; Tsagarousianou et al. 1998.
31. In early Net communications the word 'anonymous' was commonly used when 'identification' was required. Each year, organizations and individuals energetically devise new strategies for obliterating their addresses – their actual (as opposed to 'virtual') presence in the world.
32. A benefit of the 'medium' is that many users are thus regular readers who never were before – and who don't submit to the idiomatic conventions of the literature of their passing interest-areas. But on the Internet it is not uncommon to range through a dozen idioms in one sitting, *within* interest areas as well as from one interest-area to another. Individuals must adjust in seconds to the symbolism – terms, tonalities, images/icons – of each. For concrete examples of social conflict arising with the 'Net effect' see CGF. This may be a 'micro' phenomenon prefiguring the 'macro' effects of a more pluralistic (postmodern) society.

The *act of participating* on the Internet is *inherently* to experience new levels of social friction and boundary disturbance and may impart a new and still greater spin to narcissance itself. The forthcoming displacement of communication-via-text by visual and audio imaging is likely to induce not merely the end of emoticons but the development of vocal and visual disguise software.

33. Turkle in Brockman 1996: 307–8. Notionally, postmodernity and narcissance collaborate to turn Realist/Modernist 'crises' into a blessing. Like Stendhal's Julien Sorel I can play a role, but without Julien's anxieties. I can in the frank display of my role's fictitiousness both act out my self-uncertainty and defeat others' efforts to pin me down. That 'we all really play many different roles' possesses rapidly increasing exchange value in social intercourse and in media commerce where 'images are sold'.
34. It is increasingly common to celebrate a global merging of technologies – of information – inducing an indeterminacy ('irrelevance') as to whose actions are involved or who is responsible. Cyborg culture is working hard to produce ways of redesigning the human body to accommodate integrated circuitry rendering human and machine indistinguishable. For an array of representations of cyborg culture see Dery 1994; Feher et al. 1989–90; Gray et al. 1995; Haraway 1991; Kroker 1992, 1993; as well as essays in Featherstone and Burrows 1995. Haraway finds a political rationale for the dissolution of oppositions and/or the possibility of an infinite (Deleuzian) ramification, arguing that boundary-dissolving technologies make room for a new 'post-gendered' culture.
35. Clark 1995: 127; quotations from Kroker 1992 and 1993.
36. See <www.kapelica.org/stelarc/image6.htm>.
37. Unnamed male participant in the cyberpunk discussion list FutureCulture, cited by Balsamo in Dery 1994: 140.
38. Note De Landa's forecast of the possibilities of "self-organization" and transformation by means whose dominant trope is a fusion of geological and organicist models (1997).
39. E.g. Richard Falk, "Reflections on the War", *The Nation*, 28 June 1999, 11–22.
40. Where, each promoting each other, both forestall the emergence of – and engagement with – what is figural in the field. (Postmodern enthusiasms – and their commercial spin offs – appropriate confusions of this order. Recognizable links with 'escapism' are relevant.) I am grateful to Mallory Nash for this observation.
41. Kvale notes that in the postmodern "There is an oscillation [with] a cool, ironical distance" "an intense sensuous fascination". "Fascination may take the place of reflection; seduction may replace argumentation ..." (1992: 38). For Storey, attached to "the ideology of consumerism" is a Lacanian fantasy that "consumption will return us to the blissful state of the 'imaginary'" (1996: 115).
42. In a therapeutic setting, this discovery – 'I have nature in me, a spontaneous life independent of others' will that will speak and cannot be denied' – is a potentially vital stage in the 'narcissist's' 'healing'.
43. Carnegie Mellon University has published a two-year investigation, from which the following statement is quoted (editorial, *MacWorld*, December 1998: 24–5). A study by Kimberly Young, University of Pittsburg, elicited much media attention in 1996.
44. For John Biram's theory of 'teknosis' see Michael Prochak, "Gateswill to Power", *MacWorld*, December 1998: 47.
45. "Both narcotics and (excessive) narcissism deaden, attenuate sensation and feeling" (Levin 1993: 40).

46. Drug addiction, for example, was seen early by Rado (1926) as an autoerotic – 'narcissistic' – pleasure apparatus.
47. In public discussions of the 'encroachment of postmodern cultural activities', where the 'hungry, undiscriminating' assembling of raw 'undigested information' is featured, addiction is commonly invoked. Among the problems that can arise in psychotherapy itself are that "understanding alone leads to addiction. Explanation alone can lead to compliance" (Goldberg 1987, 7:184).
48. 'Narcissistic' patients describe "a nostalgia for the excitement of psychosis, and a profound dread of falling back into ... depression" (Mollon 1993: 183). For Kohut and Wolf narcissists, lacking sufficient experience of "stimulating responsiveness ... will use any available stimuli to create a pseudo-excitement in order to ward off the painful feeling of deadness that tends to overtake them ... such as head-banging in toddlers, compulsive masturbation in later childhood, daredevil activities in adolescence" as well as "gambling, drug and alcohol-induced excitement, and a lifestyle characterized by hypersociability" (1986: 184–5). Cf. what Best and Kellner address as 'the pathos of the new' in writers such as Baudrillard; see e.g. 1991: 140.
49. Note the simultaneous coming-into-favour of the words 'postmodern' and 'corybantic dancing' – "dancing yourself into abandon, ecstasy, and orgasm. One of the oldest ways to break through to the ASC [Alternate State(s) of Consciousness] experience" (Joel Homer, *Jargon: How to Talk to Anyone about Anything*, New York 1979: 179).

CHAPTER 6: LIVING THROUGH POSTMODERNITY

1. Jacques Derrida, "Ja, ou le faux-bond", *Digraphe*, March 1977, 11:103. Quoted by Leitch 1983: 205. Cf. Derrida 1996: 54–5.
2. See e.g. Norris 1987, kindly called to my attention by Christopher Norris.
3. For brief discussions of postmodernity's aversion of issues of distress, see e.g. Glass 1994 and Hoggett 1989.
4. On the psychological indispensability of conflict for self-definition and self-experience, see e.g. Mitchell 1988: 276–7.
5. On the cultivation of free-play of "narcissistic illusions", Mitchell believes that it "overlooks the extent to which they often constrict and interfere in real engagements" with others (1988: 193).
6. On whether Derrida can take an effective political stand, see the analysis of his "Remarks on Deconstruction and Pragmatism" (1996) and "<<Eating Well,>> or the Calculation of the Subject" (1995) in CED. The resonance of narcissant discursive processes in defeating political decision is pronounced.
7. For a discussion of the impeachment of President Clinton as an illustration of deconstruction put to public use in the interests of moral fundamentalism, and a consideration of the aestheticization of politics, see CGF.
8. It fails also to qualify as offering insight – e.g. regarding the historical dominance of modes of thought and speech which it aims to deconstruct – because by its own account its apparatus of observation interferes with what is observed.
9. On philosophical cynicism or what the psychologist Bion called the attitude of 'moral superiority' as a strategem for the preservation of the self, see Hoggett 1989: 34.
10. Failing to observe the difference between *meaning seriously* ('I love you') and *using seriously* ('"I love you," he said mockingly, displaying his indifference to her charms') we can confuse postmoderns' saying things they don't mean 'seriously' with – more crucially – their performatively serious pastiche of

'serious' objects and utterances e.g. to make a grave political point, to destabilize seriousness, or – as so often in narcissance – to disarm judgement of itself. This can have effects that are themselves subject to critique. For example the famous case of Reebok's advertisements seeking aggressively (for expressly counter-postmodern ends) to sell shoes by appealing to a postmodern generation's decorum of irony. As Goldman and Papson's study of the event suggests (1994), this is one of the problems postmodernism is unable to deal with. Disarming strategies can create voids into which other intentions can insert themselves that postmodern theory hasn't invited.

11. For an extended discussion of narcissance as a stimulus to and a social hazard in the caring professions, see CGF.
12. 1998: 37, 35. Child-loss figures based on evidence prior to more recent (e.g. Balkan, Chechen, Indonesian) conflicts. On wounded, whereas the UNHDP Report gives 4-5 million in 1998 for 1997, 8 million was reported by BBC Radio 4 News, 4 September 1999, showing just what two years can achieve.
13. On how the most enthusiastically forecast improvement – that in communications – can 'bring us together': is the Internet likely to be a truly global superhighway, equally accessible to all? Bill Gates, investing more than any human in global communications, says no (Gates et al. 1996); meanwhile, 80 per cent of the world's population have never used a telephone.
14. See e.g. Lasch (e.g. 1979, 1984) and David Rieff (e.g. 1998). While on or near the left a variety of voices (such as those of Habermas, Jameson, Eagleton, Dews, Sennett) have long articulated anti-postmodern protest, they have often been dependent on or implicated in either the tradition of anti-*Modernist* protest (descending from e.g. Lukács) or the theoretical discourses of postmodernism itself (with its early and now largely eclipsed adversaries). Partly for obvious recent-historical reasons, just how e.g. a 'neo-Marxism' is to build a viable opposition or to open negotiations with the postmodern is presently uncertain. Writers like Christopher Norris (e.g. 1987, 1993, 1997) have endeavoured to find a nexus between poststructuralist and political humanist thinking in the name of reason, and Anthony Giddens, whose influence on end-of-century British governmental policy was considerable, has worked to incorporate an understanding of narcissism into his account of socio-economic problems to be met. Reserving discussion on this front for CED and CGF owes not only to the fact that partisan policies are not this essay's focus but also to a sense that it would be unhelpful to indulge in the archeology of a (past) field that has already been generously excavated, and abortive (and perhaps ungenerous) to seek to dig one in which the buildings have not yet been fully erected. By 2000, spreading anti-capitalist demonstrations (e.g. Seattle, London) had replaced 'socialism' as their unifying emblem with 'anarchism', in a gesture of pragmatic alliance with a postmodern ethos bidding to leave conventional party politics inoperable.

    By 'moral conservatism' (in e.g. Lasch) I refer to forms of resistance to innovative individualism, in the name of social harmony based on fixed ethical limits. Lest it be thought only to lament postmodern indeterminism and leave pluralism alone, writers like David Rieff have launched zealous attacks on e.g. multiculturalist movements, condemning current American society's material investment in an ethic of anti-normative cultural production in opposition to selective 'quality' production.
15. For example BBC Radio 4, "Straw Poll", 4 September 1999, in a debate on the question: "The therapy culture is responsible for more harm than good".
16. The 'let's talk' idiom came in an effort to bring a kind of 'emotional' or 'relational intelligence' to contemporary social life, and is certainly no worse than religious or corporate cant, or the vernacular of contact-*avoidance* (rang-

ing from 'not now, I've a headache' to all the jargon of Unqle Trim). Like any discourse touching a common nerve, it risks stereotyping and is as bad or as good as the uses it's put to. To judge the latter, we must *listen to what's in the field*. Only to pretend to do so is as unhelpful as are any habits that relational literacy can induce.

17. Awareness of our unease with narcissance can lead to a helpful examination of ourselves. When we meet (or hear described, as it is here) the 'uncomfortable' phenomonon of narcissance, if we find ourselves impatient to the point of revulsion: this is how a narcissant frequently feels when told of needy others. *Not everyone feels this way*. If we don't feel mixed with our irritation signs of compassion, we know what it's like to experience narcissance.
18. Each individual (and movement) is more than merely the sum of its/his/her narcissance, each presenting some different and complex 'personality dominant' image. Each draws on the skills and ethos introjected during his or her specific formation (one may adopt the mode of extreme moral rectitude, another that of extreme relativistic tolerance, etc). What makes narcissance unique is that it makes itself manifest in polar opposition – e.g. radical postmodernity activates Unqle Trim's narcissance – and initiates oscillation. An important aspect of rigidified moral conservative practice is that while it attacks the postmodern violently and *without empathy*, it *also* displays unequivocal gestures of social *care*. (That is in fact its theme: postmodern selfishness is wrong because so many – not excluding the speaker – are in need.)
19. On the array of diverse vested interests shaping conflicting globalist ideologies and interventions see CGF.
20. Computers can function as icons (if not fetishes) for the compulsion to calculate and the anxiety of the incalculable, combined with the refusal to (seem personally to) calculate. (Cf. the growing complaint that 'we're leaving reason in the machine', breeding a new generation lacking the motivation to 'learn' or 'think'.) Any such process influencing our increasingly intimate and pervasive relationship with technology will make urgent a more acute understanding of narcissant thinking. The argument of Landauer (1997), endorsed by hypertextualists such as Moulthrop (1998) – that something the computer hasn't actually done is increase productivity – would reinforce this.
21. Feminist writing has powerfully but perhaps too infrequently noted how – similar to the case of the 'unhappy marriage of Marxism and feminism' (Sargent 1981) – another latent domestic scrape lies in wait for them in adopting the surname 'Postmodern'. See e.g. Fraser and Nicholson (1988). On common problematic practices for the 'massaging' of postmodernist tenets to bring them into seeming conformity with activist needs, see CGF.
22. For an analysis of an illuminating example of this circle, where current social criticism may in its apparent 'cold' observation of narcissance actually be a 'hot' performance of it, see CED on Peter Gabel's attack on industry's use of marketing tactics in "Maalox™ … & Meaning" (1999: 11–12).
23. See e.g. Thomas (1997).
24. Cf. in Loeb (1993) contemporary students' expressions of apathy. 'They' are too big for us, 'they' can't be trusted because they use power arbitrarily; students "felt unequivocally hostile to attempts at social change … disdaining anyone who did speak out" (14). The nexus of apathy and paranoia suggests an altogether different mind-style from one organized simply around concerns of practical economic circumstance.
25. Current arguments against a consumerist plural society are numerous; for introductory examples see James W. Carey, "Reflections on the Project of (American) Cultural Studies", Nicholas Garnham, "Political Economy and the

Practice of Cultural Studies", and Todd Gitlin, "The Anti-political Populism of Cultural Studies", in Ferguson and Goulding 1997.

26. Mollon 1993: 21, quoting Stolorow.
27. Starting from presumptions of fixed psychic structuration they have no useful philosophical or pragmatic function except to provide a conveniently specious target for those wishing to ground a top-heavy argument on their speciousness.
28. Jacobs 1992: 41.
29. Infants are far from lacking social power, as self-aware parents know and as unself-aware parents often show they know by various forms of child abuse.
30. A vital part of contemporary therapeutic practice is to help the narcissant see how s/he is part of a field of reciprocal influence, in which the s/he has always been an active agent. With this, there is a shift toward considerations of a "willful commitment to" his/her "subjective world. Considerations of agency do not belie or negate the experiential reality of the analysand's subjective organization; they broaden that reality by deepening the context in which it develops and operates" (Mitchell 1988: 268).
31. 1995: 197. On Derrida's conventionalism in the use of 'narcissism' see CED.
32. "These boundaries are not entities, but processes. A boundary is a process of separating and connecting", as Yontef says.

    > Effective boundaries are permeable and allow transactions between the organism and the environment. A closed boundary is like a wall in which the organism closes itself to the outside (isolation) and attempts to be self-sufficient, to nourish itself. A boundary that is too open threatens the autonomous existence of the organism via loss of separate identity (confluence/fusion). An effective boundary requires enough permeability to allow nourishment to enter and enough nonpermeability to maintain autonomy and keep out the toxic. (Yontef 1993: 206–7)

33. See Chapter 5. One of the most informed, energetic and articulate cases made for our living out alternative identities by means of recent technology is Sherry Turkle's (see especially 1995). For a discussion of its difficulties see CGF.
34. Exceptionally in the history of Western movements, a postmodern trait is an unreadiness to stress yet not mourn the instability and transience of human identity and worth (for grief is a form of failure incompatible not only with normative indeterminism but with omnipotence, and is too overwhelming in the face of its counterpart, shame). Without grieving – letting grief be, as one of the qualities of being – it is impossible to 'go on'. "What is not possible must be mourned. To heal, one must acknowledge the loss, the limits of what is possible, grieve that loss, and go on" (Yontef 1993: 456).
35. It is at the moment when we decide what an utterance means, and confront and correlate this with (what we also think to be) actuality, that it takes up for the first time its place in the universe of signs. The instant we 'close' an utterance, and never before, it becomes genuinely 'intertextual'.
36. In David Brown's view, "integrated social experience that forms both a source of inner strength and ... a moral foundation for effective political resistance", as well as "personalities and entire cultures", can on the Net be "marginalized ... systematically isolated and carefully dismantled" (1998: 191–2). On this and whether there is 'a distinction we can make use of between narcissant paranoia and intelligently aware, "reality-grounded", socially effective scepticism' see CGF. One test distinguishing the latter is that it takes in openly the responsibility of all parties – and not just 'the other' – in the network of effective action; i.e. in actual political praxis, there is no beginning until one has said 'I am' and, effectively, 'I am s/he who values X'.
37. Levenson 1991: 198. Paul Cilliers, synthesizing Derrida by way of Druscilla

Cornell's reading of him, suggests a related process (entailing "remotivation"), as does Patricia Waugh (arguing the possibility of a "truth-effect", 1992: 163–4) reminiscent of Vaihinger's 'philosophy of "as-if"'; see CGF. Problems arise in determining rules for taking 'remotivating' action; but the interminable insistence on such dilemmas at the expense of the examination of the field's specificities can disclose narcissance.

38. "The problem with many of our present social arrangements is not that they cause emotional distress, but that they fail to contain it adequately," Barry Richards believes (Free Association Bks catalogue 1998: 13, describing Richards 1989). "The intellect assumes a supportive function of incalculable value in strengthening the defence mechanisms, but behind it the narcissistic disturbance can deepen" (Miller 1986: 328).

39. It may be in part Western culture's preoccupation with, and (Judeo)Chrisianity's (and Freud's) emphasis on, guilt that kept sealed the Pandora's box of narcissant shame which postmodern thinking – in extending the Enlightenment project of 'offloading' dubious moral canons – has opened. See Morrison 1986: 353, 370 and CED.

40. Such questions may seem unorthodox and philosophically 'off the point'. The more so the better. As suggested in the section 'Wasting', wrestling with stated rationales *may be not engaging* but accepting the lure to ignore the processes that shape and drive the encounter (and that in fact produce the bristling display of ostensible 'reasons'). In such arguments unorthodox questions can help to shift the furniture around, dissolve heavily entrenched positions, and allow the fullness of what is really going on to reveal itself.

Questions can be seen as ways of calling people to account. This is never more justified than where in claiming to account for itself the postmodern poses utterances that are in fact diversified repetitions, a prime feature of narcissant deflection. (For example the now routine phrase 'to put into question' itself, inducing hackneyed procedures and stereotyped thinking.) But accountability where that means 'explaining oneself' is not the object here. Explanations can be premature leaps to self-justification, when here what is wanted is to bring into the field the experience, the problem itself that needs to be addressed, for which swift self-justification can be a cover-up and a revealing symptom of the problem, rather than an answer. Vitally, such questions, however lighthearted, are not to be delivered as rhetorical or ironic; the point is precisely that those modes obstruct engagement. It should be insisted that irony is not to be the primary idiom, and that what we ask, we ask with sympathy and respect, and a readiness to go anywhere the answer may lead. If irony is read in our question, we have to go back and feel our way through what it's actually asking. The essential is to discover and negotiate what is wanted – and not merely what is wished-to-be-said.

Model questions have been indicated throughout this essay; for full discussion and further examples see CED. For example, useful in addressing e.g. postmodern assertions of indeterminacy can be questions such as: *What makes you think we disagree? / When you say that what we say is part of the infinite play of signification, what do you 'mean'? How does that work? / Do you always feel the same? If you do, how did you choose to be uncertain with consistency? If you don't, what changes your mind? / Is there any worry that what you or I say will close the case? Or place us in danger? How did you come by this worry? / Why speak more? Would it make a difference if we didn't? / Why do you need to say that what you mean isn't 'serious'? / What's important right now? How do you know?* But prefiguring the occasion is just what we want to avoid; questions should arise out of the moment, particularly since part of narcissance's intent is to manage expectations. *Any* questions can stir grandiosity arresting exchange; be in the spirit of support and never patronizing. In response a narciss typically say 'Who are you to ask? When I want open-heart surgery I' it,' and no complaint could seem more reasonable. But a valuable und ing is that narcissants may often be calling for attention when aiming least to be thought to, and a situation-accurate response may be 'Are you sure you're not asking for it?' It is important to listen with complete and open attention. Any such questions are about getting some answers, but more about *setting in motion* the processes of awareness and engagement.

41. Miller 1986: 342; emphasis mine.

AFTERWORD

1. For example, I've not presented a theory for predicting where shifts from rigid position-taking to oscillation occur (such as some in the school of Freud do in speaking of the tension/oscillation between Eros and Thanatos or libidinal and destructive narcissism).
2. A move toward intelligent moderation is the important work of Anthony Giddens (1991). Showing a strong awareness of the force of 'narcissism' (and a sound critique of Lasch and Rieff), the study does not suggest how the moral and social-institutional reforms it recommends might address and resolve the specific problems narcissant mechanisms create. It thus provides a valuable accompaniment, rather than a direct response, to psychological analyses of the problem. (For a detailed discussion see CED.)
3. A culture bearing signs of narcissant thinking should not be thought anything so crude as the sum of a demographically widespread number of 'narcissant individuals'. The cultural adoption of a mind-style will have many and diverse personal biographical reasons behind it. The movement from 'private' process to a cultural ethos is likely to be powerfully influenced by facts not considered in previous analyses, concerning the *inter-generational* dynamic inducing narcissance. A historical account of the relations between the 'modern' and the 'postmodern' must comprehend the fact that the mental and material behaviour characteristic of narcissance is not the product of the mature individual's progressive loss of faith represented in Modernist writing. Half of the process of the development of narcissance is undergone in the generation of the parents, whose failure it is to provide faith-based structures and their accompanying sense of security, stability, continuity, determinacy, etc. Thus the generation of the 'Modern(ist)' cultural experience may be an explicit and essential background to a culture of subsequent narcissance.
4. In recent passages on distress I have treated pleasure/pain unproblematically as a category of experience. I can offer no excuse except to say that I don't know what it would mean to object to this without reference to some similar theory (e.g. of attraction/aversion), unless it were based on an idea of pure rational being whose grounds I would like to see.
5. Encouragingly positive in spirit, postmodern arguments for a pluralism that is universal (it is ultimately difficult to conceive an alternative workable sort) frequently commend an infinite array of differences, none of them privileged. Making radical use of the potential in 'splitting', propositions imply that identical room should be made for all of these as though the nature of each unproblematically claims a different species of space, or as if all can equally occupy the same space without conflict significant to the pluralist's own continued being. For examples of several more sophisticated positions in recent debate see e.g.

Archard 1996; Foster and Herzog 1994; McLennan 1995; Nicholls 1994; Rescher 1993; Taylor 1994; *Critical Review* 1997.

6. The relations between how we behave inwardly (I believe, say, that I am 'constituted by my utterances') and outwardly (Derrida also brushes his teeth), as well as the fact that I don't experience myself consistently as a bundle of utterances any more than as a bundle of neurons firing, remain unaccounted for by radical indeterminist thought. The only way of managing such a split existence must be not to sever but to maintain an unbroken contact between our discourses about both, to mediate their conflicts rather than conceal them according to taste. This indeterminist thinking itself can't achieve; it is obliged to leave that task to other modes of thinking, and ones with which it must often be in disaccord.
7. Cf. the proposition put by Philip Rieff and widely held, that (after 'deconversion') contemporary communities no longer hold categories by which to interpret experience. Quite stable postmodern interpretive categories actively convey to their users a reassuringly standardized language combined with the frisson of a once radical diction.
8. Deploring the 'loss of the family' fails to take in the evidence that many of the processes underlying contemporary problems of self arise *in* the family, and that what has been 'lost' is an ideal family characteristically fantasied specifically in narcissance. Important economic and actuarial reasons for the rising number of people living alone (including single parents) do not account for the major category of those having tried living with others and abandoned that option, whatever their age and the cost. What needs to be understood is the evolution of a mind-style that makes living together feel qualitatively less satisfactory than in the past – for people feeling an increased rather than a lightened burden in living with others. Further, as psychiatric evidence suggests, the breakup of families by choice (e.g. in divorce, affecting a third of all developed-nation marriages) contributes to the development of narcissant depression in the following generation to an extent that the historical norm – where a third of the young might be expected to lose one parent through natural causes – did not.
9. There is no question of dealing with psycho-cultural matters first and political ones later; both must be vigorously attended to side by side. But 'solutions' to the latter consistently fail to resolve the former. Etiolated notions of monolithic unitary 'hegemonies' may often veil socially perilous processes of human interaction, in just the way that the idealizing processes of narcissance are disposed to invoke monolithic 'principles' and 'enemies' to conceal the too-near-at-hand and literally unspeakable turmoils of personal living.
10. Lewis Wolpert, "A Living Hell", BBC2, 3 March 1999.
11. On Lacan's florid enactment of narcissance throughout his daily life, see Roudinesco 1997 – where it is never named as such – and CED.

    On the postmodern test of experiential richness: as developments in social management and attitudes show, when risk-concern is institutionalized (e.g. in the intensification of concern *vis-à-vis* citizens' eating habits) or is conceptually canonized (e.g. in radical indeterminism's repudiation of decidability), the weighting of the penalties increases and there is a depreciation in the awareness of the rewards that can come with decisive choice and action. Many postmodern activities *seem* to encourage risk, but their underlying anxiety patterns can lead to experiential shallowness. ("A hermeneutics of suspicion can … undermine all attempts to ground the relationship between philosophy and a real world", Goodchild 1996: 7.) The anxious sense that we humans are (now) alone in charge of the material world can give us pause. But among the chief outcomes of such fantasies of omnipotence and of consequent splitting to avoid choosing is the "marked impoverishment of the personality" of which Miller and others speak (Miller 1986: 346–7).

12. The growing popular insistence on the 'need for a sense of community' – spreading widely alongside the emergence of the culture of postmodernity – isn't a coincidence. The matter of bonding and of intimacy (including physical contact) as a support against narcissance needs active consideration. Among increasingly urgent issues requiring new societal responses are the shift in the balance toward 'living alone' (where both actuarial and attitudinal changes exert growing force); the complex relationship between sexual motives for bonding and other motives (where dominant commercial interests' iconic accent on sexuality and its stereotypes can promote increasingly conflictual social misunderstanding – particularly affecting the growing older population – and defeat efforts toward beneficial social forms of support); the interaction of traditional and new forms of social 'contact' (e.g. prostitution, the Internet and virtual reality), and the ethical status of relevant psychological concerns; the roles of work and employment as primary sources of bonding, 'belonging' and self-esteem (where fast-changing forms of work and workplace call for the reconsideration of attitudes toward the right to work and the social role and structure of work patterns). For detailed discussion, see CGF.
13. Rorty 1991b: 163. To consider in the light of narcissance is the truism (in a popular adaption of Santayana's phrase) that those who forget the past are condemned to repeat it, and that to disown our history is to disown ourselves.
14. Of both the grandiose and the depressive person: "Neither of them can accept that this loss has already *happened in the past*, and that *no effort* whatsoever *can ever change this fact*" (Miller 1986: 346). This is a theme powerfully developed also by Winnicott and others.
15. There is much evidence that many who lack faith in a higher power or meaning have 'decided against death' because they have children (or even a pet) to care for. Survival may thus draw on narcissance (the other 'will not survive without me, the world depends on me'); but realism may suffice.
16. Where, opposed to narcissance's 'impoverishment of personality' there is the possibility of "a cohesive, plentiful self which allows for self-acceptance" (Morrison 1986: 363), the beginnings of the latter lie in the feeling that, for a start, 'I can be ordinary without despair'.

Bibliography

Every effort has been made to refer to editions most readily available in English at the time of this writing. Where two editions are involved (for example, in the case of translations into English), the year of the later and normally most readily found publication is given first and is the year cited in references in the main text. Where sources originally appearing in periodicals are known to have been subsequently printed more accessibly in book form, they are listed according to the dates and publication details of the latter. Readers interested in exploring works by fictionalists alluded to in this essay will find full and detailed references in Nash 1987/1993.

Akiskal, Hagop S., et al. (1986), "Borderline: An Adjective in Search of a Noun", in Stone 1986.

Alford, C. F. (1988), *Narcissism: Socrates, the Frankfurt School, and Psychoanalytic Theory*, New Haven, CT.

Alford, C. F. (1991), *The Self in Social Theory: A Psychoanalytic Account of Its Construction in Plato, Hobbes, Locke, Rawls, and Rousseau*, New Haven, CT.

Anderson, Walter Truett (1990), *Reality Isn't What It Used to Be*, New York/San Francisco, CA.

Archard, David (ed.) (1996), *Philosophy and Pluralism*, Cambridge.

Aronowitz, Stanley, Barbara Martinsons and Michael Menser (eds) (1996), *Technoscience and Cyberculture*, New York/London.

Aurier, G.-Albert (1968), "Symbolist Art Theories, 1" (tr. H. R. Rookmaker, "Les peintres symbolistes", *Revue Encyclopédique*, Paris: April 1892), in Chipp 1968.

Balsamo, Anne (1994), "Feminism for the Incurably Informed", in Dery 1994.

Barth, John (1967), "The Literature of Exhaustion", *Atlantic Monthly*, 220 (August).

Barth, John (1969), *Lost in the Funhouse*, New York.

Barth, John (1973), *Chimera*, Greenwich, CT.

Barthes, Roland (1974), *S/Z* (tr. R. Howard, *S/Z*, Paris 1970), London.

Barthes, Roland (1987), *Sollers, Writer* (tr. P. Thody, *Sollers écrivain*, Paris 1979).

Bateson, Gregory (1972), *Steps toward an Ecology of Mind*, San Francisco, CA.

Baudrillard, Jean (1983), *Simulations* (tr. P. Foss, part-translation of *Simulacres et simulation*, Paris 1981), New York.

Baudrillard (1984), "Game with Vestiges", *On the Beach*, vol. 5 (Winter).

Baudrillard, Jean (1987), *Forget Foucault* (tr. H. Beitchmann and M. Polizzoti, *Oublier Foucault*, Paris 1977), New York.

Baudrillard, Jean (1988a), *Selected Writings*, see Poster 1988.

Baudrillard, Jean (1988b), "The Year 2000 Has Already Happened", in Kroker and Kroker (1988).

Baudrillard, Jean (1993), *Symbolic Exchange and Death* (tr. I. H. Grant, *L'Echange symbolique et la mort*, Paris 1976), London.

Baudrillard, Jean (1996), *The Perfect Crime* (tr. C. Turner, *Le Crime parfait*, Paris 1995), London/New York.

Baudry, Jean-Louis (1967), *Personnes*, Paris.

Bauman, Zygmunt (1988), "Is There a Postmodern Sociology?", in Featherstone 1988.

Bauman, Zygmunt (1997), *Postmodernity and its Discontents*, Cambridge.

Beardsworth, Richard (1996), *Derrida and the Political*, London.

Beckett, Samuel (1949), "Three Dialogues with Georges Duthuit", *Transition*, vol. 49, no. 5 (December); repr. in Esslin 1965.

Beckett, Samuel (1959), *Molloy, Malone Dies, The Unnamable: A Trilogy*, Paris.

Bellamy, Joe David (ed.) (1974), *The New Fiction: Interviews with Innovative American Writers*, Urbana, IL.

Bérubé, Michael (1999), "Of Fine Clothes and Naked Emperors", *Tikkun*, Mar/Apr.

Best, Steven and Douglas Kellner (1991), *Postmodern Theory: Critical Interrogations*, Basingstoke.

Bloom, Allan (1987), *The Closing of the American Mind*, New York.

Bloom, Harold, Paul de Man, Jacques Derrida, Geoffrey H. Hartman, J. Hillis Miller (1979), *Deconstruction and Criticism*, New York.

Bogue, Ronald (1989), *Deleuze and Guattari*, London.

Borch-Jacobsen, Mikkel (1991), *Lacan: The Absolute Master*, Stanford, CA.

Borgmann, Albert (1992), *Crossing the Postmodern Divide*, Chicago, IL.

Bory, Jean-François (1973), "Post-Scriptum" (tr. D. Higgins), in Kostelanetz 1973.

Bouchard, Donald F. (ed.) (1977), *Language, Counter-Memory, Practice*, Oxford.

Boundas, Constantin V. and Dorothea Olkowski (eds) (1994), *Gilles Deleuze and the Theater of Philosophy*, New York/London.

Bowlby, John (1988), *A Secure Base: Clinical Applications of Attachment Theory*, London.

Bramblett, Claud A. (1976), *Patterns of Primate Behaviour*, Palo Alto.

Brenkman, John (1976), "Narcissus in the Text", *Georgia Review*, vol. 30.

Brockman, John (1996), *Digerati: Encounters with the Cyber Elite*, London.

Bromberg, Philip M. (1986), "The Mirror and the Mask: On Narcissism and Psychoanalytic Growth", in Morrison 1986.

Brooke-Rose, Christine (1974), *Thru*, London.

Brooks, David (2000), *Bobos in Paradise: The New Upper Class and How They Got There*, New York.

Brown, David (1998), *Cybertrends: Chaos, Power and Accountability in the Information Age*, Harmondsworth.

Burman, Erica (ed.) (1998), *Deconstructing Feminist Psychology*, London.

Bursten, Ben (1986), "Some Narcissistic Personality States", in Morrison 1986.

Cahalan, William (1983), "An Elaboration of the Gestalt Personality Theory: the Experience of Self in Social Relations", *Gestalt Journal*, vol. 6, no.1.

Cahoone, Lawrence E. (1988), *The Dilemma of Modernity: Philosophy, Culture, and Anti-Culture*, Albany, NY.

Calvino, Italo (1970), "A Sign in Space", in *Cosmicomics* (tr. W. Weaver, "Un segno nello spazio", *Le cosmicomiche*, Turin 1965), New York.

Calvino, Italo (1969), *t zero* (tr. W. Weaver, *Ti con zero*, Turin 1967), New York.

Carroll, David (1982), *The Subject in Question: The Languages of Theory and the Strategies of Fiction*, Chicago, IL.

Castells, Manuel (1996/1997/1998), *The Information Age: Economy, Society and Culture* (I. *The Rise of the Network Society* [1996]; II. *The Power of Identity* [1997]; III. *End of Millennium* [1998]), Oxford.

Chipp, Herschel B. (1968), *Theories of Modern Art: A Source Book by Artists and Critics*, Berkeley, CA/London.

Cilliers, Paul (1998), *Complexity and Postmodernism: Understanding Complex Systems*, London.

Clark, Nigel (1995), "Rearview Mirrorshades: The Recursive Generation of the Cyberbody", in Featherstone and Burrows 1995.

Clements, Colleen (1982), "Misusing Psychiatric Models: The Culture of Narcissism", *Psychoanalytic Review*, vol. 69.

Cockcroft, George (pseud. Luke Rhinehart) (1998 [1971]), *The Dice Man*, New York.

Cohen, Phil (1980), "Subcultural Conflict and Working-class Community", in Hall 1980.

Cooper, Arnold M. (1986), "Narcissism", in Morrison 1986.

Cooper, Judy and Nilda Maxwell (eds) (1995), *Narcissistic Wounds: Clinical Perspectives*, London.

Cornell, Druscilla (1992), *The Philosophy of the Limit*, London.

Critical Review: An Interdisciplinary Journal of Politics and Society (1997), 'Pluralism or Relativism' (special issue), Fall.

Culler, Jonathan (1975), *Structuralist Poetics: Structuralism, Linguistics and the Study of Literature*, London.

Dallmayr, Fred R. (1981), *Twilight of Subjectivity: Contributions to a Post-Industrialist Theory*, Amherst.

De Landa, Manuel (1997), *A Thousand Years of Nonlinear History*, New York.

Deleuze, Gilles (1983), *Nietzsche and Philosophy* (tr. Hugh Tomlinson, *Nietzsche et la philosophie*, Paris 1962), Minneapolis, MN.

Deleuze, Gilles and Félix Guattari (1984), *Anti-Oedipus: Capitalism and Schizophrenia* (tr. R. Jurley, M. Seem and H. R. Lane, *L'Anti-Oedipe: capitalisme et schizophrénie*, Paris 1972), London.

Deleuze, Gilles and Félix Guattari (1987), *A Thousand Plateaus* (tr. B. Massumi, *Mille plateaux: capitalisme et schizophrénie II*, Paris 1980), Minneapolis, MN.

de Man, Paul (1983), *Blindness and Insight* (2nd edn), Minneapolis, MN.

Derrida, Jacques (1976), *Of Grammatology* (tr. G. Spivak, *De la grammatologie*, Paris 1967), Baltimore, MD.

Derrida, Jacques (1978), *Writing and Difference*, (tr. A. Bass, *L'Ecriture et la différence*, Paris 1967) London.

Derrida, Jacques (1979), "Living On" (tr. J. Hulbert), in Bloom et al. 1979.

Derrida, Jacques (1980), "Interview", *Literary Review* (London), no. 14.

Derrida, Jacques (1981), *Dissemination* (tr. B. Johnson), London; based on *La Dissémination*, Paris 1972.

Derrida, Jacques (1985), "Des Tours de Babel" (tr./ed. J. F. Graham), *Difference in Translation*, Ithaca, NY.

Derrida, Jacques (1986), *Memoires for Paul de Man* (tr. C. Lindsay, J. Culler, E. Cadava), New York.

Derrida, Jacques (1989), "How to Avoid Speaking: Denials", *Languages of the Unsayable: The Play of Negativity in Literature and Literary Theory* (ed. Sanford Budick, Wolfgang Iser, New York; tr. K. Frieden, "Comment ne pas parler, Dénégations", *Psyché, Inventions de l'autre*, Paris 1987).

Derrida, Jacques (1995), *Points: Interviews, 1974–1994* (ed. Elisabeth Weber; tr. P. Kamuf and others, *Points de suspension, Entretiens*, Paris 1992).

Derrida, Jacques (1996), "Remarks on Deconstruction and Pragmatism", in Mouffe 1996.

Derrida, Jacques (1998), *Resistances of Psychoanalysis* (tr. P. Kamuf, P.-A. Brault, M. Naas, *Résistances de la psychanalyse*, Paris 1996), Stanford, CA.

Dery, Mark (ed.) (1994), *Flame Wars: The Discourse of Cyberculture*, Durham, NC.

Deutsch, Helene (1942), "Some Forms of Emotional Disturbance and Their Relationship to Schizophrenia", *Neurosis and Character Types*, New York.

Dews, Peter (1995), *The Limits of Disenchantment: Essays on Contemporary European Philosophy*, London/New York.

Dickens, David R. and Andrea Fontana (eds) (1994), *Postmodernism and Social Inquiry*, New York/London.

Dixon, Joan Broadhurst and Eric J. Cassidy (1998), *Virtual Futures: Cyberotics, Technology and Post-Human Pragmatism*, London.

Dublin, Max (1992), *Futurehype: The Tyranny of Prophecy*, Harmondsworth.

Dunn, Robert G. (1998), *Identity Crises: A Social Critique of Postmodernity*, Minneapolis, MN.

Eagleton, Terry (1985), "Capitalism, Modernism and Postmodernism", *New Left Review*, vol. 152.

Eagleton, Terry (1996), *The Illusions of Postmodernism*, Oxford.

Eco, Umberto (1979), "On the Possibility of Generating Aesthetic Messages in an Edenic Language" (revised as Chapter 3 of) *The Role of the Reader: Explorations in the Semiotics of Texts* (tr. B. Merry, "Sulla possibilità di generare messaggi estetici in una lingusa edenica", *Strumenti critici*, vol. 5, no. 11, 1971).

Eco, Umberto and Constantino Marmo (eds) (1989), *On the Medieval Theory of Signs*, Amsterdam.

Edelman, Gerald M. (1989), *The Remembered Present: A Biological Theory of Consciousness*, New York.

Ehrenzweig, Anton (1993), *The Hidden Order of Art*, London.

Ehrmann, Jacques (1981), "The Death of Literature" (tr. A. J. Arnold, "La Mort de la littérature", *"Textes" suivi de "La Mort de littérature"*, Paris 1971 [published anonymously]), in Federman (1981); (different version) *New Literary History*, 1971, no. 3.

Esslin, Martin (ed.) (1965), *Samuel Beckett: A Collection of Critical Essays*, Englewood Cliffs, NJ.

Featherstone, Mike (ed.) (1985), 'The Fate of Modernity' (special issue), *Theory, Culture & Society*, vol. 2, no. 3.

Featherstone, Mike (ed.) (1988), 'Postmodernism' (special issue), *Theory, Culture & Society*, vol. 5, nos 2–3.

Featherstone, Mike (ed.) (1990), *Global Culture: Nationalism, Globalization and Modernity*, London.

Featherstone, Mike (1991), *Consumer Culture and Postmodernism*, London.

Featherstone, Mike (1995), *Undoing Culture: Globalization, Postmodernism and Identity*, London.

Featherstone, Mike and Roger Burrows (1995), *Cyberspace/Cyberbodies/Cyberpunk: Cultures of Technological Embodiment*, London.

Featherstone, Mike, Scott Lash, Roland Robertson (eds) (1995), *Global Modernities*, London.

Federman, Raymond (ed.) (1981), *Surfiction: Fiction Now … and Tomorrow*, Chicago, IL.

Feher, Michel, Ramona Naddaff, Nadia Tazi (eds) (1989–90), *Fragments for a History of the Human Body* [*Zone* 3, 4, 5], Cambridge, MA.

Fenichel, O. (1945), *The Psychoanalytic Theory of Neurosis*, New York.

Ferguson, Marjorie and Peter Goulding (1997), *Cultural Studies in Question*, London.

Finlay, Marike (1989), "Post-modernising Psychoanalysis/Psychoanalysing Postmodernity", *Free Associations*, vol. 16.

Fiske, John (1989), *Understanding Popular Culture*, Boston, MA.

Flax, Jane (1993), *Disputed Subjects: Essays on Psychoanalysis, Politics and Philosophy*, New York/London.

Foster, Lawrence and Patricia Herzog (1994), *Contemporary Philosophical Perspectives on Pluralism and Multiculturalism*, Amherst.

Foucault, Michel (1977), "Nietzsche, Genealogy, History", in Bouchard 1977.

Frank, Thomas (1997), *The Conquest of Cool: Business Culture, Counterculture, and the Rise of Hip Consumerism*, Chicago, IL.

Fraser, Nancy and Linda Nicholson (1988), "Social Criticism Without Philosophy: An Encounter Between Feminism and Postmodernism", *Theory, Culture and Society*, vol. 5, nos 2–3.

Freud, Sigmund (1957), "On Narcissism: An Introduction", *The Standard Edition of The Complete Psychological Works of Sigmund Freud* (tr./ed. J. Strachey), vol. 14, London.

Friedman, Jeffrey (1997), "Introduction: Pluralism or Relativism?", *Critical Review*, vol. 11, no. 4.

Fuentes, Carlos (1975), *Terra Nostra* (tr. M. S. Peden, Mexico (City)), Harmondsworth 1976 [1978].

Fukuyama, Francis (1992), *The End of History and the Last Man*, Harmondsworth.

Gabel, Peter (1999), "Maalox™ ... & Meaning", *Tikkun*, July/August.

Garé, Arran E. (1995), *Postmodernism and the Environmental Crisis*, London/New York.

Garnham, Nicholas (1997), "Political Economy and the Practice of Cultural Studies", in Ferguson and Goulding 1997.

Gates, Bill, Nathan Myhrvold and Peter Rinearson (1996) (2nd edn), *The Road Ahead*, London.

Gaylin, Willard (ed.) (1994), *The Meaning of Despair: Psychodynamic Understanding of Depression*, Northvale.

Gear, M. C., M. A. Hill and E. L. Liendo (1981), *Working through Narcissism: Treating Its Sado-Masochistic Structure*, New York.

Gergen, Kenneth (1991), *The Saturated Self: Dilemmas of Identity in Contemporary Life*, New York.

Giddens, Anthony (1991), *Modernity and Self-Identity: Self and Society in the Late Modern Age*, Cambridge.

Glass, James M. (1994), *Shattered Selves: Multiple Personality in a Postmodern World*, Ithaca, NY.

Goldberg, A. (1987), "A Self Psychology Perspective", in S. Pulver (ed.), "How Theories Shape Technique" (special issue), *Psychoanalytic Inquiry*, 7.

Goldman, Robert and Steven Papson (1994), "The Postmodernism That Failed", in Dickens and Fontana 1994.

Goldman, Robert and Steven Papson (1996), *Sign Wars: The Cluttered Landscape of Advertising*, New York/London.

Goodchild, Philip (1996), *Deleuze and Guattari: An Introduction to the Politics of Desire*, London.

Goodheart, Eugene (1984), *The Skeptic Disposition: Deconstruction, Ideology, and Other Matters*, Princeton, NJ.

Gray, Chris Hables, Steven Mentor and Heidi Figueroa-Sarriera (eds) (1995), *The Cyborg Handbook*, London.

Grossberg, Lawrence (1992), *We Gotta Get Out of This Place*, New York/London.

Gruneberger, Bela (1971), *Narcissism*, New York.

Guattari, Félix (1989), *Cartographies schizoanalytiques*, Paris.

Hall, Stuart (1980), *Culture, Media, Language*, London.

Hamilton, Victoria (1993) *Narcissus and Oedipus: The Children of Psychoanalysis*, London (first pub. 1982).

Haraway, Donna J. (1991), *Simians, Cyborgs, and Women: The Reinvention of Nature*, London.

Harlow, Harry F. (1971), *Learning to Love*, San Francisco, CA.

Harlow, Harry F. and Robert R. Zimmermann (1959), "Affectional Responses in the Infant Monkey", *Science*, vol. 130, no. 3373.

Harvey, David (1990), *The Condition of Postmodernity: An Enquiry into the Origins of Cultural Change*, Oxford.

Hassan, Ihab (1975), *Paracriticisms: Seven Speculations of the Times*, Urbana/Chicago/London.

Hawthorn, Jeremy (1996), *Cunning Passages: New Historicism, Cultural Materialism and Marxism in the Contemporary Literary Debate*, London.

Hebdige, Dick (1979), *Subculture: The Meaning of Style*, London.

Heim, Michael (1995), "The Design of Virtual Reality", in Featherstone and Burrows 1995.

Heisenberg, Werner (1956), "The Uncertainty Principle" (tr. C. Eckart and F. C. Hoyt), *The Physical Principles of Quantum Theory*, Chicago, IL, 1930; repr. in James R. Newman (ed.), *The World of Mathematics*, New York, 1956.

Heisenberg, Werner (1958), "The Representation of Nature in Contemporary Physics", *Daedalus*, vol. 87, no. 3.

Henderson, Sheila (1997), *Ecstasy: Case Unsolved*, London.

Hoggett, Paul (1989), "The Culture of Uncertainty", in Richards 1989.

Hollinger, Robert (1994), *Postmodernism and the Social Sciences: A Thematic Approach*, London.

Holtz, Geoffrey T. (1995), *Welcome to the Jungle: The Why Behind "Generation X"*, New York.

Howe, Neil and Bill Strauss (1993), *13th Gen: Abort, Retry, Ignore, Fail?*, New York.

Hudson, David (1997), *Rewired*, Indianapolis, IN.

Human Development Report 1998 (1998), United Nations Development Programme, New York.

Huyssen, Andreas (1986), *After the Great Divide: Modernism, Mass Culture and Postmodernism*, London.

Jacobs, Lynne (1992), "Insights from Psychoanalytic Self-Psychology and Intersubjectivity Theory for Gestalt Therapists", *The Gestalt Journal*, vol. 15, no. 2.

Jameson, Fredric (1984), "Postmodernism, or the Cultural Logic of Late Capitalism", *New Left Review*, no. 146.

Jameson, Fredric (1991), *Postmodernism, or, The Cultural Logic of Late Capitalism*, Durham, NC.

Jameson, Fredric (1994), *The Seeds of Time*, New York.

Jencks, Charles (1988), 'Profile 72', interview with Peter Eisenman, *Architectural Design*, vol. 58, nos 3/4.

Jenkins, Keith (ed.) (1997), *The Postmodern History Reader*, London.

Joseph, Jennifer and Lisa Taplin (eds) (1994), *Signs of Life: Channel-Surfing through '90s Culture*, San Francisco, CA.

Kegan, Robert (1994), *In Over Our Heads: The Mental Demands of Modern Life*, Cambridge, MA.

Kellner, Douglas (1988), "Postmodernism as Social Theory: Some Challenges and Problems", in Featherstone 1988.

Kellner, Douglas (1989), *Jean Baudrillard: From Marxism to Postmodernism and Beyond*, Stanford, CA.

Kellner, Douglas (1995), *Media Culture: Cultural Studies, Identity and Politics between the Modern and the Postmodern*, London/New York.

Kernberg, Otto F. (1975), *Borderline Conditions and Pathological Narcissism*, New York.

Kernberg, Otto F. (1986a), "Factors in the Treatment of Narcissistic Personalities", in Morrison 1986.

Kernberg, Otto F. (1986b), "Further Contributions to the Treatment of Narcissistic Personalities", in Morrison 1986.

Kling, Rob (ed.) (1991 (2nd edn), *Computerization and Controversy: Value Conflicts and Social Choices*, San Diego, CA, 2nd edn.

Kohut, Heinz (1971), *The Analysis of the Self*, New York.

Kohut, Heinz (1977), *The Restoration of the Self*, New York.

Kohut, Heinz (1986), "Forms and Transformations of Narcissism", in Morrison 1986.

Kohut, Heinz and Ernest S. Wolf (1986), "The Disorders of the Self and their Treatment: An Outline", in Morrison 1986.

Kostelanetz, Richard (ed.) (1973), *Breakthrough Fictioneers: An Anthology*, West Glover, VT.

Kristeva, Julia (1989), *Black Sun: Depression and Melancholia* (tr. L. S. Roudiez from *Soleil Noir: Dépression et mélancolie*, Paris 1987), New York.

Kristeva, Julia (1996), *Julia Kristeva Interviews* (ed. Ross Mitchell Guberman), New York.

Kroker, A. and M. Kroker (eds) (1988), *The Body Invaders: Panic Sex in America*, Montreal.

Kroker, Arthur (1992), *The Possessed Individual: Technology and Postmodernity*, Basingstoke.

Kroker, Arthur (1993), *Spasm: Virtual Reality, Android Music, and Electric Flesh*, New York.

Kvale, Steinar (ed.) (1992), *Psychology and Postmodernism*, London.

Lacan, Jacques (1974), *Télévision*, Paris.

Lacan, Jacques (1977a), *Ecrits: A Selection* (tr. A. Sheridan, *Ecrits*, Paris 1966), New York.

Lacan, Jacques (1977b), *The Four Fundamental Concepts of Psychoanalysis* (tr. A Sheridan), New York 1977 (1964; text established by J.-A. Miller, *Les Quatre concepts fondamenteaux de la psychanalyse*, Paris 1973).

Lacan, Jacques (1988), "Seminar on 'The Purloined Letter'", in J. Muller and W. Richardson (eds), *The Purloined Poe* (tr. J. Mehlman, "La séminaire sur La Lettre volée" [26 April 1955], *La Psychanalyse*, vol. 2 [1957]), Baltimore, MD.

Laing, Ronald David (1990 [1960]), *The Divided Self: an Existential Study in Sanity and Madness*, Harmondsworth.

Land, Nick (1995), "Meat (or How to Kill Oedipus in Cyberspace", in Featherstone and Burrows 1995.

Landauer, Thomas J. (1997), *The Trouble with Computers: Usefulness, Usability, and Productivity*, Cambridge, MA.

Landow, George P. (ed.) (1994), *Hyper/Text/Theory*, Baltimore, MD.

Lasch, Christopher (1979), *The Culture of Narcissism: American Life in an Age of Diminishing Expectations*, New York/London.

Lasch, Christopher (1984), *The Minimal Self: Psychic Survival in Troubled Times*, New York/London.

Lash, Scott (1990), *Sociology of Postmodernism*, London/New York.

Lavers, Annette (1982), *Roland Barthes: Structuralism and After*, London.

Leary, Timothy (1994), *Chaos & Cyber Culture*, Berkeley, CA.

Lecercle, Jean-Jacques (1985), *Philosophy through the Looking-Glass: Language, Nonsense, Desire*, London.

Lee, Jonathan Scott (1990), *Jacques Lacan*, Amherst, MA.

Leitch, Vincent B. (1983), *Deconstructive Criticism: An Advanced Introduction*, London.

Levenson, Edgar A. (1991), *The Purloined Self*, New York.

Levin, Jerome David (1993), *Slings and Arrows: Narcissistic Injury and Its Treatment*, Northvale.

Lewin, Kurt (1951), *Field Theory in Social Science*, New York.

Lewis, H. B. (1971), *Shame and Guilt in Neurosis*, New York.

Loader, Brian (ed.) (1998), *Cyberspace Divide: Equality, Agency and Policy in the Information Society*, London.

Loeb, Paul Rogat (1993), *Generation at the Crossroads: Apathy and Action on the American Campus*, New Brunswick.

Loewald, H. W. M. D. (1980), *Papers on Psychoanalysis*, New Haven, CT.

Lovell, Terry (1983), *Pictures of Reality*, London.

Lunenfeld, Peter (ed.) (1999), *The Digital Dialectic: New Essays on the New Media*, Cambridge, MA.

Lyotard, Jean-François (1984), *The Postmodern Condition* (tr. G. Bennington and B. Massumi, *La Condition postmoderne: rapport sur le savoir*, Paris 1979), Manchester.

Lyotard, Jean-François (1993), *Libidinal Economy* (tr. I. H. Grant, *Economie Libidinale*, Paris 1974), London.

McGilchrist, Iain (1982), *Against Criticism*, London.

McGuigan, Jim (1997), "Cultural Populism Revisited", in Ferguson and Goulding 1997.

McHale, Brian (1992), *Constructing Postmodernism*, London/New York.

McLennan, Gregor (1995), *Pluralism*, London.

McRae, Hamish (1995), *The World in 2020: Power, Culture and Prosperity*, Boston, MA.

McRobbie, Angela (1994), *Postmodernism and Popular Culture*, London/New York.

McRobbie, Angela (1997), "The Es and the Anti-Es: New Questions for Feminism and Cultural Studies", in Ferguson and Goulding (1997).

Magarinos, A. M., J. M. Verdugo and B. S. McEwen (1997), "Chronic Stress Alters Synaptic Terminal Structure in Hippocampus", *Proceedings*, National Academy of Sciences of the USA, vol. 94 (25), 14002–8.

Mahler, M. S. (1967), "On Human Symbiosis and the Vicissitudes of Individuation", *Infantile Psychosis*, vol. 1.

Mahler, M. S. (1986), "On the First Three Phases of the Separation-Individuation Process", in Scientific Proceedings-Panel Reports, reported by Muriel C. Winestine, *Journal of the American Psychoanalytic Association* (1971), vol. 21; cited by M. W. White in Morrison 1986: 148.

Mahler, M. S. (1975), F. Pine and A. Bergman, *The Psychological Birth of the Human Infant: Symbiosis and Individuation*, New York.

Mancia, Mauro (1993), *In the Gaze of Narcissus: Memory, Affects, and Creativity* (tr. S. S. Lanfranchi, *Nello Sguardo di Narciso*, Rome/Bari 1990), London.

Marin, Peter (1975), "The New Narcissism", *Harpers Magazine*, October.

Meissner, W. W. (1986), "Narcissistic Personalities and Borderline Conditions: A Differential Diagnosis", in Morrison 1986.

Mellencamp, Patricia (1992), *High Anxiety: Catastrophe, Scandal, Age, and Comedy*, Bloomington.

Miller, Alice (1983), *The Drama of Being a Child and the Search for the True Self* (tr. R. Ward, *Das Drama des begabten Kindes*, Frankfurt am Main 1979), London.

Miller, Alice (1986), "Depression and Grandiosity as Related Forms of Narcissistic Disturbances", in Morrison 1986.

Miller, J. Hillis (1975), "Deconstructing the Deconstructors", *Diacritics* 5.

Miller, J. Hillis (1987), *The Ethics of Reading*, New York.

Miller, James (1993), *The Passion of Michel Foucault*, London.

Mitchell, Stephen A. (1988), *Relational Concepts in Psychoanalysis: An Integration*, Cambridge, MA.

Mitchell, Stephen A. and Margaret J. Black (1995), *Freud and Beyond: A History of Modern Psychoanalytic Thought*, New York.

Modell, Arnold (1986), "A Narcissistic Defence Against Affects and the Illusion of Self-Sufficiency", in Morrison 1986.

Mollon, Phil (1993), *The Fragile Self: The Structure of Narcissistic Disturbance*, London.

Morrison, Andrew P. (ed.) (1986), *Essential Papers on Narcissism*, New York.

Morrison, Andrew P. (1986), "Shame, Ideal Self, and Narcissism", in Morrison 1986.

Mouffe, Chantal (ed.) (1996), *Deconstruction and Pragmatism*, London/New York.

Moulthrop, Stuart (1998), "Where To? A Review of *Forward Anywhere*", as of 2 December 1998, <http://eastgate.com/reviews/moulthrop.html>.

Mullan, Bob (1998), *The Self-Help Cascade*, London.

Munslow, Alun (1997), *Deconstructing History*, London.

Nabokov, Vladimir (1955), "On a Book Called Lolita", *Lolita*, New York.

Nabokov, Vladimir (1962) [1973], *Pale Fire*, London.

Nabokov, Vladimir (1975), *Tyrants Destroyed and Other Stories*, London.

Nash, Cristopher (1987), *World-Games: The Tradition of Anti-Realist Revolt*, London; see also Nash 1993.

Nash, Cristopher (1989), "Playing Havoc", *PN Review*, vol. 15, no. 4 (also, revised, as "Slaughtering the Subject: Literature's Assault on Narrative", in Nash 1990).

Nash, Cristopher (ed.) (1990), *Narrative in Culture: The Uses of Storytelling in the Sciences, Philosophy, and Literature*, London.

Nash, Cristopher (1993), *World Postmodern Fiction*, London; revised edition of Nash 1987.

Newman, James R. (ed.) (1956), *The World of Mathematics*, 4 vols, New York.

Nicholls, David (1994), *The Pluralist State: The Political Ideas of J. N. Figgis and His Contemporaries* (2nd edn), Oxford.

Norris, Christopher (1986), "Home Thoughts from Abroad: Derrida, Austin, and the Oxford Connection", *Philosophy and Literature*, vol. 10, no. 1.

Norris, Christopher (1987), "Against Postmodernism: Derrida, Kant and Nuclear Politics", *Paragraph*, vol. 9.

Norris, Christopher (1993), *The Truth about Postmodernism*, Oxford.

Norris, Christopher (1997), *New Idols of the Cave: On the Limits of Anti-Realism*, Manchester.

O'Brien, Flann (1974), *The Third Policeman*, London.

Owen, David (ed.) (1997), *Sociology after Postmodernism*, London.

Parker, Ian, Eugene Georgaca, David Harper, Terence McLaughlin and Mark Stowell-Smith (1995), *Deconstructing Psychopathology*, London.

Parlett, Malcolm (1991), "Reflections on Field Theory", *British Gestalt Journal*, vol. 1.

Peters, Glen (1996), *Beyond the Next Wave: Imagining the Next Generation of Customers*, London.

Porter, David (ed.) (1997), *Internet Culture*, New York/London.

Poster, Mark (ed.) (1988), *Jean Baudrillard: Selected Writings* (passage from 'Fatal Strategies'), tr. J. Mourrain from *Les Stratégies fatales*, Paris 1983), Cambridge/Stanford, CA.

Pulver, Sydney E. (1986), "Narcissism: The Term and the Concept", in Morrison 1986.

Rado, S. (1926), "The Psychic Effects of Intoxification: Attempts at a Psycho-analytic Theory of Drug Addiction", *International Journal of*

Psycho-analysis , vol. 7.

Ragland-Sullivan, Ellie (1986), *Jacques Lacan and the Philosophy of Psychoanalysis*, London.

Reich, Wilhelm (1949), *Character-Analysis* (tr. T. P. Wolfe, *Characteranalyse*, 1933), New York, 3rd edn.

Rescher, Nicholas (1993), *Pluralism: Against the Demand for Consensus*, Oxford.

Richards, Barry (1989), *Crises of the Self: Further Essays on Psychoanalysis and Politics*, London.

Rieff, David (1998), "Therapy or Democracy? The Culture Wars Twenty Years On", *World Policy Journal*, vol. 15, no. 2.

Rieff, Philip (1968), *The Triumph of the Therapeutic: The Uses of Faith after Freud*, New York.

Robbe-Grillet, Alain (1965), *Snapshots and Towards a New Novel*, New York (tr. B. Wright, *Pour un nouveau roman* and *Instantanés*, Paris 1962, 1963).

Robbe-Grillet, Alain (1970), *The House of Assignation* (tr. R. Howard, *La Maison de Rendez-vous*, Paris 1965) New York 1966/London 1970.

Robbins, M. (1982), "Narcissistic Personality as a Symbiotic Character Disorder", *International Journal of Psycho-Analysis*, vol. 63.

Robins, Kevin (1995), "Cyberspace and the World We Live In", in Featherstone and Burrows 1995.

Rorty, Richard (1991a), *Objectivity, Relativism, and Truth: Philosophical Papers, I*, Cambridge.

Rorty, Richard (1991b), *Essays on Heidegger and Others: Philosophical Papers, II*, Cambridge.

Rorty, Richard (1998), *Truth and Progress: Philosophical Papers, III*, Cambridge.

Rose, Margaret (1991), *The Post-Modern and the Post-Industrial*, Cambridge.

Rosenau, Pauline Marie (1992), *Postmodernism and the Social Sciences: Insights, Inroads, and Intrusions*, Princeton, NJ.

Rothstein, Arnold (1979), *The Narcissistic Pursuit of Perfection*, New York.

Rothstein, Arnold (1986), "The Theory of Narcissism: An Object-Relations Perspective", in Morrison 1986.

Roudinesco, Elisabeth (1997), *Jacques Lacan* (tr. B. Bray, *Jacques Lacan: Esquisse d'une vie, histoire d'un système de pensée*, 2nd edn, Paris 1994), New York.

Ruggiero, Greg and Stuart Sahulka (1995), *The New American Crisis: Radical Analyses of the Problems Facing America Today*, New York.

Rushkoff, Douglas (1994), *Media Virus! Hidden Agendas in Popular Culture*, New York.

Russell, Charles (1981), *The Avant-Garde Today*, Urbana, IL.

Rutter, Michael (1981), *Maternal Deprivation Reassessed*, Harmondsworth, 2nd edn.

Sardar, Ziauddin and Jerome R. Ravetz (eds) (1996), *Cyberfutures: Culture and Politics on the Information Superhighway*, New York.

Sargent, Lydia (ed.) (1981), *The Unhappy Marriage of Marxism and*

Feminism: A Debate on Class and Patriarchy, London.

Sarraute, Nathalie (1963), *Tropisms and the Age of Suspicion* (tr. M. Jolas, *L'Ere du soupçon*, Paris 1956).

Sarup, Madan (1996), *Identity, Culture and the Postmodern World* (ed. Tasneem Raja), Athens, GA.

Schafer, R. (1968), *Aspects of Internalization*, New York.

Schwab, Klaus (1995), *Overcoming Indifference: Ten Key Challenges in Today's Changing World*, New York.

Sclove, Richard E. (1995), *Democracy and Technology*, New York/London.

Scott, Alan (ed.) (1997), *The Limits of Globalization: Cases and Arguments*, London.

Sennett, Richard (1998), *The Corrosion of Character: The Personal Consequences of Work in the New Capitalism*, New York.

Shapiro, Andrew L. (1999), *The Control Revolution: How the Internet is Putting Individuals in Charge and Changing the World We Know*, New York.

Shenk, David (1997), *Data Smog: Surviving the Information Glut*, New York/San Francisco, CA.

Shields, Rob (1996), *Cultures of Internet: Virtual Spaces, Real Histories, Living Bodies*, London.

Silverman, Hugh J. and Gary E. Aylsworth (1990), *The Textual Sublime: Deconstruction and Its Differences*, Albany, NY.

Smith, Paul (1988), *Discerning the Subject*, Minneapolis, MN.

Sollers, Philippe (1961 [1968]), *The Park* (tr. A. M. Sheridan Smith from *Le Parc*, Paris 1961), London.

Sollers, Philippe (1965), *Drame*, Paris.

Sollers, Philippe (1968), *Nombres*, Paris.

Sollers, Philippe (1981a), "The novel and the experience of limits" (tr. C. Grahl, "Le Roman et l'expérience des limites", *Logiques*, Paris 1968), in Federman 1981; see also Sollers, *Writing and the Experience of Limits* (tr. P. Barnard with D. Hayman, New York 1983).

Sollers, Philippe, (1981b), *Vision à New York: Entretiens avec David Hayman* (tr. from English, P. Mikriammos), Paris.

Sontag, Susan (1969), *Against Interpretation and Other Essays*, New York.

Stern, Daniel (1985), *The Interpersonal World of the Infant*, New York.

Stolorow, Robert D. (1986), "Toward a Functional Definition of Narcissism", in Morrison 1986.

Stone, Michael H. (1986), *Essential Papers on Borderline Disorders: One Hundred Years at the Border*, New York.

Storey, John (1996), *Cultural Studies and the Study of Popular Culture*, Edinburgh.

Storr, Anthony (1989), *Solitude* (first published as *The School of Genius*, 1988), London.

Swingewood, Alan (1998), *Cultural Theory and the Problem of Modernity*, Basingstoke.

Symington, Neville (1993), *Narcissism: A New Theory*, London.

Tapscott, Don (1996), *Digital Economy: Promise and Peril in the Age of the Networked Intelligence*, New York.

Taylor, Charles (ed.) (1994), *Multiculturalism: Examining the Politics of Recognition*, Princeton, NJ.

Teicholz, Judith Guss (1999), *Kohut, Loewald, and the Postmoderns: A Comparative Study of Self and Relationship*, New York.

Thomas, Sari (1997), "Dominance and Ideology in Culture and Cultural Studies", in Ferguson and Goulding 1997.

Tobin, Stephan (1983), "Gestalt Therapy and the Self: Reply to Yontef", *Gestalt Journal*, vol. 6, no. 1.

Toffler, Alvin (1980), *The Third Wave*, New York.

Toffler, Alvin (1991), *Powershift: Knowledge, Wealth, and Violence at the Edge of the 21st Century*, New York.

Tomas, David (1995), "Feedback and Cybernetics: Reimaging the Body in the Age of the Cyborg", in Featherstone and Burrows 1995.

Tsagarousianou, Roza, Damian Tambini and Cathy Bryan (1998), *Cyberdemocracy: Technology, Cities and Civic Networks*, London.

Turkle, Sherry (1992), *Psychoanalytic Politics: Jacques Lacan and Freud's French Revolution*, New York, 2nd edn.

Turkle, Sherry (1995), *Life on the Screen: Identity in the Age of the Internet*, New York.

Twitchell, James B. (1999), *Lead Us Into Temptation: The Triumph of American Materialism*, New York.

Urry, John (1990) *The Tourist Gaze: Leisure and Travel in Contemporary Societies*, London.

Vonnegut, Kurt (1967 [1959]), *The Sirens of Titan*, London.

Vonnegut, Kurt (1991 [1969]), *Slaughterhouse-5*, London.

Wallace, Patricia (1999), *The Psychology of the Internet*, Cambridge.

Wallis, Brian (ed.) (1984), *Art after Modernism: Rethinking Representation*, New York.

Ward, Glenn (1997), *Postmodernism*, London.

Waugh, Patricia (1992), *Practising Postmodernism/Reading Modernism*, London.

Westen, Drew (1985), *Self and Society: Narcissism, Collectivism, and the Development of Morals*, Cambridge.

White, Marjorie Taggart (1986), "Self Relations, Object Relations, and Pathological Narcissism", in Morrison 1986.

Windschuttle, Keith (1996), *The Killing of History*, New York.

Winnicott, D. W. (1965), *The Maturational Process and the Facilitating Environment: Studies in the Theory of Emotional Development*, London/New York.

Winnicott, D. W. (1971), *Playing and Reality*, London.

Wolfe, Alan (ed.) (1991), *America at Century's End*, Berkeley, CA.

Yontef, Gary M. (1993), *Awareness Dialogue & Process: Essays on Gestalt Therapy*, Highland.

Zavarzadeh, Mas'ud (1976), *The Mythopoeic Reality*, Urbana.

Index

While this index, like the Bibliography, seeks to put the reader in touch with the full range of the essay's topics and authors, in the interests of economy it indicates their occurrence in the case of *primary* discussions only. Certain topics (such as 'postmodernity', 'postmodernism' and 'narcissance') are of such central concern throughout as to appear by name here only to indicate passages offering their general introduction; see more specific entries for the detailed consideration of their more particular aspects.

PERSONS

TOPICS